Thomas Hart Benton sketching on the beach, Martha's Vineyard, 1922.

An American Original

Alfred A. Knopf, New York 1989

Thomas Hart Benton

Henry Adams

This biography/catalogue was published on the occasion of the exhibition
Thomas Hart Benton: An American Original and as an accompaniment
to the PBS documentary *Thomas Hart Benton.*

The exhibition was curated by Henry Adams, organized by Ellen Goheen, and circulated by The Nelson-Atkins Museum of Art, Marc Wilson,
Director. It will open at The Nelson-Atkins Museum of Art, Kansas City,
Missouri (April 16 to June 18, 1989) and will travel to The Detroit Institute of Arts (August 4 to October 15, 1989), the Whitney Museum of
American Art, New York (November 17, 1989 to February 11, 1990),
and the Los Angeles County Museum of Art (April 29 to July 22, 1990).

The Ken Burns documentary *Thomas Hart Benton* was initiated by the
Nelson-Atkins Museum of Art and produced by Florentine Films in
partnership with WGBH Boston. It will be broadcast nationally on the PBS
system in May 1989.

**The exhibition was made possible by generous grants from the United
Missouri Bank of Kansas City, N.A., and the Enid and Crosby Kemper
Foundation.**

Additional support was provided by the National Endowment for the
Arts. The film was made possible by generous grants from the Equitable
Life Assurance Society of the U.S., The National Endowment for the
Humanities, and the Jules and Doris Stein Foundation.

This book has drawn extensively from unpublished materials from the
Thomas Hart Benton and Rita P. Benton Testamentary Trusts. Copyright
ownership of such materials is in the Trusts. The Trusts also hold the
copyright to *An Artist in America* and *An American in Art* and other publications by Benton. None of these materials can be used in publication
without permission from the Trusts. They are used here with the permission of Lyman Field and the United Missouri Bank of Kansas City, co-
trustees.

Library of Congress Cataloging-in-Publication Data

Adams, Henry
Thomas Hart Benton: an American original /Henry Adams.
— 1st ed. p. cm.

Bibliography: p.344
Includes index.

ISBN 0-394-57153-3.
ISBN 0-394-75958-3 (pbk.)

1. Benton, Thomas Hart, 1889-1975.
2. Painters — United States — Biography.
I. Title.
ND237.B47A84   1989
88-30347
759.13—dc19
CIP

Manufactured in Italy
First Edition

Contents

The symbol • at the end of a caption indicates that the work depicted will be included in the opening venue of *Thomas Hart Benton: An American Original* at the Nelson-Atkins Museum of Art, Kansas City, Missouri.

Acknowledgments

Throughout my writing I have enjoyed the support of Marc Wilson, the director of the Nelson-Atkins Museum of Art, a remarkably generous and inspiring man to work for. I am also grateful for the wise guidance provided to the museum by its trustees, particularly the three university trustees, Menefee Blackwell, Herman Sutherland, and Donald J. Hall.

This book is one of three projects initiated by the Nelson to mark the centennial of Benton's birth; the others are a major traveling exhibition and a documentary film. While I initiated all three projects, the larger part of the work on the exhibition and the film has been carried out by others.

Ellen Goheen organized the exhibition, a task that was particularly taxing because the Nelson has never before undertaken a project of this type. In addition to negotiating most of the loans, she devised loan forms, negotiated contracts, worked out the budget, wrote grant proposals, planned publicity and social events, and handled a thousand other details. I am also grateful to those who made possible the tour of the exhibition: Nancy Rivard Shaw and Samuel Sachs at the Detroit Institute of Arts; Patterson Sims, Barbara Haskell, and Tom Armstrong at the Whitney Museum of American Art; and Michael Quick and Earl Powell III at the Los Angeles County Museum of Art. Lynne Breslin, of Breslin-Mosseri Design in New York, has created the provocative, postmodern installation design, ably supported by Michael Hagler, the exhibition designer at the museum. West Associates of Kansas City have designed the posters and publicity materials. Francesca Lack of Francesca Lack & Associates, New York, has coordinated our publicity campaign.

The documentary, which was created by Ken Burns, became a reality thanks to the enthusiasm of Peter McGhee, chairman of National Productions at the WGBH Educational Foundation in Boston. My friend Elizabeth Deane, a senior producer at the station, both introduced me to Peter and first recommended that I contact Ken Burns.

Ken Burns, of Walpole, New Hampshire, and his wife, Amy, have proved wonderful good friends as well as brilliant filmmakers. I owe Ken deep thanks for allowing me to observe and to some extent participate in every aspect of the filmmaking process. Everyone associated with the documentary has been a joy to work with: Geoffrey Ward, the scriptwriter (whose phrases have occasionally crept into this narrative); Julie Dunfey, the producer; Buddy Squires, the cameraman; Roger Sherman, the sound recorder; Donna Marino, the editor; and Camilla Rockwell, the associate producer. The introductory page of this book is drawn directly from the film, and I have made extensive use of the interviews made for the film, often using sections that did not make the final cut.

Jennifer Hardin, my curatorial assistant, has worked doggedly to gather and organize materials, and to carry out the thousands of eccentric tasks that are associated with a large-scale research project. Without her unflagging assistance, this manuscript could never have been completed. Diana Gaston worked energetically on the early stages of research and then moved on to direct and supervise our catalogue of American paintings. Patricia Fidler and Kelly Ebeling helped with research, as did, on a short-term basis, two volunteers, Lea Reams and Andrea Fraley.

This project got off the ground thanks to the initiative of Mrs. John William Abbott and the group of donors she recruited to provide seed money for it: Mr. and Mrs. George Charno, Mr. David A. Stickelber, Mrs. Herbert O. Peet, Mr. and Mrs. Lester Siegel, Jr., Mr. and Mrs. Richard Frontman, Mr. and Mrs. Arvin Gottlieb, Mr. and Mrs. William Hickok, Mr. and Mrs. George B. Ashby, Mr. Thornton Cooke II, Mr. and Mrs. William H. MacLaughlin, Mr. and Mrs. Peter E. Bowers, Jr., Mr. and Mrs. Gerald Oppenheimer, and Mr. and Mrs. Donald R. Williams.

Funding for the exhibition was provided by the United Missouri Bank of Kansas City and by the Enid and Crosby Kemper Foundation. I owe a deep debt to the bank's president and chairman of the board, R. Crosby Kemper. A brilliant businessman, Crosby has done much to improve the cultural life of Kansas City and has long been a munificent donor to the American art collection of the Nelson. Shirley De Wald, Mr. Kemper's executive secretary, has facilitated our many dealings. I am also grateful to Mick Aslin, chief operating officer of the bank.

Funding for the film was provided by grants from The Equitable Life Assurance Society of the United States, The National Endowment for the Humanities, and the Jules and Doris Stein Foundation. Personal thanks are due to Benjamin Holloway, of Equitable Real Estate, whose support of the film followed logically from his purchase of Benton's mural *America Today* for the new headquarters of The Equitable in New York. I am also deeply grateful to Gerald and Virginia Oppenheimer, who arranged for the funding from the Stein Foundation which made it possible to complete the film.

The Bacchus Foundation of Kansas City generously funded educational programs associated with the exhibition.

Michael Churchman, director of development at the Nelson, has assisted with fund-raising in Kansas City. Vicky Devlin of WGBH coordinated the successful fund-raising effort for the film, ably seconded by Jeffrey Little, who handled many of the negotiations with The Equitable. Marilyn Mellowes of WGBH helped me write our successful application to the National Endowment for the Humanities. Douglass Scott of WGBH designed the corporate brochure.

Karen Johnson, the director of publishing at WGBH, the kindest and most supportive person I have ever worked with, has been this book's fairy godmother. Working in conjunction with the station's literary agent, Steven Axelrod, she masterminded the sale of the manuscript to Alfred A. Knopf. She has also supervised and participated in all the different aspects of editing and design. I am grateful to Ashbel Green, senior editor at Knopf, for his faith in the potential of the book; and to Susan Ralston, my good-humored, long-suffering, and extremely skillful editor. Marjorie Horvitz, the copy editor, was extremely helpful. Deborah Paddock has gathered the illustrations, assisted by Jennifer Hardin. Douglass Scott, under fearful time pressure, has worked out the complex and beautiful book design, with the assistance of Jeanne Lee and Constance Jacobson.

Many individuals have provided information and assistance. My largest debt is to Lyman Field, trustee of the Benton Trust and former police commissioner of Kansas City, who was Benton's lawyer, drinking companion, and intimate friend. Stephen Campbell, vice-president and trust officer of the United Missouri Bank, has ably helped us with our every request. Jessie Benton, the most delightful of raconteurs, has been unfailingly generous in providing material about her father, and has shown a grace and good manners altogether rare in this awkward age. My thanks to her and to the other members of the Lyman "family," particularly Richie Guerin, Anthony Gude, and Dick Randall. John Callison, by allowing us to consult his clippings and scrapbooks, made available materials about Benton that normal research methods would never have uncovered. George O'Maley, and Lee and Anne Constable have also supplied helpful information. George Gurley of the Kansas City *Star* provided access to useful material on Howard Huselton. Mary Jane Hickey, of the Henry Luce Foundation, has given advice and encouragement. James Rogers, who is writing his doctoral dissertation at the University of Missouri on Benton's Jefferson City mural, provided many useful corrections. Stephen Polcari, my former colleague at the University of Illinois, first introduced me to the connections between Benton and Jackson Pollock; Roger Ward, the Nelson's curator of European art, first took me to see Benton's Jefferson City mural. Margaret and Harold Hedges, Benton's old companions, guided me on a memorable trip down the Buffalo River in Arkansas.

In April 1987, we organized a symposium on Thomas Hart Benton at the museum, and I am deeply grateful to the scholars who participated: Karal Ann Marling, Hilton Kramer, Edward F. Fry, Matthew Baigell, Harry Rand, Elizabeth Schultz and Clement Greenberg.

In the art history department at the University of Kansas, Steve Addiss and Tim Mitchell have been consistently supportive, and I am also grateful to that most wonderful of librarians, Susan Craig.

Among the patient readers and commentators on the manuscript have been Tom McCormick, Mellissa Williams, Michaela Schaeffer, Mary Ellen Young, Robert Cohon (the curator of classical art at the Nelson), and Mr. and Mrs. James Berardi.

The national committee for this exhibition reflects, in an indirect way, the diversity of Benton's interests. It includes Missouri's two senators, its governor and all its living former governors, the mayor of Kansas City, the head of the New York Stock Exchange, a U.S. President's daughter, a journalist, a newscaster, the founder of Common Cause, a comedian, a painter, a librarian, a college president, a museum director, a physician, several writers, and an assortment of business leaders. Most of these individuals knew Benton or have some strong tie to his work. The Honorable Thomas F. Eagleton has served as chair of this committee. Its members are: the Honorable John Ashcroft, Professor Matthew Baigell, Jessie Benton, the Honorable Richard L. Berkley, Eleanor Lambert Berkson, Menefee D. Blackwell, Henry W. Bloch, the Honorable Christopher S. Bond, Emily Braun, M. Graham Clark, Bill Cosby, the Honorable Jack Danforth, Margaret Truman Daniel, Lyman Field, John W. Gardner, Donald J. Hall, the Honorable Warren E. Hearnes, Benjamin D. Holloway, R. Crosby Kemper, Edward D. King, Sidney Larson, Arthur Levitt, Jr., Peter S. McGhee, Franklin D. Murphy, Virginia Oppenheimer, Eleanor Piacenza, Robert Sanford, Stephen Sloan, David A. Stickelber, Herman R. Sutherland, the Honorable Joseph P. Teasdale, Mike Wallace, Linda Weintraub, Lyle S. Woodcock, the Honorable Harriett Woods, and Dr. Benedict K. Zobrist.

Landon H. Rowland, president of Kansas City Southern, has chaired our local committee, ably assisted by Cynde Brookfield, Kay Callison, and Sharon Hoffman.

I should close with two debts of a personal nature, one to Marianne Berardi, my muse, my inspiration, and my most ingenious research sleuth; and the other to Burt Lancaster, for his recollections of Tom Benton and for the most entertaining conversation I have had in many years.

To Marianne Berardi: A small tribute of affection

Prologue

Thomas Hart Benton painted America.

For more than seventy years, he painted its cities and small towns, its farms and backwoods. He painted its people too: faith healers and lovers, politicians and soda jerks, farmers and movie stars.

Most of all, Benton wanted to make his art available to the ordinary man. In so doing he shook up the art world, embroiled himself in endless controversy, and left a legacy of paintings that detail an entire age.

He showed how an American artist can succeed. And how he can fail.

Critics still argue about his work. But each year, his friends celebrate his birthday in a Kansas City saloon.

Alfred Eisenstaedt, Thomas Hart Benton Painting *Perse-phone, 1939.*

I

Chapter One
Neosho

Maecenas Eason Benton. "The western Bentons," Thomas Hart Benton wrote of his family, "were an individualistic and cocksure people. . . . My dad was a slice of the block."

"[Tom] was very sure that he was always right, and he was very talkative. At meals, my father would sometimes send him away from the table because he insisted on 'What I think,' and 'What I do,' and 'What I will do,' and it was always, as my father said, 'I,' 'I,' 'I.' My father called him 'Big I.' "

Beginnings

Thomas Hart Benton's father, Maecenas Eason Benton, did not want him to become an artist. "Dad was profoundly prejudiced against artists, and with some reason," Tom recalled. "The only ones he had ever come across were the mincing, bootlicking portrait painters . . . who hung around the skirts of women at receptions and lisped a silly jargon about grace and beauty. Dad was utterly contemptuous of them and labeled them promptly as pimps." This view was shared by most of the other inhabitants of Neosho, the small southwest Missouri courthouse town where Tom was born. With an exaggeration that seems pardonable in light of his own long struggles, he declared that the environment of his youth manifested "the most complete denial of aesthetic sensibility that has probably ever been known."

Indeed, it is hard to grasp fully what impelled Tom to become an artist, against the full force of his father's will. Certainly many factors played a role. If Maecenas Benton, for example, had not been elected to the U.S. Congress, his son might never have looked beyond southwest Missouri and set off to live the artist's life in Chicago, Paris, and New York. But the principal catalyst for this decision was undoubtedly Tom's mother, Elizabeth, who always supported her eldest son in his struggles against his father, as if doing so provided an outlet for her own frustrations.

To understand Tom Benton's artistic drives, one must know something of his parents and of their conflicts. These conflicts shadowed him throughout his life, and he eventually compressed his feelings about them into his greatest paintings. As an old man, he wrote that his parents often "annoyed, embarrassed or even outraged me." Yet he asserted that over the years, he had gained "a profound sympathy for them and for the unhappy ways in which they ended their lives."

The story begins a few years before Tom was born, with an ambitious lawyer, a grand mansion, and a beautiful young woman from Texas.

Maecenas Eason Benton (known as "M.E.") was born in 1846 on a small plantation in Tennessee and studied law in St. Louis. In September 1869, he moved out to Neosho, a town on the fringe of the Ozarks that boasted a population of 612. Only two men subscribed to the town newspaper, one of whom, a local storekeeper, would stand on a horseblock and read it to the farmers and hangers-on who collected. The coming of the railroad, however, brought thousands of new people to the town, and thanks to the turreted brick courthouse in the center of the town square, there was plentiful business for a lawyer.

Soon M.E.'s business was flourishing and he had become prosperous—the most successful lawyer in all southwest Missouri. As he grew portly and substantial, he came to be called "Colonel," after the Southern fashion of the time. In 1887 he built a grand mansion, "Oak Hill," on a four-acre eminence just two blocks south of the courthouse. It had towers and porticoes, and the first coal furnace and indoor plumbing in town. Neosho had never seen anything like it.

Shortly afterward he began his fateful courtship of Lizzie Wise. Miss Lizzie normally lived with her parents in Waxahachie, Texas; but she had just come up to Neosho for a long visit with her older sister Emma. M.E. was a thickset bachelor of forty-one; Lizzie was a pert, good-looking girl of twenty-three, with a talent for singing and tinkling the piano keys. On June 24, 1888, at the Baptist church in Waxahachie, the Colonel and Miss Lizzie were locked in matrimony.

Probably M.E. expected, in the simple naïveté of his male soul, that this fashionable creature would quietly settle into his home and form a cozy familial unit with his siblings, Fanny, Dolly, and Sam. In this, he was mistaken; his young bride asserted her personality from the start. Perhaps a conflict was inevitable, for Miss Fanny, the elder of the two sisters, was a square-faced, hook-nosed redhead with adamantine opinions and an imperious demeanor. The battle, however, was no contest, for Lizzie had youth, sexual attractiveness, and a fierce conviction of righteousness on her side. "Throw them out of the house or I'll go back to Texas," Lizzie told her new husband. Within a month she had ousted her rivals; Fanny, Dolly, and Sam beat a hasty retreat down to the valley, where they moved into a dwelling close to the courthouse and the town square. By the time her first child was born, Lizzie had domestic affairs firmly under her own control.

The hopes of both parents were centered on this child, Tom, who came into the world on April 15, 1889. "The boy is worth his weight in gold," M.E. told Dr. Wills, who officiated at the birth. He marched to the bureau, opened a strongbox, and took out several gold pieces, which he handed to the doctor in payment. Three more children were born to the couple—Mary Elizabeth ("Mamie," 1891–1953), Nathaniel Wise (1893–1946), and Mildred (1896–   )—but for both Tom and his parents they were just afterthoughts.

Neosho. The central landmark of Neosho was the courthouse, placed smack in the center of the town square.

Detail from A Social History of Missouri, *egg tempera and oil on linen mounted on panel, 1936. "My father was a political figure in the state," Benton once recalled, "and I got acquainted very early with a kind of flamboyant early political life of Missouri." An ardent supporter of the Populist cause, Colonel M. E. Benton was elected to the U.S. Congress in 1896. In his mural for the Missouri state capitol, Benton showed his father delivering a political speech in front of a poster of Champ Clark.*

Senator Thomas Hart Benton.

The newborn was given the most prized name in the Benton family, that of his great-uncle Senator Thomas Hart Benton. The senator's biographer, President Theodore Roosevelt, described him as possessing "a perfect type of Western statesmanship," and noted that he exhibited "the tenacity of a snapping turtle." His career was one of continual turmoil: he nearly killed Andrew Jackson in a brawl and once murdered a man in a duel. Yet he sat for thirty years in the United States Senate, the longest term served up to that date. Just before the Civil War, he was finally defeated, because he opposed the extension of slavery.

For Maecenas Eason Benton, the course of his son's life seemed clear. Tom would become a lawyer and politician, as the Bentons always had. M.E. would never entirely forgive his son for choosing a different path.

Early Childhood

Until the age of six, Tom was cared for by a remarkable woman, Aunt Maria Watkins. The daughter of a black slave and a white doctor, she was renowned for her medical skills throughout southwest Missouri. She lived to be 101 and became famous as the woman who had adopted and raised George Washington Carver, the distinguished black scientist.

Tom always remembered her with great affection. Queen of the household, Aunt Maria would arrive at the Benton home each morning in her little carriage, pulled by a small palomino pony; she had often been up all night delivering a baby. Despite her considerable bulk, Aunt Maria was amazingly agile and could carry two buckets of hot water up the back stairs without losing a breath, or run down a chicken before it knew it was being chased. She watched over Tom as she carried out the household tasks: it was she who fed, clothed, washed, and whacked him.

M.E.'s younger brother, Sam, had managed to remain exempt from Lizzie's wrath, and although he moved with his sisters down into the valley, he continued to keep his hunting dogs in the Colonel's woodlot and train them in the yard. Once Tom became old enough, Uncle Sam would drive him around the country in a wagonette, accompanied by the dogs. From time to time they would stop and run the dogs in the fields.

One of Tom's most vivid early memories was of being taken by Uncle Sam to see the "petrified man," a celebrated hoax that was kept in the back of the Neosho saloon, where visitors paid ten cents to see it. The dark room and the strange eyeless corpse so upset him that he began to throw up and had to taken out. Even after Tom learned that the exhibit was a fraud, made of cement, the frightening memory haunted him for weeks.

After Fanny and Dolly both married, Sam moved back into Oak Hill. Before long, however, he developed tubercular symptoms and migrated to the warmer climate of Arizona. There he died, leaving a legacy that later allowed his nephew to study art in Chicago and Paris.

Pappy Wise

Early every spring, generally when it was still cold in Missouri, Lizzie Benton headed down to Texas with her children to visit her father, who was known to his offspring and to his neighbors as Pappy Wise. He lived in a white two-story house surrounded by sheds and farm buildings of raw wood, gray and warped by the Texas sun. In the center of the packed dirt yard stood a tall windmill and a water tank. There was a small garden, which contained rickety bean and tomato poles and a section devoted to okra.

In the 1890s, Pappy had retired from business and moved to this cotton farm outside Waxahachie. He didn't work the land himself but leased it to others and kept

Thomas Hart Benton, aged three, 1892. The first and smallest of four children, Tom was named for his great-uncle, Missouri's first senator.

himself busy manufacturing violins. The Wises possessed musical gifts, and every member of the family either played an instrument or sang. Pappy often got up at four in the morning and played his violin until breakfast time. He believed in direct communication with God, and while alone in his workshop would often talk to Him.

In his maturity, Tom Benton made several paintings based upon his Texas visits. *Spring Tryout* of 1943 records an attempt to ride a frisky sorrel with another boy; it shows Tom falling off, while the other boy struggles to hang on. *Fire in the Barnyard* of 1944 was also based on a memory of a visit to Waxahachie. A neighbor's barn caught fire, creating a light so bright that the elders talked of the end of the world. Tom later remembered that "We all visited the place next morning and heard tell of how the farmer and his sons had got the scared horses out of the barn. Such things are immensely impressive to young 'uns."

Both the Benton and the Wise family had been Southern hill folk—Piedmont people—and thus were frontiersmen rather than tidewater aristocrats. The families, however, had very different traditions. The Bentons had been lawyers and planters, and except for brawling, they avoided physical effort. The Wises liked to work with their hands.

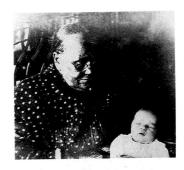

Aunt Maria Watkins. Until he was six, Benton was cared for by Aunt Maria, who had also raised George Washington Carver, the distinguished black scientist.

Family and Friends

Tom learned very early that a mysterious tension existed between his parents. The Colonel, in fact, possessed a dual personality. Outside the house he ruled assertively. In his office on the town square, he was a jovial teller of stories and a man whose opinions led to action. Out in the yard, he confidently bossed the hired hands. Inside, though, he was upstaged by his wife; his manner was ineffectual, suspicious, and irritable. In the house only Aunt Maria Watkins, who was proud of her association with the famous "lawman," treated him with respect.

"Maybe the problem existed from the first night," Tom later speculated. M.E. was a man of coarse sensual appetites, while Lizzie was fastidious, with a squeamishness about sex that had been encouraged by her early religious training. In physical appearance the two made a dramatic contrast. The Colonel was short and thick-necked, with reddish skin, a red beard, and a protruding belly. Though he was only five foot three, his weight burgeoned—thanks to hearty meals, little exercise, and numerous toddies and juleps—to some two hundred pounds. Lizzie, on the other hand, was a dainty, good-looking woman. Later on, when the couple lived in Washington, they came to be known as "Beauty and the Beast." After Mildred, their fourth child, was born, Lizzie slept with her until Mildred left home. By keeping the child in her bed, she kept her husband out.

But despite her distaste for sex, Lizzie Benton loved masculine attention, and as her husband's political power and influence grew, she made her home a place to which men, and men of high importance, came eagerly. The house was generally filled with arguing, expostulating politicos, great, burly men with loud voices and big appetites, who smoked fat cigars, the ends of which they chewed. As a little boy, Tom sat pop-eyed at breakfast, watching Champ Clark and William Jennings Bryan, still allies in the Populist camp, devouring poached eggs set on baked potatoes—engulfing a whole egg and half a potato in a single bite.

Although she had grown up in the provincial milieu of Waxahachie, Lizzie Benton knew how to perform as a great lady. She loved to dress up in St. Louis finery and display her brunette good looks before the friends her husband brought home, swallowing their compliments like nectar. Her sisters Emma, Lara, and "Aunt Duck" were generally excluded from these parties, and so were other women—she wanted all the men to herself.

M.E. was proud of his wife's social gifts and enjoyed playing master of the house.

Elizabeth Wise Benton. The artist's mother, nineteen years younger than his father, was a beautiful, high-strung Texan with artistic and social ambitions. This photograph, taken in Washington, D.C., shows her in one of the gowns she ordered from Paris.

He would become expansive and genial; his customary at-home irritability would not reappear until after the guests had gone. Then he would retreat in moody silence to the library, where he would lose himself in the mysterious practice of adding and subtracting long columns of figures. Mildred recalls once asking her mother: "Why can't we have company every night? It makes Father happy, and when he's happy we can be happy."

The Bentons were not churchgoers, but reading the Bible after supper was a family ritual. The religious meaning of the text was not discussed, and in fact the point of the exercise was never explained. In *An Artist in America*, his autobiography, published in 1937, Tom made a joke of this, claiming that he once inquired about the whore of Babylon, "who glorified herself and lived deliciously," but was told to hush up. "I don't recall ever having any desire to talk about any of it," recalls Mildred, who like Tom started to join these gatherings when she was about six years old. "I remember having a craving to read aloud. I suppose that started as pride at being able to read at all."

Most of the menfolk would dodge these sessions. Uncle Ed, Lizzie's oldest brother, was openly skeptical. Uncle Jim McElhany would generally be off somewhere horse trading. Uncle Sidney, who had married "Aunt Duck," a particularly holy sister, would generally be taken with the recurrent malaria he had contracted when he took part in William Walker's abortive expedition to establish an empire in Central America. Only the Colonel took an active part, probably less because he loved religion than because he loved the sound of his own sonorous voice.

Tom learned at an early age that it sometimes pays to break the rules. After learning that the class above him in school had more entertaining books, he announced to his parents that he had been promoted to it. The falsehood was soon discovered, but he did get to keep the books they had bought for him.

The split in M.E.'s personality led him to treat Tom quite differently outside the house than at home. At Oak Hill, his father was a nitpicker and faultfinder who criticized nearly everything Tom did. In public, on the other hand, he encouraged the boy's argumentative traits. While Tom's features and coloring strongly resembled those of his mother, the Colonel liked to suppose that his disputatiousness derived from the Benton clan. He frequently introduced Tom at public gatherings as one who was destined to be another lawyer and politico—a fighter for the rights of the people.

Once, when Tom was seven or eight, his father was scheduled to speak at a country fair in Cassville, Missouri. Just as he was about to begin, Tom climbed on the platform and cried, "Hold on, Dad! Hold on! Gimme a quarter to ride the Spinnin' Jenny!" There was a burst of laughter from all within earshot and one old fellow called out, "He's got you, M.E.!" The Colonel laughingly shelled out the quarter, and Tom got his ride. Later, the incident was humorously reported in the local newspaper. Thus Tom learned at an early age that creating a disturbance can generate publicity, a lesson he applied very effectively later on.

As part of his political fence-building, M.E. often went out into the country to hunt and fish, and he generally took Tom along. They would frequently stay overnight with farmers. Sometimes they would undertake a river trip with a group of companions, camping for days in the woods.

When Tom was only six or seven years old, his father gave him a .22 rifle and, after setting him for a while at target practice, assigned him the task of shooting the blue jays that pecked into the eaves of the house. Tom cheerfully assassinated a few, but one bird he shot fell to the ground and hopped around in misery, its wing broken. This so upset him that he could no longer bring himself to shoot to kill—whether blue jays or other game. To his father's disgust, he soon developed a reputation as the most game-shy hunter in the region.

Through his expeditions with his father, Tom befriended Johnny Smith, son of a local farmer, with whom he went on his first possum hunts, running through the woods at night with a lantern, trying to follow the barking dogs. The other "best friend" of Tom's childhood was Wellesby Benton—not a relation—whom he met in memorable circumstances when he was seven or eight years old. Tom had been sent into town to pick up groceries and was ambling along beside a placid old farmer who carried a bushel basket of potatoes. Without warning, a paper sack filled with water came sailing down from above and exploded on the sidewalk. The farmer soared into the air like a jumping jack, dropping his basket and scattering potatoes all over the walk. Tom became so convulsed with laughter that he nearly wet his pants.

He looked up, to see a carrot-topped head, freckles, and a big grin poking out of a second-story window. This was Wellesby Benton. But as Tom looked, a huge moon-like face appeared behind the boy and an enormous hand grabbed him by the hair and pulled him back. A few moments later, Wellesby trotted down a flight of steps by the side of the building and helped the farmer pick up the potatoes. Tom joined them at

Thomas Hart Benton, Spring Tryout, *lithograph, 1943.*

Thomas Hart Benton, Fire in the Barnyard, *lithograph, 1944.*

7

the task, and he and Wellesby became immediate friends. The farmer proved to be a good-natured fellow, whose only comment was: "Next time you do that, sorrel-top, do it to my old woman!"

Early Drawings

At the age of six or seven, Tom began to show a remarkable talent for drawing. There was no ancestral precedent for his visual gifts. "All little children try to make some sort of pictures," his sister Mildred Small has commented, "but his were better than the average child's and my mother decided very early in his life that he had more talent."

"My first pictures were of railroad trains," Benton later recalled. "Engines were the most impressive things that came into my childhood. . . . I scrawled crude representations of them over everything."

Tom's childhood friend John Robison told the reporter Bob Sanford of the first drawing he saw Tom make—a locomotive roughly one hundred feet long, which he sketched in charcoal on a concrete drain (already he liked to work large). Mildred Small still vividly recalls a train that Tom drew on the wallpaper by the third-floor landing at Oak Hill, which remained visible until the house burned down in 1917. Evidently Tom also made a drawing on the first floor which he later reluctantly erased. He wrote:

"When I was six or seven years old our house was newly papered in some light cream-colored paper. We had a stairway which went around a landing from the lower hall to the second floor. My first mural consisted of a long freight train in charcoal which went up this stairway on the new paper. It began with the caboose at the foot of the steps and ended at the top with the engine puffing long strings of black smoke —because of the heavy grade. The kind of appreciation afforded this early effort was the first intimation I received of the divergency of view on the subject of mural decoration. The question of appropriateness, which later on and on other occasions I was to hear a lot about, was then brought up for the first time. Decision in this case was against me and, after a good lecture, my labors were obliterated with bread crumbs."

As it happens, Tom's earliest surviving drawing also shows a train. It was made when he was nine, in Vinita, Oklahoma, while idling on the front porch of a family friend, Mrs. J. B. Saunders, during a stopover on the way to Texas. The lady was so impressed by the sketch that she saved it all her life. It shows three views of the Katy Flier—the locomotive in profile, and two perspective studies of the whole receding train, as seen from a vantage point behind the caboose.

For a child of nine—and indeed for an artist of any age—the skill of the draftsmanship is remarkable. The perspective is handled with unhesitating confidence. The sketch of the engine shows an amazing understanding of the vehicle's working parts— the cowcatcher and truck wheels, the funnel puffing smoke, the boilers and whistle, the bell on top filled with sand (to be dropped on the track on slippery grades), the rods and driving wheels, the cab, the couplings and connectors, the coal car, and the first boxcar, which is inscribed with the letters "MKT" (for Missouri-Kansas-Texas— usually shortened to "Katy"). Even the handling of atmosphere is remarkable—witness the billowing puffs of smoke. The boy had somehow internalized the workings of a train so that it became for him an active, breathing presence.

The sketch is so accurate, in fact, that two Kansas City railroad experts, Tom Carter and Harold Vollrath, have been able not only to determine the make of locomotive but to identify the specific engine: MKT number 14, constructed by the Pittsburgh Locomotive Company in 1870—a machine that was already an antique when Tom recorded it.

The locomotive was scrapped on Demember 1, 1899, so the drawing could not

have been made after that date. It seems clear that, despite its amazing quality, Tom indeed made the drawing when he was nine, and did not redate his work for reasons of self-interest, as so many artists do.

Politics

The most exciting moments of Tom's childhood came when he accompanied his father on political tours, activities that soon led to a dramatic shift in the family's way of life.

The late 1880s and early 1890s were tough years for Midwestern farmers. Overproduction and new cheap railroad transportation brought a sharp drop in agricultural prices. Bad weather and locusts worked further havoc (a calamitous drought drove away half the settlers in Kansas); and the Panic of 1893 caused such confusion in the American economy that many small towns virtually did without money and carried out transactions through either barter or credit. The Benton home buzzed with talk, fascinating but mysterious to a small boy, of Grover Cleveland, Indian lands, Senator Vest, Eastern bankers, railway rights, and Free Silver 16 to 1.

"My father was a Populist in a true sense," Mildred recalls. "He was trying to fight off modernization and keep an agricultural focus in the center of the nation." In his party affiliation, M. E. Benton remained a loyal Democrat, but ideologically he embraced the Populist cause. He was one of the first to throw his support behind William Jennings Bryan. In 1896, after Bryan's famous "Cross of Gold" speech electrified the convention, the Democrats nominated him as their presidential candidate.

M.E.'s chief political mentor was George Graham Vest—like himself a former Confederate and a lawyer—who became a United States senator in 1877. George Vest's political career, as a recent writer has noted, "was characterized by a disinclination to recognize new developments and new issues in American life; he adhered largely to bygone principles and precedents." Vest had a remarkable ability, however, for passionate speechifying, a talent he displayed early in his career, when he worked as a country lawyer. Indeed, he probably never surpassed his moving address to the Court of Common Pleas in Warrensburg, Missouri, on the heartless murder of the hunting dog Old Drum. This brought tears to the eyes of the jury and has been called "the greatest speech for the dog in all history."

Like Senator Vest, M. E. Benton enjoyed delivering loud declamatory orations, and he expended his energy to the fullest in the great campaign of 1896, one of the most passionately waged campaigns in American history. Young Tom accompanied his father, who was running for Congress, into the backcountry. He attended rallies and listened to speeches. He marched for his father and for Bryan in dramatic night-

The Benton children. Little Tom did not look happy when a photographer in Washington snapped him standing beside his siblings, Mary, Nat, and Mildred.

Oak Hill. Colonel M. E. Benton's residence was the grandest mansion that had ever been constructed in Neosho.

Thomas Hart Benton, Custer's Last Stand, *pencil on paper, 1896–98. One of his many early drawings of this subject, inspired by a large color lithograph distributed by Anheuser-Busch, which hung in saloons and barbershops.*

Thomas Hart Benton, Katy Flier, Vinita, Oklahoma, *pencil on paper, 1898. At age nine, during a stopover on the way to visit his grandparents in Texas, Benton made this sketch from life.*

time processions around the main square of Neosho, in which the participants carried flaming torches made of gunnysacks on sticks dipped in pine pitch. Just about everyone in Neosho was sure that Bryan was an easy winner.

When it was all over, Bryan had lost his race for the presidency—even though he carried all the states of the old Confederacy. But Colonel M. E. Benton had attained his seat in the House of Representatives.

Washington

Thanks to M.E.'s victory, Tom spent most of the next eight years in Washington, D.C. Mildred recalls teasing him about the popular conception of his hillbilly background when he was in his seventies. "Tom," she exclaimed, "what's all this nonsense about you being Huckleberry Finn?" He laughed and replied, "You're absolutely right. I was a Washington city boy."

During their first year in the capital, the family lived at 216 A Street just behind the new Library of Congress. Tom was just eight and a half when they moved in. He did not go to school that year but was educated at home, with his sister Mamie, by a female tutor. This woman would repeatedly hug and embrace him, to his annoyance and embarrassment. His father, when not at his office, would entertain his cronies at cards in a room at the back of the house, which was always filled with cigar smoke. Periodically his mother would bring them a tray of juleps. The men, to her pleasure, would rise, bow, and exclaim with wonder that the ugliest man in Congress had the prettiest wife.

During this period the family did little socializing. Tom greatly missed the Indian pony he had been given just before he left Neosho, and sometimes wondered what all the speeches and torchlight processions were good for if in the end he didn't even get a yard to play in.

After a year or so, the family's way of life started to change. Lizzie Benton discovered that the Benton name was known in Washington, and she began to attend parties, receptions, and musicales. She bought new dresses and persuaded her husband to acquire some proper evening wear. She soon learned that they did not live in a fashionable part of town; when she paid calls on fine ladies, they were often reluctant to return the visit. The Colonel was satisfied with where they lived, because he could walk to the Capitol, but Tom became aware that tension was brewing between his parents. Once, after overhearing angry words between them, he came into the parlor to discover his mother prostrate on the floor, with only the whites of her eyes showing. His father, red and grim-faced, hurriedly explained that she had fainted and pushed the boy out of the room.

The result of this particular conflict was the family's move, in autumn 1899, to a residence more than twice as large, at 1723 Q Street, a much more fashionable location. The new home required new dishes, silverware, and furnishings to meet the standard of Washington society. New Paris gowns were required. "Missuz, you are ruining us!" the congressman would exclaim, but his wife had taken the bit between her teeth, and there was no stopping her.

Lizzie Benton quickly mastered the proper forms of etiquette. In Neosho, for example, the handsome black servant, Berry, had placed the entire dinner on the table at once and then had stood by to help with the serving. In Washington, the family adopted the French method of serving the food course by course, with wine in between. Within a few months, Lizzie Benton, the homegrown girl from Waxahachie, Texas, had become Mrs. Elizabeth W. Benton, with engraved stationery and calling cards to prove the point. By the end of their stay in Washington, she even had a carriage, which was kept on call, with a driver and a footman.

Eager for self-improvement, Elizabeth took music lessons from Ernest Hutchinson, who later became a distinguished concert pianist. Once a week she would ride the train up to Baltimore to study with him. The Colonel could see no point to the scales that she diligently plunked out for hours and would exclaim, "Missuz, why don't you play a tune once in a while!"

An avid reader, Tom would go with his mother to the Library of Congress, where, quite by accident, he stumbled on an adult version of *The Arabian Nights*. He checked it out, unaware of the sexually explicit stories it contained. There was a row when his father discovered the volume, but after it was confiscated, Tom managed to get hold of it anyway by the simple device of having it checked out by his friend John Rixey. Tom's bedroom, on the third floor, had a bay window adjacent to a window on the Rixey house; he and John were able to pass back and forth the forbidden *Arabian Nights*, along with cigarettes, pulp novels, and copies of the *Police Gazette*.

Tom's enthusiasm for mural painting started at this time, when he became acquainted with the murals at the new Library of Congress. Indeed, these paintings provided him a small victory over his hypercritical father. One day, the congressman was taking a delegation of prominent Missourians through the building, and somebody inquired about the subject of one of the murals. Tom promptly butted in to reply

The Library of Congress, Washington, D.C. Here Benton's enthusiasm for mural painting was born. The building opened to the public in the year he moved to Washington. The critic Royal Cortissoz christened the edifice "our national monument of arts."

and ended by delivering a little speech describing the whole narrative program. When one of them asked how he had obtained his knowledge, he responded, "Well, I read books once in a while." "That boy don't waste no time, does he, M.E.?" the man exclaimed.

About this time, Tom became locked in combat with his father, a battle in which his mother almost invariably took his part. "He struggled against our father all the time," Mildred recalls. "He wasn't struggling against anybody else in the house. Our father had ideas about what he was to do in the world, and they were not Tom's ideas.

"[Tom] was very sure that he was always right, and he was very talkative. At meals, my father would sometimes send him away from the table because he insisted on 'What I think,' and 'What I do,' and 'What I will do,' and it was always, as my father said, 'I,' 'I,' 'I.' My father called him 'Big I.' . . .

"He cared about himself. He wanted to make himself felt everywhere—at home, in the streets of Washington. He fought in the street as a boy. He was always very, very forceful—always trying to force himself against everybody except our mother. He never misbehaved in any way at all in our mother's presence. All his life he was very quiet and very solicitous, very tender, with our mother. She was the only person he really loved, I guess. And he was the only person she really loved. . . .

"I was always very admiring of my mother, but I never liked my father, and he never did anything to make us like him. He was a very Victorian father, which is the worst thing a parent can be."

Shortly after the family moved to Q Street, Tom began formal education at the nearby Force School. M.E. decided that it was time his son began preparing to be a lawyer and statesman, and gave him two college textbooks, one about the structure of government and the other a very dry, conventional history. To these he added his own copy of Senator Thomas Hart Benton's *Debates of Congress*. The gift didn't have the desired effect. Though the Colonel nagged Tom to read these ponderous books, the boy did not: they were just too dull.

Despite their conflicts, M.E. seems to have tried to be helpful to his rebellious son. Mildred recalls: "In Washington, in eighth grade, they had manual training for boys and cooking schools for girls. Tom said that he wanted to go . . . with the girls. My father used political influence to get him into the cooking class."

Tom pretty much kept himself apart from his siblings at this time, and saw them mainly at meals. Poor Nat had developed a remarkable physical resemblance to his father, with red hair and protruding gray-blue eyes, and his mother developed a coldness toward him that bordered on outright disaffection. He would often come to her for help or attention when she was busy, and she would rudely push him away. The girls picked up on her impatience and began calling him the family "dumbhead." If he lost control and hit them, they would run to their mother and complain. Nat would be banished to his room, where his father, who slept there also, often found him crying. M.E. sometimes angrily protested, but his father's support did Nat no good. It only reinforced his mother's distaste.

Indians and Art

Along with railroad trains, Tom loved to draw Indians. One of his favorite subjects was "Custer's Last Stand," inspired by a popular barroom print. Curiously, despite his contempt for Tom's drawing, M.E., who served on the House Indian Affairs Committee, encouraged his interest in Indians. He gave Tom all the Indian reports of the Bureau of Ethnology, in thirteen or fourteen volumes.

This gift became a long-lasting artistic influence. Through his early teens, Indians remained Tom's favorite subject matter, and even after he had grown up he kept the volumes with him as he moved from one apartment to the next. After he married, he got tired of carting them around, and gave them to the City and Country School in New York, run by his friend Caroline Pratt. But the influence of the books did not end. Jackson Pollock worked briefly at the school as a janitor, thanks to Tom's recommendation. He stole the volume on Navajo sand painting, and it was found in his studio after his death.

Tom drew Indians enthusiastically until 1904, when he attended the St. Louis World's Fair and paid a quarter to meet Geronimo. He was so disillusioned by the sight of the tired old man, who gave bored answers to the visitors' questions, that he ceased drawing Indians and moved on to other subjects.

By the time Tom was twelve or thirteen, his skill at drawing was attracting attention, and his father was beginning to feel concerned about the course of his future. For guidance on the matter, he consulted the Rixeys next door, an old tidewater Virginia family. Undoubtedly, M.E. assumed that they would take his side in the matter and dismiss Tom's scribblings as foolish. But on the contrary, after looking at the work, they declared that it was remarkable for one so young and that the boy should be provided with instruction.

At the recommendation of the Rixeys, Tom took lessons from a sweet old lady who made decorated place cards. He dutifully turned out a couple of dozen cards, but afterward went to his father and told him, "I don't want to do this stuff. It's sissy." "Of course it is," his father agreed. "Why don't you quit it? I'll talk to your mother." The lessons were discontinued.

Rather than abandoning art, Tom just moved in a new direction, teaching himself to make pen-and-ink caricatures in the style of the Washington *Post* cartoonist Clifford Berryman. "When my father would take me up to the House," Tom later recalled, "I'd sit there for hours sketching the congressmen, especially Uncle Joe Cannon, the famous speaker. I'll bet I drew him a hundred times."

Tom's drawings impressed his schoolteachers, and he was allowed special time off to work on them. At the suggestion of the principal at the Force School, his mother enrolled him in classes at the Corcoran Art Gallery, beginning in 1901. There a mild-mannered old woman set him to work drawing geometric shapes from wooden models, a task he found excruciatingly boring. He soon went back to drawing battles and Indians. Possibly, however, this early training affected his mature work, for in the 1920s, when he became fascinated with compositional arrangement, he found that a feeling for geometric form was lying buried in his unconscious, as if it had been planted there.

Quite on his own initiative, Tom took up sculpture as well, as Mildred vividly recalls. One day, there was a great commotion on the stairs, and Cretia, the family servant, came into the dining room, propelling Tom by the shoulder. She had something in her hand, and a sobbing Nat trailed behind her. Cretia thrust Tom up beside his father's chair and put the thing on the table. It was an idol Tom had made, about fifteen inches high, carved out of wood and painted. He had been making his little brother kneel down and worship it. Nat had seemed tearful for several mornings when he came down to breakfast, but nobody had paid much attention. This was the explanation.

Summers in Neosho

Throughout his childhood, Tom was shuttled back and forth between two homes: winter was spent in Washington, summer in Neosho. During this period, the Missouri house was being made over to reflect Elizabeth Benton's new, sophisticated East Coast ideas. But nonetheless, the atmosphere in Neosho remained very rural.

In the summer of 1903, M.E. entrusted Tom with the care of the family cow, Bluey, for which the Colonel had a remarkable fondness. This helped prove to the

Neosho country boys that Tom wasn't just a sissy. The best link with these rapscallions was provided by Tom's little pony, which had been trained by Indians out in the Oklahoma territory. It would buck if a saddle was placed on it, but it did not mind being ridden bareback and would stop if a boy fell off. Tom and his friends would climb on, two and three at a time, for wild Indian gallops around the pasture or jaunts to the local swimming hole at Hickory Creek.

The youngsters took to staging circuses in the barn, rounding up an audience of small fry, mostly their brothers and sisters. They dressed up as clowns, acrobats, or Indians, and presented performances on a makeshift stage. Tom would print up programs for these theatricals, one of which caused hilarity among the grownups.

It read:

CIRCUS AT BENTON'S BARN
1. John T. Shannon—Skinning the Cat.
2. Thomas Hart Benton—Hanging by the Legs.
3. John Smith—Walking on Hands.
4. Indian War Dance and Burning at the Stake.
   Wellesby Benton to be Burnt Alive.

For the climax of this performance, Tom had saved up his packages of Fourth of July powders, which burned red, green, and orange. All the boys but Wellesby painted themselves up like Indians, with stripes of red clay, pokeberry juice, and charcoal. Then they set the powders on a big sheet of tin and placed Wellesby in the middle, tied to a four-by-four stake. After setting a match to the powders, the Indians began dancing around the prisoner, yelling at the top of their lungs. Unfortunately, the flames got too close and began to burn Wellesby's bare legs. He picked up the stake and ran off, howling, "No you don't, you! Somebody else has got to be burned at the stake!"

Despite this unplanned conclusion, the audience was delighted by the performance, and Tom's sister Mamie, who attended, vividly described it at the dinner table. M.E. was far from pleased by the recital. "Why, you damned young scoundrels, you might have set the barn afire!" he roared. Tom had to promise that no more Indians would be burned in the barn.

When he was thirteen, Tom began working in the summers as a strawberry picker. He would hasten to fill his quota and then would rush back to the shed and draw a humorous picture on the door. The others would scramble after him to see what he had done.

In 1900, when he was eleven years old, Tom joined his father after school let out on his campaign trips around the district. The long-anticipated climax of the summer was a floating and fishing trip on the Gasconade River in the upper Ozarks. During this expedition, Tom seriously injured his foot; it became infected, and the whole party pulled up camp to rush him to a doctor. The raft he was on capsized as they ran through a rocky chute. He swam ashore without difficulty, was loaded onto another raft, and floated to a railroad bridge, where the party flagged down a passing train. The concern M.E. showed when Tom's raft overturned, and again after they finally reached the doctor, showed the boy that his father cared deeply for him. But it was to be their last intimate association until Tom spent three months by his father's bedside in 1924.

Political Defeat

Tom's mother, meanwhile, was successfully scaling the heights of Washington society. She reached the peak when Theodore Roosevelt stepped into the presidency after the assassination of McKinley in September 1901. Though a Republican, Roosevelt proved most hospitable to the Bentons; in 1886 he had written a biography of Senator

Thomas Hart Benton. The Colonel and his pretty wife were frequently invited to White House parties and musicales, and there Elizabeth shone graciously, chatting with the President and showing off her good looks, her good manners, and her cultural attainments. She had a chance to demonstrate her knowledge of music, which was quite extensive by Washington standards. This was probably the happiest time of her life.

M.E.'s days as a politician, however, were numbered, for his thinking had not kept pace with that of the younger generation. He had vigorously supported President Cleveland's bloody suppression of the Pullman strike in 1894. He approached issues from the standpoint of the farmer, and he did not understand the needs of miners, merchants, and industrialists, or those of the workingman.

Elizabeth Benton's behavior did not help, for her fancy Washington ways estranged her from the women of Neosho, who resented being outclassed. From his friends Tom picked up snatches of gossip, reflecting what they had heard at home, that the Benton family had become "mighty uppity." The Colonel constantly admonished Elizabeth to rein in her behavior, to dress less splendidly, to keep things simpler, and above all not to talk about "how we do it in Washington." "It's these folks that send us there, Missuz," he would say. "Don't shame them." The couple would often bicker about this at dinner. "Don't criticize me before the children, Mister," Elizabeth would reply, and she would lean back in her chair and wipe her eyes.

As the election of 1904 approached, the conflict between Tom's parents died down, but the mood at home grew subdued and somber; M.E. was being reelected by narrower and narrower margins. In 1904 Teddy Roosevelt ran for the presidency and swept Missouri with him in a Republican landslide. In a stinging rebuke, the Colonel was defeated by a Republican lawyer from his own hometown of Neosho.

Despite this defeat, Tom's mother was eager to stay in Washington. She wanted her husband, who was not yet sixty, to take up legal practice in the city. She enlisted her children, particularly Tom and Mary, to apply pressure on him, bribing them with

Thomas Hart Benton, Valentine, ink and watercolor on paper, circa 1906. Made for his mother just after the family's return to Neosho. Benton showed himself in the background as a pipe-smoking cherub.

Thomas Hart Benton, Christmas Card, ink and watercolor on paper, 1905. When he was sixteen, during his last year in Washington, Benton made this card for his mother.

affection, and in Tom's case with a beautiful box of pastels. But M.E. stubbornly resisted. Perhaps he was too set in his ways to embark on such a new venture, perhaps he was too fond of Neosho.

Tom thought little about the move until his sixteenth birthday, when his mother organized a party for him. In the midst of it, she broke into tears. "Tom, do you realize that this is your last birthday in Washington?" she blurted out, and hurriedly left the room. His friends exclaimed in surprise, "What, you won't be on the team next year?" It suddenly came home to Tom that he was about to leave. A few weeks later, the Benton family began packing up their household goods for the return to Missouri.

Return to Neosho

Elizabeth Benton suffered a nervous breakdown after her return to Missouri and spent much of her time in bed. She was finally pulled back to health by her elder sisters, who came to Oak Hill to care for her and called upon religion for assistance. They got down on their knees in her bedroom and prayed for her welfare, an event that was reported to Tom by his awestruck little sister Mary, who told him, "They asked God to come in the room!"

By the end of the summer, Elizabeth had pulled herself together and was taking pleasure in unpacking her Washington possessions, impressing her sisters with them. She had even located an elegantly turned out piano teacher, Mr. Calhoun, who came down once a week from Carthage to chat about culture and teach music. He took a great interest in Tom, admired his drawings, and told him that he ought to study art in Paris.

Tom, like his mother, had "adjustment problems" when he returned to Neosho, although he expressed it differently: he began getting into fights with the local kids. On a Sunday evening in June 1905, he was strutting around the town square in his finest Washington attire—a shiny silk shirt and colorful tie, a blue blazer with mother-of-pearl buttons, and white flannel pants. As he walked past the Bank of Neosho, some boys taunted him, and one of them, Harry Hargrove, smeared his foot on Tom's white pants.

Tom responded with a punch that bloodied Hargrove's nose. Hargrove then rushed him, and the two fell in a tangle on the ground. Tom put a scissors hold around his opponent's head and began to cut off his breath, but before he could do much damage, a deputy marshal arrived and broke things up. The next day, the two were hauled into court. Tom was fined a dollar plus court costs, a total of eight dollars, while the Hargrove boy was acquitted. The Colonel was away when the fracas occurred, but upon his return he for once took Tom's side. "The damned scoundrels," he exclaimed, "trying to get at me through my boy. They can't fine a kid like that for getting into a kid fight."

He advised Tom to stay off the square, but his advice was ignored and more tussles took place. In the meantime, M.E. had protested to his friends, so Tom's adversaries were fined also. Unlike Tom, they had to pay out of their own earnings. To avoid the police, the boys challenged Tom to come down to Big Spring Park, and there they fought without interference. Tom, however, had trained in boxing and wrestling at the Force School, and this stood him in good stead. He came out of these contests pretty well. One of his Neosho friends later recalled Tom's amazing ability to withstand pain. He would shrug off a punch with the words, "It don't pay me no mind." By the end of the summer, Tom had convinced the town boys that despite his fancy clothes he was definitely not a sissy.

That year, he did poorly in school. Although most of his fellow pupils were unambitious country boys, Tom came out at the very bottom of his class. Outside of school, however, he was an avid reader.

A local ritual in which the town took considerable pride was the annual high school football game with the town of Seneca. Neosho, a larger town, was usually the victor, but in 1905 the rumor got around that Seneca was taking older and larger boys, nineteen and twenty years old, away from work and putting them on the team. Neosho decided to do likewise. Though Tom was an aggressive player, he was small, so the coach decided to replace him.

He decided to attend the game anyway, with his chum Sterling Price, whose father owned a dry-goods store called the Golden Eagle. Sterling brought with him a bottle of rock-candy whiskey, a brew heavily sweetened with sugar to conceal its bitterness. The two polished off the entire bottle and in the euphoria that resulted drove their wagon right onto the Seneca playing field. They were so intoxicated that when they were stopped, they could hardly stand up. This caused considerable commotion and led to an unflattering editorial in the Seneca newspaper.

To punish him, Tom's parents kept him home in the evenings. There he did a great deal of reading, as he did also in the home of Wellesby Benton, whose father had the finest library in Neosho. In his friend's living room, Tom savored delicious books forbidden elsewhere in town, such as the romances of Alexandre Dumas (then not considered suitable for the young), the lurid stories of Edgar Allan Poe, and a grimly fascinating treatise on the torture methods of the Spanish Inquisition. There, also, Tom first read Mark Twain's *Huckleberry Finn,* a book most people in Neosho regarded as indecent because of its frank presentation of the friendship between Huck and Nigger Jim.

During his last summer in Neosho, eager for more adventure, Tom decided to jump a freight train with his friend Johnny Smith. Each told his parents that he had gone to stay with the other, and they successfully caught a train headed south. They sat in an open boxcar watching the moon fade and the dawn come as they crossed the border into Arkansas. In the chill of early morning, however, they were spotted by a tough, diligent brakeman, who threw them off. After hanging around most of the day by a desolate railroad spur, they hopped onto a northbound freight late in the afternoon and returned home.

Joplin and the House of Lords

With the end of the 1906 school year, the question arose as to what Tom would do that summer. His first cousin Willie McElhany (son of his mother's sister Emma) had established a surveying outfit in Joplin. In May he wrote to offer Tom a job. Joplin was on the boom, thanks to the discovery of lead and zinc in the area.

Thomas Hart Benton, Turn of the Century Joplin, *acrylic on canvas mounted on panel, 1972. At age eighty-three, Benton painted this work for the Joplin Municipal Building, showing himself in the center as a cub newspaper cartoonist. "After I took the lines out of my face," he commented ruefully, "there wasn't much left."*

The Bentons underwent much soul-searching. Though named for a high-minded minister, Joplin was filled with saloons and painted women. Willie McElhany's own brother Roy was running a fancy brothel, filled with girls of different nationalities. Fortunately, Willie did not associate with his brother, and after a good deal of family debate, Tom was allowed to go.

The finest saloon in Joplin was the House of Lords, which had a seventy-five-foot frontage at 319 Main Street. One Saturday night, Tom went in and ordered himself a beer. Over the bar hung a large gilt-framed oil painting that was famous in the locality; it depicted a nude woman with a black mask, lying on a divan. She had just been stabbed, and her assailant was in the process of turning the knife on himself. Supposedly the young man had picked up the girl at a costume ball and slept with her, only to discover that she was his sister.

Tom was looking at this work with intense interest, when he was startled out of his reverie by the awareness that a bunch of men at the other end of the bar were kidding him. Their jocular obscenities made him blush with embarrassment. He hastily explained that he wasn't interested in the subject matter; he was gazing so intently because he was an artist. "So you're an artist, shorty?" one of his tormentors asked skeptically. "Yes, by God, I am!" Tom replied. "And I'm a good one."

"I don't really remember the conversation that followed," Benton wrote in *An Artist in America,* "but those kidding roughnecks with their good-humored, amused faces, lost as they are to me in the vague memory of the shining bar at the House of Lords, with its bright lights, glittering silver and glassware, determined in a way the life I was to follow. Their bantering skepticism about my claims to artistry tied together the loose strings of all the purposeless activities of my adolescence. They threw me back on the only abilities that distinguished me from the run of boys, those abilities which I had abandoned for more active things. By a little quirk of fate, they made me a professional artist in a short half-hour."

Ben Reese and Thomas Hart Benton, in Joplin, 1906.

One of the men mentioned that there was an opening for an artist across the street at the city newspaper, the Joplin *American,* and that Tom should try for it. Unable to back down, he went across the street with them and up a steep, narrow stairway to the newspaper office, which reeked of printer's ink, hot iron, and oil. There a man with a short gray beard and a kindly face sat alone, reading. Tom explained his business, and the man heaved himself out of his swivel chair, took him over to the window, and pointed across the street to where bright lights were burning. "Listen, son," he said. "That's Jim Keena's. You go over and draw Jim so we'll recognize him, and you're hired."

Keena's place was full of lead miners busily pouring nickels into a row of gambling machines. Tom made his sketch and returned to the office. There were several men there this time, and they passed the sketch around. One of them asked: "Can you do that in ink?"

"Yes," Tom said, "I can. I've done a lot of pictures in pen and ink."

"Where'd you learn to draw like that?"

"Nowhere. I've always drawn."

"Have, huh? Well, you're hired. Fourteen a week. What's your name, by the way?"

"Thomas Hart Benton."

The pay was four times what Tom had been getting as a surveyor. He was always proud that they gave him the job before they learned his name and discovered that he was Colonel Benton's son.

For the rest of the summer, Tom worked under the hot tin roof of the Joplin *American,* drawing a daily cartoon portrait of a prominent Joplinite. In the fashion of the time, he would draw big heads on small bodies and then surround the people with

the implements of their profession. Completely untrained in portraiture, he would start with the nose and hang the rest of the features on that. Somehow the drawings came out all right. He quickly made friends with a cub reporter who signed on at about the same time, Ben Reese, who later became managing editor of the St. Louis *Post-Dispatch*. They made a striking contrast, for Tom was only five feet three, whereas Ben was six feet two. Not long after starting the new job, Tom moved into a cheap boardinghouse on the south side of town on the corner of Moffet and Third, where he shared a room and a bed with Ben.

Tom discovered some things about sex while he lived in Joplin. One of the first calls he paid was to Mr. Calhoun, his mother's music teacher, who took him out to dinner and plied him with wine and Benedictine. Mr. Calhoun said that he soon would be going to Europe to visit Berlin and Paris. He talked enthusiastically about Tom's artistic talent and declared that Paris was the only proper place for a man of such natural ability to receive training. Would Tom like to join him? At first Tom listened to this with pleasure, but at some point in the middle of the meal he became aware that Mr. Calhoun was making eyes at him, as if he were a girl. He got up in embarrassment, hastily excused himself, and made a point of never seeing Mr. Calhoun again. He later wrote:

"I remembered for years the sad and defeated look on the face of this usually so self-possessed man when I departed. I almost felt sorry for him. Years later, losing caution with age, he carried his homosexual activities too far for the Joplin area to stomach and was run out for corrupting young boys. Vice was an accepted part of Joplin life but not Mr. Calhoun's kind."

Girls proved to be a more dangerous temptation. Tom had already gained a voyeur's knowledge of sinful ladies in Washington, where he had saved up quarters to go to the burlesque on Saturday afternoons with some older boys. Now he began to visit the local brothels with Ben Reese and other friends. He would sit in the parlor and sip beer at a dollar a bottle, until one night, after drinking a good deal, and spurred on by the taunts and challenges of his friends, he lost his virginity to a black-haired harlot in a red kimono, who did up her hair in curls like a little girl. Afterward the woman led him back downstairs, pushed him forward like an exhibit, bowed to the assembled beer-drinkers, and laughingly announced, "The kid has been fucked." The experience turned Tom's stomach, and it was several years before he made love to a woman again.

Chapter Two
Chicago

Clifford Berryman, Teddy Bear, *pencil on paper. Benton modeled much of his early work on Berryman's Washington* Post *cartoons, which featured figures with little bodies and big heads.*

"I dressed in the half light that came from the street lamps, feeling disgusted with my naïveté but also kind of sorry for Hud. I said, 'Hud, I can't sleep tonight. I guess I'll be going.'"

Military School

The job at the *American* gave Tom's rebellion a new force and credibility, for the fourteen-dollar salary was much greater than a law clerk's. Moreover, he had received a substantial bequest from his uncle Sam, $3,500, more than sufficient for any kind of education. Tom began pressuring his father to let him use this money to pursue artistic studies. As usual, his mother took his side against M.E. Finally, a compromise was reached. Tom quit his job at the *American* and agreed to attend military school for a year. His father promised that once he had graduated, he could begin studying at the Art Institute of Chicago, in order to become a newspaper cartoonist, which would pay well. By the end of September 1906, Benton was enrolled at Western Military Academy in Upper Alton, Illinois.

Tom's first letter from the school, dated September 21, complained, predictably: "The restriction of this life is something awful, one is never free for a moment; I am going to try to stand it; it's pretty trying to have a boy no older than yourself punching you in the stomach to make you hold your head up." He cheerfully reported that on the first day he had knocked one of his tormentors down and that "they have been partly civil to me since although they treat the other boys pretty badly."

Accounts of football fill up much of his correspondence. On October 28, for example, he devoted a long letter to a description of a game with Central High, in which the military academy was defeated. "Nearly every man on our side was hurt," Tom told his mother, "and I expect all of theirs. One of them broke his wrist and another that I know of must have had some teeth knocked out as he was bleeding at the mouth a great deal." He himself had been injured, he reported. "Two fingers on my left hand I can't move and my leg is badly swollen."

Other than football, Tom's chief interest was *The Reveille*, the school magazine; he was soon listed on the masthead as "Illustrator." "I was the maker of nearly the whole magazine," he boasted.

As usual, young Benton marched out of step with the academic program. Oddly, given the strong geometric patterns of his mature paintings, he flunked geometry, which he declared seemed exactly contrary to his way of thinking. He excelled in English and struck up such a friendship with his English teacher, Mrs. Dodge, that he began studying Browning's poetry with her in the recreation period after school.

He felt deeply frustrated, as he confessed to his mother: "I never seem to be able to say what I wish," he wrote. "I try to let you know and understand the feeling which riots within me, and yet when I read what I have written I invariably feel like casting it away. It was that way when I wrote you last week and it is that in what I have just written Dad, incoherency, a whole mass of words expressing nothing, honestly I sometimes feel like kicking down the house and resisting from attempting explanations of things that I scarcely understand myself.

"It is the same way with my art, I have inspiration, conception and lack execution. Let me once but conquer the last—but enough, why repeat what is all ready said."

To demonstrate his artistic gifts, Tom covered his letters home with cartoon sketches, drawn in a bold pen-and-ink style loosely based on the work of Clifford Berryman. Significantly, he did not hide these drawings in his letters but drew directly on the envelopes; in several cases he ingeniously used the postage stamp to represent a flag in his design. Already he wished to make his drawings public—to communicate not just with his parents but with the postman as well. While hastily drawn, these sketches betray remarkable skill both in capturing outline and in using crosshatching to indicate textures and shading.

Reprieve came unexpectedly, with the help of his friend Mrs. Dodge, who wrote a long letter to his parents arguing that Tom was meant to be an artist. Early in January, M.E. agreed that he could leave the school immediately and enroll at the Art Institute of Chicago. Tom bubbled with enthusiasm and wrote in excitement to his father:

"I believe at last that you have come to realize the greatness of the gift which Providence has thrust upon me. I don't believe that you ever thought of it as more than a mere pastime . . . and now I believe that you too begin to recognize the value of my gift.

"I am bound to be successful. I have the fullest confidence in myself. Ask anyone capable of judging my work what he thinks of my genius. He will tell you that the greater artists' work done in their boyhood does not equal mine. Everyone tells me that and I have seen and compared the earlier work of Abbey, H. Jones and others with mine, and without boasting I find it lacking. So do others who are authorities.

CENTRAL HIGH FEARS THIS ELEVEN'S PROWESS.

WESTERN MILITARY ACADEMY TEAM.

Lower row: George Karr, right half, Belleville; Jack Bratton, quarter back, East St. Louis; Capt. J. M. Daniels, left tackle, Leavenworth; Spencer Harlow, full back, St. Louis; M. C. Taylor, left half, Carthage, Missouri.

Upper row: A. S. Dowell, right end, Walnut Ridge, Ark.; P. H. Arbuckle, coach; Earl Hackney, right tackle, Carthage, Mo.; M. Myres, right guard, Chicago; Roy Black, center, Manito, Ill.; W. P. Callahan, left guard, Dayton, Ohio; S. B. Stevinson, right guard, Fort Smith, Ark.; C. R. Gray, Jr., manager, St. Louis; T. H. Benton, left end, Neosho, Mo.

Western Military Academy Football Team, 1906. Although small, Benton starred in football at the military academy and later played on a semiprofessional team in Chicago. He can be seen on the far right, just below the boy with a cap.

*Thomas Hart Benton, Bad
Dreams,* pen and ink on paper,
*from a letter to Hienie Hietz,
circa March 1907. When Hienie
Hietz had appendicitis, Benton
sketched "a pleasant and helpful
dream" for him.*

*Thomas Hart Benton, Cartoons,
pen and ink on paper, 1907.
Benton's letters to his mother
included cartoons of himself
sketching on a pier and in the
guise of a detective. He also
enclosed a sketch of the family
dog, "Bay."*

"I want you Dad to come up as soon as possible and let me talk with you. I will do my best to learn other things, but what is science and mathematics when compared to Nature and I know that I have a touch of nature. So send me to study that which is to be my life work and I shall do that which will never make you regret it."

Arrival in Chicago

Tom Benton took his first automobile ride when he arrived in Chicago, early in February 1907, and took a cab from the station. He had seen a few horseless carriages in Joplin, but they were so rare that the sight of one coming down the street would empty out all the stores. When he had left Washington in 1905, it was still a brick-and-stone, horse-and-buggy town. In Chicago he entered the modern age, the age of automobiles and skyscrapers. "This is certainly a big city," he reported in his first letter home. "The buildings are regular mountains, making the streets look like footpaths. Everything is rush and bustle."

M.E. had procured a room for Tom with an old business acquaintance, a dry, cautious man named Sidway. Mr. Sidway had once been an agent for farm properties in Missouri but had since grown wealthy through the sale and management of Chicago real estate. A widower, he lived on the third floor of a four-story brownstone with his son Harry, who was in business with him. The house was on the far south side of town, near a big park that faced Lake Michigan. To get to the Art Institute, which was five or six miles away, Tom took a streetcar. Although they had a kitchen, the Sidways ate at cheap restaurants in the neighborhood, and Tom often joined them, getting breakfast for a dime and lunch or dinner for forty or fifty cents. A frugal man, Mr. Sidway saw to it that everyone paid his own bill.

The Sidways, as Benton noted in one of his letters home, were "all business." During his first year in Chicago, his most interesting acquaintance was a bank officer named Mr. Hudspeth, who lived downstairs. About forty years of age, Hudspeth came from Canada, dressed impeccably in a tweedy style, and spoke with a distinctly British accent. His apartment, in contrast to that of the Sidways, was elegantly furnished, with dark wood bookshelves and a Persian carpet. Benton began seeing him often. He was a great reader and introduced Tom to the latest developments in literature, such as the writings of Ibsen, Shaw, and Wilde. As they got to know each other, Tom began calling him "Hud."

Benton later recalled: "By the time April came and my eighteenth birthday, Hud was the best friend I had in Chicago, much more interesting than any I had made at the Art Institute among the students. He was also the best informed one I ever had and during my 1907 friendship with him greatly advanced my education, in all directions."

Nearly every week, Hud took Tom out to dinner at one of the fancier Chicago eating places, and a number of times they went afterward to concerts or the opera. He thus encouraged the young man's musical interests, which had already been sparked by his mother. When the nights became warm, he introduced Tom to German beer gardens, familiar to Chicago. Together, they went several times to one on the far south side, a place so popular that tables had to be reserved. During the intermission, people strolled up and down on the gravel walks between the rows of tables underneath the trees, and Tom observed that among them were male couples who paraded with an affected military walk. They stood out because of their elegant dress and arrogant manner. Occasionally one of these fellows would stop and talk with Hud, who might get up and walk too. But he never introduced Tom. "They're the German crowd, not *our* kind at all," he would explain. Tom felt relieved, for he suspected that they were "queer." He only once mentioned his beer garden visits in his letters home, and on that occasion he did not mention Hud.

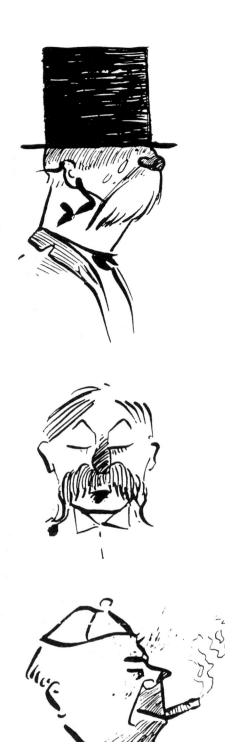

Thomas Hart Benton, Heads, pen and ink on notepaper with the letterhead of the Joplin American, *August 1906. Benton's drawings for the Joplin* American *have been lost, but these sketches in a letter to his friend Hienie Hietz reveal his wit as a caricaturist.*

Classes at the Art Institute

Although Chicago was giving birth to modern forms of architecture and had perfected a new building type, the skyscraper, the curriculum of the Art Institute, whose students mostly went on to careers in commercial art, did not reflect modern developments. During his stay in Chicago, Benton seems to have been unaware of the most progressive painters in Europe, except for Whistler.

His enthusiasm for art died quickly when he walked into his first class and confronted the task of copying plaster casts. The students met in a cold gray room with a few easels. The dull, kindly old woman who taught the course, Mrs. Vanderpoel (the wife of the head of the drawing department), was unimpressed by Tom's journalistic credentials. When he asked her why he needed to draw casts, she responded, "It is the way everyone has to begin. You'll see why later."

Benton dutifully set to work copying the head of a goddess with a broken nose and blank, expressionless eyes, but he soon grew bored. "I was not very good at it," he confessed later in life to the scholar Paul Cummings. He had always drawn subjects that had dramatic meaning, and he asked Mrs. Vanderpoel which goddess the plaster head represented. She didn't know. Moreover, he was accustomed to drawing with pencil or with pen and ink. His sticks of charcoal smeared and wouldn't keep their points.

Occasionally John Vanderpoel, a hunchback who had trained in Paris under Jean-Léon Gérome, would come into the classroom and examine the students' work. "He'd come and look at your drawing," Benton later recalled, "and say, 'It's no good. Do it again.'" He never touched Tom's drawings, although he sometimes corrected the work of the older students. Undoubtedly the experience was a blow to Benton's self-esteem, for a few weeks after he had arrived in Chicago, he wrote to his mother with uncharacteristic modesty: "I am beginning to think that there is no such thing as a born artist."

Tom's frustration with plaster casts, however, did not hold him back for long. After a week or so, he learned that a life drawing class, taught by Allen E. Philbrick, met at the same time. The following day, he went into Philbrick's class and rapidly produced a large, flashy pencil drawing, which the other students admired. He was in a cocky mood as the instructor came over to investigate. When Philbrick asked him where he had studied, he declared, "No wheres," and then boastfully launched into an account of his experiences as a *paid* newspaper cartoonist. The teacher listened with tight lips and then pointed to the drawing. "Of course there's ability here," he noted to the little group that had assembled. "But it's not artistic. Newspapers are bad places to begin. Bad for writers but worse for artists."

"Why isn't it artistic?" Tom shot back, half defensive and half genuinely eager to learn. Philbrick flushed. "Because it isn't," he replied, and abruptly turned away. After class, a group of students gathered around Tom; one of them commented, "Philbrick couldn't do what you did this afternoon to save his neck. Don't let what he said worry you." "I am drawing a little interest for some reason or other," Benton wrote ingenuously to his mother shortly afterward. "I don't know what it is."

Philbrick could never bring himself to compliment Tom's work. He took an immediate dislike to him and never gave sympathetic or helpful criticism. He was fair enough, though, to include Tom's drawings in the weekly exhibitions of student work, where they attracted attention.

One day, one of the instructors, Frederick C. Oswald, introduced himself to Benton in the corridor and began questioning him about his ambitions. Tom replied that he had worked for pay as a newspaper cartoonist and intended to return to that line of work when he had improved his drawing. Oswald looked disapproving. "You

Thomas Hart Benton, Self-Portrait Sketch, *pen and ink on paper, 1907.*

know, you could be some kind of artist," he commented. "Did you ever think of that? Have you ever tried painting?"

Not long afterward, on an afternoon when he felt bored with Philbrick's model, Benton wandered into Oswald's studio and became so entranced with watercolor that he decided to switch classes again. As a matter of courtesy, he told Philbrick of his move, but this only stirred up trouble. Instead of being pleased, as Tom had expected, Philbrick accosted Oswald in the corridor, where all could hear, and accused him of stealing one of his best students. He carried this accusation to the office and put the transfer in jeopardy, but luckily Benton had befriended Martha Moline, a fellow student, who was a woman of influence in Chicago. She put in her voice, and Tom had his way.

With Mrs. Moline's encouragement, he began attending other life classes, even though he hadn't been passed on. He would leave just before the instructor came in to give critiques. No one objected, and he soon got into the habit of dropping into any class whose model interested him.

During the breaks between poses in life class, Benton got to know a large, stocky boy from Iowa, Bob Everhardt. Bob was a few years older than Tom and had been in Chicago longer, so he knew his way around. Through him, Benton learned about oil painting. One day after lunch, Everhardt invited him into the painting room, where easels were grouped around various still-life arrangements. Bob was working from one consisting of a copper bowl, a couple of lemons, a red pepper, and a stuffed fish. Until that moment, it had never occurred to Tom that still life could be a subject for painting.

Although it was well advanced, Everhardt's study was quite dark compared with the watercolors Benton had been making in Oswald's class. In fact, the pepper was rendered in greenish brown rather than red. Puzzled, Tom asked why, and Bob explained that it was just underpainting. Then he picked up his palette, stained with patches of dried color, found a tube of vermilion paint, and squeezed out some pigment. Grabbing a big brush, he stuck it into the vermilion and with one stroke smeared it into the still wet greenish brown of the pepper. An inexplicable thrill rushed through Tom's body. "God a mighty, that's something I've got to learn about!" he exclaimed.

Everhardt painted by himself in his room on Saturdays and Sundays and agreed to take Benton on as a pupil. The next weekend, Tom watched him paint a still life, and shortly after this demonstration he purchased a big box for oil paints, a palette, and a dozen or so tubes of color. One afternoon, he skipped Oswald's class and took his equipment to Bob's place so that he could have Everhardt's guidance while he worked.

"I have never forgotten the nervous excitement that enveloped me when I began squeezing out the colors," he later recalled. "Why this mechanical act should have occasioned the emotional rocking it did is hardly explainable. . . . From the moment I first stuck my brush in a fat gob of color I gave up the idea of newspaper cartooning. I made up my mind that I was going to be a painter."

Every weekend through the spring, he experimented with the new medium, sometimes in Everhardt's room, sometimes outdoors in one of the south side parks. It had never occurred to him before to work outdoors, but he picked up the idea from Bob and his friends.

Once, the two of them took a trolley far out to the southern lakeshore and attempted to paint an old sailing vessel that lay on the beach. Bob went to work with moderate success, but Tom could only come up with smears. Fortunately, Everhardt was kind, and only commented, "Maybe you're trying to use too many colors." On his subsequent painting excursions, Benton shifted to watercolor, a medium he could handle more easily.

Thomas Hart Benton, Carica-ture of the Quartermaster at the Western Military Academy, *pen and ink on paper, autumn 1906.*

Thomas Hart Benton, Humor-ous Self-Portrait, *pen and ink on paper, from a letter to Hienie Hietz, March 1907. Benton por-trayed himself sitting on the throne of leisure and smoking his pipe in his bathrobe while preparing to go to bed.*

25

For all his efforts to master painting, he remained most skillful at drawing from the imagination, the talent he had developed as a child. In one of his letters, he reported an encounter with Mr. Timmons, a well-established Chicago artist who taught classes at the Institute. One day, Benton was sketching by a window in the corridor when Timmons walked by, picked up a drawing, and asked, "Is this from the imagination?" "Yes, sir," Tom replied. Timmons turned the paper over and looked at the sketch on the reverse. "And this too?" Tom replied it was. "Well," said the artist, "you are all right, you're all right; you're going to make good."

Summer in Neosho

On July 9, Benton wrote home that he had made the class for which he had stayed on in Chicago and that he had just completed "the best thing I have ever done in pastel." But he was not yet satisfied with his work. When his mother suggested that she might come up for a visit, he replied: "I would rather you would come when Benton is a name a little better known, for I am but newly initiated to the artistic and am just 'catching on' as they say. Next year I am going to have that exhibit loaded with my stuff for I haven't done all I can do."

Later in the month, he returned to Neosho and rejoined the round of small-town activities—picnics, parties, and excursions to swim in the creek. He made a studio for himself in the attic of Oak Hill and arranged his paintings from Chicago on the bracing timbers. He did a good deal of landscape painting outdoors, much to the astonishment of the village boys, who would sneak up in the bushes behind him to watch him at work.

"Neosho was a whiskey town for Oklahoma then, you know," his friend Phil Ratcliff recalled. "Tom and I and some of the others used to go to the saloons here. You didn't have to be twenty-one, you just had to look like you were grown. There used to be a mint bed down by the Big Spring park, and Tom and I would go down there and pick some mint. Then we'd take it to a saloon on Spring Street, and Tom would draw a picture of the bartender, who was a great big fellow with a mustache. In return for the picture, the bartender would give us a mint julep made with the mint we'd picked."

Jack Rushmore, another Neosho friend, who later became an oil executive, remembered Benton's passion for boxing: "We used to box in the evenings in the basement of one of the buildings on the square. Well, I don't know whether you could really call it boxing—we used to put on the gloves and rough each other up."

In August 1907, Benton was nearly killed when he hit his head on a rock while diving into the aptly named Shoal Creek from an overhanging tree. He had been showing off to some girls. Fortunately, one of his friends had an extra-fast horse, so he galloped Tom into town to the doctor. The accident laid Benton up for several days and gave him a nasty scar for life.

Little was said of Tom's artistic efforts in the family, and he did not encourage inquiry because he was still struggling with oil. His mother accepted with enthusiasm, his father with indifference, the shift in his interests from illustration to painting. His relationship with his father remained cordial but distant; the Colonel spent most of his time in his office in the town square and was frequently absent from town on legal or political business.

Return to Chicago

Benton returned to Chicago in late September and was quickly caught up in the excitement of starting to work again. Already he felt infinitely more sophisticated than the first-year students and was eager to prove his talent. He had learned to affect the look of artistic genius, growing his hair down over his ears and collar. He wore a derby hat, a very baggy pair of peg-top corduroy trousers, a black flannel shirt, and a red tie. Sometimes he even carried a cane. In a letter of October 1, 1907, to his mother, he declared:

"I am excited and restless and everything. I can just feel the power in my hands and brain, to draw and paint. For the first time I have absolute confidence that I have that in me, I haven't the egotism to call it genius, which will enable me to realize on paper or canvas the pictures which are on my brain, which I can see and am just gaining the power to execute. It won't be many years before I'll be absolute master of my hand, and then with imagination which I know I have, is there any reason why I cannot be great?"

He did not return to the Sidways. Mr. Sidway had been disapproving of his friendship with Mr. Hudspeth, and encouraged Benton to move uptown with his student friends. He even wrote a letter to Neosho in support of the move, so that when Tom announced his change of residence, neither parent raised objections. Tom moved into a brownstone at 291 Michigan Avenue, where the Hotel Stevens later stood. His friends Bob Levett and Bill York had found the place before he arrived, and they were joined by a new first-year student, a big, handsome blond fellow named "Jack" Armstrong, who would achieve renown as a creator of calendar girls. All four shared a shabby room on the top floor. They had only a couch and two beds to sleep four people. Benton, because of his short stature, was awarded the couch; York, who was bony and restless, got the single bed; Levett and Armstrong shared the double.

The place soon became a popular hangout for evening debates and fan-tan playing, and a rendezvous point for nocturnal excursions. The boys frequented the old Congress Café and ate at all kinds of ethnic restaurants—German, French, Italian, and Chinese. They went to dance halls to hear Negro bands up from New Orleans, who played ragtime, jazz, and blues. At a poker game with some newfound "friends," Tom was lured into gambling away his monthly allowance. They also visited the brothels but mostly just gawked at the girls, who were tender toward their youthful timidity.

That fall, Benton played semiprofessional football for five dollars a game, until the weather grew too cold for the games to attract a crowd. In the company of his teammates, he began going to a gymnasium, where young prizefighters trained. Since he had a bit of experience with boxing, he was easily lured into two-minute sparring rounds with the young hopefuls who were near his weight. He was good enough that the young pugs began laughingly to call him "Kid Benton." He wore headgear, and so was never badly marked up—unlike his friend Armstrong. Jack, who had also studied boxing, but was larger and more arrogant than Tom, was severely battered one afternoon by a young light heavyweight—an experience that permanently ended his interest in working out with professionals.

At the Art Institute, Benton finally graduated from plaster casts to the men's life class, an event marked by an elaborate induction ceremony lasting from six in the afternoon until long past midnight. After the secret rites, the initiates stripped to their underwear and marched down Michigan Avenue carrying a coffin with a skeleton in it. Tom wrote his mother: "I am still alive. I have been through the most horrible of initiations and am thanking my stars that I have its effects off my mind. The ceremony came off Thurs. night and I have spent the time since in cleaning the paint off my body."

In late October 1908, Benton left the brownstone on Michigan Avenue. His place was taken by a boy from Arizona, Ross Santee, who later became well known as a writer and illustrator of cowboy stories. Tom had grown tired of the continual racket and was dismayed that none of his friends did any serious reading, except for an

Thomas Hart Benton, Self-Portrait in Caricature, *pen and ink on paper, 1907–08.*

Thomas Hart Benton, Self-Portrait Sketch, *pen and ink on paper, 1907–08. From the scapbook of his classmate Claire Stadeker. In Chicago, Benton wore baggy peg-top trousers and let his hair grow long. "I began to be regarded as a genius among my companions," he recalled. "My garb was proof of it."*

occasional magazine. They all wanted to become illustrators for the magazine or calendar market and had little understanding or sympathy for his high-flown aspirations.

When he applied for a room at 4556 Vincennes Avenue, the landlady, Mrs. Hamer, looked at his remarkable attire with surprise. "Are you a religious man?" she asked. "No, ma'am," Tom replied. "I'm an artist." Her face beamed. "Oh, how nice. I'm an artist myself." Her oeuvre consisted of copies of sentimental prints and magazine covers, but it was enough to make her feel an affection for the boy, and she showered him with attention, bringing him little gifts of tea and homemade cookies when he worked at home on weekends.

The neighborhood children looked on Tom's artistic mannerisms with less affection. He walked quickly, swinging his shoulders in a cocky way, and his clothes set him apart. During the first week of his stay, as he was walking home, he passed a group of pretty girls sitting on a stoop. "Look at that crazy freak," one of them declared as he walked past, and as he strode on, he was greeted by gales of female laughter and the catcalls of a gang of boys across the street. That night he slipped out and got a haircut, and thenceforth he kept his eccentric clothes in his locker at the Art Institute. This helped a little, but nonetheless he was constantly on the verge of street brawls.

Some of his classmates resented his manner as much as the neighborhood toughs. A clique against him had begun to form after his conspicuous first day in Philbrick's class, and after the fracas over the transfer to Oswald's camp, several students began to kid him unkindly. "Oh, look at the precious boy! Oh, the little Jesus!" they would say.

An Evening with Hud

In Benton's second year, a hulking six-footer who was studying commercial art joined his detractors. One day early in the fall, when Tom was showing off his prowess in Oswald's class, the fellow poked his head through the doorway and called out sarcastically, "Is Oswald's pet showing off again?" Normally Tom would have responded to such a jibe and perhaps resorted to his fists, but his adversary was so big that he held off. This only encouraged the bully, who continued to needle him on every possible occasion. Gradually Tom's anger heated to the boiling point, until the day he stepped into the men's room and found it filled with students smoking cigarettes, his tormentor among them. As Benton stepped up to the urinal, the giant made a disparaging remark about his size. Though stung, Tom concentrated on his business, but as he came out he saw his enemy walking down the corridor a few steps ahead, and a wave of anger washed over him. Impulsively he ran up behind his adversary, grabbed his foot, and with all his force flipped him down hard on his face onto the stone floor.

"You little bastard, I'll shake your guts out," the boy exclaimed as he scrambled to his feet. Fortunately for Benton, Bob Everhardt was following a few steps behind. As the hulking fellow rushed toward Tom, both arms outstretched to throttle him, Bob rushed forward and hit the boy squarely in the pit of the stomach, winding him. Down he went once again, falling next to a coal shaft that led down to the furnace room in the cellar. Tom twisted the lid free and jerked his assailant's head and shoulders over the hole. Bob instantly took the hint, lifted up the boy's legs, and dropped him down the chute. Had the bin been empty, his neck might well have been broken. Fortunately, he landed on a bed of powdered coal, where he was discovered a few moments later—bruised, black with coal dust, and crying from pain and humiliation.

Moments later, Bob, Tom, and their tearful black-faced adversary confronted each other in the school manager's office. The inquest did not take long. Everhardt and Benton were told to pack their things and leave; they were expelled. A thousand unhappy thoughts rushed through Tom's mind. Would this mean the end of his artistic career? What could he tell his parents? He calmed himself a little with the thought that perhaps he could seek newspaper work in Chicago.

Going to his classroom to gather his paints, brushes, and papers, Tom ran into Fred Oswald, who had already heard what had happened. "You leave your things here," Oswald said. "Come back for them when I tell you to. There are sides to this the office doesn't know about. I know how this fellow has been treating you, and I'm going to tell them."

Benton went home and waited. Two days later, Bob Levett told him that he and Everhardt were wanted at the Institute. They were given a lecture and allowed to come back. Their enemy left the school, probably ashamed to return.

Only a few days later, Tom had another disturbing experience. One evening, he decided to call on his former landlord, Mr. Sidway, and report on his doings. He arrived at the house about eight o'clock and spent an hour with Mr. Sidway and Harry. Then he went downstairs and knocked on the door of his old friend Hud, who grasped him by the hand, patted him on the shoulder, and pulled him into the sitting room. "Well, well, let's hear all about you," he said. "Sit down and we'll have a little nip for old time's sake. I've missed you and have been wanting to hear from you."

Hud chipped some pieces of ice out of the chunk in his icebox and they sat down together with a big bottle of Scotch and a siphon of soda. Hud began pumping Benton for news, and as Tom liked nothing better than to talk about his projects, he was soon going full speed. When he slowed down, Hud slipped him another nip of Scotch and a fresh question and started him up again. He wanted to know about Oswald and whether Tom went out with him in the evening; about Tom's roommates; about his artistic endeavors.

The doses of whiskey must have gotten larger and larger, because when two hours had gone by and it was time to go home, Tom found that he could barely stand. "Why, you're tipsy," Hud said. "Better sit down again." Hud had a strangeness in his eyes, which Benton couldn't quite place. He seemed different from the Hud he had known,

Thomas Hart Benton, Classroom Drawing Under the Instruction of Peixotto, *pen and ink on paper, 1907. Benton gave this pen-and-ink study from Ernest Peixotto's course in illustration to one of his female classmates, Myrtle Irwin, of Carthage, Missouri.*

Thomas Hart Benton, Upper and Underclassmen *(illustrations, the University of Missouri yearbook), 1908. "The new students are all very funny," Benton wrote to his mother at the beginning of his second year in Chicago. "They fail to understand things and in a half-afraid style are continually asking questions of the older ones."*

but Tom wasn't quite sober enough to understand what was going on. All he could think was, "Old Hud's drunk too."

They talked a bit more, and once again Benton tried to rise. He staggered, and Hud took him by the arm. "You can't go out on the street, Tom," he said. "You'd better stay here tonight. My bed's big enough for both of us."

"I guess that's right, Hud," said Tom, and he allowed himself to be ushered into the bedroom, where he stripped down to his undershirt and climbed into the bed. His later description of what ensued expresses forcefully the revulsion he felt. He wrote in an unpublished memoir:

"Hud undressed in a little alcove adjoining the bedroom but when he came out and turned off the light I noticed, in spite of my drunken drowsiness, that he was stark naked. But I was too far gone to think much of it and began to doze. I did not get fully asleep, however, and after a bit became aware that one of Hud's hands was on my penis trying to get the foreskin back. Still the only thought that came to me was that he was drunk and did not know what he was doing so I turned over to my other side. Then, all of a sudden he stuck a greased finger up my rectum. He'd probably stuck it in a pot of vaseline because it went way up. I jumped, like a hot poker had been shoved in me and leaped clear out of bed, instantly stone sober, well knowing now what he was up to.

"I dressed in the half light that came from the street lamps, feeling disgusted with my naiveté but also kind of sorry for Hud.

"I said, 'Hud, I can't sleep tonight. I guess I'll be going.'

"When I arrived downtown all my roommates were asleep and I tiptoed to my couch, pulled my clothes off, and lay down. I had hardly got stretched out when my rectum began to itch and then suddenly I was overwhelmed with a furious need to get to the bathroom stool. This was on the floor below and when I got to my feet I knew I could not make it. Either the vaseline left from Hud's finger, or the overdoses of whiskey to which he had subjected me, had produced one of those instant diarrheas which brook no delay. We had a metal slop jar in the room for midnight necessities so taking off its lid I plopped myself over it and let fly, using the pages of a magazine for toilet paper when I was finished.

"When I woke up in the morning my roommates were gone. With what water they had left in our crockery wash pitcher I cleaned up and prepared to go myself. Just as I was about to leave the woman who did our cleaning came in. She was a big gawky Negro girl from the South who took care of all the rooms in the house and was probably overloaded with work. Somehow she went straight to the slop jar and feeling it heavier than usual pulled off its lid. With the stench boiling out she clamped it right back and turned to me.

" 'Who done dis?' she asked.

" 'Maybe I did,' I said, 'I was sick last night.'

" 'Well y'all just take dat pot downstahs and impty it out yo'self. Ise uh piss chambuhmaid all right but I ain't no shit chambuhmaid.'

"I took the vessel downstairs to the bathroom and cleaned it out. So ended my friendship with Hud."

Frederick Oswald

Benton's training in Chicago was remarkably haphazard, as he attended whatever class suited his fancy. When drawing from the model, he worked in unorthodox ways, using pen or pencil rather than charcoal, sketching rapidly, and frequently changing his position in relation to the model. He did not attempt a photographically literal rendering but searched for those configurations of bone and muscle that provide the expressive essence of human action.

He already treated the making of art as a kind of performance. He was at his best working quickly, under pressure, slapping on paint with gusto in front of a crowd of gawkers and fellow students. Nerve, impulsiveness, the desire to show off—these were essential parts of his creative talent.

A number of his drawings survive from his time in Chicago: two pen-and-ink pieces that he gave to young women in his illustration class, five illustrations for the University of Missouri yearbook, and a number of sketches in his letters. Showing a finer, more atmospheric use of line than his earlier drawings, they were influenced by his study in the fall of 1907 with the illustrator Ernest Peixotto and by the example of the Spanish draftsman Daniel Vierge. Frederick Oswald introduced Benton to the work of Vierge simply by taking him to the library and showing him a volume of *Don Quixote*. "Take a look," was all he said. The instruction took care of itself.

No oil paintings survive from this period and, sadly, no watercolors—the medium in which Benton most excelled. Apparently the watercolors were free and wet and bold in color. One can get some idea of what they must have been like from the watercolors he executed just after he returned from France, such as a view of Central Park with a blue tree in silhouette, which he gave to his friend the cartoonist Clarence Batchelder.

Benton never saw Hud again after their traumatic evening encounter. The experience only brought him closer to Frederick Oswald. As with Hud, the relationship with Oswald contained a strange sexual undercurrent. The teacher didn't like the idea that Benton might associate with women. When Tom changed his attire because of the ridicule of the neighborhood urchins, Oswald immediately noticed the change. One day, he abruptly asked Tom if he was courting a girl. When Tom said no, he looked relieved and said, "Avoid that of all things. It could ruin your career." Something about his look reminded Benton of Hud and Mr. Calhoun, and he resolved not to go out with him if he was invited.

In fact, Oswald openly expressed a physical affection for him, and when Tom stayed after class to talk, as he often did, the teacher would throw his arm over his shoulder. Later in life, in speaking of Oswald to Paul Cummings, Benton stated: "I think he was a homosexual—there was no question of it. His interest in me may have been more than just artistic. But he never showed it too much."

The Art Institute of Chicago: Illustration Department.

In later life, Benton waged a violent campaign against homosexuals in the art world. Yet it was his early contact with three homosexuals that enabled him to transform himself from a small-town boy with small-town ambitions to a serious artist. They opened up to him a side of his personality that he had difficulty sharing with the boys in Neosho or his father's business acquaintances the Sidways. It was Calhoun who first inspired him to take his artistic gifts seriously and think of art as a possible career; it was Hud who introduced him to the literature and thought of the modern age; and it was Oswald who took his raw and rambunctious talent and turned it in a serious direction.

Of the three, Frederick Oswald had the greatest influence. While in mid-life, when he had outgrown Oswald's teachings, Benton tended to discount them, as an elderly man he grew increasingly appreciative of Oswald's influence. He wrote: "I now see that entering Fred Oswald's painting class was one of the crucial moves of my life. In a short while it changed my whole outlook, redirected my ambitions and made me conscious of my basic inclinations and character potentials, made me find myself that is."

And later: "Oswald was the perfect teacher for me. He knew how to handle a sort of innate rebelliousness in my character which made me resent instruction from above." Toward the end of his life, Benton told Paul Cummings: "I've always felt— well, sort of grateful to have had the luck to have run into that kind of a guy when I was just starting, rather than some drillmaster."

Thomas Hart Benton, Baseball, 1908. Among the few finished illustrations by Benton to survive from his period in Chicago are a group he made in the spring of 1908 for the University of Missouri yearbook. He obtained the commission through a friend on the yearbook's staff.

Benton's classmate Vaclav Vytlacil would state: "There's no question about it, Tom was the star of Fred Oswald's watercolor class." Tom's letters home to his mother report as much. On January 20, 1908, he wrote: "Every day now, when I leave school I have the satisfaction of knowing that I am the very best watercolorist in the place and that others know me as such, even though jealousy prompts many of them to discourage the growing reputation. At the end of this year I am going to have the students exhibition so full of my work that outsiders will be inquiring to see who I am."

By June 8, Tom could write with pride: "Everything is coming my way, the watercolor exhibit is simply a one man thing and I am the one. Everything I have done since Xmas has been hung. All my large watercolors have been framed separately. My pastels are all hung separately and I have a great many pen & ink drawings. . . . This has been the best year of my life and everybody here is expecting me to do great *things.*"

Once a week, Oswald gave a short talk about the "science" of picture-making. While he felt that "arrangement" could be done intuitively, he believed that "composition" was a "science" by which disparate objects were unified into an ensemble, and that this had to be taught. Probably he followed the ideas set forth in Arthur Wesley Dow's handbook *Composition*, which had been published in 1899.

Oriental art was popular at this time, largely through the example of Whistler, and while Oswald did not show his own work to his students, he did show them Japanese prints. At first Benton was puzzled as to the relevance of Japanese prints to the sort of realistic, descriptive watercolor painting that interested him. But when he challenged his teacher, Oswald didn't argue back; he just said, "Keep looking." After Tom had made a few rough pencil copies of the prints, he began to understand what Oswald was getting at.

Oswald's point was reinforced by a huge loan exhibition of 659 Japanese prints at the Art Institute, March 5–25, 1908. Spread through six galleries, the show was installed by Benton's future friend Frank Lloyd Wright, who owned many of the works. Tom studied the display carefully, and it permanently affected his ideas about design. He quickly absorbed the notion of "controlled composition," the planning of

the whole design before starting work on it. For the first time, he realized that it was possible to explore the disposition of lines and colors apart from the issue of representation—in other words, that it was possible to explore issues of form apart from those of meaning.

Oswald also had theories about color, which he had probably derived from the current literature on French Impressionism. He advocated the use of complementary colors, particularly in shadows—for example, the introduction of a dark green into the dark side of red objects or red into the dark side of green ones. He used a color wheel in his demonstrations; Tom was naive enough to suppose that Oswald had invented it, although he later saw many similar ones in France.

Benton also slipped into an advanced portrait class conducted by an elderly artist, Frederick W. Freer, who taught his students to draw with a brush and use a limited palette. Freer became ill toward the end of the winter (he died in the spring of 1908), and his place was taken by Louis Betts, a painter of society ladies and their tycoon husbands. Fred Oswald resented Betts, whom he dismissed as a "trickster," but Tom couldn't resist attempting to imitate his bravura, even though it had a disastrous effect on his emerging concern with compositional structure. He was accustomed to the translucent medium of watercolor, in which, to darken a tone, one simply applied

Thomas Hart Benton, Central Park, *watercolor on paper, 1912. None of Benton's Chicago watercolors survive, but they must have looked similar to this view of New York's Central Park, which he made just after he came back from Paris. Benton gave the painting to the cartoonist C. D. Batchelor, one of his friends in the Lincoln Arcade.*

33

successive washes. In oil, on the other hand, it was necessary to get both color and "tone" with the first stroke. At the end of the year, he still had not worked out his difficulties. "I am having a terrible time painting in oil," he confessed to his mother.

His technical abilities still lagged behind his ambitions, but he was growing increasingly attentive to the Whistlerian beauties of tone and color around him, and he wallowed in an intensely felt if somewhat jejune romanticism. As he wrote his mother: "Every hour, every day brings me more and more into the realms of the ideal, into the beautiful. Where a few months ago I would gaze and pass on, I now gaze and ponder. The beauty of the sun, falling at evening in the smoke of the city, leaving all indistinct, blue and rose, soft and mysterious, will hold me for an indefinable period. Just the other night I was crossing the Chicago river and was so impressed with the marvellous coloring, as the day drew to a close, that I stood and watched for a long time, saw the sky and the buildings turn from gold to rose and from rose to a most delicate blue from which the masts of the ships rose into the sky like vast spider webs, it was divine, and looking at the soft harmony of the whole, I could feel the power of the Infinite, and I could rejoice that I was one of the few who can hear the music that comes from a harmony of colors as from a harmony of sounds. To me color is music and music is color."

His ideal at the time (surprisingly, given that his own mature work developed a very different character) was the work of Whistler. He wrote: "My art is not to be the art of realism. I am not to put things as they are, but more beautiful than they are. The art of James McNeill Whistler has left an impression on me that has shown me what is really and truly artistic. Tone, colors harmoniously arranged, a certain quality, a certain lightness of line, whether you can distinguish one object from another or not, whether the thing painted looks like a man, woman, or dog, mountain, horse, or tree; you have harmony, and that is the grandest artistic aim, it is the truly artistic aim. One of the reasons that I must go to Paris is to see the greater works of the Whistler I speak of, he was the greatest of all modern painters and may be ranked with the grandest of the old masters."

By his last year at the Art Institute, he had become well aware of the nature of artistic genius. On March 9, 1908, he wrote: "I feel in my very soul that I was born to be great, born to do things in which other men have failed. Those men here who call me 'promising' know not the magnitude of the 'promise' which the gods have given in the later hours of the night, when the hum of the city is hushed in stillness and the winds are dead, and thought and I commune alone. They know not the greatness that has come upon me at these times, when the mind has leapt beyond the real and soars unrestrained in the mysteries of the infinite."

The task would not be easy, he recognized. In an earlier letter, he had observed: "Of course I don't expect to be hailed as a remarkable artist for 8 or 10 years yet, even more than that, 15 comes nearer to it, but I am building now the foundation of my real work, which is to come later on, and then I expect to be successful, to have fame and money, and know and be friends with the world's greatest of men." Brash words for a young man! But Benton was eventually to make good on his boast, though it took him not fifteen years but roughly twenty-five to accomplish this ambition.

He seems to have developed the ambition of going on to study in Paris soon after his arrival at the Art Institute. He felt dissatisfied with the atmosphere of Chicago. On January 27, 1908, he wrote to his mother: "Money, money, money. The more I get the more I want: in these few words I see and understand Chicago. Of course this can't hurt me, because I know my character is strong enough not to let it hurt me, but nevertheless I long for a better atmosphere during my student days, and I shall get it."

"The only art you will be able to practice here is commercial art," Oswald told him, "and that is no art at all. Chicago offers no opportunities for an artist like I think you are going to be." Though he seems to have known nothing of the modernist revolution going on in Paris, Oswald sensed the adventurous spirit of the place, and he spoke of it so often that Tom chided him for not going there himself. "I don't have the money to stay there yet," Oswald replied. "But when I do have it I'll go."

Benton echoed these sentiments in his letters home. In February he wrote: "Only those who have studied in Paris, only artists, can understand what the two words Latin Quarter mean. It is there that the great men of the artistic world have been shaped, Whistler, Jerome [sic], Rodin, and the others who have risen to great fame. You can't know how I long for this land where all is art, and all quest is that for beauty, whether it be in painting, architecture, literature, or music." By March 9, he could tell his mother: "Paris has been the favorite dream of many months." At some point that spring, he persuaded his parents to finance his studies there for the following academic year.

Many months before they gave their approval, in the fall of 1907, Tom reported that he was taking French lessons. But he made slow progress. "Ton fils avec aimer," he signed a letter to his mother, adding boastfully, "You see I'm getting to be quite a Frenchman." But as this specimen of his proficiency suggests, his ability to speak French remained very limited.

In mid-June 1908, Benton packed up his things and returned to Neosho to prepare for his embarkation for France. Just before he left Chicago, Oswald sent Mrs. Benton a letter, probably at Tom's behest, saying that her son "has been my strongest student." Benton never saw Fred Oswald again.

Tom had a girlfriend in Neosho at this time, Fay Clark, on whom he projected the romantic ideals of perfect womanhood that had been so rudely overturned by the prostitute in Joplin. An undated note to her indicates the intensity of his interest: "The pink dress was more than a dream, it was divine, truly sweetheart, you were the loveliest, sweetest, most darlingly, dazzling, delicious, charming thing Sat. night that I have ever seen, a real Queen of the Fairies, come to earth and bringing with her all the quivering, trembling, lucid translucent memories of her fairy kingdom, of warm streams and soft, caressing, amorous, fragrant breezes, of fairy arms, and fairy eyes, fairy lives and fairy kisses, and more than all memories of the divinely, glorious sweetness of a fairy love. (That's yours dearest)."

To celebrate her son's departure for Paris, Mrs. Benton decided to hold an "Oak Hill Hop"; she printed cards for the affair and had a dance floor constructed on the back lawn. It was an oddly inappropriate way to see him off, for Tom, being so short, did not like to dance. A few days later he took the train to New York and boarded the French liner *Le Lorraine*. Not long afterwards, Fay Clark received a note scrawled across two postcards, which became intelligible when they were placed side by side. "Have been in Paris two days," Tom wrote. "Fascinating beyond all dreams is its life. I already am becoming enraptured with its ways. Everything is glorious, doubly glorious being new. Remember me as being happy."

Chapter Three
Paris

Thomas Hart Benton, Self-Portrait, *pen and ink on paper, 1908.*

"When the pains came Jeanette screamed and screamed. . . . The actress got up, pulled down the covering sheet and pushed Jeanette's knees apart. There before my horrified eyes was a small protruding human foot."

Arrival

The *Le Lorraine* left New York in late August 1908. Benton soon realized that despite his efforts to learn French in Chicago, he couldn't understand a word of what was being said around him. As soon as the ship passed Sandy Hook, he became violently seasick; since his second-class cabin had no toilet, he rushed to the men's room to vomit into a urinal. As he was retching he felt a hand under his armpit and a voice speaking French. When he did not respond, it shifted to English: "It don't last long, this seasickness," the voice said. "Come up on deck and you'll get over this right away."

Thus did Tom meet Ali the Turk. On deck, when he had recovered a little, he introduced himself. "I'm going to Paris to study art," he said. "I'm an artist. My name is Benton. I come from Missouri." It turned out that they were cabinmates. Ali was headed for the Middle East to buy tobacco, which he would sell to cigarette makers in New York. But he planned to stop off in Paris "to have a good time." He was a rather handsome man, about thirty-seven years old, a little balding above the forehead, and distinguished by penetrating, shiny black eyes.

Recognizing Benton's helplessness, Ali took him under his wing. He always called him "artist," when they were alone and when he introduced him to others. For the rest of the voyage, Tom conversed almost solely with Ali. When not with Ali, he remained glued to his deck chair, grimly scrutinizing a French grammar.

The ship docked in Le Havre. Benton gathered his bags to board the train and started to say goodbye to Ali. "No, artist. I'm going to see you through to Paris. I'll tell you goodbye when I get you settled among the other American students there." With Ali's help, Tom found a cheap artist's studio at the Passage Guibert, acquired some simple furniture, learned how to shop for his basic needs, and made contact with a few other American artists, who congregated at the Café du Dôme. Ali then bade him farewell, and Tom was on his own in Paris.

His closest friend during these early months was a young painter from Cleveland named Abe Warshawsky, who arrived in Paris on Thanksgiving Day, 1908. Warshawsky went directly to the Passage Guibert, hoping to find Leon Kroll, whom he had known in New York. Kroll was not in, but Abe was warmly greeted by Benton and another artist, who were celebrating Thanksgiving with a sumptuous meal of steak and red wine. They invited Abe to join in, and he hungrily devoured the feast, exclaiming that the steak was delicious. "Roars of laughter greeted my reply," Abe recalled. "They told me I had been eating horsemeat! For a moment I felt as if I would

Thomas Hart Benton, Châtaignier [Chestnut Tree]—Contre Soleil, *oil on canvas, 1910. One of the few paintings to survive from Benton's sojourn in France is this pointillist study executed in the summer of 1910. The colors have now darkened as the result of drier used in the varnish.*

be sick. . . . A deep-rooted prejudice and a fondness for the noble animal spoiled the feast for me that evening."

In the next few months, Abe Warshawsky became Benton's closest confidant. He was a large, square-jawed hulk, built like a boxer, but blessed with soft, gentle eyes that revealed his personality, for he was a gentle man. Abe had studied painting in Cleveland and New York and had arrived in Paris with his style essentially formed. He combined solid, academic draftsmanship with candylike Impressionist colors, in picturesque views of the tourist highlights of Paris and other localities in France.

Temperamentally, Abe could not have been more different from Tom—calm and cautious where Benton was pugnacious and reckless. Nor was he interested in theories about painting or in modernist experiments. "It's all right for you," he once commented. "But I need to make paintings I can sell." From the beginning, his work sold well to American tourists, and he enjoyed substantial patronage from the Jewish community back in Cleveland.

During Tom's first three months in Paris, he spent much of his time getting drunk in the cafés, where he would pick fights and quarrel with the women. He drank Grog americains (rum mixed with lemon and water, generally served hot), and these, plus his loneliness, often put him in a sorrowful mood and made him shout insults and stir up trouble. Because of his diminutive stature, he quickly became known as "le petit Balzac." Abe always did his best to pull him away when he was making a nuisance of himself. Once, when Tom was spoiling for a fight, Abe held out his jaw as a target. Tom actually took a swing, but Abe just held his ground without resistance until he calmed down. Years later, he recalled: "Many a night I'd walk [Tom] about for miles, trying to restore him to a normal and cheerful mood."

John Thompson. Benton's neighbor at the Passage Guibert, who introduced him to the impressionist masterpieces at the Luxembourg.

The two men decided to study together and pooled funds to hire a female model. To Benton's great regret, the girl would not pose in the nude but brought her mother with her and sat nursing her child, part of one breast showing. Nonetheless, he was so high with the excitement of it all that he surpassed himself. Abe, impressed, called in the neighbors, John Thompson, Julius Josephs, and Leon Kroll, all of whom were amazed that a mere nineteen-year-old could produce such work.

But Tom could not repeat the performance. When they hired another girl, he did nothing but fumble, and he had the same experience with the third model, an over-muscled young man. To his great pleasure, however, word of his first painting got around and people sometimes pointed him out when he entered a café.

Unlike Kroll, who was a star pupil at the state-run École des Beaux-Arts—a difficult school for an American to get into—Benton proved a complete flop in his drawing class, at the Académie Julian. For a while he was even obliged to draw plaster casts with the novices. When he got back to the live model, his work did not improve. At Julian's, the drawings were always the same size, on the same type of paper, and executed the same way, with small sticks of charcoal. Places were assigned, and it was not possible to change them. "Those patterns of the nineties were consistent," Benton later told Paul Cummings. "You went to the Académie Julian, you learned to do what they called 'draw,' then you went into the next class and learned how to color that drawing. That's the way it was . . . it was standard academic drawing . . . and it's a bore. The model stayed there for two weeks. You got tired of looking at it." Fortunately, Tom's failures did not cause comment in his circle, for there were no other Americans in the class.

Things improved later in the year when, at John Thompson's suggestion, he shifted from the drawing to the painting class at Julian's. With his knack for catching a likeness quickly, Tom achieved some recognition and success. He got in the practice of going in the evenings to the cafés around the Gare Montparnasse, seating himself in the corner with a little sketchbook and making pen-and-ink drawings of the customers and their lady companions. A few individuals took offense, but for the most part, people were delighted to be drawn, and he often attracted a small crowd that would look over his shoulder and chuckle while he drew their friends. His Passage Guibert friends called these sketches "clever." He did not yet know that this term had a condescending implication for a painter.

It took only a month for Benton to strike out on his own. Early in the winter, Abe Warshawsky introduced him to the Collarossi sketching studio. It was a shabby place, with no instruction, but a model was always available. One would seat oneself wherever one wished, and by coming early one could get close enough to see. Tom began going there two or three afternoons a week.

Just after he arrived in Paris, Benton was deeply impressed by the work of the Spanish realist Ignacio Zuloaga, and for a brief period he attempted to imitate his

Thomas Hart Benton, Self-Portrait in the Artist's Paris Studio, pen and ink on paper, 1909. He enclosed this sketch in a letter to his mother.

Thomas Hart Benton, The Park Bench, pen and ink on paper, 1908–09. During his stay in Paris, Benton made many humorous sketches of life on the boulevards and in the cafés.

style. But when John Thompson, who had studied color theory with Percyval Tudor-Hart, introduced him to the Impressionist masterpieces in the Luxembourg Gallery, the French painters replaced Zuloaga as Tom's ideal. His favorite picture in the Luxembourg was Pissarro's sunlit scene of red tile roofs and backyard gardens. He imitated its effect in the one painting that survives from his first months in France, a little impressionist sketch looking out the back window of his studio to the rooftops of Paris. Tom made it early in the winter, when a dusting of new-fallen snow caught his attention.

He became fascinated by the use of bright colors, often in complementary opposition, and, in the solitude of his studio, made still-life paintings depicting apples, pears, and other fruits in bright hues. In designing these works, he was influenced greatly by Japanese prints. He had already learned about them in Chicago, and very good ones could be had for small sums of money in the bookstalls along the Left Bank of the Seine. Benton avidly collected them, and they lined the walls of his studio. He never painted a still life without including one of the prints in the background, and he tried to design the shape patterns of his compositions in a similar style.

He had no wish to return home. His letters speak condescendingly of Americans; in one he railed angrily about a "big fat dowager" he had encountered who was "smoking a cigarette in a very stupid washerwoman-like way and flashing a big red bediamonded hand in everybody's face, talking at the top of her voice and making herself altogether the most prominent person about the café. People like that ought to be tied up in a pen, it hurts Americanism terribly."

His pursuit of different and contradictory directions, however, seems to have made his work extremely uneven. In April 1909, he confessed to his parents that he had been feeling discouraged with his progress and added: "Most of my friends, such as they are, have a laughable opinion of me, but since my friends don't have artistic power either their ideas and opinions don't bother me too much. I will be an artist and I will be something other than mediocre." His first six months in Paris were terribly lonely ones. Then he met in succession three individuals who changed the course of his existence: George Carlock, Jeanette, and Stanton Macdonald-Wright.

George Carlock

One day as Benton emerged from Collarossi's, a young man with wiry, uncontrollable black hair approached him, sizing him up as he did so. He introduced himself as George Carlock. "Your name's Benton," he said, "and I've heard about you. They say you're the best ever. I'd like to come to your place and see what you're doing." Carlock had eyes of an indeterminate color, with streaks of green, hazel, and blue in them. "I'd like you to come," Tom replied, for he had already heard about Carlock from Thompson. He was a nephew of Elbert Hubbard, whose popular philosophizing in the *Roycrofter Magazine* had a wide following in the Midwest among would-be sophisticates, not only schoolboys but lawyers and doctors as well. Carlock had been in Paris for some time and was reputed to be very knowledgeable.

Tom spent some time preparing for the visit, as he wanted to make the best possible impression. He thumbtacked a number of his paintings to the wall, beginning with his study of the mother and child, which still looked good to him. Along with head studies from the Académie Julian, he included some of his personal impressionist experiments. He spread a selection of his café drawings on the table.

Carlock arrived promptly at the appointed time. Benton opened the door and said hello, but Carlock did not acknowledge the greeting. He stood staring at his host without opening his mouth; just as the situation was getting uncomfortable, he strode silently into the room and began examining the work. Once he had Tom's nerves thoroughly on edge, he turned to speak. "Benton," he said, "I'm completely disillusioned. This is awful." He paused a moment to give Tom time to absorb the pain and then launched into a more detailed critique.

He explained that Benton not only had no knowledge of how to paint properly but also had no integrity. No painter of integrity could simultaneously produce academic studies and impressionist experiments. When Tom protested that some of the artists at Julian's seemed to like his portraits, Carlock laughed cynically and replied, "Artists at Julian's? There are no artists at Julian's. If anybody *there* likes your stuff you can be certain that it's no good." You couldn't learn to draw at Julian's, Carlock declared; you could only learn to copy. But what of his café drawings? They weren't academic studies, Tom protested. "Newspaper pictures," Carlock explained. "Sort of clever but nothing to 'em. Nothing wrong with sketching people if you know how to draw. But you don't."

Seeing that he had succeeded in completely crushing Benton's feelings, Carlock then relented a little. "What I say is for your own good," he asserted. "I don't think you haven't got *any* talent. I just don't think you know what you're doing."

After Carlock had left, Benton hastened over to his neighbor John Thompson and told him of the ordeal he had been through. Thompson just laughed and said that Carlock's performance was typical—he did that to all the new people. But he added that it would be a mistake to write him off. Carlock, he felt, knew a lot—he was even consulted at the Louvre about old-master drawings.

Benton kept this judgment in mind when he next ran into Carlock at Collarossi's. Several weeks had gone by, and the assault on his pride had worn off. Carlock acted delighted to see him and wrung his hand in the friendliest manner, as if they were old friends. Benton was growing dissatisfied with the Académie Julian and felt that he had ceased to make progress. The one class that had been helpful was anatomy, in which the instructor lectured from charts, a skeleton, and a living model. It cost a few francs extra, but it had given him a better understanding of the inner workings of anatomical forms. He wondered if it would not be possible to approach other kinds of drawing in a way that would similarly build up a body of useful knowledge.

He meekly asked Carlock for advice about how to study. Carlock replied that the best way to learn was from the men who really knew how to draw—the old masters. Study the drawings in the Louvre, he advised. Take a pad and copy them.

Tom was skeptical. He had already been bored nearly to death in Chicago copying plaster casts. Nonetheless, he went down to the Louvre one afternoon with a drawing pad. He began to copy one of the paintings that had most impressed him, Titian's large *Entombment*. He found it extremely awkward to stand with a pad in one hand and draw with the other. His copy was inexact. But he also realized that he was seeing things in the painting that he had never noted before—that he was starting to understand its principles of composition and movement. He was quite literally learning to see more deeply into it, to comprehend it in terms not only of lines and contours but of forms arranged back into depth.

He put in a number of afternoons making such sketches, trying to apply some of the ideas he had picked up about composition from analyzing Japanese prints with Fred Oswald. In one study he would concentrate on outlines and contours and in another on the light and shade—the chiaroscuro—of a picture. When he had exhausted all the approaches he could think of, he went back to Carlock and showed him what he had done.

Carlock, as usual, was critical. Benton was on the wrong track, he declared; he was starting with something much too complex. He should begin by studying drawings and work up to more complicated problems by degrees. Perhaps they should meet together in the Louvre. There Carlock would be able to give him a few pointers.

This meant giving up a portrait head at Julian's that was coming along nicely, but

Tom agreed. They met at the Louvre, and Carlock led him to a room where old-master drawings were laid out in vitrines. "Benton," he announced, "everything you need to know about drawings can be found in these rooms." He then told Tom to pick out a drawing and make a study of it. He himself had an appointment in the offices to discuss a new Raphael. When he got through, he would drop by and see how Tom was doing.

Always acutely sensitive to one-upmanship, Tom realized that Carlock had deliberately arranged the appointment to demonstrate his own importance at the Louvre and thus clinch his ascendancy. Still, he obediently looked at the drawings and after a few moments went to work. He chose a work by Annibale Carracci showing a male figure with vigorously defined muscles in the chest and stomach. He tried to draw the contour of the figure to contain these muscles but couldn't get the proportions right. Once again he found it difficult to draw and hold his pad at the same time. He was at his fifth or sixth try and totally absorbed in his work when Carlock returned. In fact, he didn't realize that Carlock was standing beside him until he spoke.

As before, Carlock was brutal in his comments. He began by criticizing Benton's taste in choosing a model of such academic flavor. He then explained that Tom was starting in the wrong way. Although what had appealed to him about the drawing was the forceful definition of the chest and stomach, he had begun with the outline. Carlock advised him to work from the inside out. He should make drawings that were built up from an understanding of inner structure.

Frustrated, Tom handed Carlock his pad and pencil. "Show me how you would start to study this thing," he said. Carlock promptly handed the pad and pencil back. "It's you that's got to learn, Benton," he said. "Won't do you any good if somebody else does your work." The suspicion ran through Tom's mind that Carlock might not be able to do it, and the other man must have recognized that he was having this thought. "Yes, Benton," he said, "I'd have to work at it just like you." The humble tone of his voice as he confessed this made Tom more tolerant of his little cruelties.

Benton began seeing a great deal more of Carlock—who probably was desperately lonely too, for he never introduced Tom to anyone. Tom quit his class at Julian's and began to draw daily at the Collarossi studio, where he would chat with Carlock between poses. Thanks to Carlock's influence, he became primarily concerned with discovering the relationships between the forms he studied and those he copied. He began to search out the basic principles of "form organization," which he finally managed to systematize in the 1920s.

He and Carlock would frequently walk back together from Collarossi's to Benton's studio, where, usually joined by John Thompson, they would eat salt fish, bread, and cheese, drink cheap wine, and talk late into the night. After a while, Carlock got in the habit of casually dropping by the Passage Guibert with part of a cheese or a bottle of wine, and they would have lunch or dinner together.

Carlock was not a skillful talker; in fact, he was remarkably inarticulate, but he had ideas. The only modern artist for whom he had any attachment was Cézanne. "This was too much for me at the time," Benton later recalled. "But remembering his remarks about Cézanne in later years I realized they were penetrating and uncannily accurate." And he noted that Carlock "gave me, through his introduction to the values of the classic masterpieces, something to cling to and to return to." For the rest of his life, Benton remained a student of the classic form of the old masters. Even during his most modernist phase, he thought of himself as a "classicist."

Despite the two men's frequent contact, Carlock remained extremely secretive, perhaps as a way of maintaining his position of dominance. He would never allow Benton to look at his work; at Collarossi's, he always closed his sketchbook when

Tom came by. And when Tom asked to visit his studio and see his paintings, he replied, "Benton, you are not ready for that yet—not nearly ready," and strode off. When Benton asked Thompson about it, he replied that though he had known Carlock for two years, he had never been allowed to see his work.

Benton found it difficult to paint when Carlock was around. In addition, a little incident somewhat undermined his ascendancy. One morning, Carlock came into the studio and found Tom immersed in Balzac's *Splendeurs et Misères des Courtisanes*, with a dictionary beside him and a pad of paper on which he wrote the meanings of the words he did not know. Nearby were several other books he was working his way through at the time, including a romance novel for housemaids, *Olympe*, and a volume of Verlaine's poetry. Carlock promptly launched into an attack on literature, declaring that painters should stay away from it. Tom had grown up with books around him and was shocked. He began to notice how Carlock stuttered and stumbled when he tried to explain things. "It's because he hasn't read enough to have a language," he concluded.

But what finished off Benton's association with Carlock was his relationship with Jeanette. After she moved in, Tom was no longer free to travel as he pleased. He was unable, for example, to accompany Carlock to Italy. More than that, Jeanette disliked Carlock and did her best to undercut his influence. After he returned from Italy in the autumn of 1909, he no longer came to Tom's studio, for he was afraid of Jeanette. The two men met only occasionally, at Collarossi's or the Dôme.

"*C'est un peintre prétendu*," Jeanette said, "*qui parle mais ne peint pas.*" ("He's a phony painter, who talks but doesn't paint.") Perhaps she was right. "I never knew for sure about Carlock," Benton later wrote. "But whether or not, I always remembered his 'pointers.' They opened paths for me I would long continue to explore."

In 1916 Carlock visited the United States, and Tom met him at Alfred Stieglitz's place in New York, where all kinds of artists congregated. He said, "Well, Benton, I hear how you're the best ever. I'd like to come see what you're doing." Remembering his similarly worded request at the time of their first meeting, Tom didn't invite him over. After the war, he learned that Carlock had been killed doing ambulance work in Italy. None of his paintings seem to have survived, and there is no record that any of his friends ever saw them.

Jeanette

During his first seven months in Paris, Benton had no female companion, and his one attempt at sexual adventure was embarrassingly unsuccessful. He followed a woman to her hotel room and gave her twenty francs, but before she had even taken off her shoes, her "husband" and the desk clerk came in and ordered him out. When he tried to get his money back, they called a gendarme, who pushed him out into the street in a most humiliating way.

It was Abe Warshawsky who introduced him to more solid companionship. In April 1909, about a week after his twentieth birthday, he went to a party given by Abe, who had taken up with a red-haired girl of the quarter and was celebrating his liaison. Tom partook heavily of wine and cognac and, thus fortified, began flirting with a friend of Abe's paramour.

A few days later, Warshawsky told him that the woman was available if he was looking for a mistress. This offended Tom's sense of delicacy, but not long after, he invited Abe, the redhead, and her friend, Jeanette, to have tea in his studio. This worked out so well that he encouraged a second meeting, which proved so jolly that the foursome extended it into dinner. The girls went out to a rotisserie, where they collected a leg of lamb, salad, bread, cheese, and fruit, while Tom and Abe purchased

Thomas Hart Benton, Land-
scape, Southern France, *pencil
on paper, 1910. The landscape
sketches Benton made in the
south of France strongly reveal
the influence of Cézanne.*

wines and a bottle of champagne. After dinner, Tom became drunk and invited Jeanette to sleep with him, and they spent the night together, uncomfortably sharing his tiny cot.

Jeanette was one of those working-class women who supported themselves by establishing liaisons with foreign students. She was older than Tom and had already lived with a German sculptor, who left her his furniture when he returned home. The very morning after her first night with Tom, she hired a cart and moved the furnishings of her apartment into his studio. Soon the place was transformed. She brought curtains for the windows, a rug for the floor, commodes for clothes, tables, chairs, and even a tin bathtub, which fitted under a three-sided bench. After the austerity of his existence, Tom liked all this.

Yet he knew that his parents would never approve of Jeanette, a lower-class woman with a sexually tainted past. Indeed, he was often embarrassed to reveal her existence to his friends. He fell into the relationship because it was comfortable and convenient, not because of deep love or any commitment to the future.

Once Jeanette moved in, Benton stayed home at night rather than getting drunk in the cafés. Naturally, he never mentioned her in his letters. But by May he was reporting to his mother that he had suddenly become much more proficient in French. Jeanette also increased his expenses. Fifty dollars a month would have been enough for a single art student living frugally; it was hardly enough for two. Shortly after he arrived, he had written home that in Paris "everything is reasonable." A month after Jeanette moved in, he began to report that he was going into debt.

Benton followed a fairly regular working routine through the spring of 1909, at Collarossi's in the mornings and in the Louvre in the afternoon. If the weather was good, he would paint outdoors in the parks. That summer he went on several sketching excursions into the country.

While painting near Chartres, he met an artist who was looking at the landscape through little squares of colored glass, and though Tom's French was a bit thick for technical discussion, he managed to ask him about it. He learned that because the glass took the color out of the scene, it helped establish the "values," the tonal grada-tions from light to dark. When he returned to Paris, he hunted up a *verrier* and purchased some small squares of colored glass for himself. With these he made quick, roughly brushed-in landscape studies in which he attempted to reduce the scene to broad patterns of color relationships. All his friends thought these sketches looked funny, but the procedure had a lasting impact on his thinking about color and form.

Toward the end of autumn, Jeanette's mother started to come by the studio for long visits. She was a woman of sixty or more, her kindly face deeply marked with lines of trouble and that look of resigned hopelessness so common to members of the Parisian poor. After her third visit, Benton asked Jeanette what was up. "Are you sick?" he inquired. "Tommy," she replied, "I'm pregnant."

As Jeanette's pregnancy advanced, she grew increasingly fearful that Tom would abandon her, and to set this fear at rest he spent more and more time at home with her. Eventually he gave up his classes at Julian's and his sketching classes at Collaros-si's—even his visits to the Café du Dôme. He read and painted in his apartment, going out only for short walks along the neighboring streets.

Jeanette was visited regularly by a doctor named Chevelarius, who tended to the poor people in the quarter and always looked drawn and tired. One day, Chevelarius took Tom aside and questioned him about his financial means, listening with a sad expression while Tom confessed that his assets were slender. Chevelarius responded, *"Il y a du courage au moins."* ("Well, at least you're brave.")

The next week, late in the night, Jeanette went into labor. Benton later recalled:

"When the pains came Jeanette screamed and screamed. Thompson and his actress who by this time were aware of the situation came over. While they stayed with Jeanette I ran for Dr. Chevelarius. He was out on a call but I left a note with a sleepy house maid telling him the time had come. When I got back only the actress was there. The ordeal was too much for Thompson. Jeanette was quietly asleep. But this did not last long. The pains came back and with them the screams. Finally about two o'clock in the morning, in a moment of fear and agony, Jeanette cried out, 'Help me. See what's happening to me.'

"The actress got up, pulled down the covering sheet and pushed Jeanette's knees apart. There before my horrified eyes was a small protruding human foot. The sight paralyzed me. With my little experience of the basics of life I could only apprehend it as some impossible deformity. I retched and vomited. At that moment Dr. Chevelarius arrived. In a short time with the help of the actress he made the delivery. We had a small corpse in the studio. It was put on a drawing board and covered with a towel.

"Dr. Chevelarius looked at me. '*C'est dommage, jeune monsieur,*' he said. But his eyes spoke differently. They said, 'It's much better that it happened like this.' When he got up to leave he picked up a small still life I had painted. 'Souvenir,' he said and took it with him. He never asked any money of me during or after this affair.

"The next day the police authorities came and, after questioning me for awhile, took the tiny corpse away."

Adrift

Once the dead infant had been disposed of, Benton was free to return to his normal routine. He celebrated the end of his ordeal by going to a prizefight, but for a month or two after the event his work went slowly and his mind was consumed by strange anxieties. The sight of the protruding foot had so horrified him that he was no longer able to engage in sex with Jeanette. They slept apart and grew ever more distant. While Jeanette was recovering, her friend Madeleine came in regularly to cook meals, and others came by from time to time to help with the shopping and to socialize. The

Thomas Hart Benton, Self-Portrait, *oil on canvas, 1909. Soon after his arrival in Paris, Benton painted this awkward but intense self-portrait.*

45

sleeping balcony became the locale of long whispered conferences, and Benton began to feel slightly out of place as the lone male in a kind of sexless harem.

He had lost his sense of artistic direction in the month he had been cooped up with Jeanette, and the enthusiasm he had felt at the end of the previous summer had been superseded by a deep depression. In early January 1910, when he sent home some photographs of his recent paintings, he fell into a fit of despair. "I very nearly cried when I first saw them," he wrote of the photographs to his mother. "Had the blues for two days and didn't work at all." He confessed: "The photographer is not at all to blame, the fault lies with the pictures, the pictures are bad not only bad but miserable. This has been the most horrible wakening up that I ever had, these photographs let me see what I amounted to brought me face to face with my incapability, with the utter lack of honest sincerity in my work."

In his despair, he decided to re-enroll at the Académie Julian, despite the laughter of his friends. He also set to work on a portrait, which he hoped to submit to the spring salon. He promised that his progress would soon be apparent. "I am going to be an artist and not an ordinary one either, but it will take time." This effort to win academic honors soon fizzled. A week later he reported in discouragement: "I am getting desperate over my work again. I never seem to get my things up to a satisfying point. Sunday is the last day to send things to the Salon and I see no hope of being able to properly finish my picture. I attempted too big a thing and though distressing it is my own fault."

Stanton Macdonald-Wright

Before long, Benton was plunging again into modernist experiments. No doubt his academic ambitions would have dried up in any case, but this process was hastened by a new friend he made at this time, Stanton Macdonald-Wright, who had just arrived in Paris from California.

The two men had met early in the winter of 1909, while sitting at the Café du Dôme. Wright's physical appearance was repellent. He had pale, pasty, unhealthy-looking skin, his shoulders drooped, and his watery gray-blue eyes looked bilious. He had an oddly shaped face with a sloping brow and a fat, pointed nose, which always seemed to be sniffing something. The chin receded and the mouth turned down with a premature weariness. His whole face had a cunning and distrustful look, and written all over it was self-esteem. But Benton forgot his reservations about Wright's curious appearance when he began talking. He spoke fluently, with wry, irreverent sallies that kept Tom laughing.

Benton did not follow up this first meeting with Wright, for it was only a week later that he learned of Jeanette's pregnancy and became progressively more confined to his studio. Once Jeanette was on her way to recovery, however, he dropped in at the Dôme. There he found Macdonald-Wright sitting at a table, conversing with the waiter. He had a phrasebook in his hand and was going over sentences with him, with an accuracy of pronunciation that Benton found astonishing.

Benton called out, "Hi, California!" and Wright hastily stuffed the phrasebook in his pocket, stood up, and came toward him. He grasped his hand enthusiastically. "Where the hell have you been?" he inquired. "I've asked everybody around here about you. Nobody knew where you lived or what had become of you."

"I've been sick," Benton replied.

"By God, you look it," Wright responded. "You look like a ghost." They sat down together and were soon chatting about the studios of Paris. Wright had a lemonade and Benton a beer. "Met any artists about?" asked Tom.

"Yes, a few. All fatheads," Wright replied. "I made the rounds, looked in at Julian's, tried to get in the Beaux-Arts but couldn't. Didn't want to anyhow. Opened the doors on Friesecke and Miller. Both places stunk. Tried old Carol Delvaille's class. But what can you learn from him?" He ran on and on, like a wound-up talking machine, listing every teaching studio in Paris and enumerating their deficiencies, occasionally interjecting apt and witty French phrases, always perfectly pronounced. Tom knew there was no way that Wright could have tried so many places in a month, but he listened on in amazement, impressed by Wright's brilliance and by the effrontery of his lies.

Sensing Benton's skepticism, Wright broke off and asked him how he had gotten started in Paris. Despite his flamboyance, Wright proved a good listener and sat attentively while Tom enumerated his experience in the schools, his impressionist experiments, his studies in the Louvre, his sketches in the cafés and at Collarossi's, the theories he had picked up about color values. When he finally tapered off, Wright commented, "Benton, you're great, really great. You are the only intelligent man I've met in Paris."

They saw much of each other after that. They met several times at the Dôme, and Benton introduced Wright to Collarossi's. Unlike Carlock, Wright was not reluctant to show his work. One day, Benton suggested that they quit talking about what they were attempting and show each other what they were painting. "By God, I've been waiting for you to say that!" Wright replied. "Want to come to my place now?"

His place, as it happened, was only a few short blocks away—a big, impressive studio, handsomely furnished, which he described as "my camp." As Wright entered, he whistled loudly, and a moment later, a frail, timid-looking American girl came in—his wife. "Sweetheart," Wright said, "this is Benton, the artist I've been telling you about." She made a little finishing-school curtsy. "I'm pleased," she said. "I hope to see you often." With another little curtsy, she went back out the door that led from the studio into the apartment.

A look at the paintings convinced Tom that for all Wright's posturings, he did indeed possess astonishing talent. Canvases lay stacked against the wall, several of them five or six feet high. "Just exercises," Wright remarked, with a half-deprecatory gesture, "but an intelligent person like you will understand." None of them was highly finished, but their confident execution took Tom's breath away. The style was realistic, rather in the manner of Tom's Académie Julian exercises, but they were far more dexterous, with brushwork based on William Merritt Chase, John Singer Sargent, and especially Robert Henri. Most of them showed female models in colorful costumes, a sort of class exercise that was much in vogue at the time because it attracted students.

Though Wright kept pestering him, it took Benton some time to reciprocate, for he was afraid that his friend, a married man, would be shocked to discover that he kept a mistress. He finally arranged for Jeanette to be away from the studio one afternoon and gave Wright a precise time and directions for finding the Passage Guibert.

His elaborate precautions, however, were a waste of time. Wright arrived on the minute, even more elaborately dressed than usual, sporting a new gold-headed cane. He surveyed the studio for a moment, his head held high, like a conquering general. His inquisitive nose sniffed a little. "There's a woman here," Wright exclaimed. Tom was thrown completely off guard. "No. Yes. Not now. But there is one," he stammered.

"Don't be a fool, Benton," Wright exclaimed. "I know about these things. I know about you, too. Everybody in the quarter does. You don't have to be sneaky with me."

For a moment Tom felt deeply offended and almost ready to throw Wright out of the studio. "What a nervy bastard," he thought. But Wright, with his remarkable quickness, immediately sensed his annoyance and completely shifted his approach. His stiff body drooped, and his arrogant expression became pleading and sad. "I came to

Benton painting Macdonald-Wright, 1961. Benton painted Wright seated in front of one of his characteristic Synchromist works. "Tom was out here during the whole process," Wright recalled, "with a pan of water near him. He chewed tobacco with great rapidity and used this pan of water to spit in, to save himself from having to go to the edge of the porch. . . . I'm very fond of Tom and always have been; he's a very sweet fellow."

Thomas Hart Benton, Stanton Macdonald-Wright, *oil on canvas, 1961–62.* •

see your work," he said, in a conciliatory tone. As he looked around the studio, his eye caught the study of the mother and child that Tom had painted in his session with Abe Warshawsky.

"That's a fine thing over there," Wright commented. "As fine a thing as I've seen around Paris. When did you do it?"

"That's the first thing I did in Paris," Tom replied. "But I don't work that way anymore."

"No," Wright replied. "I remember you told me you were an Impressionist. Let's see your new pictures—the impressionist ones." Though still eager to get rid of Wright, Benton went over to the corner and pulled out a couple of paintings from a stack of canvases. Wright looked at them with interest. "Let's see more of these," he said. "Help yourself," Tom replied, and they went to the corner and one by one went through the stack of pictures. Wright carefully examined them all, asking questions and making friendly comments.

By April the two had become constant companions, at Collarossi's, at the Louvre, and at the cafés and art exhibitions. They would spend long hours painting in the Bois de Boulogne or the Parc Saint-Cloud. Wright was related to the Huntingtons, the California railroad family, and was financially well off. Whenever they stopped at a restaurant or café, he picked up the bill, and while at first Tom protested, he soon came to accept this practice.

They had many points in common. Both had quit high school at the age of seventeen, convinced that they could better educate themselves. Both were addicted to poetry—Poe, Byron, Swinburne, Rossetti, and the *Yellow Book* poets. Very soon Wright became amazingly proficient in French, and they would read Baudelaire, Verlaine, and the Symbolist poets together, each standing up in turn and declaiming a work. (With his gift for mimicry, Wright had learned the language better in a few months than many Americans who had lived in France for years.) They shared a repugnance for academic teachings, and they both enjoyed theorizing, often on the basis of very scanty knowledge.

In other respects they were very different. Benton was a Democrat raised in the populist atmosphere of Missouri, and his reading of Bernard Shaw and other writers had pushed him toward the left. "My sympathy is with the Anarchistic and Socialistic theories," he once wrote to his parents. Wright, on the other hand, had developed right-wing ideas of the most peculiar sort. He occasionally launched into political monologues, full of brilliant and witty insights but built upon the slenderest possible foundation.

He believed that "the people" should be kept in their place and should serve the wealthy and wellborn, among whom he naturally counted himself. In his eyes, the Civil War was a tragedy, which had destroyed the slave system necessary for the maintenance of an aristocratic class. He looked forward to the day when Americans would recognize their mistake and re-enslave the blacks. While he admired French culture, he despised the egalitarianism of French politics and looked forward to the day when the Germans would conquer France and restore to it its "noble soul."

Facts did not trouble him much. Once Benton asked his age. Wright paused a

Robert Delaunay, La Tour Eiffel, *oil on canvas, 1910.*

moment and then asked, "How old are you?" "Twenty," Tom replied. "But I'll be twenty-one in April." "About the same age as me," Wright replied. "I'm twenty-one now." As he spoke, Benton recalled that one of Wright's friends had told him that Wright was nineteen; years later, he confirmed that Wright had indeed lied about his age. In the competitive atmosphere of the Parisian art world, Wright did not wish to be the younger of the two.

His behavior at times could be astonishing. For example, he came up with the idea of having his picture taken in front of the important monuments of Paris and hired a photographer to perform this task. When Tom saw some of the results of this project, he became curious and followed Wright to a photo session on the Pont Neuf. It was a sunny day, and Wright planted himself in the center of the bridge, with the towers of Notre Dame right behind him. Folding his arms like some conquering Siegfried, he stared with contempt at the passing train of French secretaries and petty functionaries. Though he drew a crowd of amused spectators, they did not faze him—he was living in his own dream world.

With his exaggerated behavior, his cynical wit, and his general impatience with fools, Wright did not find it easy to make friends. He was too opinionated, flamboyant, and independent to get on with most art students. Thanks to his wealth and wit, he was often invited to parties on the Right Bank, but he didn't fit in with the conventions of the diplomatic crowd and was dismissed as an oddity.

Wright often precluded the possibility of being insulted by starting out with an offensive remark of his own. And he could be strangely callous. When Benton told him of Jeanette's delivery, he burst into laughter at the part about the protruding foot. "Funniest God damn thing I ever heard of," he howled. "God damn crazy funny."

Yet even when his notions were mad, Tom found Wright's imagination, intelligence, and wit remarkably stimulating. By the spring of 1910, Gauguin and Cézanne had become household names; Matisse and the Cubists had come into prominence. Benton and Wright dived enthusiastically into the modernist adventure, starting new experiments one after another before they had a chance to finish a canvas.

In an interview toward the end of his life, Macdonald-Wright, quite unsolicited, put in a tribute to Benton's talent. He declared: "Tom Benton is one of the sweetest people, and to me one of the finest painters in the country. We have nothing in common when it actually comes to painting. But he's a great painter. . . . People insist on looking on him as 'old hat,' and so forth and so on. He's actually a great painter." Few people but Stan Wright would have thought to describe Tom Benton as "sweet." Tom, in turn, once wrote that Wright was one of the two best friends he ever had, and was "the most gifted all-round man I ever knew."

Benton's affection for Wright was not shared by any of his friends. Jeanette took an instant dislike to him. Having missed her on his first visit, Wright turned up at the studio shortly afterward, uninvited, when he figured that she would have to be around. Jeanette was *en déshabillé* at the time, with her hair in complete disorder, and deeply resented the intrusion despite all of Wright's mollifying phrases. Typically, he was elaborately primped up, and she felt outclassed by his fancy clothes and pretentious manner. After he left, she commented, "Tommy, you need a new suit."

Jeanette never got over this initial unfavorable impression, and while she saw a good deal of Wright after that, she would never use his name. He was always "Monsieur L'Épateur," "Monsieur Polisson," "Monsieur Sournois," or "Monsieur Pesteux" ("Mr. Bigshot," "Mr. Sleazebag," "Mr. Shifty," or "Mr. Nuisance").

Jeanette was more complimentary than John Thompson, who always referred to Wright as "that pasty-faced prick." And George Carlock, with his need to dominate, couldn't stand Wright's presence, nor his quick, sardonic wit. Even the mild Abe

Warshawsky clearly worried about Wright's influence, though he skirted around the topic and did not attempt to interfere.

Abe reported to Tom, however, that rumors about Jeanette and her pregnancy had reached the diplomatic crowd, along with gossip about the crazy smears he was making as a painter. Tom should be careful, or someone might write back to his parents, who certainly would cut off his funds if they knew the true nature of his artistic experiments and his way of life.

The South of France

The sister of Jeanette's friend Madeleine was married to a ceramist, Gabriel Bernadou, who worked in the tradition of the French fifteenth-century master Bernard Palissy, making vases and bowls with little sculptures on their sides, mostly of animals and butterflies. Bernadou was an exuberant, laughing fellow, about twenty-six years old, who like many Frenchmen of the time sported a square black beard. Unlike most, though, he spoke quite good English. He had his kilns on a small estate in the hills at Saint-Augustin, near the little city of Tulle, and he spoke with such affection of the beauty of the landscape that Benton decided to spend the summer there with Jeanette.

Tom had been saving up money for a new suit for himself and a dress for Jeanette, but they decided to give these up in favor of an excursion to the south. Early in August, they boarded the night train to Tulle. They spent a long, uncomfortable night, sleeping only in snatches on the hard wooden benches of the second-class carriage. Nonetheless, Tom felt elated when they disembarked the next morning in the midst of a hilly landscape entirely unlike the north of France, embellished by puffy, pillowlike clouds touched by pink sunlight.

They hired a cart to take their suitcase and painting supplies to Saint-Augustin, a few miles to the northwest. For sixty cents a day, they found accommodation (meals included) at the local hotel, an unsanitary but picturesque establishment with horses, cows, and manure on the first floor, the kitchen on the second, the salon and dining room on the third, and the guest bedrooms on the fourth. People stared at them as they unloaded, but after a while their friend Bernadou came with his wife and they had a hearty lunch of fresh lamb, black bread, a round ball of hard cheese, and the wine of the region.

In the country atmosphere of Saint-Augustin, the café gossip of Paris soon passed out of Benton's mind. The inn, following the pattern of peasant life, brewed its coffee before dawn, and Tom was always out early, in front of his selected motif, while the forms were still clearly defined by the slanting morning light. He would paint until midday, when the mounting sun flattened the forms. Then he would stop for lunch, the largest meal of the day, followed by reading or a siesta. In the late afternoon, when the light again began to slant, he would head out to paint some different motif, until the sun went down. When not painting, he struggled to make drawings of trees, rocks, flowers, and the effects of running water.

He kept up this life until the cold winds of November made outdoor work impossible, and then regretfully returned to Paris. Jeanette, who also filled up her time with painting, was as disappointed to leave as he. This was the happiest period of Benton's stay in France and also the most productive: he managed to complete about a dozen canvases. All but one of these paintings were lost in the fire that destroyed the family home in Neosho, but one rendering of a chestnut tree, *Contre Soleil*, survives to document his accomplishment. These trees had great significance to the people of the region, not simply for their decorative qualities but as a source of food.

Unfortunately, the painting has dulled somewhat as the result of the ill-advised use of siccative, or drier, in the painting medium. It was originally brightly colored, with ultramarine and violet shadows and yellow-green and orange highlights. The previous spring, Benton had admired an exhibition of the work of Paul Signac, and *Contre Soleil*, a fully pointillist work, clearly reveals this influence. Apparently some of the other Saint-Augustin paintings were not pointillist but broadly brushed renderings of light and colored shadows, like the sketches Signac and the other pointillists often used as preliminary studies. Benton's paintings were similar to these sketches, except that he did not later rework them with dots but treated them as finished canvases. In contrast to the previous summer's work, he did not abandon paintings midway but carried each piece through to completion, filling up the entire surface rather than leaving bare patches of canvas. In fact, he was hoping to produce exhibitable and salable works. "I expect to prepare nearly all of my exhibition here," he wrote his parents.

These paintings represented an attempt to capture the "values" of nature, through symbolic equivalents rather than through direct imitation. Benton used warm colors, such as orange and vermilion, to indicate the light values; and cold ones, such as blue or blue-violet, to represent the darks. Various shades of green occupied the positions between light and dark. In this system, the actual color of an object might barely survive. The modeling of a red apple, for example, might end up as a cluster of color spots ranging from yellow to blue, with only small patches of red.

First One-Man Show

Benton returned from Tulle elated by his accomplishments. "All my friends who have seen the work I did in the country are agreed that I have made enormous progress," he reported. He was desperate to find a way to remain in France, and in several of his letters to his mother he proposed sending paintings home for sale. At first he favored "a few private exhibitions" in "a well lighted hall in Kansas City, Joplin, and Springfield." As his thoughts developed, he focused on having Mr. Calhoun arrange an exhibition in Joplin. "If by chance I sell them all," he wrote enthusiastically, "we will see if we can't arrange a month for Mamie in Paris."

As a prelude to an American tour, he decided to show his work in Paris. There were few galleries in the city at this time, and none would have risked showing the work of a young and unproven American painter. Remembering that portrait painters sometimes held a tea to show off a newly finished likeness, Tom decided to stage such an affair in his studio. He printed up a few dozen cards and distributed them to his friends and to the cashier at the Café du Dôme, to pass out to American artists.

After considerable discussion, he and Jeanette decided to get new clothes for the occasion. Tom had a blue serge suit made and Jeanette a skirt and jacket. They cleaned up the studio and arranged his pictures around the walls. Jeanette bought cakes and borrowed teacups from her friends so that they would have enough.

As the fateful hour of four o'clock approached, tension built up in the studio. At three, Jeanette burst out with "I'm not staying. I don't want to see all these people. You can pour tea for them as well as I."

She left. Four o'clock came and passed, and no tea drinkers came. Tom waited and waited, paced the floor, and smoked one cigarette after another. The hour approached five, and the light began to fade. Finally, his next-door neighbor John Thompson came in with his mistress. She had no interest in the paintings and left almost immediately, but Thompson stayed and looked around. Tom's neo-impressionist style, though not of the most advanced sort, had a decidedly radical flavor in 1910. It was clear that Thompson didn't much like what he saw—he had never approved of Benton's impressionist experiments—but he was polite and managed a few compliments.

While the two men were talking, Carlock arrived. To Benton's surprise, he spoke curtly to Thompson, and Thompson replied in kind. Clearly some strain had developed between them. Conversation died, and the atmosphere in the studio became uncomfortable.

It became a lot more so a few moments later, when Stan Wright arrived, dressed in his usual affected manner. At the sight of Carlock and Thompson, the only other visitors, both of whom he disliked, he stiffened and assumed his most aristocratic stance, nose in the air and backside flared out, his hands folded over his Whistlerian cane.

Thompson, without a word, walked around Wright and out of the studio. Because of some childhood injury to his left leg, he walked with a slight limp. As soon as he was out of earshot, Wright commented, "Well, we've got rid of that cripple." He then turned to Carlock. "Hello, Curly," he said. "How's the great authority?"

"How's the fashion plate?" Carlock responded, and then, exactly like Thompson, walked around Wright and out the door. Just after he had exited, he turned around for a moment and poked his head back in. "Say, Benton," he shouted. "I'll come back when the air is better."

Wright and Benton then stood alone in the studio in the fading light. "Where's the party?" Wright inquired. "So far, this is the party," Benton confessed.

Wright fell silent and turned to look at the paintings on the walls. "Benton," he exclaimed, "this is great stuff. I can see *that* even in the dark." He looked a little longer and then commented, "Benton, you acted stupidly, but you *are* a man of talent. It doesn't make any difference whether you get in the salon or not." And then, unexpectedly, he added, "When you need money, you tell *me* about it. I'll find it for you."

Morgan Russell.

Sculpture in Morgan Russell's studio.

Tom was too startled to follow up this offer.

After the failure of his tea party, Benton lost his momentum as a painter and shelved his plans to send his paintings to America. He spent a lot of his time reading art criticism and discovered the work of Hippolyte Taine, which would be useful later on but for the moment seemed only to fog up his vision of the future and make him question the legitimacy of his modernist experiments. Taine's insistence that great·art reflected the cultural forces of its time presented him with a dilemma:

"Weighing my situation, it seemed to me that I must make a choice. Either I would paint in the realistic traditions of Western art with some kind of identification with the natural world, and thus risk being 'unprogressive,' or I would follow the new movements toward an unknown goal, a goal which a number of farsighted critics were already saying might turn out to be an empty square of paint."

By this time he had grown bored with Signac and was even less impressed by Henri Martin, who was just then making a splash with his own rendition of the pointillist style. Tom had put expensive frames on two of his paintings from Tulle, and not too long after the maddening tea party, he submitted them to the government Salon. He hoped that some sign of official recognition would persuade his parents to let him stay in Paris longer. But his canvases were rejected, and the experience deepened his discouragement.

In addition, in the early spring of 1911, Macdonald-Wright found a new friend, Morgan Russell, and this cut into his association with Benton. While they continued to see each other often, they were no longer inseparable. Russell was twenty-five at the time, older than Benton and Wright, and he had come more directly in contact with modernist developments than they had. He had been in Paris since the spring of 1908 and had already studied Michelangelo in the Louvre and learned about Cubism from the Steins.

Russell treated Benton quite coldly, but he courted Wright assiduously, and one reason for this soon became apparent. Benton had brushed aside Wright's offer of financial support, which ran against the traditions of his family. Morgan Russell, however, was soon living off Wright's largesse. In fact, he relied on Wright's assistance for the next thirty years or more. The arrangement suited Wright, for it gave him power and placed Russell in a position of dependency.

If Benton did not care for Russell as a person, he was ready to acknowledge his talent. He was particularly intrigued by Russell's ability as a sculptor, and greatly impressed by a torso in wet clay that he encountered in Russell's studio. Under its influence, in fact, he took up modeling in clay himself and made several small figure studies.

With Wright, Benton visited a Russian collection of Cézannes in a mansion in the Parc Monceau. This led him to try to develop his own methods and theories of the handling of color to generate form. He tried out some of these ideas in a portrait of Jeanette that he began in February 1911, but it proved maddeningly difficult to carry out.

During the early part of 1911, he began to make a large number of new artistic acquaintances. He met Arthur Lee, Lee Simonson, and Sam Halpert—all of whom he encountered later in New York. He met the Mexican painter Diego Rivera, who in the 1930s became his chief rival as a muralist but at the time was completely immersed in Cubism. Through Morgan Russell, Benton and Wright met Leo Stein and had a long talk with him at the Dôme—or rather, listened to Leo talk, for it was hard to get a word in edgewise. Leo was still painting and invited them to his studio. Wright later paid a visit to the Steins, but Tom lost his nerve and did not go. Perhaps this was just as well, for Wright's cockiness annoyed Leo and Gertrude, and the evening was not a success. When Wright later discussed the encounter, he described Gertrude to Tom as "that fat-assed kike."

A Family Reunion

Mildred Benton Small can still vividly recall a self-portrait that Tom sent home from Paris toward the end of his stay there. It looked very much like the paintings of the German Expressionist Emil Nolde, with brilliantly colored shadows of purple and orange. Benton was twenty-one at the time. It showed him with a full beard and was a very good likeness. His mother hung it in the library, but took it down after a while because visitors thought it looked odd. She also told Tom to shave off his beard before she came to visit him, which he did. Mildred had only known paintings of the "brown gravy" sort, which didn't seem very interesting to her as a child; this portrait was the first to excite her artistic interest.

Tom had remained Elizabeth Benton's favorite child. Mildred recalls coming upon her in 1909 quietly weeping over a photograph he had sent home from Paris; she said she wept because Tom had come to look like her brother Toby, who died young.

During this period, the Benton family's financial situation was changing in ways that would very shortly have great impact on Tom's life and personal relationships. The Colonel lost a good deal of money in an unsuccessful political bid. Just after the election, he wrote Tom an alarming letter informing him that the sum set aside for his education was almost entirely depleted and that he would have to come home soon. Shortly afterward, however, Pappy Wise died, and Tom's mother inherited some money, a windfall that gave her complete independence from her husband. Naturally, Tom hoped that some of it might come his way and allow him to stay in Paris longer.

On March 1, 1911, when he went to the bank to pick up his allowance, Benton discovered to his surprise that he had been sent 350 francs rather than the usual 250. In a cheerful mood, he stepped outside to read the accompanying letter. Opening it, he received a nasty shock. His mother announced that she was coming to Paris with his two sisters. She would arrive at the Gare du Nord at seven o'clock in the evening of March 3—only two days away. The envelope had been sitting at the bank for two weeks, but Tom had neglected to pick it up.

What could he do about Jeanette? His entire savings, including the extra dollars

Leo, Gertrude, and Michael Stein, circa 1906. The expatriate American Gertrude Stein played a major role in the discovery of Picasso and Matisse. Benton had several long talks with her brother Leo at the Café du Dôme.

just added to his March allowance, would not suffice to set up a place for her, even during the period of his mother's stay. Perhaps, he hoped, Jeanette would know what to do. Certainly he had no option but to discuss the situation with her. But when he did so the next day, she proved unwilling to give up her relationship with him or disappear. "We will go together to meet your people," she said.

Tom tried to explain to her that her social class was an insuperable barrier, but this turned out to be the worst thing he could have said. Jeanette lost control. Her mouth tightened, her chin jutted out, and her eyes bulged with anger. She let loose a flood of obscenities, screaming that Tom's mother and sisters were "not fit to kiss my ass" ("à me baiser le cul") and similar insults. When she had exhausted herself, she collapsed on a chair and began to cry and moan and rock herself back and forth.

This torrent of tears and insults lasted until two in the morning, when Tom finally collapsed still fully dressed on the couch and caught a few hours of sleep. When he awoke in the early gray of dawn, he found the oil lamp still burning. He blew it out, stirred up the fire in the stove, made some coffee, and sat down to think. About nine o'clock, Jeanette came down from the balcony fully dressed and left the studio without a word. She was gone all day. About five o'clock, Tom put on a clean white shirt and the blue serge suit he had purchased for his unhappy tea party. No sooner was he dressed than Jeanette came in. "I'm sorry for last night, Tommy," she said, "but I'm going with you."

"Do as you please [comme tu veux]," he replied. So she climbed on the streetcar with him and followed him to the station. But Benton guessed rightly in assuming that in the end her sense of propriety and of social distinctions would play in his favor. At the last moment, she lost her nerve. When he stepped forward to greet his mother and sisters, she did not follow him.

Benton's sister Mildred, then fourteen years old and the lone surviving witness of these events, recalls that none of them recognized Tom at first—his clothes and demeanor had become so foreign. He was dressed in the dark suit of the Parisian art student, with a black cape and a round black hat with wide brim and low crown. The one nonblack accent was a flowing white satin tie. Tom's gestures had become animated and exaggerated, and he spoke English with a strange accent and with occasional mistakes of grammar. (His French was fluent, rapid, and idiomatic, though marred by an execrable accent.)

He dropped off his mother and sisters at an apartment they had rented near the Place de l'Étoile and returned to his studio for the night. The next morning, he had another frightful argument with Jeanette, who refused to leave. She declared that the furniture was hers (which it was) and that Tom had no right to throw her out. But she finally agreed to visit Madeleine for the afternoon. After she left, Tom rushed through the place, hurriedly trying to hide the indications of a woman's presence.

He then went to meet his mother and sisters at the Place de l'Étoile. After a leisurely lunch, they hired a horse-drawn hack to take them to the Passage Guibert. There was much laughter and joking on the way. When they arrived Tom spotted Jeanette and her mother standing on the corner, but he pretended not to notice. Once again Jeanette lost her nerve. She did not follow him inside.

"What a nice place," Tom's sister Mamie said as she walked into the studio. His mother looked around curiously. She paid no attention to Tom's pictures but set out to explore the apartment. First she went over to the chest in which Jeanette's clothes were hidden and opened it. Tom explained that he was keeping some things for a friend and his wife, who were away in London. Then she came to the curtain that hung below the stairway to the balcony. When she pulled it aside, she discovered Jeanette's cosmetics sitting on a shelf, and a douche can with a telltale nozzle hanging from a nail. "Oh, Tom, it's true!" she exclaimed. He realized that someone must have told his mother of his mistress.

Mrs. Benton retreated to a chair and collapsed. The girls were confused and puzzled. Tom finally got them all back to their apartment, where his mother put on more tears and fainting spells and tried to persuade him to stay overnight.

He returned to the studio late that evening and immediately became involved in another argument with Jeanette. "What are you going to do about me?" she queried. He told her that he would somehow provide for her, and then, quite suddenly, her approach shifted from combative to reasonable. She had discovered where the family's apartment was located, and observed, "It takes a lot of money to live there." They discussed what she would need to live on and finally agreed that Tom would give her three hundred dollars. This was a pretty good sum at a time when rent was generally eight or ten dollars a month and a single person could live on twenty dollars a month or even less.

The next day, he tried to persuade his mother to lend him the three hundred dollars for Jeanette, but she flatly refused to oblige. In desperation, he went to Macdonald-Wright and asked for a loan. He was sure he could repay it after he got back home and had a chance to explain the situation to his father. "Yes, this is for men, not women," Wright agreed. When Benton mentioned the amount, he asked, "Why give the bitch so much?" but he forked it over, only requiring that Tom write up an IOU. He seems to have had no fear that the debt would not be paid.

When he dismissed Jeanette, Tom lost the furniture in his studio, which belonged to her and which she and her friends cleared out. Soon afterward he gave up the place and slept in the maid's room of his mother's apartment. With brutal ease, his mother stripped him of all vestiges of independence.

Benton's anxieties at this time were not apparent to his youngest sister. Mildred recalls that "Tom seemed wholly at ease with Mother and Mary and me," and that he "was like an eager boy showing us Paris, which city he obviously loved unreservedly." He was "consistently pleasant," which "he never had been before and he never was again." As a young girl of fourteen, she remained completely ignorant of Tom's mistress, and was not aware of his conflicts, embarrassments and subterfuges.

Benton's recollections of this time were very different. The month of March 1911, he recalled, "produced so many shameful and humiliating experiences that they could not be adjusted to, or put into any acceptable pattern of memory." It was filled with "disconnected and senseless disturbances of my peace of mind."

He pleaded with his mother to let him stay on in Paris for further study, but she would not hear of it, even though Wright forcefully argued his case. In July, the Bentons embarked for the United States. The boat was delayed two weeks in Liverpool for engine repairs, and Tom spent most of his time studying an English manual on perspective.

Disembarking in Boston, they spent two days there before they could get railroad accommodations through to Neosho. Benton, already interested in large wall paintings, insisted on going to see the celebrated murals by Puvis de Chavannes at the Boston Public Library. "I never understood," Mildred comments, "why such a turbulent person was interested in such placid painting."

Chapter Four
A Misfit in New York

Thomas Hart Benton, Portrait of Maecenas E. Benton, *oil on canvas, 1912.*

Thomas Hart Benton, Self-Portrait, *oil on canvas, 1912. After an abortive attempt to settle in Kansas City in the spring of 1912, Benton returned to Neosho and executed a series of dark portraits, somewhat influenced by Manet. Most of these paintings were destroyed when the family home burned down, but this one was hanging in his father's office and survived. The gold-topped cane was given to him by his mother in Paris.* •

"My God, man," Stan Wright wrote to Benton from Paris. "When I think of what there is yet to be done in painting I rear and pant like a war horse smelling powder. It puts new life into me."

Neosho and Kansas City, 1911–12

Benton got back to Neosho late in July 1911, just under three years after he had left it. His homecoming was not pleasant, for the Colonel was outraged by the strange splotches and splashes his son had been creating in Paris. To demonstrate that his time in France had not been entirely wasted, Tom painted several portraits in the Rembrandt-like, almost monochromatic style he had learned at Julian's. The likeness he painted of his father provides no hint of the tension in their relationship. He chose a side view, his subject looking off into the distance, and did not even show the Colonel's intense gander-blue eyes, which bugged out of his head and made his stare uncomfortably penetrating.

The course of Tom's future remained unclear. Shortly before Christmas, he went shopping with his mother in Kansas City and happened to run into one of his Chicago friends, Frank Zimmerer, a chubby, good-natured man who had just become head of the Kansas City Art Institute. "Just what we need," Frank commented, "a Parisian artist," and suggested that Tom come to Kansas City to teach.

In January 1912, Benton moved to Kansas City, and in the first week of February the Kansas City *Star* ran a feature story about him. The piece opened with a vivid description of his appearance—"an agile, nervous little man," with long, disordered black hair under a rakish, baggy velvet cap. He wore a long black tie, which cascaded over his soft negligee shirt, and sat in an ancient rocking chair, beside a candle in a brass candlestick, which he used to light his cigarettes. His studio contained a battered grand piano, some canvases, an unfinished painting of a dark-skinned girl, and an ancient brass warming pan, in which a few apples and wizened oranges nestled together. The journalist commented:

It sounds like the beginning of a Leonard Merrick story, doesn't it, and as if a French phrase might be sprung at any time, or an offhand allusion to the Latin quarter? Well, it isn't, and it wasn't even in the Bohemian quarter of New York that the little man was holding forth, but right here in Kansas City, out in a well-to-do residence neighborhood. The studio is at Fortieth and Penn streets, in an old building that was once a Presbyterian church, and the little man, despite his long hair and velvet cap and generally exotic appearance is a native Missourian and his name is Thomas Benton. "Tommy" Benton they call him down in the little town of Neosho, Mo., where he was born twenty-three years ago, and where his father, an ex-congressman, still lives.

Balcolm, Tommy Benton, Late of Paris. *In February 1912, a staff artist from the Kansas City* Star *sketched Benton in his Parisian painter's attire.*

But for all that he's the kind of artist you read about and see on the stage, and for settings it would be hard to beat the studio in old Westport. For three years "Tommy" Benton has been studying art in Paris—learning to paint. Now he has come back to put into practice here in the Middle West the things he learned in the art center of the world.

Maybe some of the things will startle the Middle West a little, too, for Mr. Benton belongs to the impressionistic school of painting. That means that he's lavish with his colors; also that he sometimes sees different colors than the rest of us do. The man who painted the purple cow, you know, was an impressionist—the one who caused Gelett Burgess to shriek wildly:

> I never saw a purple cow,
> I never hope to see one;
> I'll tell you one thing, anyhow,
> I'd rather see than be one.

After reading that impassioned stanza, who can doubt that the impressionist was successful in his attempt? He made an impression on Gelett if on no one else.

WHY, HERE'S A BLUE-HAIRED WOMAN.

But to get back to Mr. Benton. There are no purple cows in his studio, but there's a blue-haired woman, with a russet skin. He explained to an ignorant person who wandered in the other day that the hair of the model from whom he was painting didn't really look blue to him even in his most downcast moments; however, comma, that "realism is not an exact copy of any part of Nature but an effort to reproduce in paint a replica of the sensation received."

The ignorant person began to understand then. He looked again at the blue-haired woman, and it made him feel very blue. The longer he looked at her the bluer he felt, and thus he realized the power of impressionism.

But Mr. Benton paints other things besides blue-haired women; because, if the truth were known, the market for them is rather restricted in this part of the world. Therefore he turns his facile brush to landscapes, now and again, and for these he generally goes to Neosho, where the landscape is extensive and blue-haired women exceedingly rare.

However, Neosho does not interest Mr. Benton very much. In fact, he left there about as soon as he was able to.... "My art," he says, "so far as it has developed, has been an effort toward the presentment of life. I believe that this can be truly given only through the passionate massing of line and color, especially color. Color is the only quality within the realm of painting capable of producing sensation. Life is all sensation and the painting productive of the greater amount of sensation comes nearer being life."

A CUP OF TEA THAT NEVER CAME.

He paused, lit another cigarette at the candle that flickered in the big draughty room, and shook a vagrant lock of black hair back from his face.

"Wouldn't you like some tea?" he asked the ignorant person. The I.P. admitted that that would go very well and the artist hurried into a room back of the studio and lit the fire under a teakettle. Then he returned to talk some more about art. It had been hard to get him to talk about his own life and experience, but art—that was another matter.

He talked on, through clouds of cigarette smoke, of his art and his ambitions, and he saw no more reason why a real artist should not succeed in the Middle West than anywhere else, if he had it in him. Then suddenly he remembered the tea.

"Aha," thought the material minded person in whose honor the tea was being made, "I wonder whether he'll serve lemon with it. Lemon is certainly more esthetic than cream. Undoubtedly it will be lemon."

In the back room there was a scrabbling and a noise of moving about. Then Mr. Benton appeared, lemonless and tealess.

"I'm so sorry," he apologized, "but there isn't any sugar in the place, so I guess we can't have any tea. Stupid of me not to think of it."

Tom's attempt to bring Paris to Kansas City didn't last very long; he stayed a mere three weeks. He later explained: "At that time Kansas City was a vaudeville and carnival exchange center, and it was a place where the chorus boys would be stranded for weeks at a time. And somehow or other, Kansas City had become a quite developed homosexual center, and it had reached into the art institute. Now listen, I had been to Paris, and I'd never seen anything like that. It shocked the hell out of me. They had a party for me, and they all came in women's underwear and all that stuff. That was something I was absolutely innocent about, and I couldn't stay there."

He made no secret of his disgust. As a consequence, he did not receive the job offer he expected, and returned to Neosho in a state of emotional confusion. He tried to explain to his father what had happened, but M.E. did not believe him and thought he was just fabricating excuses. For the next eight months he hung around the house, painting realistic canvases with a limited palette—dark, solid paintings, a bit reminiscent of Manet but more sculptural in their handling of form. One would never have guessed from them that he had just returned from the coloristic explosions of Paris.

Benton's friends and family walking about Neosho, 1912. Benton was wearing his best clothes from Paris when his friend Garland Price snapped this photograph. Thomas Craven, who met Benton a few months later, recalled: "He was a sight with his tight French clothes, his flat French hat and his Balzac stick—the antithesis of everything American."

Oak Hill on fire, 1917. In the spring of 1917, the Benton family home burned to the ground. Most of Benton's early work, stored in the attic, was destroyed in the fire.

Thomas Hart Benton, The Fish Hatchery, Neosho, *oil on canvas, 1912.* •

Only one of these paintings survives, a self-portrait, which was hanging in his father's law office on the town square on the day the family home burned down. Tom stares grimly ahead, dressed in his Parisian attire, with his flat, wide-brimmed hat in his right hand and the gold-tipped cane his mother had purchased for him in the left.

He worked for eight months in this manner—the longest time he had ever pursued a single artistic course. But at the end of that time, a very different side of his character demanded expression. Spring came, and the brilliant colors of the flowering fruit trees led him to abandon his somber exercises. He made a group of Fauvist landscapes outdoors, sketching them in with blue outlines and then boldly filling in the whites and pinks of the blossoming dogwood and redbud. The most beautiful of these to survive is *The Fish Hatchery, Neosho* (the hatchery was located about half a mile from Oak Hill). The well-dressed young woman in the foreground was probably Tom's girlfriend of the time, Fay Clark.

Tom had many long discussions with his parents about his future. With great effort, he convinced them of his ability to support himself as a portrait painter in New York, making likenesses such as those he had produced for them. According to Mildred, one factor in their decision was Tom's increasingly intense relationship with Fay Clark.

In Paris, he had grown used to living with a mistress, but in Neosho sexual mores were extremely strict. His liaison with Fay became the subject of such gossip that her father paid a call on the Colonel to inquire about his son's intentions. The Colonel replied that Tom had no intentions, for he had never been able to support himself and showed no indication of ever being able to do so. To put an end to the affair, shortly afterwards, in June 1912, the Bentons bundled Tom off to New York, with train fare and $150 to get started.

New York, 1912

Tom soon found a studio at the old Lincoln Arcade, at Sixty-fifth Street and Broadway, a ramshackle building filled with prizefighters, dancers, actors, models, commercial artists, painters, sculptors, astrologers, and muscle builders. The place was infested with bedbugs and cockroaches, as he discovered the night he moved in; rats raced above the metal ceiling. He learned to keep the legs of his bed resting in pans of water, so that the bedbugs would drown when they tried to crawl up to the mattress.

Still immersed in the ideals of French culture, Benton seemed totally out of place in the metropolis. Thomas Craven, who met him at this time, remembered him as "a sight" and "the antithesis of everything American," with his tight French clothes, his flat French hat, and his Balzac stick. "He was only twenty-three," Craven recalled, "but he looked old and sad: his face was deeply lined and drawn, and I cannot remember that he ever laughed. He was, I felt, the victim of some strange irregularity of development."

Thomas Hart Benton, Upper Manhattan, *circa 1917, oil on canvas, Benton probably painted this Cézannesque landscape in 1917, when he was working in the movie studios at Fort Lee, New Jersey.*

63

For a while after his arrival, Benton tramped around the city with several books of pen drawings he had made in Paris, attempting to solicit commissions. But he soon grew tired of this, for he was unable to drum up work—the style of his drawings was evidently not in fashion. His Chicago roommate, handsome, facile Jack Armstrong, was earning a good living making heads of pretty girls for the movie magazines. Tom had no enthusiasm for this line of work. "I sometimes get thoroughly disgusted with the whole thing," he wrote his mother, "especially when I see these half-witted talent-less imbeciles who tickle up the vapid, simpering abortion called 'The American pretty girl.' "

"I have been so engrossed in my work since the arrival of the thirty-nine dollars," he further wrote, "that I have lost all sense of time . . . . When I have the money to buy paint and live models the artist in me gets the better of everything else . . . . We must do our best to find some teaching position for I am mentally too far away from this commercial world to be ever able to make a success therein.

"I will have to develop alone and on my own ground (as, in truth, I have always done) . . . . I am helpless before the world. My strength is in abstractions. If I have not genius I am utterly worthless. Art is not lucrative at first (sometimes it never is) but at least its devotees have a purpose in life, which is more than most men have."

On July 10, he wrote: "My outlook at present is far from bright. I can find no work whatever, my designs do not seem to be popular so I have had no more orders of that sort, and as for illustration I know nothing about it and could hardly hope to compete with men of experience in that field . . . . The illustrators are not artists, they are rarely men of anything more than mediocre intelligence, but they have certain clever tricks . . . . Sham, . . . hypocrisy of any sort is always better paid and with the mass more respected than sincere work.

Jack Armstrong and model. When Benton moved into the Lincoln Arcade, he met up with his old roommate from Chicago. Armstrong made a good living drawing girlie pictures, many of which were reproduced on cal-endars. His favorite medium was pastel.

"I can't even get a job as a scene painter . . . . Isn't it awful to have a son so practically worthless? I would be willing . . . to do anything (even hard work) for the sake of my own living if I could find something to do. Anything that doesn't degrade my artistic ideals. . . .

"I am sure every day that I am a great man. There is no young man here that can do what I can. There are many talented men, but none with a personal viewpoint. It will only be a matter of time—'en attendant' the fight for sausage and beans is hard. If you can let me have 5 dollars more my stomach will praise you thrice daily as long as it lasts."

Despite the hardships of his existence, he remained devoted to his work. In July 1912, he wrote: "I am working slowly (when I can afford the paint) toward decorative fields—the demand for such work is large and it affords the greatest scope for the expression of poetic thoughts. I am *absolutely* sure of myself as an artist, if I can stick it out until I have made a name for myself I believe that I will not find life so hard."

Practically the only person besides his mother who believed in his talent was Stan Wright, who to Tom's envy was still in France, painting in a villa, "Rose du Ciel," near Cassis on the Riviera. Wright was at the peak of his productivity, filled with enthusiasm for his new color discoveries and in the process of developing the Synchro-mist style that would make him famous. "My God, man," he wrote. "When I think of what there is yet to be done in painting I rear and pant like a war horse smelling powder. It puts new life into me." He continued: "I have all the faith in the world in your future . . . . I'm damned glad that you are in N.Y. It is the only place in America possible for an artist & you are one."

New York Friends

Within a month of his arrival, Benton met Thomas Craven through Stan Wright's half-brother, Willard Huntington Wright, who had just become editor of *The Smart Set* in New York. Soon after their meeting, Craven moved into Tom's studio at the Lincoln Arcade and paid the rent. They got along well. In July 1912, Benton wrote to his mother: "In Wright and in Craven, the poet, I have two very sympathetic and sure friends, two men that I can count on for the defense of my Art from the non-aesthetic vulgarity of the common painting and literature."

Craven had grown up in Kansas, but like Benton he had done his best to put the Midwest behind him. Indeed, he had wandered even more widely than Tom, failing in everything he tried. He had lived for a while in Paris and kept a French mistress. He had been a newspaper reporter in Denver, a schoolteacher in California, and a night clerk for the Santa Fe Railroad in Las Vegas. When Benton first met him, he aspired to be a poet, signed his name "Jewell," and was deeply immersed in the spirit of the *fin de siècle*. Shortly after he arrived in New York, he sold two poems to the *American* magazine, but for the next eight years he was unable to sell a single manuscript.

Craven often taught in prep schools when he needed money, but for the next decade, whenever he and Benton were both in New York, they either lived together or had adjoining apartments. Benton later commented: "He was a good cook. He'd cook and I'd wash the dishes. They used to think we were a couple of homosexuals because we were always together. But it was for the convenience. I've always liked the association of males anyhow." Richard Craven has commented: "I would say my father and Tom were as close, as inseparable, as two men could be with one another."

Tom had two other friends who helped him to survive the next decade. Both of them would become famous and very rich in the 1920s, a period that for Benton was full of hardship. Ralph Barton, a tiny man with a large head, had grown up in Kansas City. His friendship with Benton was cemented when they discovered that Senator Benton, Tom's namesake, had shot and killed one of Barton's ancestors in a duel. After his arrival in New York, Barton transformed himself almost overnight into a dandy, a boulevardier, a ladies' man, and an ardent Francophile. He was soon making sketches for *Life, Judge, Puck,* and the movie magazines. "He had a fancy for me," Benton later recalled, "and carried me through many tough moments. He was clever, made money easily, and spent it—no small amount on me. I was always living in studios or apartments for which he had paid the rent." Most of Benton's friends disliked Barton, who could be vain and petty and was subject to nervous crises. But Tom put up with his foibles, and not only because he was so generous. "Underneath the pretensions of his vanity," Benton later wrote, "it was plain to see that he suffered."

Rex Hitchcock, an athletic, temperamental, and remarkably handsome young Irishman, was taking classes at Yale University. He aspired to be a sculptor but also had some talent as an actor. He often came to New York to take part in boxing matches, go to the theater, and visit the movie studios. During these excursions, he would frequently stay in Tom's atelier.

By chance, Tom ran into Samuel Halpert, who like himself had just come back from Paris. Sam, who also had his studio in the Lincoln Arcade, was a few years older and as a consequence had never paid much heed to Tom in France. But back in New York, as fellow veterans of the Paris art world, they immediately became close friends. At this time, Benton was much influenced by Halpert's rather decorative adaptations of Cézanne. He began making copies of the photographs of Cézanne's paintings that Sam had collected, and making paintings of his own based on still-life arrangements, in which he broke up the surfaces in gradated planes of color. Because of their stay in

Ralph Barton. The society cartoonist helped Benton survive through the lean years in New York. Despite his success, Barton suffered from melancholia; in May 1931, at the age of forty, he blew his brains out with a revolver in his Manhattan penthouse.

Ralph Barton, Caricatures of Benton and Ingram, *ink and wash on paper, circa 1912. When he arrived in New York, Benton looked "old and sad," according to his friend Craven. "His face was deeply lined and drawn, and I cannot remember that he ever laughed. He was, I felt, the victim of some strange irregularity of development."*

Thomas Hart Benton, Portrait of Thomas Craven, *oil on canvas, circa 1912. Benton painted this portrait soon after they met.*

Thomas Hart Benton, Still Life with Fruit and Vegetables, *oil on board, 1912–14. During the early years in New York, Benton executed many still-life paintings modeled on the work of Cézanne.* •

France, he and Sam felt superior to the other artists in the Arcade. Tom got in the habit of dropping by Sam's studio in the late afternoon to chat and reminisce.

On one of these occasions, he made an enemy who would plague him for the next fifty years. One day when he came into Sam's studio, he found the floor littered with charcoal drawings in a rough style reminiscent of Robert Henri—the work of a young artist with an arrogant, pudgy face and slicked-back hair. Sam introduced him in a bored way as Stuart Davis.

Though young, Davis knew a lot about the Ashcan School style, for he was the son of Edward D. Davis, the art editor of the Philadelphia *Press*, who had employed John Sloan, William Glackens, George Luks, and Everett Shinn, back in the days when they had been newspaper illustrators. While still in his teens, Stuart had made the pilgrimage to New York to study with Robert Henri. He was very full of himself as he discussed his drawings, and Benton, who was easily annoyed by such behavior, told him that he was pretty presumptuous to push himself before two Parisian veterans. "Go to Paris and try to learn something," Tom told him acidly.

He regretted the nasty snobbery of this comment as soon as he had said it and saw the look on Davis's face. As it happened, it was the best advice to have given Stuart Davis. He did eventually go to Paris, where he absorbed the work of the Cubists more fully and intelligently than any other American artist. Through this exposure to French art, Davis transformed himself from a provincial into a significant painter. Nonetheless, he never forgave Benton his arrogance; for the rest of his life, he remained Tom's bitter enemy.

In October 1912, Tom was called back to Missouri. His mother had become seriously ill. When he arrived, he discovered that she was undergoing a nervous breakdown. The relationship between his parents had grown even more tense: his mother still missed Washington and felt imprisoned and unhappy; his father was curt and irritable and was drinking heavily. Because of this trip to Neosho, Benton missed the Armory Show, the first major exhibition of European "ultra-modernist painting" to be held in the United States. After an uncomfortable and unproductive seven months, he returned to New York in June 1913, exactly a year after his first attempt to move there. His father had no money to give him, but his mother, dipping into her inheritance, provided his train fare, along with $150 to get him started. When he asked for more, she told him that he had to make his own living.

Not long after he had settled in, Mrs. Benton followed him to New York, bringing the other children with her but leaving the Colonel in Neosho. She arrived in October and rented an apartment in the Pointsiana, an elegant building with a doorman. According to his sister Mildred, Tom lived in the apartment with his mother and the family and ate most of his meals there. "He doesn't tell that in his books," she notes. Thomas Craven often joined them. Once, Tom went on a long walking trip in upstate New York and came back looking like a tramp, with shaggy, uncut hair and ragged clothes, his toes sticking through the tips of his shoes. His mother had to come downstairs and vouch for him before the doorman would let him in.

At this time, Tom made a portrait of Mildred, who was then a freshman at Barnard College. "I think it's a very beautiful painting," Mildred has commented. "I think it looks like a Manet. Nobody thought it was a very good likeness of me because he has coarsened my features so much it looks a lot like him. But I think all portrait painters do that. If you get twelve Rembrandts lined up together of twelve different people, you can see Rembrandt in every one of them." The National Academy of Design rejected this portrait when Benton submitted it for their annual exhibition. But he showed it with the works of other *refusés* from the Academy display, and it attracted favorable comment. Not long afterward, it was reproduced in a national magazine, *Collier's*, his first significant publicity.

Tom kept secret from his mother his relationship with a redheaded dancer named Lysle, who posed for him around this time. Eager to earn some money, he decided to do pretty-girl pictures for the magazines and arranged with Lysle to pay for her services by splitting his earnings with her. His first effort was a success; it wound up on the cover of a movie magazine and earned him an impressive hundred dollars—fifty, once he had shared the take with Lysle. Soon after, he painted a full-sized nude of her, with bright colors and a Cézannesque background. He felt proud of the result, and even Sam Halpert thought highly of it. But after these first successes he began to flounder. Despite many further efforts, he could not manage to make any more paintings that fit the commercial formula. The relationship apparently ended when Lysle stabbed Tom in the back. "She surprised me," Tom later recalled. "She'd have never gotten close enough to cut me if I had thought she was mad."

In autumn 1914, Mrs. Benton and the girls returned to Missouri. (Mildred had been expelled from Barnard at the begining of the term.) Tom and his brother Nat abandoned the apartment at the Pointsiana and moved the furniture to a much cheaper place, on 242nd Street in the Bronx, not far from the subway. They were joined by Thomas Craven. Because he could no longer afford it, Benton abandoned his studio at the Lincoln Arcade. They were all very hard up. Craven got a small remittance from his father, but for the most part, all three lived off the money that M.E. sent to Nat to pay his college expenses at Columbia. Their poverty was temporarily relieved when Tom ran into an old Chicago friend, "Mac the Drunk," an alcoholic with a talent for

Thomas Hart Benton, Portrait of the Artist's Sister, Mildred, *oil on canvas, 1913. In the fall of 1913, Benton painted his youngest sister, Mildred, then a freshman at Barnard College. "I think it's a very beautiful painting," Mildred comments, adding, "Nobody thought it was a good likeness." After Tom exhibited the canvas, it was reproduced in* Collier's, *his first significant publicity.* •

writing advertising copy. But Mac soon disappeared, and their funds got so low that they had to steal food to survive.

Through Bob Everhardt, his old friend from Chicago, Tom got a few small jobs doing sign painting, layouts, and lettering, but he discovered that he wasn't very good at it. Most of his paintings seemed crazy to his friends. The Armory Show of 1913 had attracted so much controversy that magazine articles and books about Parisian art began to circulate about New York. Tom came across reproductions of Braque's still-life paintings in muted colors, and this led him to paint several Braque-like compositions of flowers. Since he didn't have the money to buy plants, he abstracted them from a seed catalogue, stylizing them in flat, decorative patterns.

Early in 1914, Tom stayed for about two weeks at Coney Island with his friends Bert and Ellen, who were professional dancers. By chance, the owner of the dance hall downstairs happened to see one of his florals and commissioned him to paint five large panels in a similar style for the dance hall, for thirty-five dollars apiece. This was the first time Tom had ever sold a painting. Though not much money by later standards, at the time he could stretch it a long way. Sadly, these decorative paintings were destroyed when the dance hall burned down, in about 1917.

Benton invested some of the proceeds of his work in porcelain bowls and plates, which he decorated in the flat manner of the florals. He sold everything he produced, and consequently kept up with this ceramic work for several years. He was not painting but was busy decorating these plates when Stan Wright came back from Paris and gave his morale a much needed boost. "I taught Tom Benton," Macdonald-Wright boasted to Betty Hoag in 1964. "He had given up painting when he came back to America." For his first two years in New York, Tom had not known many artists. This began to change in 1914, the result of Stan Wright's tonic influence.

Thomas Hart Benton, Sketch of Willard Huntington Wright, pencil on paper, circa 1914 (now lost). Willard Wright, an arrogant Nietzschean and the editor of The Smart Set, energetically promoted the paintings of his half-brother Stan. His book Modern Painting had a major influence on Benton's thinking about art. After a nervous breakdown in 1925, Willard shifted to writing detective stories under the pseudonym S. S. Van Dine.

Willard and Stan

Wright had used up his money in France, thanks in part to his generous support of Morgan Russell, and was now flat broke. When Benton first saw him, Wright attempted to get back the three-hundred-dollar loan. He claimed that Tom was "playing poor" and threatened a lawsuit against his father, but finally realized that Tom was in financial difficulties also. "Forget it," Stan said, and he never asked for the money again. Unable to afford an apartment of his own, Stan moved in with his brother Willard. For two weeks or so in 1914, Benton moved in as well.

An enthusiastic reader of Nietzsche, Willard maintained a pose of studied arrogance and shared Stan's views about keeping the lower classes in their place. Unlike Stan, he possessed a streak of deliberate cruelty. In their apartment building, for example, there was an Italian boy he disliked, who ran the elevator and kept his overcoat hanging there. Willard put a silver spoon in the coat pocket and then went to the police with the complaint that his silverware was being stolen. The detective sent to investigate the case discovered the spoon in the boy's coat, and he was promptly fired.

Stan and Willard fought constantly, but they clearly loved each other; each called the other "Bud." They looked rather similar, even to the Vandyke beards they grew to cover their weak chins.

In France, Stan, along with his friend Russell, had created a new artistic movement called Synchromism—"with color." Synchromism used the cubist vocabulary of fractured forms in combination with brilliant prismatic colors. Though visually the effect was quite similar to another Parisian movement, Orphism, the artistic intention was different; in Synchromism, color was used to build form and had a constructive significance. Stan Wright and Morgan Russell trumpeted their works, in a series of manifestos, as a turning point in the history of Western art.

69

Stan had returned from France with a large number of his Synchromist abstractions and was anxious to mount an exhibition. He had a hard time finding a place to display them, but finally, with Willard's money, he hired the Carroll Galleries, a small space in a converted brownstone on Forty-fifth Street. He had the show mounted by March 1914, only about a month after his return.

Willard took over the task of "public relations." Since Tom was still going around in his French attire, Willard decided to create an effect by introducing him to the press as "a young Parisian artist." To maintain this illusion, he told Tom and Stan to converse with each other only in French. Unbeknownst to them, he also told the reporters that Benton was a Parisian gangster in flight from the police, who went by the name "Kiki la Souris" ("Kiki the Mouse"). The fiction didn't hold up very long, and when it collapsed it affected the credibility of Stan's painting—and later on, of Tom's as well.

Whether because or in spite of Willard's antics, the show did attract a fair amount of interest, and Benton got in the habit of dropping by the Carroll Galleries. "After all," he recalled, "this was part of the smell of Paris. . . . The first impression I received, all the pictures being large and crowded together, was like an explosion of rainbows. However, as an act of friendship I visited the show nearly every day and soon found myself interested."

While flawed as an artistic solution, Synchromism was singularly rich in its artistic challenges. It demanded a new approach not to one but to three of the major issues of painting: form, color, and figurative expression. As regards both form and color, Synchromism relied on modernist sources. Its handling of form was derived from the fragmented shapes of the Cubists, and its use of brilliant prismatic colors must certainly have been influenced by the example of the Orphists, despite the claims of Macdonald-Wright and Russell that they had created a new and entirely different style.

The figurative emphasis of the Synchromists, however, was rooted in the Renaissance. It was from the sculpture of Michelangelo, which both Macdonald-Wright and Russell hugely admired, that they derived their enthusiasm for muscular tension and movement, and for tightly wound spiraling forms. Most Synchromist paintings, in fact, were not true abstractions but ultimately based on some sort of figurative reference, usually one that explored muscular tension and movement, as is the case, for example, with Macdonald-Wright's *Arm Organization* of 1914.

Benton was most strongly attracted to precisely this figurative element of Synchromist work, which tended to produce an ordered but spatially energized, highly motive form very much at odds with the planar, blocky, and relatively static world of most abstract painting. As he noted: "What captured my interest . . . was the Synchromists' use of Baroque rhythms, derived not from Cézanne's work, as was the case with most of the Parisian painters who had experimented with such rhythms, but from the more basic source of Michelangelo's sculpture. Through its use of these rhythms, Synchromism seemed to offer a more logical connection between the orderly form of the past and the coloristic tendencies of the present than any other of the Parisian schools. . . . I could look more sympathetically at the Synchromist effort than most of the New York artists who came to see it. I could not accept the repudiation of all representational art, which was the core of Synchromist dogmas, but its procedures were interesting enough to induce experimentation."

While seemingly the most reactionary aspect of Synchromist work, it was this figurative element that was to prove most pregnant with significance for the future of modernist painting. For it was Stan Wright's interest in figural rhythms, particularly the dynamic interaction of "the hollow and the bulge," that most influenced Tom Benton; and it was through these same muscular rhythms, enlarged and abstracted, that Jackson Pollock found the organizational principles for his grand and sweepingly gestural "action paintings."

Wright's show provided a forceful stimulus to Benton at a time when he had begun to lose his sense of artistic direction. In addition, it threw him into contact with large numbers of New York artists. Robert Henri, John Sloan, George Bellows, and others of that generation came by, though none of them liked the show much because it was so brash. Tom also met Andrew Dasberg, who took an immediate dislike to him. Dasberg had roomed for a time with Morgan Russell in Paris and felt that Macdonald-Wright was stealing the credit for Synchromism, so he stayed all day at the exhibition "to defend Russell's interests."

One day, Sam Halpert, who had dropped by to view the exhibit, introduced Benton to John Weichsel of the People's Art Guild. It was at this time, also, that Tom first got to know Alfred Stieglitz, who in 1914 was exactly twice Benton's age, fifty to his twenty-five. Stieglitz's art gallery, 291, located in the small attic of a brownstone on Fifth Avenue, had long been the chief showplace of modernist art in New York.

Thomas Hart Benton, Constructivist Still Life, *oil on paper, 1917–18. The noted collector of modernist painting Ferdinand Howald took this early Constructivist design to a local picture framer but never bothered to retrieve it. Many years later, the framer donated the painting to the Columbus Museum of Art.*

Thomas Hart Benton, Constructivist Still Life, *oil on cardboard, 1917–18. Around this time, Benton created a group of abstract compositions, based on maquettes that he constructed out of wood, paper, and wire. •*

This flurry of interaction with other artists did not last long. Shortly after the Carroll Galleries exhibition closed, Stan Wright headed back to France, using the money he had earned from the show. Early in 1915, Ralph Barton also left for Paris, sending his wife and his five-year-old daughter back to Kansas City. He left Tom in possession of his studio. "Knowing I was broke he paid the rent for a year in advance," Benton later remembered gratefully. According to the New York Directory, in 1915 and 1916 Tom lived in a house at 1 Arden Street, just off Broadway, which he shared with Thomas Craven.

It was not a good neighborhood. "Some of my friends were semi-gangster types," Benton said later. "They thought I was a smart guy but they couldn't understand why a smart guy would paint pictures." On one occasion these friends held an opium-smoking session on the roof, but left in a hurry when they got a tip that the police were headed their way.

With most of his friends gone, Benton devoted himself to the grim struggle to earn money to survive in New York. He did so thanks to one of his old roommates at the Lincoln Arcade, Rex Hitchcock—who had just changed his name to Rex Ingram. He had become a movie director, and starting in 1914, he hired Tom for seven dollars a day to work for him as a set designer and general assistant. For the next three years, Benton supported himself primarily through movie work.

At that time, the movie business was very loosely run and was not unionized. The actors would meet at Lüchow's for dinner to figure out what they were going to do the next day. Filming was carried out across the Hudson, in Fort Lee, New Jersey. Tom did various odd jobs, such as finding props; for one film he lent Rudolph Valentino his black cape and gold-tipped cane. His main activity was to go down to the public library and draw an Irish castle or some such setting, then go home and make a sketch. Assistants would paint a large black-and-white backdrop in fast-drying distemper paints; when filmed, it generally looked remarkably real behind the actors. This was Benton's first experience at painting on a large scale.

The Forum Exhibition

Willard and Stan Wright returned to New York in 1915, and Willard quickly picked up a job writing a column for the New York *Sun*. Stan at this point had no money at all and lived with his brother. Benton, also hard up, moved in with the two. He covered some of his expenses by illustrating *Europe After 8:15*, a chatty travelogue written jointly by Willard Wright, George Jean Nathan, and H. L. Mencken. But the book was a commercial flop: the World War was raging, and no one was interested in reading about nightlife in Berlin and Paris.

Willard and Stan were both smoking hashish, and Stan later confessed that some of his major paintings, such as *Oriental Synchromy*, were inspired by his experiences with narcotics. Tom found the habit too expensive to take up, but he probably at least sampled the drug. In fact, one of his many female companions of this period tried to turn him into the Revenue Service for opium smoking.

Willard had spent much of his time in Paris, learning about the new movements in painting, and he was hard at work on a book titled *Modern Painting*, based principally on Stan's ideas. The brothers argued incessantly, with Tom in the middle. Though the dialogue sometimes got heated, it remained fairly good-natured until Stan picked up a girlfriend, Edith, who quarreled with Willard's girlfriend, Claire. At the time, Willard was providing Stan's entire support, and while he didn't mind paying for his brother, he objected when his money also sustained Edith, "that damn no good bitch." Things eventually got so uncomfortable that Benton moved back to Lincoln Square; a few weeks later, Stan took a studio near Tom's.

Thomas Hart Benton, Figure Organization No. 3, *oil on canvas, 1916. Benton's most ambitious painting for the Forum Exhibition was this figure composition, loosely based on Michelangelo's relief* The Battle of the Lapiths and the Centaurs. *The painting, now lost, was reproduced in the Forum catalogue.*

In autumn 1916, Mrs. Benton returned to New York from Neosho, bringing Mildred with her. They settled in an apartment on 113th Street, just off Broadway; Mildred began studying music with private teachers. She recalls that Tom ate and slept there. Craven, who had become a favorite of Tom's mother, very often ate with the family as well.

Stan Wright was eager to exhibit again, although he had already displayed most of his pictures in the Carroll show. He and Willard eventually came up with the idea of doing a grand survey of modernist painting, like the Armory Show, limited to the work of American artists. Willard had been cultivating Stieglitz, and they began meeting at 291; after much discussion, they formed a selection committee of six. Stieglitz, a great manipulator, endeavored to gain control of the exhibition and did manage to get into it all the artists whom he supported. Thanks to Willard Wright and John Weichsel, however, he was unable to dominate it fully, and the Synchromist group was also strongly represented.

Unlike the Armory Show, the Forum Exhibition (as it came to be called) was highly selective. The committee sifted down a list of artists from fifty or more to sixteen, and then carefully screened each painting that these individuals submitted. The final show contained quite a mix of stylistic approaches, but nearly all the works stressed considerations of color, line, and form over those of subject matter. A good many of the paintings were entirely abstract.

While Robert Henri wrote a note for the catalogue, defending the cause of expressive freedom in art, the show marked a break with the sort of social realism that

Thomas Hart Benton, Figure Organization, oil on canvas, 1917. In the period just after the Forum Exhibition, Benton returned to painting figure pieces. These were often very French in appearance. The brushwork of this lost canvas was modeled on the work of Cézanne; its friezelike composition derived from Puvis de Chavannes.

Pierre Puvis de Chavannes, Doux Pays, oil on canvas, 1882.

he and the other members of "The Eight" had espoused. Benton, who eventually came to feel a bit embarrassed by his role in the enterprise, later commented, a little wistfully: "Sloan, Bellows, Henri, Glackens, had . . . been in touch with American life. They still kept the touch. We people who were represented in the Forum Show were expatriates who came back thinking we were above these people. In fact, we scorned them as old hat, no good. At least they had some attachments. And I didn't. None of us had. Not any of us."

Naturally, politics played a large role in deciding who was included. Benton got into the show through his friendship with Stan Wright, who invited him to make some Synchromist paintings specifically for the exhibition. Stuart Davis, however, was not included. Tom nearly lost his place by getting in a quarrel with Willard Wright. Willard had purchased two paintings from him, and Benton took them back without permission and completely repainted them. Willard was so angered that he wanted to exclude Tom's work from the show, and he was backed by Stieglitz, who had never had much interest in Benton's explorations of the mechanics of organizing form. Fortunately, Stan took Tom's side and patched up the quarrel. Strong support from Weichsel also helped Tom's position.

Most of the work Benton submitted was figural, but to placate Willard he made a large abstract color synchromy, similar to those Stan Wright had been painting two years before. Stieglitz and Weichsel excluded this canvas, however. Apparently they thought it derivative, and felt that Tom was being an opportunist.

The paintings Tom displayed contained figure groupings based on Michelangelo —who had also inspired the first Synchromist paintings. Benton employed a rainbow

Thomas Hart Benton, illustrations for Europe After 8:15, *1914. Written by Willard Wright, George Jean Nathan, and H. L. Mencken, the book sold badly because of its poor timing: no one was interested in European nightlife after the outbreak of the World War.*

palette like that of Russell and Wright, but unlike them, he retained the sculptural solidity of the forms rather than dissolving them into the mist of color. "I just simply did Renaissance compositions with spectral color," he later told Paul Cummings. "That's all it was. But it looked strange at the time." He added: "I did exactly what you see in those drawings of Jack Pollock's only with bright color."

Despite the haste with which Benton produced his paintings, the press gave them a lot of attention. They were realistic enough to be understandable but colorful enough to seem wildly eccentric. Because of their strong outlines, they looked good in newspaper reproduction. The critic for the New York *Tribune*, Royal Cortissoz, singled out Benton's works as the best things in the show: "His treatment of form, like some distant echo of the tradition of Michelangelo, suggests a large and flowing conception of truth, a feeling for life, and even in some vague way, a feeling for beauty. His queer color, now hot, now livid, is, we suppose, a kind of sacrifice to the cult with which he is here associated."

Perhaps the fullest review of the exhibition was a long article in *The Forum* magazine by Willard Huntington Wright, which evaluated, alphabetically, each of the artists included. Of his brother, he wrote: "In all of Macdonald-Wright's work I feel a magistral creative ability." His praise for Tom's work was more measured but full of enthusiasm. Moreover, thanks to the position of the letter *B* in the alphabet, Benton was treated nearly at the beginning of the review, second only to Ben Benn. Willard declared: "Benton is one of those few painters who are searching for the meaning of great composition." He concluded: "He has a brilliant future, provided he attacks his problems of color and form-harmony more at length."

Thomas Hart Benton, Three Figures, *oil on canvas, circa 1916. One of the few surviving Benton paintings from the Forum Exhibition, it reveals the bold coloring of his work at that time.* •

Such tributes, of course, infuriated Stuart Davis, whose work had not been accepted by the committee. Long after most people had completely forgotten about the exhibition, he was still spreading accusations that Benton was an unscrupulous opportunist for participating in it.

In addition to the Michelangelesque compositions that were displayed in the Forum Exhibition, Benton painted some Synchromist abstractions at this time. The large canvas of color disks that he painted specifically for the exhibition has disappeared, but one purely abstract Synchromist work survives, a painting now known as *Bubbles,* which was purchased by H. L. Mencken. Benton later recalled that the Synchromist color system, which was based on the theories of Percyval Tudor-Hart, employed "a spectral wheel so divided that triads of harmoniously related colors could be automatically determined." The subject of *Bubbles* is simply this color system; the painting relates closely to earlier works by Macdonald-Wright, such as his *Abstraction on the Spectrum (Organization No. 5)* of 1914.

H. L. Mencken.

Mencken was largely indifferent to art, but he enjoyed things that stirred up discussion. One of his favorite pieces was a drawing made by his friend Max Broedel, a gifted medical artist from Germany. It depicted a cancer of the uterus, and according to Mencken, it was a beauty. He alarmed his mother by threatening to hang it on the wall of his home at Hollins Street. Possibly, Mencken considered Benton's *Bubbles* humorous. Gail Levin has written that the title *Bubbles* "indicates Benton's stated determination not to renounce representation." At this time, however, Benton had not yet renounced abstract art. Probably, in fact, the title wasn't provided by Benton himself, who at the time was describing all his paintings as "organizations." Most likely, Mencken named it as a joke.

By taking part in the Forum Exhibition, Benton allied himself with those who opposed literary subject matter in art. Indeed, in his catalogue statement he had declared: "I wish to say that I make no distinctions as to the value of subject matter. I believe the representation of objective forms and the presentation of abstract ideas of form to be of equal artistic value." Ironically, the chief consequence of the Forum Exhibition is that it reawakened his interest in subject matter and social themes, for around this time he became intimate with John Weichsel.

Benton's attraction to Weichsel was partly due to his disenchantment with Alfred Stieglitz, the manipulative, egotistical leader of modernist tendencies in New York. The son of a cultured and highly successful cloth merchant, Stieglitz had enjoyed the advantages of elite schools, private music lessons, and European travel. After studying photographic chemistry in Berlin, he had returned to New York, where he pursued a career as a photographer, edited the adventurous periodical *Camera Work,* and opened an art gallery. He gradually squandered both his own inheritance and that of his more conventional wife, the heiress to a brewery fortune, who became first puzzled by and then estranged from her husband's activities. Unlike Robert Henri, who attempted to direct art toward the masses and to deal with social themes, Stieglitz always insisted that true artistic achievements could be appreciated only by a small group of the cultured and well-educated elite.

Both in his lifetime and today, Stieglitz attracted the sort of reverent worship that might be accorded a religious sage. One admirer compared him to "a Japanese teacher who produced illuminations by jolts, contradictions and rudeness." He was not tolerant, however, of dissension within the ranks of his followers. "If they crossed him in any way," Georgia O'Keeffe once commented, "his power to destroy was as destructive as his power to build—the extremes went together. . . . He was the leader or he didn't play. It was his game and we all played along or left the game. . . . For me he was much more wonderful in his work than as a human being."

Benton had an easy *entrée* into the Stieglitz group, for he had known Stieglitz's protegé John Marin in France, but he did not find the cliquish atmosphere at all congenial. "Although I was there all the time I was not in the center of it," he later recalled. "I didn't get on with the chief ones." In an interview with Paul Cummings, he said of Stieglitz:

"I thought he was a pain in the neck. He talked all the time. You never could get a word in. I like to talk a little myself. . . . Stieglitz was no intellectual. He was thoroughly ignorant. He knew nothing whatever about the background of painting or of anything that he showed there. . . . He'd out-talk these intellectuals. It's really amazing how men of vastly more education and so forth would just simply yield to his flow of language. . . . Even Leo Stein gave him attention. Now Leo was really educated. There's a great case. Stieglitz could out-talk Leo Stein. And Leo was a talker.

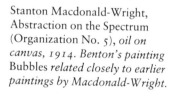

John Weichsel, the founder of the People's Art Guild introduced Benton to Socialism and Marxism, as well as to the writings of John Dewey and Sigmund Freud.

Stanton Macdonald-Wright, Abstraction on the Spectrum (Organization No. 5), *oil on canvas, 1914. Benton's painting* Bubbles *related closely to earlier paintings by Macdonald-Wright.*

"He had a terrific ego, a great sense of self-projection. . . . Just through association or, say, exposure to art I think he became in a certain way sensitive to certain aspects of it. . . . He was a hell of a photographer in a way. . . . I don't know whether he was a good thing for American art. I think he was."

Because of this disenchantment with Stieglitz, Benton took to associating with Weichsel, who had become the central figure of a very different sort of artistic group, the People's Art Guild. As Tom later commented, gleefully: "John Weichsel was a full intellectual, highly educated, a German professor. . . . Stieglitz didn't get very far with him." He had met Weichsel before, at the Carroll Galleries show, but they first became friends a year or so later, when Abe Walkowitz and some other artists took Tom up to Weichsel's home in the Bronx, where the People's Art Guild had its meetings.

Benton always objected to Stieglitz's murky use of language and to his long sentences, which, transcribed, would have run on for pages. But Weichsel was no better. Trained in Germany, he applied German grammar to English, writing abstruse essays on such topics as "The Rampant Zeitgeist," "Cosmism or Amorphism," and other matters of cultural import. Yet if Weichsel's rhetoric was garbled, his essential message held a deep appeal for Tom, who from his childhood had learned to think of the world in social and political terms.

Weichsel was a Marxist socialist, who wanted to get art back into some cultural relationship with the masses and hoped to do so through the labor unions. "I wasn't a Marxist and I didn't know anything about it," Benton later stated. "But I learned a lot from John Weichsel. . . . I had been in a political family but I had never seen that side of it. I knew about Eugene Debs and the Socialist movement in general but this time I got in the middle of it and some of its theory. So it was of great benefit to me. In fact, I was very friendly with John Weichsel, perhaps more so than any other artist in this crowd."

Thomas Hart Benton, Bubbles,
oil on canvas, circa 1916.

Rex Ingram with Clara Kimball Young. Benton's friend the handsome young sculptor Rex Hitchcock changed his name to Rex Ingram and became famous as a director. Here he provides guidance to a well-known star of the silents.

At Weichsel's home, Benton learned about Sigmund Freud, John Dewey, William James, and Karl Marx. With Weichsel and other radical friends, he began attending labor union meetings, where he got to know the Marxist group associated with *The Masses* magazine, such as Robert Minor, Mike Gold, and Max Eastman. "WE TEACH THE PEOPLE TO BUY GOOD ART AND TO KNOW GOOD ART," Weichsel boasted in a broadside, adding that "ours is a distinctly up-to-date, non-partisan, intensely practical though idealistic program." By November 1915, the Guild had sponsored six exhibitions; Tom showed a "figure organization" at their exhibition at Madison House in that month.

1917–18

Benton got good publicity from the Forum Exhibition, but no money. To make a living he had to rely on his movie work with Rex Ingram. In the spring of 1917, he moved out to Fort Lee, to be near the movie studios. He designed sets and painted portraits of the queens of the day—Theda Bara, Clara Kimball Young, Violet Mercereau, and others. "I knew Warner Oland and Stuart Holmes," he later recalled. "With the latter I had a great knockdown and drag-out fight over a drunken party argument about who should entertain the ladies present on a player piano."

For a brief period he took up acting himself: "One time Rex got it into his head that I might be made into an actor and gave me a part in a barroom scene with Paddy Sullivan and Jimmy Kelly and a lot of the other pugs of those days who put on the fights for the movies. When that picture came out it went into theaters in Missouri and some friends of my father's saw it, recognized me, and told him about it. The old man was outraged and wrote me a scathing letter about where my artistic ambitions were leading me."

A number of artists lived in Fort Lee, the leader of whom was Walt Kuhn, one of the organizers of the Armory Show, whose family owned property there. Benton found Kuhn domineering, but he did enjoy the company of George "Pop" Hart, the free-spirited watercolorist. Once the weather became warm enough Tom and Pop went out together to paint watercolors on the Palisades of the Hudson. Always energetic, on those mornings when studio work was slack, Tom would swim across the Hudson, rest a while on the New York side, and then swim back.

In the summer of 1917, when Benton still living in Fort Lee, John Weichsel found him a job teaching art at the Henry Street Settlement, a union-controlled and subsidized settlement house on New York's Lower East Side. For keeping the place open for the public, teaching afternoons and alternate evenings, and putting up exhibitions, he was paid fifty dollars a month.

In the summer of 1917, Rex Ingram was fired. Tom quit his movie job and moved back to New York, to a house at Twenty-third Street and Seventh Avenue, not too far from the Henry Street Settlement. For thirty-five dollars a month, he rented an unheated four-room apartment, whose big front room was his studio. There was no bath. Thomas Craven was living in New York at this time, so he moved in too, and paid half the rent. There were often brawls in the saloon below, and once a man was shot.

The job at the settlement house led to a position with the Chelsea Neighborhood Association. A "People's Art Gallery" was established as an experiment in art appreciation, and Benton was offered the directorship. He kept the gallery open on Sundays and on alternate afternoons and evenings. To supplement his income, he taught drawing classes for adults in a neighborhood public school. "I had some very interesting Jews, Italians," Tom later recalled. "Young people would come in there. Like my wife came as a young girl seventeen or eighteen years old."

Rita Piacenza, just seventeen years old, was still in high school. She was slender and very beautiful. She later recalled that at her first art class with Tom, she brought along copies she had made of museum paintings. He took one look. "These are no damn good," he said. "But why?" she asked, offended by his abruptness. "Because they're not yours, that's why." He set up a still life of potatoes, some onions, and a knife for her to paint. "It's so dull," Rita complained. "Why should I?" But she painted it anyway.

Not long afterward, Benton asked Rita to stay after class if she had time. "If you're not in a hurry to go home . . . I'd like to talk to you for a few minutes." Once the others had gone, he began to look her over very carefully, then he picked up a pad and began drawing. He drew for ten or fifteen minutes. "That's enough for today," he said. "Come back tomorrow. We'll do some more." She posed several times. A month or so later, she came in and found a large hunk of plaster of Paris sitting on the table, a bust of herself that Tom had made. Her dramatic profile and long neck had been worked into a sinuous pattern, like that of ocean waves. On the base, he wrote: "From Tom, to Rita." He gave the piece to her, and she carted it around for the next fifty years, finally making some casts of it in 1961. It is the earliest piece of his sculpture that survives.

Benton was also experimenting at this time with abstract sculpture. As he told Paul Cummings: "I began making small sculptures shortly after my Synchromist experience in order to give more impact or reality, we might say, to abstractions. I found out that my still-lifes that I painted direct from objects had more impact than the abstractions that I made from imagination. So I began making these sculptures, constructions. I made them out of wire, paper, cloth, all kinds of things. This was before construction became an art in itself. I did it for the purpose of improving an abstract painting, giving it more impact, making it seem real."

In March 1917, Tom put on an exhibition of his work at the Chelsea Neighborhood Association, with a handsome brochure to promote it. He showed Michelangelesque figure compositions, similar to those he had submitted to the Forum Exhibition but less brightly colored, with brushwork reminiscent of Cézanne's. When Rita Piacenza happened to run into Robert Henri and asked him what he thought of Tom's work, Henri replied, "Oh, he's too Michelangelese," and dismissed the subject.

George Hart, Walter Kuhn, and Gus Mager at Fort Lee, New Jersey. When he worked in the movie studios at Fort Lee, Benton got to know Walt Kuhn and his circle. He found Kuhn tiresome but enjoyed the company of "Pop" Hart, with whom he often painted watercolors on the Palisades.

Rita Piacenza Benton.

Thomas Hart Benton, Bust of Rita, *plaster, 1918, cast by Roman Bronze in 1961.* •

At this time, *The International Studio* published the first article devoted to Benton's work, written by his friend Willard Huntington Wright. Willard stated that he considered Tom's show "the most important modern exhibition of the month," though he noted that the artist's emphasis on figurative subject matter would probably lead him to be dismissed as "not modern" by many critics. He praised Tom's "classical *élan* toward the complexities of profound composition," and concluded: "when an artist at times actually achieves rhythmical line sequences, then a vital aesthetic force has been set in motion." While the exhibition does not seem to have resulted in any sales, it marked an advance in Benton's reputation among artists.

He was still seeing a lot of Stan Wright, who lived near him, on the other side of Seventh Avenue. During the first phase of Synchromism, Wright had largely followed Russell's lead and pushed his designs toward an ever greater degree of abstraction. In the United States, however, Wright returned to explorations of the human figure—no doubt partly because of the influence of some lessons in figure drawing from Benton. He began producing a group of enigmatic, Michelangelesque figures wrapped in diaphanous veils of color, which are probably the best paintings of his career.

In 1917 Wright exhibited these paintings at Stieglitz's 291, where they attracted considerable attention, and in the following year he showed them at the Daniel Gallery. Despite these successes, he was out of money most of the time. He survived chiefly

82

off occasional handouts from Stieglitz, who had sold a few of his works to an adventurous collector of modernist paintings, John Quinn.

Wright often ate with Benton and Craven, leaving them to pick up the bill. They would gripe about the art world and New York, and discuss America's entrance into the war and the impending draft. Wright penned a hysterical letter to John Weichsel, which doubtless conveys the tone of his conversations with Benton and Craven: "Why dammit it is a fact that artists, not merely painters, have no more esteemed place in their friends' and public's heart than whores and that society hates both classes as pariahs with the obvious preference for the whores (at least they travel in automobiles and have charge accounts)." He concluded bitterly, "I have no address."

Finally, in October 1918, after a severe break in his health, Wright moved to California. "I'm tired of chasing art up the back alleys of New York," he declared. "I'm getting out of here." "I depended on Stanton Wright's friendship," Benton later recalled. "I had a sincere regret when he departed for the nut state." Wright's move to California marked the end of his significance as a painter; he never again produced major work.

Tom's life was also very difficult. He was unable to sell his paintings, and his family life was going through unhappy changes. In the spring of 1917, Oak Hill was destroyed by fire. The Colonel stood among the oak trees and watched the house that he had built burn right down to the ground. "It must have been the top emotion of his life," Mildred Small comments. Most of Tom's early work, including nearly everything he had painted in Chicago and Paris, had been stored in the attic and was lost in the inferno.

Fortunately, the house had been completely insured, and shortly after the disaster, M.E. came east to discuss the situation with his wife. He seems to have hoped to persuade her to return to Neosho, but he did not adequately anticipate her resistance. After much discussion, he gave her most of the insurance money to purchase a house in Great Neck, Long Island, while he himself went back to Neosho, where he lived in rented rooms. At this point, Tom's contact with his father almost ceased; he continued to rely on his mother for support.

In the spring of 1918, he wrote to his friend John Weichsel, explaining that he was completely out of money and had moved out to Great Neck with his mother. He was expecting to be drafted, he said, but this was just as well, as none of the art dealers had any use for his work.

"I have made a few watercolor landscapes since I have been out here," he wrote, "but do not know where to take any of them for exhibition. In fact, I am quite at a loss where to show anything now as none of the dealers seem to care anything either for me or my work. Stieglitz suggested that I bring something up to his place. I left a small painting with him but have since discovered he had no use for it. I expected as much, for Stieglitz, beyond a pleasant enough exterior for everyone, has respect only for those who care enough for his personality to tolerate his loquacity. Stieglitz takes it upon himself to judge the value of all art, which is especially irritating to me as he knows nothing about what I myself am trying to do.

"Mr. Daniel has evidently come to the conclusion that a man with classic aspirations has no claim to respect as a modern artist so I feel as much left out with him as I do with Stieglitz. Mr. Montross twice refused to have anything of mine last winter (this was after the Daniel Ex.) and I am therefore not anxious to approach him again.

"Thus I stand both in relation to war and to the art world. I am in good physical condition and am perfectly indifferent about the future. When the war is over I shall continue to paint as I see fit."

In a subsequent letter to Weichsel, Benton noted that he felt too stale to paint.

Chapter Five
"My Husband Is a Genius"

"We didn't approve, to be honest. . . . You know, the Italians, they have a very funny way about that. They expect the man to support the wife, not the wife to support the husband."

Navy

Both Benton and Craven were eager to avoid being drafted in the infantry and sent overseas. They decided that a spot in the Navy, safely off the battlefield, would suit them perfectly. Tom decided to get around the hurdle of his insufficient stature by making use of the Colonel's political influence. In *An Artist in America*, he left a jocular description of his trip to Washington to visit his father's old political crony Governor Dockery of Missouri, now assistant postmaster, who helped him get the navy berth he wanted. According to his sister Mildred, he left out one very significant point: he went down to Washington with his mother, and she helped him plead his case.

Tom's first naval assignment did not prove as easy as he had hoped. After reporting for duty in Norfolk, Virginia, he was sent on to study naval signaling at the quartermasters' school on Cherrystone Island in Cape Charles. But he arrived at a bad time, for the base received its allotment of coal every four months, and one had just arrived. He later recalled: "My call finally came, but through some mix-up in my papers it led me to the coal pile and I found myself, not in a swivel chair, but down in Virginia with a shovel, loading boats with dirty coal."

Despite this mishap, his letters to his mother were amazingly cheerful. In New York, he had lived under the combined strain of artistic discouragement and poverty. For six years he had not been able to eat three square meals a day. Consequently, the tone of most of his letters from Cape Charles and Norfolk is that of a schoolboy on vacation. Containing neither the desperate pleading nor the grandiloquent boasting of his letters from New York, they gleefully describe the ease of naval life, the softness of the beds, and the plenitude of food. "I think of little save food since I entered the service," one of his early letters to his mother reported.

He soon found a way of maintaining a permanent distance between himself and the coal pile: he participated in boxing matches. "I am getting to be somewhat of a privileged character on the island," he gloated to Mildred. "I escape all the daily jobs and am able to do whatever I please to get a rowboat or canoe for exploring trips. This is accounted for by the fact that I go into all athletics and that I am generally known, by now, as an artist unlike the usual type. The popular idea of an artist is summed up by a consumptive appearance coupled with feminine habits. The fact that I do not fit that idea has given the boneheads a better opinion of the profession and consequently singled me out as a person worthwhile."

He was even cockier in a letter to Craven, who had been less lucky in his naval

Thomas Hart Benton, Self-Portrait with Rita, 1922. Shortly after his marriage, Benton painted this double portrait of himself and his new wife on South Beach. The empty face of his wristwatch alludes to the timelessness of art. •

assignment. "A hitch in the Navy prepares a boy for three walks of life," Craven later bitterly remarked, "the night watchman, the laundress, and the janitor."

Tom wrote to him: "Well, Craven, old top, I have fallen into a much softer dump than yours. . . . With the exception of three hours in the morning which I put in on the 'blinkers' and flags, with a decent instructor (who doesn't object to tobacco in class), I spend my entire time here swimming, rowing, sailing and sleeping. This is not a regulation camp and my garb is limited as a general rule to a pair of bathing trunks. To leave the island and go over to the mainland clean 'whites' are necessary but here on this little 5 acres of sand and seaweed anything goes. I can get a little rowboat anytime and prowl around the inlets, anytime, that is, from 5:15 to 9:30 on weekdays and from 12 on Sat. to 9:30 Sunday night. Lights are out, of course, at 9:30 but that does not necessarily mean bedtime in the school bunks. You can sit on the sand and smoke if it pleases you. And the nights here are the real kind, white moon and cool breeze.

"I am being taught to handle a cutter in the afternoons. We cross the bay to the mainland, get in some inlet or on the beach, signal for a while, smoke, swim, fish for clams or crabs and then row the cutter back. All this is not very hard. In fact, I am having a real vacation and am getting tough as a nigger. I am sunburnt worse than I was at Ft. Lee."

He later noted that it was a relief to get away from the high-strung, overrefined, and often effeminate characters of the art world and associate with real men. "Down there in Virginia," he later wrote, "I was thrown among boys who had never been subjected to any aesthetic virus." His letters from Cape Charles confirm that he got on well with his companions, though they express this in less than flattering language. As he wrote to Craven: "I get along splendidly with the bone-headed southern boys who make up the camp."

Early in September, he was transferred back to Norfolk, where he was assigned to make descriptive drawings of the naval base: "Better fortune has come to me. I have been relieved of the tedium of mechanical work and am to be given a position more in accordance with my taste. The commandant of this section revoked my transfer to another department and is keeping me here to make perspective drawings of the new construction. All this new work will be free hand and though it must be more accurate than artistic will not be unpleasant. It will make me practically master of my time which is rare enough in the Navy and well worth a little extra care in making my sketches accurate. . . . The food here is much better than that at Cherrystone."

Thomas Hart Benton in his Navy uniform, 1918.

A week or so later, he wrote: "I am now no longer at the base. No longer a clock puncher even. I am now officially listed as 'camoufleur' and have a nice quiet room in Norfolk and an office in which to work. There are two more 'camoufleurs' in the office with me, a photographer and a young would-be artist. They are both already practically under my thumb. . . .

"The work is easy and bids fair to be exciting at times. Twice a week I leave the office at Norfolk with the fellow who takes the photographs. We go on board a 40 foot motor boat (motor sailer) and cruise around the bay making sketches and photographs of newly arrived camouflaged ships. The sketches are finished back at the office (the colors of the camouflage are put in) and along with reports giving name, type, tonnage, etc., of each ship are sent to Washington to be filed. This is done so that if the ship should be torpedoed or lost in any way all the facts concerning her appearance etc. can easily be found.

"The other days of the week I am *supposed* to spend finishing up my sketches!! But I can finish them perfectly in from half to three quarters of an hour. I shall have plenty of time to paint and with my new pass I can work anywhere I please.

"I have a good room, clean, two windows, a bath just below. My landlady is Norfolk Irish and friendly."

Benton later declared that this job of recording the buildings, ships, and machinery of the base marked a turning point in his development as an artist, for it shifted his attention back to the objective world. He wrote: "This was the most important thing that, so far, I had ever done for myself as artist. My interests became, in a flash, of an objective nature. The mechanical contrivances of building, the new airplanes, the blimps, the dredges, the ships of the base, because they were so interesting in themselves, tore me away from all my grooved habits, from my play with colored cubes and classic attenuations, from my aesthetic drivelings and morbid self-concerns. I left for good the art-for-art's-sake world in which I had hitherto lived."

In addition, at this time he began to reconsider the issue of subject matter and its relation to formal issues. As he later remembered: "During the latter part of my sojourn in the Navy I had been permitted to live 'off base' in a Norfolk lodging house. In the parlor there I had found an old-fashioned four-volume history of the United States by J. A. Spencer, written in the middle of the nineteenth century and plentifully

Thomas Hart Benton, Norfolk Harbor, *watercolor on paper, 1918.*

Thomas Hart Benton, Impressions, Camouflage, WWI, *watercolor on paper, 1918.*

illustrated with engravings in the various styles of the period. Having nothing to do at night, I read and reread this work and examined its illustrations with increasing interest. They reminded me that similar pictures had often promoted the amateurish efforts of my high school days, when history reading had been a favorite pursuit, and I began to ask myself questions. Why could not such subject pictures dealing with the meanings of American history possess aesthetically interesting properties, deliverable along with their meanings?"

In his spare time, Tom worked at his own painting. He sent his mother detailed reports of his progress. "I find time every day to do something for myself and expect by Christmas to have enough things together to make a good exhibition."

Return to New York, 1918–20

Benton got out of the Navy late in November 1918 and headed for New York to renew his artistic struggles. Though he had worked solidly at painting for a decade, he had little to show for it. He had no patrons, and most of what he had produced had been destroyed in the Oak Hill fire. Once again he was out of money; he had to borrow fifteen or twenty dollars from his sister Mary in order to make his way back to the city, where he worked on the wharves, first as a longshoreman and then as a cooper, until he had saved up enough to go back to painting. Again he shared a flat with Thomas Craven. Mildred Small recalls that their place was located over a saloon and "was the most desolate place you could possibly imagine, with three rooms and no plumbing."

Craven later wrote of Benton's work up to this time: "From the day I met him to the end of the War, I do not believe he painted a single consistent picture. He had enormous energy and determination, but his productions were not his own—nor were they frankly of any school. He made his bow to the current isms, but without grace or that ease of mind which lends the illusion of conviction to imitation. For ten years his painting was so labored and unpromising that most of his confreres were secretly of the opinion that he was outside his field. His most gracious defender was Macdonald-Wright who steadfastly maintained that buried in his halting, badly imitative, and crude performances, were the seeds of genius."

One of the first things Tom did after his return was to look up John Weichsel, to see if he could get some sort of artistic employment. To his surprise, he found that the People's Art Guild had disbanded. During the war, artists had stopped coming to the meetings, and the whole organization had gradually collapsed. Weichsel did not seem deeply disturbed by this turn of events, however. He had apparently come to realize that the labor unions cared little about artistic creativity, and he had probably grown tired of artistic squabbles.

Tom also reestablished contact with Rita Piacenza. Since neither he nor Craven had the money to buy good food, they got in the habit of visiting the Piacenzas on Sundays to fill themselves up. Most of the family spoke only Italian, a language that neither of the young men knew, so there wasn't much talking—just eating. Benton later recalled of his early visits with Rita: "When I came back to New York from the Navy I used to go to her home for Sunday dinner. Tom Craven would go with me. We'd sit in silence and stuff ourselves with great Italian courses, get in a stupor with wine, and then rise silently and go away. We never said a word."

In December 1918, Charles Daniel staged an exhibition of Tom's navy watercolors, which focused on the machines and structures of the Norfolk base. They bore such titles as *The Hydroplane, The Observation Balloon, Storage Houses* and *Sand Piles*. Benton later maintained that he "threw away his French underwear in the wartime navy," but contemporary reviewers commented on the modernity of his work. The *New York Times* critic declared that Tom's "marked modernist tendency is well known" and described the pieces as "a cubist's holiday." He noted that Benton had painted the machines of the modern age and had managed "to convey the energy and stimulus of launching these great innovations upon a startled world." The New York *Herald* reviewer was even more strongly enthusiastic. After alluding to the artist's "unruly temperament," he praised the dynamic energy of his synthesis of color, movement, and force. "Taken all in all," the writer stated, "this is the best one-man exhibition that has been produced by an American as a result of recent experiences."

Despite such positive write-ups, however, Benton felt lonely and confused—so lonely, in fact, that he looked up Alfred Stieglitz. At 291 Fifth Avenue, as at John Weichsel's place, the prewar atmosphere of artistic excitement had changed. Stieglitz had run through his money and was talking about giving up his gallery. Benton found none of the old hangers-on who had packed the place before the war, but only Stieglitz himself, all alone—feeling sorry for himself but as garrulous as ever and eager to tell a long tale of wartime woes. There was no interest in art, Stieglitz told him; America would not support a living art; Americans were too insensitive aesthetically.

Had Stieglitz seen Benton's show of wartime watercolors? Yes, indeed he had, but he had not liked them. In Stieglitz's view, Tom had not freed himself, as Marin had. His watercolors were tinted drawings, colored outlines. He still depended on a framework of rigid lines. Benton was not pleased by this, but he held himself in, for he could recognize that it contained a grain of truth. For once, Stieglitz's manner was

Thomas Hart Benton, New York Construction, *ink and wash on paper, 1923. One of many sketches of city life Benton made in the early twenties.*

Thomas Hart Benton, New York Stock Exchange, *ink and wash on paper, 1923.*

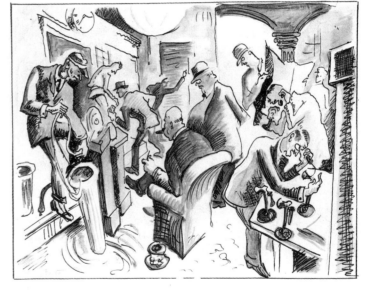

kindly—more so than it had ever been before. Not too long afterward, Benton dropped in again at 291 and Stieglitz pulled out some paintings by Georgia O'Keeffe. Not knowing of the intimate relationship between them (O'Keeffe had just become Stieglitz's mistress), Tom commented: "Stieglitz, these pictures are nice in color, but they are even harder in their outlines than mine." Stieglitz bristled and promptly informed him that he was not enough of an artist to make a criticism of O'Keeffe. The exchange that resulted put an end to their renewed association.

Nevertheless, Tom was affected by Stieglitz's advice, which had been delivered with impressive seriousness, and decided to try it out. He began by making still lifes with no preliminary drawing; in the spring of 1919, he went out and began painting freely splashed watercolors along the Palisades near Fort Lee. The results did not satisfy him. On September 21, 1919, he complained in a letter to Stieglitz: "In an endeavor to loosen up my work, probably too soon for the end to which I look, I have fallen into a sort of naturalism. I have been trying to compose for the last six months or so without my guiding lines or rather without their being in evidence in the finished thing. In doing this I became more and more dependent on the actual values of the object from which I painted with a consequent structural loss which is to me more than the equivalent to the gain in spontaneity."

After a while, Benton decided to forget what Stieglitz had said and push forward on an entirely different track. Late in life, he complained to Paul Cummings that Stieglitz never responded to his explorations of form. "He thought that all this kind of stuff I was doing was purely academic—the kind of stuff you see that Pollock did, which I did also before that."

In Norfolk, Benton had conceived the notion of painting a history of the United States, but despite his Synchromist efforts at figure composition, he had not found a means to create the sense of concrete reality that he desired. In early autumn of 1919, he read an article on Tintoretto, which described the artist's procedures in the Venetian church of Santa Maria della Salute. In order to plan his paintings there, Tintoretto had constructed a sculptural model, which he employed to work out the spatial relations of the figures and to give them a realistic and logical distribution of light and shade. As he examined Tintoretto's work, Tom became convinced that all his paintings had been planned and composed in this fashion.

Benton had already experimented a little with clay sculpture and had made some cubified compositional studies, under the influence of a German book John Weichsel lent him, which reproduced drawings by Luca Cambiaso. Now he began creating clay dioramas. None of Tintoretto's sculptures had survived for him to study, but he had seen the diorama-like sculptural groups in the portals of French cathedrals. In addition, he possessed detailed photographs of the famous doors that Ghiberti had made for the Baptistery in Florence early in the Italian Renaissance.

Tom's first clay sculptures were projected very deeply and possessed blocky, cubified shapes. Thus they articulated, strongly and schematically, the position of objects in space. Benton soon learned that it was difficult to make the transition from sculptural to pictorial treatment. He would construct a clay diorama and make numerous drawings from it, sometimes filling up a whole sketchbook. If the sculptural form did not translate into clear *pictorial* organization, he would remodel it and make a new suite of drawings.

He spent several months working on these experiments—autumn 1919 through early 1920. Little by little, he learned to make models that were not fully three-dimensional but occupied a tipped-back space, a kind of compromise between sculpture and painting. "You have to have a certain kind of knack to make them," he told Paul Cummings. "Even some sculptors can't make them if they don't have a sense of perspective in drawing."

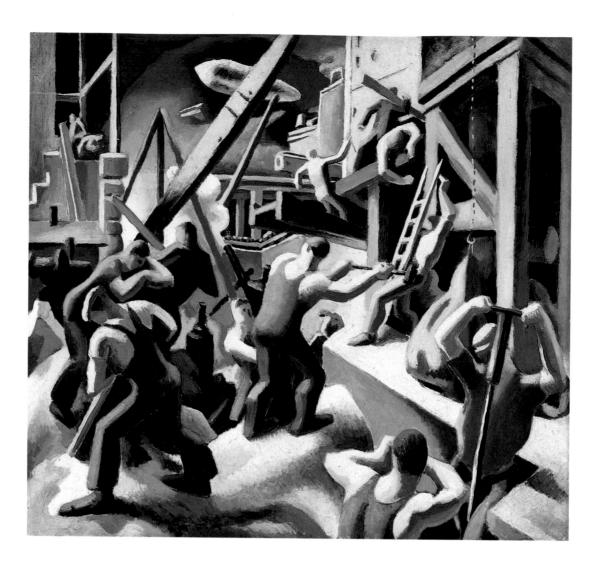

Thomas Craven and "The Dial"

For eight years after his arrival in New York, Thomas Craven had scribbled furiously
but had been unable to publish his work. In autumn 1919, however, a chance meeting
with Clarence Britten set him on the pathway to success. Britten was an editor of *The
Dial,* one of the great magazines of this century; it published the best writers of the
time and reproduced new work by modernist sculptors and painters.

Britten talked with Craven at length, plowed through the stacks of manuscript he
had piled up, and then sent him a book to review on the academic mural painter Frank
Brangwyn. "I had never reviewed a book," Craven later recalled, "and having nothing
to lose, gave Brangwyn the drubbing of his life. I could not do so well today, even
though my dislike for the Welshman increases with each wall that he bespatters."
Craven's review was more than an assault on a mediocre talent; it was a spirited
defense of the modernist movement in art, and of the achievement of such recent
French masters as Renoir, Gauguin, Cézanne, and Matisse. "Modern painting,"
Craven declared, "has rehabilitated the pictorial vision." Throughout his review, he
compared Brangwyn's work with that of the modernists—much to Brangwyn's
disadvantage.

Today, of course, such judgments have become old hat, but in the early 1920s,
modernist art was still highly controversial. Few critics of the time spoke so warmly
and intelligently in its behalf, and of those who did, none imbued their prose with
such feeling or wrote with such sensuousness of description and engaging richness of
word choice. Scofield Thayer, *The Dial*'s publisher, was delighted, and Craven was
commissioned to write more reviews. For six years, until December 1926, Craven
wrote regularly for *The Dial,* working in harmonious partnership with this country's
most dedicated apostles of French modernist painting.

Thus Thomas Craven became an art critic, a field in which he could act as a direct spokesman for Tom Benton's ideas. Indeed, many of his essays, particularly the early ones, were written with Tom's assistance. Craven slipped complimentary references to Benton into several reviews, and in July and September 1925, *The Dial* carried reproductions of his work.

Craven even wrote a novel, whose protagonist was modeled on Benton. "Craven has sold his first novel and is of course in fine humor," Tom wrote to Alfred Stieglitz in July 1922, just after the book appeared. "Its title is 'Paint' and it contains plenty of defamatory gossip concerning people of our acquaintance—I hope you will read it."

Craven's reviews consistently lauded the French modernists. He praised Picasso as "the outstanding figure" among the Cubists; in an enthusiastic review of the English critic Roger Fry's *Vision and Design,* he commented that "the illustrations alone are enough to convince us that he knows his business." In May 1924, he wrote a positively glowing review of the work of Matisse, praising his "brilliant artistry" and terming him "one of the most distinguished painters of modern times." He declared: "The poetic vision of Matisse is rich and plastic; the grace of his draughtsmanship masterly and inimitable. He alone, of all living modernists, enclosed his sensuous vision within the boundaries of pure design. It is a wise beauty that he gives us, firmly tempered and perfectly poised."

In general, Craven most admired those figures who concentrated on the mastery of form. He took issue, for example, with Howard Butler's claim that "Cézanne did nothing to aid in the rendering of the third dimension." On the contrary, "Cézanne's treatment of landscape is eminently justified. Pictorially the interaction of line and mass does not always conform with correct geometric perspective; the most successful painter of depth is he who combines his lines and masses so that the inherent dynamism is one with the special problems of recession and relief. He is a sort of sculptor in great extensions, carving in light and shadow and colour insted of marble. Cézanne was such a painter."

Craven also had the insight to appreciate Seurat, whom he considered "quite as important" as Cézanne. Craven termed him "a composer of experiences in the purest classic sense" and admired his mastery of the "architectural components of design, precisely fitted to a purposive structure."

To be sure, Craven's objections to the "excesses" of modernism had begun to stew beneath the surface. He disliked the arcane character of Cubism and lashed out at the sensationalism of Futurism. In April 1924, he criticized Katherine Dreier, a collector of modernist art, for "making modernism difficult" and objected to her insistence that geometric shapes were the carriers of mystical meanings, "the emblem of metaphysical spasms." But two months earlier, he had penned a glowing tribute to Scofield Thayer's modernist portfolio, declaring that it "must be considered as a definitive repudiation of the cursed fetish of naturalism." The watercolors by John Marin and Charles Demuth, he asserted, fittingly represented the finest achievements of contemporary American art. He regretted that the work of his friend Thomas Hart Benton had not been included, but in listing the other significant omissions he cited only modernist painters: Marsden Hartley, Stanton Macdonald-Wright, Edwin Dickinson, and Georgia O'Keeffe. Evidently, as late as 1924, Craven still regarded Benton as a modernist figure and viewed himself as a critical spokesman for modernist ideas.

Martha's Vineyard

In the summer of 1920, Rita Piacenza invited Benton to stay with her on Martha's Vineyard, where she was renting a room from a chubby, good-natured widow from Providence, Ella Brug. He arrived there early in July with Thomas Craven and Rollin

Tom Benton, Ella Brug, and Tom Craven. Ella Brug rented a space in her barn to Benton and Craven during their first summers on Martha's Vineyard.

93

Thomas Hart Benton, Martha's Vineyard, *oil on canvas, 1925. Benton sold his painting of Beetlebung Corner to the Whitney Studio Club in 1927. The white building is the Chilmark Town Hall, where the Bentons often went for Saturday-night square dances.*

Crampton, a New York artist. Rita stayed in the farmhouse, and Tom, Craven, and Crampton slept in Mrs. Brug's barn. Tom was overwrought at the time, the victim of some sort of nervous exhaustion, and Rita seems to have sensed that a country atmosphere, such as he had known as a child, would restore his tired spirit.

In this she was right. For the remainder of his life, he returned every summer to the island, and for the first half of the 1920s, Martha's Vineyard provided the subject matter for nearly all his major paintings. In 1923 he persuaded his mother to come, and in 1927 he and Rita purchased property on the island.

In the 1920s, the town of Chilmark was as isolated and inbred as the Ozark communities of southwest Missouri and Arkansas. Incorporated in 1694, it was still chiefly populated by descendants of the original settlers, who lived there year round, making a bare living from fishing, farming, cutting firewood, and grazing sheep. The solitude of the island bred a stubborn, silent people, with such eccentric habits as putting gin on their breakfast cereal or shooting mosquitoes with a shotgun indoors.

For his first decade on the Vineyard, Benton lived in a barn with a dirt floor, without heat, telephone, electricity, or running water. To get enough light to paint, he had to open the barn door. His feet were his only means of transportation, for neither he nor any of his friends owned a car. Rita did the cooking over a small burner, and well into the 1940s, the only illumination was provided by kerosene lamps. They gathered a good deal of their food: mussels, clams, fish, blueberries and blackberries, beach plums and grapes. Rita discovered that if she got down to Menemsha harbor when the boats came in she could get fish and lobster shorts for free. Frank Tilton, a retired whaling captain, often gave her an armful of fresh vegetables.

Thomas Hart Benton, Chilmark, *oil on canvas, circa 1923. Painted just as he was starting his* American Historical Epic, *it reveals his increasing interest in sculptural values.* •

Because of inbreeding, approximately half the population of the Chilmark end of the island suffered from hereditary deafness. To Rita, this widespread affliction was a blessing, for people who could not hear did not make fun of her unusual musical speech. She had known only Italian until she came to America at the age of thirteen,

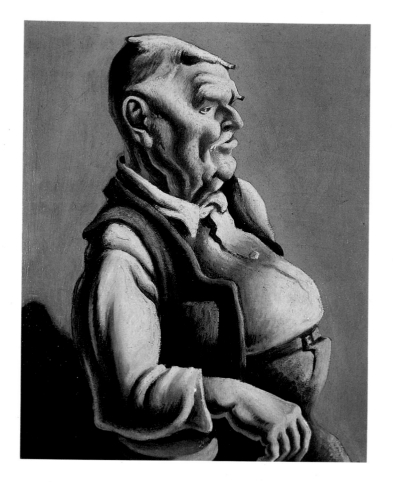

Thomas Hart Benton, Frank Flanders, *oil on canvas, circa 1924.*

Thomas Hart Benton, Portrait of Frankie, *oil on canvas, circa 1923.*

and was first taught to speak English by a teacher with a thick Scottish burr. In Chilmark she could get by with sign language and expressive Italian gestures.

Benton soon set to work making drawings and paintings of the island old-timers, who possessed for him the nobility of medieval saints. "His pencil drawings of these old people," his friend Gilberta Goodwin noted, "are exquisitely tender in feeling, despite the full-bodied form." As was often the case with his best work, his execution was rapid. "Usually they'd sit three times for half to three-quarters of an hour at a time," he recalled. "Sometimes I'd get it the first time but that was unusual. After that, I'd just look at them every time I went down to the store." Following the practice of the French cartoonist Daumier, he modeled many of the faces in clay, then tinted the statuettes in black and white to indicate the distribution of values.

His models were near at hand. Frankie was a destitute old lady, with only one front tooth, who lived in a rocking chair on Ella Brug's front porch, where she thumbed through old magazines. Frank Flanders worked during the winter months as a caretaker but devoted most of his time to playing cards or board games in the corner of Reed's General Store. Dan Vincent ran a carpentry, blacksmith, and boat shop down by the harbor in Menemsha, with a railway nearby for hauling boats out for repairs. His little shop overflowed with tools, rope, wood shavings, anchors, and lobster pots. Chester Poole, a lifelong bachelor, lived high up on Chilmark hill, in a house surrounded by a fortresslike stone wall that he had built himself. He was a convinced teetotaler, and when bootleg liquor washed ashore, he would go out on the beach with a crowbar and smash any bottle he found, despite Tom's vigorous protests.

The most colorful of the lot was Billy Benson, a weathered rascal who lived in Ella Brug's woodshed and did odd jobs around the property. As a young man, he had been arrested for stealing sheep and had tried to poison his parents with arsenic. While he was posing, he gave Benton some hard-earned advice: "When a cop comes at you, Tom, do what I say and move fast. Hit him in the shin bones as hard as you can with your boot or a stick, and run fast. It'll work every time."

The most famous of Benton's Vineyard portraits, *The Lord Is My Shepherd,* showed George West and his wife, Sabrina, both deaf, who lived just down the hill from the Brug barn, toward Bettlebung Corner. A hardworking man with large hands, George supported his three children, two of whom were deaf, by fishing, farming, and the sale of firewood. Though most viewers surely don't realize that the Wests were both deaf, the painting conveys a sober mood of hard work and eternal silence. Benton later commented: "I could, on hind sight, say that I saw something in these deaf mutes from an artist's point of view that one didn't see in a normal person." Unlike most of the other Vineyard portraits, the concept of this one matured over several years. Tom first sketched the Wests in their kitchen in the summer of 1922, but he didn't complete the painting until 1926.

Thomas Hart Benton, The Lord Is My Shepherd, *tempera on canvas, 1926. Benton originally titled the canvas* The Meal. •

Thomas Hart Benton, Portrait of Dan, *oil on canvas, circa 1924.* •

Tom, Rita, and T.P., Martha's Vineyard.

The one encroachment of New York sophistication on the Vineyard at the time was the Barn House, a vacation camp for radical intellectuals, located just down South Road from Ella Brug's barn. Presided over by Stanley King, a Boston businessman of very liberal views, it consisted of an eighteenth-century farmhouse, a large barn, which was used for parties, and a number of chicken coops that had been transformed into sleeping quarters. Eugene Debs and Norman Thomas, the Socialist candidates for President, came to stay in these coops. So did Roger Baldwin, founder of the American Civil Liberties Union; Felix Frankfurter, Supreme Court justice; Julian Huxley, biologist; Walter Lippmann, Van Wyck Brooks, and Bernard De Voto, writers; and Leopold and David Mannes, musicians. Benton later recalled: "We used to go over to the Barn House parties all the time in the 1920s. . . . They always had a punch made out of bathtub gin and I got quite drunk on occasion."

Drunk indeed. Craig Kingsbury, a Vineyard farmer, recalled: "I used to bring him and some of that gang up there their liquor from Oak Bluffs, where they had a bottling operation in the cellar of a hotel. One of the selectmen was running things and it cost a dollar a quart. You'd mix a quart of the good stuff with one gallon of native moonshine, add five quarts of water and three ounces of glycerine to smooth it a bit. They'd rebottle it and charge a dollar a quart. The strong stuff cost a dollar and a half, and we'd try it out on the coal stove first to see how it flared up.

"I used to bring it up to Tom, and if we brought along our own food Rita would cook it up for us—but we had to bring our own food. They were some hell-raisin' parties, but if things got too rough, Rita would throw us out of the house, and wouldn't let Tom go. We'd go on to somebody else's place, and Benton would find a way to sneak out when Rita wasn't looking and join us. Benton was funny as hell, a tough, wild drunk I tell you. He'd fight anybody, but he got his a couple of times. He was so small he'd go for the belly every time. He was really tough. I saw him beat up Max Eastman one night, but then Max couldn't fight worth a damn."

Embroidery designed by Benton, circa 1922.

Thomas Hart Benton, study for embroidery, mixed media on board, circa 1922. During the early twenties, Benton made many embroidery designs, which his mother executed in silk thread. They often bring to mind the work of such French artists as Jean Cocteau.

At one of these drunken parties, Tom met red-bearded Boardman Robinson, the socialist cartoonist and painter, known to his friends as "Mike." Robinson had recently revolutionized cartooning and newspaper illustration. He was the first to dispense with the fussy crosshatching of the turn-of-the-century pen virtuosos and to draw with a bold sense of caricature in heavy, blocky forms. Combined with his bold graphic style was a powerful social message. He had traveled through the war-torn regions of Russia and the Balkans with the leftist journalist John Reed; he knew and admired Debs and Thomas, and was a close friend of the socialist cartoonist Bob Minor, who was then attempting to organize an American Communist party. Like John Weichsel, Mike Robinson and his friends felt that the "modern" art of the postwar world lacked social value and was falling into decadence. They espoused a more socially relevant art, not yet foreseeing the logical extension of this viewpoint in the propaganda of Stalin's cohort Radik. At the time, Benton was sympathetic to such views, for while he had come to see Taine's writings as overeffusive, they had prepared him to think of art in social terms, as the outgrowth of social patterns.

Lewis Mumford still vividly recalls the party at which Tom first met Boardman Robinson, for shortly afterward one of his female neighbors knocked desperately on his door. Benton and Robinson were drunk, she reported, and had made passes at assaulting her. A moment later, the two men appeared and stalked around the house,

Thomas Hart Benton, The Cliffs, *oil on canvas, 1921. Benton's first drawing on Martha's Vineyard. He often painted the Windygates Cliffs during his early years on the island.*

100

demanding to be admitted. Frustrated, they knocked over the outhouse. "I never knew what a stink philosophers could make!" Benton exclaimed. Mumford adds: "Perhaps the present generation is unfamiliar with privies, so let me add that the walls and roof form a unit and can be overturned without removing the more functional base. No problem there!"

Often, after these drinking bouts, Tom and Mike would stay up all night, perched on the Windygates Cliffs and staring out to sea, discussing artistic principles. Once it was light enough to see, Tom would go to work, painting watercolor after watercolor until he found a composition that satisfied him.

The topic of composition frequently came up, for at the time the art world was filled with crackpot theories of design. George Bellows, for example, had been converted to Jay Hambridge's theories of "Dynamic Symmetry," and other artists were working with the "Golden Section." Hardesty Maratta, a persuasive salesman for the tubes of color he manufactured, was disseminating complicated color charts. Denman Ross at Harvard was trying to produce general laws of composition and color harmony. Benton, unlike most of the rest, was not looking for a mechanical scheme based on some geometric grid structure, a system of proportion, or a chart of color relationships. Rather, he sought a means of creating an ordered sequence of forms so as to fill up an illusionistic space according to rational principles. Robinson later remembered: "Though Benton's technique was not flawless, he did work intelligently and I profited by his keen reasoning. Benton and I often spent afternoons analyzing the old masters' compositions: El Greco, Rubens, Titian, Tintoretto, and Rembrandt. Rubens appealed greatly to Benton; Rembrandt to me."

In his search for a better understanding of pigments and materials, Benton covered hundreds of little panels with paint to learn how different methods of application held up. "He did the first experiments I knew anything about," Robinson later recalled, and Benton commented: "We wasted precious effort in a hunt for the basic techniques

which were the stock-in-trade of any second- or third-rate craftsman in the sixteenth-century Florentine studio."

Most New Yorkers came to the Vineyard to relax, but during his summers there, Tom pushed himself hard. Gilberta Goodwin, who met him in 1924, remembered: "Benton worked as though all the demons of the nether regions were after him. He started work at five o'clock in the morning, eating nothing till eight or nine. He said he could work better before breakfast than at any other time of day. This did not stop him from working all day and every day. He would take an hour off at the end of the day for a swim in the ocean, his only recreation when he was working steadily which was the general rule."

Love and Poverty

Rita lived with Tom on Martha's Vineyard in the summers of 1920 and 1921, but she didn't move in with him in New York until the fall of 1921, shortly after she had graduated from high school. Thomas Craven, who had been living with Benton for years, moved out to a small house in Brookhaven, Long Island, which he shared with the Synchromist painter William Yarrow.

It is probable that no American-born woman would have been willing to endure the hardships of living with Tom Benton. The Piacenzas had come to this country from Verono Brianza, a small town north of Milan. Their house had only two rooms. On the ground floor stood the kitchen, which had a fireplace where all the cooking was done, and about half the space was devoted to Mr. Piacenza's copperworking shop. His forge was located in the front yard. Upstairs, in the single bedroom, the entire family slept together. They subsisted mostly on rice; meat was a great rarity.

Conditions were better in the United States, and by the early 1920s the family had become quite comfortable. Rita's older brother, Santo, had a good job at Billy Parker's restaurant, and Mr. Piacenza was employed by a French copperworking firm, where

Thomas Hart Benton, Study of Rita, *pencil on paper, 1922. This study for* Self-Portrait with Rita *once belonged to Charles Pollock, Jackson Pollock's elder brother.*

The Piacenza family. Ettore and Maria with their children, Rita, Santo, and Louis.

Thomas Hart Benton, Picnic, *egg tempera and oil on canvas mounted on panel, 1952. Benton's love of Martha's Vineyard is evident in this scene of himself and his family with his friends Henry and Peggy Scott, and Frederic and Diana James.* •

the workers were as well paid as any in New York. The family came to own a six-room house in the Bronx. They had a front yard with a vegetable garden and twenty-five chickens. Much of the land around them was still open, and the subway was just twenty minutes away.

One day, Santo recalls, his father took him to visit Tom and Rita, in their apartment on Twenty-first Street between First and Second avenues. It had no hot water and no heat except for the stove in the kitchen. There were two tiny rooms, kitchen and bedroom, and only four pieces of furniture—a table, two chairs, and a bed. "Jesus!" Mr. Piacenza said. "This is worse than the way we lived in Italy!"

In February 1922, Tom and Rita were married in New York City, at St. Francis Xavier Catholic Church. After a small reception at the Piacenzas', they took a taxi out to Great Neck. They stayed with Mrs. Benton until June. Their only source of income was a sewing column that Rita wrote for the *Ladies' Home Journal,* for Tom had given up teaching and could not sell his paintings.

Tom's parents were deeply distressed that he was marrying an Italian immigrant, and Rita's family also regretted the match. Santo recalls: "We didn't approve, to be honest. We thought that he didn't have a job; the things that he was painting he couldn't sell; and Rita had to support him. You know, the Italians, they have a very funny way about that. They expect the man to support the wife, not the wife to support the husband. That's the Italian feeling. But as long as they were going to get married, we have to make the best of it. So my father cooked the dinner. He was a great cook."

In the fall of 1922, Rita found an apartment on the top floor at 42 Union Square. For heat, Tom carried coal up five flights of stairs; for light, they relied on kerosene lamps. As Santo has commented: "They began very poor, that's for sure. . . . When he was getting fifty dollars for a painting they thought that was a lot of money." Nonetheless, Rita seems never to have been distressed by a sense of poverty. Thomas Craven's wife, Aileen, once came by for a visit and was appalled. "I don't understand how you can live under these conditions," she exclaimed. To which Rita replied, with confidence and a touch of hauteur, "My husband is a genius."

Late in his life, Benton confided to Santo that he never would have succeeded without Rita's support: "It's been very hard to live with your sister all these years, a hard woman to get along with, but if it wasn't for her—I was a bum, I would still be a bum and wouldn't have a dime to my name."

In 1936 Benton said: "Until about twelve years ago, I threw away everything I did when I finished. Now my wife looks after them for me." This is confirmed by his daughter, Jessie, who remembers of her mother: "She never faltered from her one purpose, which was: he was a great artist, no matter what. She saved all the money and saved all the paintings. Sometimes, you know, my father would make a painting and then he wouldn't like it, so he'd make another painting over it. But she'd run out in the studio and steal them before he could do that, so that she'd have them to sell. I don't think he would have lived without her. . . . The incomes, of course, would vary from year to year. Sometimes we were very poor. Sometimes we had lots of money if we sold a painting. But the life in the house never changed, and that was my mother's genius."

Along with Rita, Tom gained another helper at this time. Among John Weichsel's friends was a socially-minded doctor named Alfred Raabe, who enjoyed the company of struggling artists, such as Benton, the two Zorachs, Jerome Myers, Preston Dickinson, and the Soyer brothers. These hungry people would visit his Bronx home, raid the icebox, and then settle into companionable evenings of talk, drinking, and dancing.

Dr. Raabe did carpentry in his basement as a hobby and started making frames for Tom's paintings. "He felt sorry for the poverty," Tom recalled. "He'd pick these

Dr. Alfred Raabe.

Dr. Albert C. Barnes. The noted collector of modern painting initially befriended Benton, then unexpectedly turned on him. "He was a vicious bastard," Benton later recalled, "but he did love art."

things up off the floor. They would have been destroyed if he hadn't." After framing the works, Dr. Raabe would lend them to his patients and sell them on various installment plans. "It will make you feel better," he'd say, as he hung one on the wall over their protests. People learned to enjoy the paintings and eventually paid for them. Most were sold for five or ten dollars. In the 1970s, when Benton mentioned these prices to Paul Cummings, Cummings commented: "That's incredible. They got bargains, didn't they?" Benton replied: "Well, it turned out to be. I got a bargain too, because I got the money."

He later wryly remarked that he owed much of his early success in New York to the use of calcimine paint. Many people painted their walls with it, and it faded in the sunlight. When Dr. Raabe lent a patient a painting, the wall would gradually fade around the work and the borrower would be forced to purchase the painting—or a larger one—if he did not want to repaint the room.

Dr. Albert C. Barnes

In the early 1920s, Benton finally began to achieve some recognition as a modernist, among both critics and collectors. One of his most useful friends at this time was the painter Arthur Carles, whom he had known slightly in Paris—a hollow-cheeked bohemian with deep-set eyes and a long, unkempt, dusty beard. Carles was a colorist and an expressionist, whereas Benton's work was monochromatic and dealt with the logical organization of form. Nonetheless, Carles worked hard to promote it. Through Carles, Benton got to know Tom and Sarah Kelly, wealthy Philadelphians who had moved to New York. In 1919 they purchased the large figure composition *Garden Scene,* based on Benton's new sculptural methods of organizing form. In addition, through the intervention of Carles, Benton was invited to contribute to a modernist exhibition held in the spring of 1921 at the Pennsylvania Academy of the Fine Arts. He sold three works from this show, all of them based on sketches he had made at Martha's Vineyard the previous summer.

One of the purchasers was Dr. Albert C. Barnes, a millionaire twenty times over, who had worked his way up from abject poverty through the manufacture of a widely used local antiseptic, Argyrol. A gruff, heavyset man, Barnes became interested in art early on, perhaps in part because of his friendship with William Glackens, the Ashcan School painter, with whom he had played baseball at Central High School in Philadelphia. Barnes built up an amazing collection of modernist paintings, with dozens of masterpieces by Cézanne, Picasso, and Matisse, and over two hundred works by Renoir. But he allowed few visitors to see his collection, his private citadel, from which he waged a running battle with the stuffed shirts of Philadelphia and the supporters of the Philadelphia Museum of Art. Barnes's libelous letters were notorious.

Barnes immediately became Benton's strongest supporter. In 1923, for example, when he showed one of Tom's paintings at the Pennsylvania Academy, he wrote an effusive commentary in the catalogue. "Corot has never revealed to me," Barnes declared, "a composition as satisfying to a critical analysis as is the composition in a painting by a young American, Thomas Benton. But to compare Corot at his best with Benton would be an offense to the exquisite sense of values, the fine intelligence which created the forms in Benton's picture."

"Barnes was a very complex person," Benton later recalled. "He was both friendly, kindly, hospitable and at the same time a ruthless underhanded son-of-a-bitch." When William Schack wrote to him asking for information for a biography of Barnes, Tom concluded his reply with the admonishment: "For God's sake don't do a *Sat. Eve Post* job on the old boy—he's too magnificent a son-of-a-bitch for that."

Shortly after his purchase of Tom's work, Barnes invited the artist to his home in Merion, Pennsylvania, and was so impressed by his intelligence and knowledge of compositional construction in painting that he invited him back several times. They saw each other and corresponded for over a year. The last time he visited, Benton brought along Thomas Craven. Warming to them both, Barnes suggested that they come to Merion every weekend to discuss projects for his Barnes Foundation. He needed a writer, he said, for a book on painting, and Craven would fit the bill perfectly. He might also employ Tom.

But the three men did not always agree. Benton did not share the doctor's enthusiasm for the Impressionists, and Craven was openly hostile to them. Tom brought Barnes some of the cubistic drawings he had made from his sculptures and explained to him that similar diagrams might explain the formal basis of the great masterpieces of the past. When Barnes asked him to discuss the compositional structure of some impressionist works, Benton replied, "Well, that's kind of difficult. There isn't much form there." Since a good part of Barnes's collection consisted of impressionist paintings, he was probably offended by this offhand dismissal.

Benton was never sure exactly why Barnes broke with him, for they parted on affable terms. "Barnes was a poor talker in man to man discussion," he later recalled, "but he brooded on his deficiencies and exploded in his notorious letters." He had no warning that the doctor intended to turn against him: "The facts are that after parting on the best of terms before his departure for Paris he wrote me one of his scurrilous letters after he'd been there for a while. . . . Barnes was also an amateur psychologist and he could really be devastating. Briefly, what he said was that my cockiness with regard to the arts derived from the fact that I was only a runt anyhow, and runts like me are always combative. He was a vicious bastard, but he did love art."

Ethel Whiteside

Fortunately, about a year after his marriage, Benton found a supporter to replace the disenchanted Dr. Barnes—an extroverted actress named Ethel Whiteside, who purchased hats from Rita. She starred in "The Follies of Coontown," which the Hartford *Courant* described as "one of the best 'pick' acts that vaudeville has ever seen."

Ethel lived with her paramour, Denny—"a criminal lawyer, tenderloin style"—in a lavish Riverside Drive apartment, where bohemian parties took place almost every night until the early hours of the morning. At the first of these affairs that Tom attended, he got the better of a jowly old judge who launched into a tirade against artists. A crowd gathered, and Tom was the center of attention.

Ethel Whiteside.

After this triumph, Tom and Rita remained regulars at Ethel's place for about three years. Ethel induced Denny to buy Tom's pictures, and soon the brocaded walls of her apartment were full of them. Their major purchase was a large figure composition of half-naked figures playing with a red beach ball, which Benton had painted in 1922. The title, *Figure Composition*, didn't suit Denny's crowd, so after several sessions of spirited discussion, aided by copious amounts of liquor, the painting was retitled *Basketball in Hell*.

Denny was eager to push Tom's career, so he arranged for him to paint Benny the Alderman. Tom went up to the Tammany Club just on the outskirts of Harlem, and was led through rooms filled with cigar smoke and lounging men to Benny himself. After some protest, he sat Benny down in a chair, set up his easel, laid out his paints, and slashed out a striking likeness.

Benny's henchmen were not pleased by the result—which showed him with a jauntily cocked derby, a broken, flattened nose, and an uptilted cigar in his fat lips. Benton responded by covering his sketch with retouching varnish and then painting it over to look more flattering—fixing the broken nose and splotchy complexion and making the whole effect more glamorous. As soon as he got home, he carefully scraped off this surface layer, bringing back the original sketch, which was only slightly damaged. When Denny saw the painting, he was sore. "Can't help a nut," he said. "You threw away a gold mine." Later, he confided to Ethel, "Tom sure nailed that mug."

The Death of the Colonel

In 1924 Colonel M. E. Benton, then seventy-seven years old, learned that he had throat cancer and came east to consult a specialist. He had not adjusted gracefully to changing times. As a young man, he had gained success by pushing the pension claims of old Union soldiers, but there were not many Civil War veterans left to represent, and he had not managed to develop another such lucrative form of business. Except for Nat, who had moved out to Missouri to practice law, he had seen little of his family in many years. He slept in the little room behind his office, a thickset, lonely man with his best years behind him; he drank quite heavily.

The doctor decided that it would be best not to operate. The only chance to save the Colonel's life, and it was a slim one, would have involved removal of his vocal cords, leaving him without a voice. "He's an old man," the doctor told Elizabeth Benton. "I think he's ready to die. I think we should let him die." In March, Tom accompanied his father back to Missouri—not to Neosho but to Springfield, where Nat had his practice. He left Rita in New York. They stayed in a rented house until the Colonel's condition worsened and he was moved to a hospital. He could talk only in a whisper, though he told rollicking stories until the end.

Elizabeth Benton had arranged to rent the house in Great Neck for the summer, and she stayed an extra six weeks or so to ready the place for the new tenants. Consequently, Tom was alone with his father for a month and a half before his mother arrived. She did come out to Missouri for the final days, though both Mary and Mildred stayed on the East Coast.

Benton had had little contact with his father since 1912, when there had been considerable friction between them. "His father was little more than a picturesque memory," Thomas Craven later commented, "so many years had they been separated." Now his father's illness made the issues that had divided them seem insignificant; it threw Tom into the kind of intimacy with his father that he had known as a small child.

In the mid-1970s, he was questioned about the role that his father's death played in reshaping his life and art. He brusquely evaded the question. "Skip that part," he said. "It's too complicated." He hinted at the significance of the event in *An Artist in America:*

"I cannot honestly say what happened to me while I watched my father die and listened to the voices of his friends, but I know that when, after his death, I went back East, I was moved by a great desire to know more of the America which I had glimpsed in the suggestive words of his old cronies, who, seeing him at the end of his tether, had tried to jerk him back with reminiscent talk and suggestive anecdote. I was moved by a desire to pick up again the threads of my childhood. To my itch for going places there was injected a thread of purpose which, however slight as a far-reaching philosophy, was to make the next ten years of my life a rich texture of varied experience."

"Probably it was only at this time," Mildred Small has commented, "the time of his death, that the sorrow of his father's life came home to Tom. . . . It's a shame that Father never had a chance to see his son's success. While he would not have understood it, he would have appreciated it." She adds: "I don't know why my father was so late in understanding his child. I guess he never thought it was necessary to understand children, you just told them what to do and they did it. But here was one who never did what he was told to do."

The annual state Democratic convention took place in Springfield that year, and while it was in progress troops of delegates stopped by to pay their last respects to the

Colonel. One day, a Kansas City group appeared, headed by the notorious boss Tom Pendergast. Silently, one by one, they went into the Colonel's room to shake his hand. Pendergast was the last. When he returned to the anteroom, he reached a big half-closed fist out toward Benton, and as Tom grasped it he felt a hard object slip into his palm. "This is from his friends for any little things he might need," Pendergast said, and walked out.

Tom was dumbfounded when he discovered that the hard object was a tight roll of bills, eight hundred dollars in all. He dared not tell his father of this gift, for he knew he would feel humiliated. Shortly afterward, however, he told Nat, knowing that he would have to account for his possession of the money. "Why the hell did you take it?' Nat asked him. Tom explained that he hadn't realized what was happening until it was too late. "Well," Nat commented, "we can damn well use the money, but for Christ's sake don't ever say a word about it to anybody."

The Colonel died late in April, and Elizabeth Benton, Tom, and Nat attended his funeral; neither Mary nor Mildred was there. After the burial, Tom sorted through his father's personal effects and discovered among them a box containing dozens of faded love letters from women whom M.E. had courted while he was rising to success, letters that revealed a romantic streak in the Colonel's disposition, which he had always concealed from his son. Several made references to poetry he had quoted.

In autumn 1925, the Colonel's sister Fanny wrote to Elizabeth Benton from Little Rock, Arkansas. She had been back to Neosho, she reported, had visited the cemetery, and had been shocked to discover that "Brother was lying in an unmarked grave." When Elizabeth showed the letter to Tom, her old anger boiled over. She launched into a tirade against the imperiousness of Fanny and her sister, Dolly. Shortly afterward, the Colonel's grave got a marker.

His father's death coincided with a significant change of direction in Benton's career as an artist, as well as a significant shift in personality. In Missouri, he produced a group of watercolor studies of local characters. He showed them in autumn 1924 at the Daniel Galleries, under the title "In Missoura." It was the first time he had exhibited any work of this type, for his portrait of Benny the Alderman and his Vineyard character studies had not yet been shown.

Until that time, the work he displayed had revealed Benton as an ingenious and thoughtful student of the formal side of painting. These watercolors, on the other hand, had an almost raucous liveliness. He had finally circled around again to that natural talent for humorous drawings which he had displayed as a young boy, and which he had put aside for years in order to follow the higher pathways of art. Lloyd Goodrich, writing in *Arts* magazine, immediately recognized the show's importance, declaring that it "presents a new side of his artistic personality." After noting that Benton had "a natural flair for caricature, somewhat akin to that of the comic strip artist," Goodrich concluded: "He has struck a rich vein, and it is to be hoped that he will continue to work it." The remark was a prescient one, for these "In Missoura" watercolors marked out the Regionalist course that Benton would follow until his death.

Chapter Six
"The Mechanics of Form Organization"

"For the development of a complete rhythm extending through large masses of sculptural form, modern art has uncovered no gift like that of Thomas H. Benton, a painter who seems to belong neither to his own department nor to the domain of sculpture."

Benton's Analysis of Abstract Form

In the 1930s, Thomas Hart Benton allied himself with the Regionalist movement and became notorious for his attacks on French abstract styles. As a consequence, most writers today view him as a foe of modernist painting. To those holding this belief, his long and well-documented association with Jackson Pollock has been simply an embarrassment, something it is best to overlook.

Benton's relationship with modernism, however, was more intense, more complex, and more richly contradictory than has generally been supposed. In the beginning of his career, he ran through the whole gamut of modernist styles—including Impressionism, Pointillism, Cézannism, Synchromism, and Constructivism—and during the early 1920s he was consistently treated by both his foes and his defenders as a modernist figure. His chief artistic concern in this period was to devise a means of unifying and interlocking the forms in his paintings into an aesthetic unity. In 1926 he summarized his discoveries in a series of articles on "The Mechanics of Form Organization," which describe the fundamental principles of abstract composition.

For Benton, the mastery of such abstract organization was simply a way station on the road to the mastery of representational painting. While he never abandoned his use of abstract principles, his paintings after 1930 contain such powerful and controversial subject matter that their control of formal organization has been largely overlooked. His pupil Jackson Pollock, on the other hand, used Benton's compositional principles as a launching point for radical experiments in abstract form. Pollock vigorously rejected Benton's insistence on realistic subject matter; the underlying structure of Pollock's abstractions, however, can be clearly traced back to his teacher's compositional diagrams of 1926.

Benton's intensive study of formal issues, his rigorous analysis of how shapes interlock and interrelate, was almost unique in American art of the teens and twenties. Alfred Stieglitz, the most forceful influence on modernist American painters of that generation, related to art emotionally and intuitively, and had no interest in it as a form of intellectual discipline. The painters whom he supported most strongly—John Marin, for example—mimicked the fractured forms of the European Cubists and Futurists in a spontaneous, emotive way, without a solid understanding of the principles underlying these new devices of pictorial structure. Only one other American artist, Stuart Davis, shared Benton's interest in the systematic exploration of formal relationships.

Although they hated each other all their lives, Benton and Davis had many affini-

ties of temperament. Indeed, their animosity was probably triggered by certain fundamental similarities. Both were stubborn and aggressive, even belligerent, personalities. Both liked to create a pictorial world that was crisp, clear, and hard, almost completely lacking in tonal subtleties or "atmosphere." Both liked to work out their compositions precisely, through large numbers of preparatory studies, and to create paintings with a polished, immaculate surface. Both loved American music and were inspired by it in their work, although Davis favored urban jazz and Benton the country music of black blues singers and Ozark fiddlers.

Both were concerned with exploring fundamental principles of pictorial construction—of mastering the mechanics through which shapes can be made to relate to each other in complex rhythms and harmonies. They differed from each other, however, in their handling of space. Although Benton made a few designs that are flat, his primary ambition was to orchestrate pictorial rhythms in depth. Davis, who was chiefly inspired by the French Cubists, wished to reassemble the three-dimensional world onto a flat plane.

Both had a theoretical bent and a gift for writing a tough, slangy, vigorously

Thomas Hart Benton, Color Study, Martha's Vineyard, *oil on paper mounted on board, 1922. The so-called Suitcase Bentons, which once belonged to Charles Pollock, have won the enthusiastic approval of such New York critics as Clement Greenberg and Hilton Kramer. Kramer has written that they reveal Benton as "an enthusiastic and accomplished modernist."*

American prose that cut through pretensions like a knife. Davis, however, while wonderfully articulate, expressed his ideas through aphorisms and slogans, many of which are contradictory. He seems to have been incapable of extended rational argument. Benton worked out a rigorous and coherent philosophy of art.

"Modern Painting"

Benton's ideas about the handling of form were derived from the book *Modern Painting* by his friend Willard Huntington Wright. More correctly, his ideas derived from the conversations that generated the book, for it was written when he was living with the Wright brothers, and he participated in the heated discussions that brought the volume to birth.

Modern Painting was a heavily slanted account, for one of its main goals was to demonstrate that the Synchromism of Morgan Russell and Stanton Macdonald-Wright represented the culmination of Western painting. Consequently Willard Wright's critical judgments were sometimes way off the mark. Most modern readers would share his admiration for Delacroix, Turner, Courbet, Daumier, Renoir, and Cézanne, but his assessment of his brother's rivals was far more fallible. Thus he described Matisse as a mere decorator, downplayed the importance of Cubism, castigated Kandinsky as a "decadent," and abruptly dismissed the Orphists, the Synchromists' chief rivals.

The lasting significance of Willard Wright's book, however, lies less in its critical evaluations than in its underlying ideas. Wright was the first writer in English to attempt a history of modern art organized around aesthetic principles. The central theme of the book was that painting should devote itself not to illustration but to formal qualities. "Painting," Wright wrote, "has been a bastard art—an agglomeration of literature, religion, photography and decoration. The efforts of painters for the last century have been devoted to the elimination of all extraneous considerations, to make painting as pure an art as music."

For Wright, the central characteristic of great painting was the rhythmic organization of form, "not rhythm in the superficial harmonic sense, but the rhythm which underlies the great fluctuating and equalizing forces of material existence." Such form should not be flat. "Significant form must move in depth—backward and forward, as well as from side to side. . . . It must imply an infinity of depth."

In modern painting such mastery of form was found most fully in Cézanne, "the pre-eminent figure in modern art." Among the old masters it was found in the work of Michelangelo, Rubens, and El Greco. To Wright, "Serious modern art, despite its often formidable and bizarre appearance, is only a striving to rehabilitate the natural and unalterable principles of rhythmic form to be found in the old masters, and to translate them into relative and more comprehensive terms."

Thomas Craven

Willard Wright's ideas about form were picked up in turn by Thomas Craven, who used them as the basis for two essays on "The Progress of Painting," which appeared in *The Dial* in April and June 1923. The first essay surveyed the development of pictorial techniques up through the work of the old masters; the second, the genesis of modernism. Both essays were written in collaboration with Benton; they represent the fullest exposition in one place of Craven's aesthetic principles.

For Craven, the key element of art was "form." As he wrote, "The rendition of form—form undisguised by the allurements of naturalism, as in primitive art—lays bare the whole creative skeleton." He particularly admired the Renaissance masters who "opened up a new and voluminous world of ordered space . . . by releasing objects from a single plane." Compositional organization thus became richer, because "design, the foundation of the decorative arts before Giotto, was intellectualized, was

conceived as running back and forth through a sequence of recessive planes as well as laterally."

This approach, Craven stressed, was not a mechanical or photographic transcription of visual appearances but was generated by the human imagination. It was "a unified abstraction of experience and not . . . literal representation." He noted: "For a long and magnificent period the genius of the artist was concentrated on the study of form. . . . Pure form, as delineated from Masaccio to Michael Angelo, was an *artistic* reality. It was not an imitation."

This progression came to an end, in Craven's view, when painters began to introduce textures into their designs and to concentrate on surface values rather than form. In their desire to transcribe visual reality, painters became "wholly uncreative" and "undermined the foundations of plastic art."

Because of his belief in the preeminence of form, Craven disdained the contributions of the Impressionists. In his view, "Monet, Sisley, and Pissarro . . . left the validity of a formless art uncontested, and . . . made no inquiry into the aesthetics of design." But he supported the modernist movement, which he defined in a somewhat idiosyncratic fashion: "Modernism made its first public appearance as a revolt against the formless productions of the Impressionists. . . . Modernism gives precedence to ideas; it stands specifically for creative thought as opposed to imitation of nature, and in this respect it is the most significant movement in art since the Renaissance."

Like Willard Wright, Craven most admired the work of Cézanne, who "held all flat art in contempt. His goal was a reality, a full, rich, tri-dimensional world in whose mass and depth we might encounter subjective experiences comparable in force with the experiences of practical life." Rather more surprisingly, Craven also admired Cubism, despite his distress that "Cubism disintegrates design." He wrote: "Cubism advocated form. . . . There are few modern painters who have not profited in one way or another by its teachings. Cubism implies the diametrical opposite of imitation."

Like Wright, Craven disdained forms of art that were flat. His initial definition of painting stressed the manipulation of form in three dimensions rather than on a two-dimensional plane. "Painting, as a creative art," he wrote, "is the revelation through colour of form more extended in its space than sculpture." This definition applied perfectly to the work of Benton, of whom he said: "For the development of a complete rhythm extending through large masses of sculptural form, modern art has uncovered no gift like that of Thomas H. Benton, a painter who seems to belong neither to his own department nor to the domain of sculpture."

In essence, Craven restated the aesthetic principles of Willard Wright, but with a subtle shift in emphasis. Whereas Wright saw the work of the old masters as a pathway leading toward the Synchromists, Craven hoped that the extravagances of modernism would eventually lead to a mode of expression with the tactile, sculptural qualities of the old masters. And whereas Wright modeled aesthetic principles on the work of his brother, Craven modeled them on the work of Benton.

"The Mechanics of Form Organization"

Benton's artistic fixation in the teens and twenties was to develop mastery of the sort of rhythmic form of which Willard Wright wrote. During his discussions with Dr. Barnes, he sketched out his thoughts about the organization of form, and in 1926–27 he finally published this material in a series of articles in *Arts* magazine. Recently Edward Fry, an authority on Cubism, expressed his admiration for this series. "Benton," Fry wrote, "was a much more acute student of European art than almost anyone else among his generation of Americans in France. . . . His relationship to European modernism, particularly of the Cubist period, was much more penetrating than most people have given him credit for . . . . His insight into the forms and structures of the European tradition was really without equal."

Benton began by dividing composition into two types, that organized on a flat surface and that conceived in depth. Throughout his essay, he maintained a significant distinction between shape and form. For him, the physical characteristics of shape remain ambiguous, whereas form possesses mass and takes up physical space. Curiously, he did not speak of the properties of negative shapes or of the interaction of figure and ground. His central preoccupation lay in the handling of shapes that had sculptural attributes—in the mastery of form.

He posited three primary factors in successful compositional structure. The first is *equilibrium*, the balancing of visual forces. In painting, the frame serves as a stable, immovable element, which defines the character of all other lines as either static or dynamic. Horizontal and vertical lines, which run parallel to the frame, are static because of their similarity to other elements. Lines that are not parallel to the sides of the frame, however, have a dynamic quality and tend to "tip over" unless met by opposing lines. The simplest means of achieving balance is symmetry, but this is the most boring. It may also be achieved through variety, the harmony of disparate elements—for example, by balancing two small shapes against one large one.

The second fundamental principle is *sequence*, or *connection*. In successful composition, the eye is led from one element to another down a visual pathway. Perceptively, Benton noted that the eye tends not to push straight onward, in the direction that a line points, but rather to focus on dynamic points of connection, where opposed lines meet and interact. Thus, for example, there is a tendency to ascend or descend a vertical pole along the opposed directions of the dynamic lines.

The third fundamental principle is *rhythm,* which, Benton noted, "is a projection from our inner selves and does not exist in the structure of the object." He defined rhythm as "the repetition in a dynamic sequence, at alternating intervals, of similar factors." Symmetry achieves a kind of static balance, but dynamic equilibrium is asymmetrical. Many compositions combine static, repetitive elements with dynamic, asymmetrical ones. The elements of a composition can be organized centripetally, so that the forces flow into each other, or centrifugally, so that the forces bounce off the opposed surfaces. Most compositions contain both principles, operating simultaneously.

Curiously, the eye can follow the interaction of elements in a vertical sequence far more easily than it can horizontally. To follow an extended lateral rhythmic sequence

Thomas Hart Benton, Organization, *oil on metal panel, 1944. Throughout his career, Benton occasionally painted pure abstractions concurrently with his better known "Regionalist" canvases.* •

Thomas Hart Benton, Twelve Planes and a Silver Egg, *egg tempera on board, 1934. In 1926 Benton wrote a highly critical review of Brancusi's work for* Arts. *Eight years later, however, he paid indirect tribute to Brancusi's egglike sculpture,* The Beginning of the World, *in this tiny abstract composition.* •

with comfort, the eye needs to divide it up into rhythmic sets. Generally such rhythms are best organized around a series of real or implied vertical poles.

A rhythmical order of masses rather than lines introduces another element into the picture, for to hold the rhythmical flow of line, the edges must interlock. In both sculpture and painting, composition can be most effectively organized around a vertical pole of equilibrium. Sculpture differs from painting, however, because to maintain a homogeneity of mass it needs to restrict itself to a single central pole of equilibrium. Painting, on the other hand, can employ several poles. In addition, because painting works from one viewpoint, it is possible to construct forms in which the movement in one plane of space is completed on another, perhaps far removed, plane of space. Thus it is possible to construct an organization whose parts function in an infinitude of depth.

Benton stressed that composition in depth depends not merely on the recognition of depth but on the ordering of forms in the sculptural fashion that suggests "cubic values." Interestingly, he used the term "cubic" as a substitute for "voluminous," since a cubic shape is the one in which volume can be most easily apprehended. For purposes of analysis, he noted, any form can be reduced to a series of cubical units.

In his fourth essay, Benton discussed human anatomy both as an illustration of the movements and countermovements that control compositional organization and as the empathetic means by which we extend ourselves into a relationship with nature. With a diagram, he demonstrated that the muscles of the human arm follow, in a general way, the principles of compositional order he had discussed. They are organized around a central vertical, the bone, and possess an organized system of movements and countermovements, or bulges and hollows. Significantly, the shape of the arm gives expression to dynamic movement, for when the arm moves, its bulges and hollows move, although they continue to form a clear rhythmical pattern.

In an extraordinary leap of logic, Benton extended this metaphor to suggest that all compositional organization is based on a fundamental harmony with body movement. "In the 'feel' of our own bodies, in the sight of the bodies of others, in the bodies of animals, in the shapes of growing and moving things, in the forces of nature and in the engines of man the rhythmic principle of movement and countermovement is made manifest. But in our own bodies it can be isolated and understood. This mechanical principle which we share with all life can be abstracted and used in constructing and analyzing things which also in their way have life and reality." It was exactly this conception that later provided the impetus for the gestural drip paintings of Jackson Pollock.

In the final article, Benton proposed to reveal the fundamental principles of artistic organization with just two simple kinds of compositional diagram. The first consisted of lines drawn through the center of forms to indicate their rhythms on the surface; the second reduced forms to cubical blocks to reveal their arrangement in depth. Any complex composition, he noted, such as a painting by Rubens or El Greco, needs both types of diagram to unlock its structure.

As remarkable as Benton's essays are the diagrams, nearly all of which present cubistic or abstract compositions. Several of them directly anticipate Jackson Pollock, the compositional structure of Pollock's early work being expressed in diagrams 22 and 23; that of his later work in diagram 24.

Pollock's fundamental ideas about art history and about form were established when he studied with Benton. Contrary to what many writers have implied, he never completely abandoned them. Alfonso Ossorio recalls that around 1948, not long before Pollock died, he "gave me a three-hour lecture about the contemporary American art scene, beginning with the chauvinist critic Thomas Craven, a Benton champion." Harry Jackson reports: "It's a lot of crap about Jack not talking much; he talked my goddam ear off one long night, drinking beer in the kitchen. Jack brought out *Cahier d'Art* and analyzed Tintoretto in great detail, explaining the composition of this and that; what he was doing was bringing me pure Tom Benton: Venetian Renaissance to Tom Benton, Tom to Jack, Jack to Harry. Then he analyzed Braque, Picasso, Juan Gris, and Matisse, but he wasn't that crazy about Matisse. He talked especially about composition that night, and Lee [Krasner] came down several times to say, 'Jackson, come to bed—you're going to be so tired and you've got this and that to do,' something like that. But we went on until dawn, with Jack describing Tintoretto and weaving a spell: 'See, it goes back over there, and then over here, and it never goes off the canvas.'"

Benton was undoubtedly hurt that Pollock had repudiated his own belief in representational form. Yet he also took pride in Pollock's success. Alfred Stieglitz had condemned Benton's explorations of form as boring and pedantic; Jackson Pollock demonstrated their significance to modern art. Through Jackson Pollock, Benton reestablished his own claim to modernity.

Benton's Figure Organizations

Despite Willard Wright's endorsement of their work, the Synchromists, in actual practice, did not achieve the three-dimensionality he advocated. Synchromism does not clearly articulate form but discloses it gradually through a process of discovery. In Stanton Macdonald-Wright's Synchromist figures, for example, the eye is first attracted to starlike clusters of color rays and only gradually manages to interpret these as the points of intersection of planes of color. These planes in turn articulate spatial volumes, which interrelate with each other in a harmony of spiraling movements.

Jackson Pollock, Going West, *oil on fiberboard, 1934–38.* •

Jackson Pollock, Troubled Queen, *oil and enamel on canvas, circa 1945.*

Thomas Hart Benton, Going West, *1930, illustration for Leo Huberman's* We, the People. *Pollock's early painting* Going West, *which has often been compared with the work of Ryder, was obviously based on Benton's illustration of the same subject for Huberman's Marxist history of the United States.*

Jackson Pollock, Summertime, *oil and enamel on canvas, 1948.*

Synchromism, in short, is built on a conflict between color and form rather than on a conciliation of these elements.

Thomas Hart Benton sensed this conflict from the first, for when he made his canvases of brightly colored figures for the Forum Exhibition, he found that the highly saturated colors tended to flatten the forms and to put all of them on the same level. Consequently he did not push forward in the direction Willard Wright proposed, toward an art of misty color expression. Instead he looked backward toward the fundamental principles he had articulated. He studied the masters whom Wright had singled out for their mastery of three-dimensional organization—Michelangelo, Rubens, Tintoretto, and El Greco. After a brief phase of painting rainbow-colored disks, in emulation of his clever Synchromist friend, Benton began to examine and analyze the fundamentals of pictorial construction, increasingly eschewing color in favor of form.

His interest in multifigured compositions developed early in his career. From his association with George Carlock he became interested in the old-master compositions in the Louvre, and while still in France, he seems to have developed the ambition of reconciling modernist techniques with "classic composition." One of Macdonald-Wright's early letters to Benton from Paris seems to allude to this classic direction of his work, and by 1913 Benton had begun making groupings of nude figures, more or less inspired by the bathers of Cézanne.

By 1914 he was beginning to develop a form of composition that worked in depth as well as on a flat surface. His illustrations of that year for *Europe After 8:15,* while awkward in many respects, reveal the germ of what became his favorite device for organizing forms: building up spiraling compositions that rotate around a real or implied central visual pole. The paintings of 1916 for the Forum Exhibition exploited this technique in combination with bright, prismatic colors—colors that served to emphasize the relatively "abstract" and arbitrary manner in which he had rearranged the human body into rhythmically interrelated sequences.

The paintings he made just after the Forum Exhibition continue this same rhythmic scheme but abandon the bright color. They look very French. While the figure of his large *Bather* of 1917 alludes to Michelangelo, the brushwork recalls Cézanne. Even more French in feeling is a large beach scene that Benton painted in the same year, which is set against a backdrop based on the Palisades of the Hudson. In conception, this work grew directly from the Cézannesque bather scenes that a number of Parisian artists—Picasso, Derain, Othon Friesz, and others—turned out in the teens and twenties; Benton saw many of them while he was still in Paris. The way the figures are rolled flat against the picture plane recalls the nineteenth-century muralist Puvis de Chavannes; as in the work of Puvis, the figures are draped in a funny combination of modern and classical attire. The brushwork, however, resembles that of Cézanne, particularly in the tree and the background landscape. A nice decorative touch is the flat sailboat at the upper left.

In 1917–18, Benton made a number of constructivist still-life paintings, two of which survive, which were painted from models he made out of paper, wood, and wire. As he progressed, these "abstractions" grew more and more "realistic," with

more emphasis on the sculptural and tangible properties of the shapes. *Rhythmic Construction* of about 1919 reveals that from making these paintings, Benton developed the ability to interlock shapes into complex rhythmic sequences. As Richard Gruber has noted, Benton may have conceived this piece as an architectural decoration, for the rectangle at the lower right suggests a door opening. Each shape in the composition directs the eye onward, in unbroken movement, until it has covered every element of the design. This visual pathway leads the eye not only over the surface of the composition but into depth as well.

Not too long afterward, in 1919, just after his return from the Navy, Benton began to make sculptural models as studies for his figural compositions. This new procedure transformed the character of his work and created a distinct stylistic break between the work before 1920 and that made afterwards. His paint handling grew somewhat slicker and drier, and he abandoned his Cézannesque brushwork. No doubt he felt that surface effects distracted from the apprehension of sculptural form. But he grew more adept in his control of spatial organization. In a 1964 interview with Milton F. Perry, Benton commented that he used these models to "turn . . . abstractions into tangible forms and spaces, things I can see and refer to."

Benton's first exercise with this new method was the *Garden Scene* he sold to Tom and Sarah Kelly. He achieved full mastery of his new techniques in two beach scenes that he painted during his first two summers on Martha's Vineyard—*The Beach* and *People of Chilmark.* These works differ in size and proportion, but in conception they might be viewed as mates. The composition of each rotates around a large beach ball in the center. *The Beach* treats the theme of repose; *People of Chilmark* that of energetic action. Thomas Craven was writing enthusiastically at this time about the Post-Impressionist Georges Seurat, and the problem that Tom set himself brings to mind the work of Seurat, who strove to evoke emotions through the relationship of shapes and the calculated balance of diagonal, vertical, and horizontal lines.

In many ways the more beautiful of these works is the earlier *The Beach*, but it is less well known, for it has not been exhibited or reproduced since the early 1920s, when it caught the attention of Dr. Barnes and was purchased by one of his friends.

Thomas Hart Benton, Garden Scene, *oil on canvas, 1919. The first figural painting that Benton designed as a clay model; it marks the transition into his mature pictorial style. The painting was purchased as an overmantel decoration by Tom and Sarah Kelly, well-to-do Philadelphians who patronized modernist artists and composers. •*

The design grew out of a number of studies of a figure reclining beside a boat, reminiscent of the reclining figures of Henry Moore. Benton balanced this figure with that of a reclining woman, and added others, which complement these two. He chose an unusual proportion for the painting—a perfect square, forty by forty inches—both as a compositional challenge and because it reinforced his general theme of repose, balance, and equilibrium.

In contrast to the placid behavior of the figures in *The Beach, People of Chilmark* shows a Rubensian scene of frenetic activity. Four men, four women, a boy, and an excited dog cavort frantically by the waterside—launching a boat, tossing a beach ball, waving their arms, and rowing. Rita and her brother Louis, their neighbor Peggy Owen, and Thomas Craven posed for the painting—Craven looking nervous and out of place in this hedonistic frolic. None of the figures have enough room to move freely, but clearly Benton was less concerned with narrative logic than with visual balance and organization. His preparatory sketches for the painting show that he designed it in jigsaw-puzzle shapes, like a sculptor drawing on a block of stone. The design was rigorously organized as a series of flat decorative planes, arrayed at different levels of depth.

In 1972, when this painting was exhibited at Rutgers University, John Canaday wrote of it: "The most interesting picture in the show for me is a strange affair painted about 1922, 'The People of Chilmark,' not because it is a good picture but because it reminds me of the kind of compositional exercises still being assigned to art students (hopefuls for the Prix de Rome) late into the 1930s. There is a bit of everything here, with Géricault's 'Raft of the Medusa' as one limit and Raphael's 'Fire in the Borgo' as the other. It is so typical an academic machine that you can all but hear the wheels grinding. Yet it is the dividing line beyond which Benton becomes an original painter. And in its scheme, if you reduce it to a diagram, it is also as proto-Pollock as any pictorial composition you can find anywhere."

"Form and the Subject"

In June 1924, a few weeks after his father's death, Benton published the essay "Form and the Subject," which marked the beginning of his break with the modernist movement. He may well have been polishing this piece while he sat by his father's bedside.

Eight years before, in a brief statement for the Forum Exhibition, he had said that he did not believe in the significance of subject matter. Apparently, however, this was not based on deep conviction: in a letter of 1971 to Matthew Baigell, he confessed that the assertion was tacked on at the suggestion of Willard Wright. In "Form and the Subject," he specifically repudiated this point of view. "Real form," he argued, "demands an obvious imposition of will on the elements of experience. Form is a characteristic of the human mind; it has no prior existence in nature.... We must have in clear outlines the human imagination actually disposing and ordering relationships.... The connection between form and the subject is far more vital than is commonly supposed."

Benton went on to criticize implicitly the Cézannesque still lifes that he himself had produced in the early teens. "We can afford to ask," he declared, "whether a table-cloth and an apple, in terms of human value, are worth all the effort expended in trying to make them pictorially interesting." With farfetched but ingenious logic, he linked the work of the modernists with the rituals of the Ku Klux Klan. "When the creative life is barren or starved," he noted, "the mind tends to dignify insignificant actions with high-sounding and impressive nomenclature.... America is unfortunately the home of an inordinate amount of sublimation of this order, and we see the ceremonies and the rigamarole of the Ku Kluxers and the various lodges eagerly

Thomas Hart Benton, People of Chilmark, *oil on canvas, 1922. Benton's friends and neighbors, including his wife and Thomas Craven, posed for his second major figure organization.*

123

grasped as a cover to spiritually naked lives. A spurious hurrah and mystery are the compensatory indulgences offsetting the average life of little and rather monotonous affairs. In the world of art, not only in America but also in Europe, we have a parallel condition. We have a weary professionalism existing utterly apart from the sweep of common interests, and covering a futile endeavor with big talk or a minute and querulous concentration on details which, to a healthy mind, would be regarded simply as a matter of course."

Two years later, in a review of a Brancuşi show, Benton reiterated this point of view and directly took aim at one of the revered figures of the modernist movement. Benton came close to a direct quotation of the words of Willard Wright when he challenged the view that the artist should struggle for "the release of art from the common vulgarities of representation and its elevation to a condition of absolute purity." While praising Brancuşi's work as "ingenious" and "nearly impeccable" in taste, Benton dismissed these elements as "academic virtues." In his view, "It is interest in the world, its fact and plain poetry, and not in fine-spun notions of essential essences and strained perfections that gives the electric charge to form and sends it streaming and spluttering into the future."

Given such forceful statements from Benton, one would expect Thomas Craven to have followed suit. Indeed, just nine months after "Form and the Subject" appeared in *Arts,* Craven published a forceful essay in *The Dial* on the French cartoonist Daumier, whose work, he proclaimed, "is living testimony to the profound importance of subject matter. . . . The French painter's straightforward narrowness of response to his environment has always seemed to me to be decidedly advantageous to individual expression. . . . The Frenchman is proud of his provincialism." Here, in crude form, Craven first put forward the philosophy of Regionalism.

"The American Historical Epic"

Both *The Beach* and *People of Chilmark,* although they contain figurative elements, are essentially abstract in conception. Both paintings stress pictorial organization; the actions and gestures of the figures do not convey narrative meaning. The next logical step was for Benton to introduce subject matter, and he did so in an ambitious history series now known as *The American Historical Epic.*

Thomas Hart Benton, Second Chapter: The American Historical Epic, oil on canvas, 1924–27. Planters; Slaves.

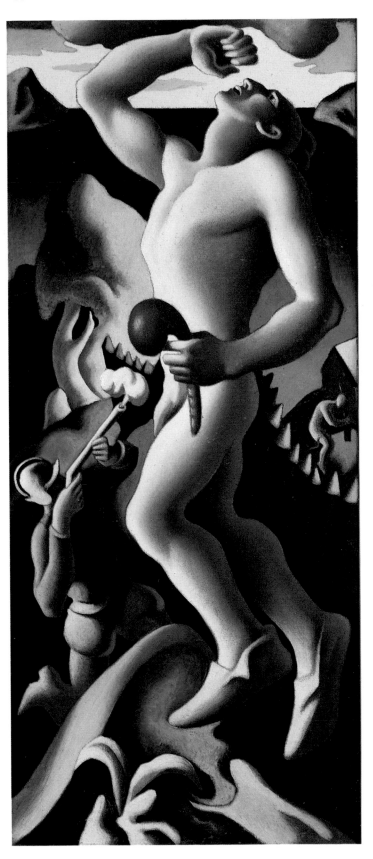

Thomas Hart Benton, First Chapter: The American Historical Epic, *oil on canvas, 1919-24.* Aggression. •

Thomas Hart Benton, Third Chapter: The American Historical Epic, *oil on canvas, 1924-26.* Jesuit Missionaries. •

Thomas Hart Benton, Third Chapter: The American Historical Epic, *oil on canvas, 1924–26.* Over the Mountains; Struggle for the Wilderness. •

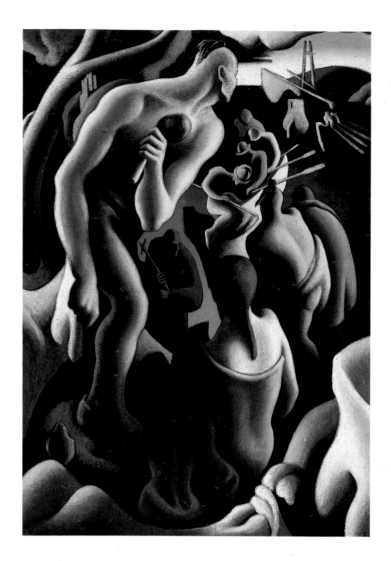

Thomas Hart Benton, First Chapter: The American Historical Epic, *oil on canvas, 1919-24.* Discovery; Retribution. •

He conceived this series while he was in the Navy, when he came upon a volume of Spencer's *History of the United States* that belonged to his landlady. The original seeds of the idea go back even further, to when he was a boy of seventeen at Western Military Academy and wrote to his mother of his ambition to create a series depicting "The Explorers and Adventurers of Early America."

He now planned a series of seventy-five paintings (he completed only about eighteen). His first "chapter" of five paintings showed the arrival of the settlers and their conflicts with the Indians. The second chapter showed the conquest of the mountainous interior regions of the United States, and included a battle scene from the French and Indian War. A third, incomplete chapter portrayed the economic life of the early colonies.

Before Benton, American muralists followed a nineteenth-century mode established by Puvis de Chavannes. One of the fundamental principles of this manner was that the picture should remain relatively flat, so as to harmonize with the wall. The colors were pale and unobtrusive, and the subject matter was tranquil—generally some allegory represented by a female figure in white cheesecloth.

Benton's style was directly opposed to all these tendencies. His *Epic* was aggressively three-dimensional, so that the figures seem about to push out of the wall and intrude on the space of the spectator. His colors were bold and strident. His subject matter was active—filled with battles and scenes of conflict.

In all three chapters, Benton depicted racial conflict and economic exploitation. "Discovery" showed war between the white man and the Indian; "Mountain" continued this theme and also pointedly illustrated the exploitation of the blacks; and the "Economic" chapter included an overseer whipping a black slave, as well as an Indian who had been despoiled of his land, standing with a whiskey bottle in his hand.

Benton later recalled that he wished "to present a people's history in contrast to the conventional histories which generally spotlighted great men, political and military events, and successions of ideas. I wanted to show that the people's behaviors, their *action* on the opening land, was the primary reality of American life. Of course this was a form of Turnerism, but it was first suggested to me by Marxist-Socialist theory. . . . This socialist theory treated 'operations' and 'processes' as more fundamental than 'ideas.' It also maintained the theoretical supremacy of the 'people.'

"I had in mind, following this theory, to show that America had been made by the 'operations of people' who as civilization and technology advanced became increasingly separated from the benefits thereof. I would go in my history from the frontiers, where the people controlled operations, to the labor lines of the machine age, where they decidedly did not."

In composing his scenes, Benton relied on the principles of arrangement that he had developed earlier, in particular the idea of arranging his forms in rotation around some real or imaginary visual pole. In *Palisades,* for example, the whole composition revolves around the vertical accent of the fence post being thrust into the ground by the figure in the center.

The American Historical Epic lays out the essential elements of Benton's mature work, in both its American subject matter and its manner of organizing forms. What it lacks is a sense of vividly observed texture and incident. The forms are generalized and in some cases downright peculiar. For example, the hunter's powderhorn in *The Pathfinder* hangs magically from his side without a thong; the Indian in *Retribution* appears to be naked, except that the bottom of his leg shows a cuff, as if he were wearing pants.

Thomas Hart Benton, Third Chapter: The American Historical Epic, *oil on canvas, 1924–26.* The Pathfinder. •

Thomas Hart Benton, Third Chapter: The American Historical Epic, *oil on canvas, 1924–26.* Lost Hunting Ground. •

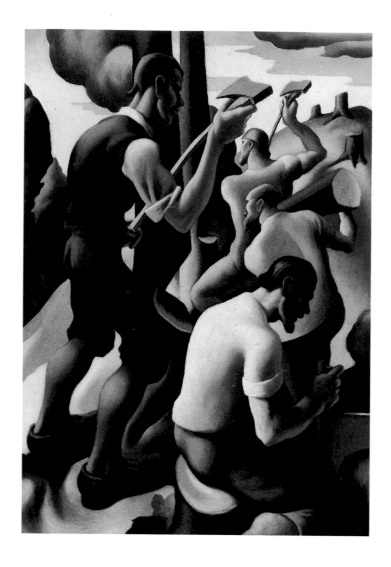

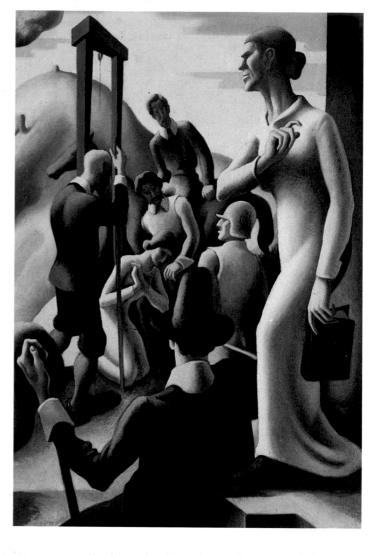

Thomas Hart Benton, Second Chapter: The American Historical Epic, *oil on canvas, 1924–27.* The Axes; Religion. •

Between 1923 and 1926, Benton worked on the first three chapters of the epic. By the winter of 1926–27, however, he had grown tired of colonial themes and wanted to record the life of the present day. Accordingly he painted *Bootleggers*—his first large-scale image of a contemporary subject and by far the most impressive composition in the series. Instead of a central, dominant figure or figural group, *Bootleggers* contains a number of competing motifs—a truck robbery, a gentleman in a top hat passing money to a gangster, a charging locomotive, a parked car, and two airplanes, one on the ground and one in the air. In many ways, the fragmentation of the design brings to mind analytical cubist painting; and its wild dispersion of compositional energies vividly evokes the rush and confusion of contemporary life.

The Suitcase Bentons

Although his main effort went into his "figure organizations," Benton worked in a variety of styles in the early twenties. Some of his paintings were remarkably abstract. The majority seem to have been destroyed, but one large group survives—the so-called Suitcase Bentons.

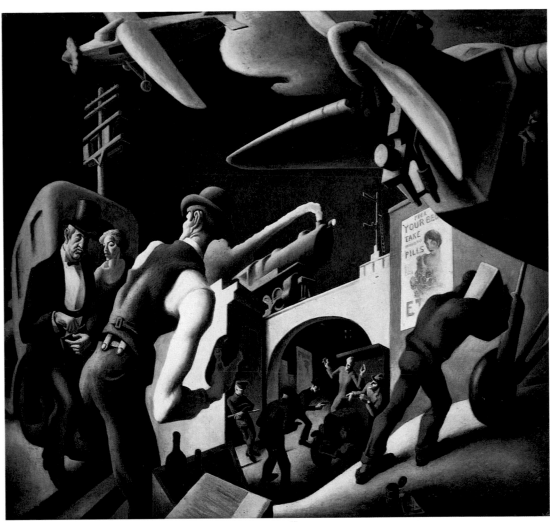

Thomas Hart Benton, Bootleggers, *egg tempera and oil on canvas mounted on masonite, 1927.* •

Thomas Hart Benton, Colonial Brides, *egg tempera/oil on canvas, 1928–30.* •

131

Thomas Hart Benton, Cookie Tin, *oil on tin, circa 1923.*

In autumn 1929, Tom and Rita moved to an apartment on Eighth Avenue. Charles Pollock, the brother of Jackson, took over their place at 42 Union Square, which they had occupied since 1922. In one of the closets, Pollock found a suitcase filled with sketches, which he appropriated and took from place to place with him for the next five decades. They were eventually acquired by the Salander-O'Reilly Gallery in New York, which exhibited fifty of the more abstract oil studies in January 1982.

The first art historians to examine this trove, Matthew Baigell and Gail Levin, dated most of the sketches between 1915 and 1920. Clearly, however, they are later, for a number of them portray Martha's Vineyard, which Benton did not visit until 1920. Several are studies for paintings that can be dated to 1922. It seems most likely, in fact, that the entire group was painted in the summer of 1922. Probably at the end of that summer, Benton threw all his sketches into a suitcase, which he took back with him to New York.

A number of critics not normally very positive toward Benton's work were bowled over by these little paintings. Clement Greenberg, one of the first advocates of the Abstract Expressionists, judged the paintings "good—really good," and noted: "I never realized before his gift for color." Hilton Kramer, in an enthusiastic piece for the *New York Times,* described them as "utterly fascinating" and declared that they established Benton's significance as "an enthusiastic and accomplished modernist."

Thomas Hart Benton, Abstract Screen, *mixed materials, circa 1930.*

Thomas Hart Benton, Autumn Leaves, *oil on panel, circa 1923–24. In this painting, Benton deliberately inverted normal color relationships, rather in the manner of a photographic negative, in order to emphasize the rhythmic interaction of the shapes.*

Kramer was particularly struck by the small, completely abstract paintings. "These," he observed, "must be counted among the most radical paintings of their day. They anticipate to an uncanny degree the work of certain color-field abstractions of the 60's and 70's in everything but their size. (They are particularly close in structure and manner to certain works of the Canadian painter Jack Bush.) Composed of nothing but irregular blocks and oblongs and improvised touches of color locked into a space that echoes the space they assume, these tiny abstracts are far more extreme than the Synchromist paintings of the period. They are closer to certain works produced contemporaneously by the Russian avant-garde."

One or two other works survive from this period that show a similar exploration of abstract principles. One of these is the lid of a cookie tin that Benton painted for his mother about 1923—a floral design, reminiscent of Braque, in which the forms float weightlessly, linked by swirling ribbons of color. Probably this piece is similar in style to Benton's lost dance-hall decorations of 1914. Another surprising little painting is *Autumn Leaves* of about 1923, in which Benton deliberately inverted normal color relationships, treating light forms as dark and dark as light, rather in the manner of a photographic negative. This inversion makes the sculptural form less palpable but emphasizes the rhythmic interaction of the shapes.

Decorative commissions seem to have encouraged him to work in an abstract manner. In 1925, for example, for the living room of a Mr. Briggs, he designed a screen with a boldly geometric wave design, loosely modeled on Japanese prints. The screen opened to reveal Mr. Briggs's fish trophies and photographs. In 1930 Benton made an even more boldly abstract geometric screen, whose design was carried out in contrasting textures of paper, wood, colored sandpapers, emery board, and grass. With relentless logic, he extended the asymmetry of the design to the outline of the screen itself, which was slanted and irregular.

During the 1920s, Benton created a number of abstract and semi-abstract designs for his mother, who transferred them to embroidery. Mildred Small recalls that around 1930, she and her mother fabricated a number of modernistic bath mats from Tom's designs. He was convinced that these utilitarian objects would bring his art to a broad public and make him wealthy, but unfortunately the broad public showed no interest in buying them.

A special problem that intrigued him at this time was the creation of a weightless design that could be looked at from any side, as it lay on the table or the floor. In 1930, for example, he transferred a drawing he had made in 1926, of a locomotive emerging from a tunnel, to a circular bath mat. The train swirls around the rug in a truly dizzying fashion. Perhaps even more intriguing is a tile he designed in 1923, loosely based on *Autumn Leaves*. In it, he transformed the foliage shapes into completely abstract rhythms, remarkably similar to some of Jackson Pollock's early paintings.

Hilton Kramer has suggested that Benton may have been "a little frightened" by the radical nature of his ventures into abstract art. "Benton's work as a modernist I thought was really strong," Kramer has remarked. "I would never have put him up in the first class, but it was apprentice work. It was the work of a young artist discovering new ideas which clearly scared the life out of him because he made certain later on that he never had to deal with a new idea again. He unquestionably dropped out of the modern movement because he couldn't handle it."

Thomas Hart Benton, Two Trains, *design for a rug, linocut, circa 1930.*

Tile with abstracted floral design, designed by Thomas Hart Benton, executed by Rita Benton, 1924. This tile (which was given to Mildred Small as a Christmas present in 1924), transforms the compositional elements of Autumn Leaves into a multisided abstract design, with no single directional orientation or focus. Its swirling, energetic design suggests the direction of Jackson Pollock's later work. The design was painted on the tile by Rita, who later taught Pollock how to dribble ceramic glazes.

Chapter Seven
On the Road

"Place opens a door in the mind."

Taking Off

Something snapped inside Tom after his father's death. He began taking lone walks over in New Jersey and up into the Catskills, but rather than being satisfied by these excursions, his wanderlust only grew stronger. From 1925 to 1928, he disappeared every summer. When he set off on these jaunts, he told no one where he was going and set no itinerary. Even Rita did not know where he was or how to reach him. "Every year since we were married he has taken a trip by himself," she told a reporter in 1942. "I never know where he's going nor how long he will be away. I don't hear from him. He doesn't write. Sometimes he has stayed away two weeks, sometimes three months."

Rita once bluntly told Polly Burroughs, a Vineyard journalist: "He's the worst husband and worst father that ever lived. No American woman could have been married to Tom. You have to leave him alone and let him come and go as he pleases. If you bother him, heaven help you—he just won't talk, that's all." At one point in the mid-1920s, according to her friend Rachel Scott, Tom was away and Rita didn't have enough money at the end of the summer to return to New York from the Vineyard. She ended up doing some sewing to earn ticket money.

At the time of his visit to his dying father, Benton began to sketch Missouri characters. The first of the subsequent roamings, the excursion of 1926, centered around southwest Missouri and northwest Arkansas, where he had traveled as a boy during M.E.'s campaigns. As time went on, he traveled in a wider and wider circle around this region. Initially, his central motivation seems to have been a desire to wander, to reexplore the world of his childhood, rather than a desire to make art. During his first trip through the Ozarks, he would hike fifteen or twenty miles a day, which did not leave much time for sketching. But as he journeyed, his activity developed into an artistic mission—to make a visual record of the entire face of America, and particularly to discover the hidden pockets of old-fashioned culture that still existed in a world of their own, isolated from the bustle of the cities.

For a while, he just drew in pencil, but he discovered that as he hiked, the pages of his sketchbook rubbed together, smudging and obliterating the pencil lines. Consequently, he got into the habit of going over his drawings in the evening with pen and wash, which made the designs more durable and also enhanced the sculptural forcefulness of the effect. He would often draw a scene twice, concentrating once on the overall aspect and once on some element within the ensemble that caught his eye. He intended to use the drawings as material for his paintings, and he made the spatial relationships so clear that most of the drawings could easily be translated into clay sculpture. Though the sketches often reveal considerable virtuosity, he did nothing to polish the effect, to give it the suave and elegant look of the French modernist drafts-

Thomas Hart Benton, Cotton Pickers (Georgia), *egg tempera with oil glaze on canvas, 1928–29. Based on sketches he made in the cotton fields of central Georgia in the summer of 1928.* •

men we have come to admire. He did not bother to clean up shaky outlines or to erase the pencil guidelines. He emphasized form and sculptural clarity rather than elegance of line. Usually he employed a scratchy crosshatching that is rough and unpolished in effect. He probably prided himself to some extent on the crudeness of the general look, both because its roughness had a strongly American character and because it indicated that he had drawn the pieces on the spot, from life, rather than from photographs or studio models.

He was more comfortable with men than with women. "Women are extremely touchy about being regarded as old-fashioned or out-moded," he noted. They were inclined to feel that he intended ridicule when he asked to sketch them. With men it was different: "Male vanity soars above all the conditions of correctness in dress or manner. The man, like the barnyard rooster, is well satisfied with himself whether he is on a dunghill or in a modern coop. He may see plainly that he is no roaring success, but he puts the blame for that on circumstances. . . . As a consequence of this, men are easy to draw." Probably this preference for men over women had deeper roots. Through his travels around the United States, he sought to rediscover the world he had shared with his father. This had been almost entirely a man's world, in which his mother played no part.

There was one important precedent for Benton's examination of the American scene—the paintings of the watercolorist Charles Burchfield. In 1924 Burchfield began

Thomas Hart Benton, Cotton Hoeing, *pencil, ink, and wash on paper, 1926. During his walking trip through the Ozarks in 1926, Benton made many sketches of old-fashioned methods of hand agriculture.*

Charles Burchfield. The watercolorist from upstate New York helped inspire Benton's interest in small-town America.

showing his paintings regularly in New York. Thomas Craven once noted: "It is not too much to say that without Burchfield's pioneering discoveries Benton would never have found himself."

1926–27

In the spring of 1926, with the money he had received for decorating a sportsman's den, Benton headed west. "After five summers I felt I had pretty well exhausted the Vineyard as subject matter for my pictures," he later commented. Rita went up to the island and lived in the Brug barn. She did not hear from Tom, and when fall came could not decide whether to stay or return to New York. At the urging of a friend, she went back to the city, where she waited for Tom. "I guess I was gone for about five months," he muttered when at the end of his life he was questioned about this period. He then quickly changed the subject.

He seems to have left New York in late April or early May and traveled by train to New Orleans. From there he came up the Mississippi on a towboat to Helena, Arkansas, where he took the train to Little Rock. At one of the railroad crossings he made a quick sketch of an elderly black man with a donkey cart, which served as a basis for the painting and lithograph *Lonesome Road.*

From Little Rock he headed north on foot. He seems to have followed the course of the Buffalo River as far as Advance, where it joins with the White River, and then followed the White River up to Springfield, Missouri. He delighted in the broken, rutted roads, the crude log houses, the stores of undressed boards, the quaint speech and customs of the isolated hillbilly people. He enjoyed their simple meals of fried pork, corn bread, and molasses.

The small mountain hotels lacked steam heat or modern plumbing. Guests would usually gather around in ample time to answer the dinner bell, for all the food was set on the table at once and latecomers were likely to be out of luck. For a while Benton traveled with an old-fashioned salesman, who had a rickety car with a great boxlike cupboard filled with trinkets in the back. He would trade a cheap grade of coffee and three-for-a-penny candies for ginseng root and walnuts. He covered the dirt back roads, wherever a car could go, dickering for long hours, telling stories, making himself at home with and part of the life of the country people.

Mostly, Tom would walk fifteen or twenty miles a day, knapsack on his back, and put up in small mountain hotels or in the homes of the farmers. "To a person who is not dressed up like a dude," he boasted, "contacts with the people are easy to make. . . . The plain people of the hills, like all plain people in lonely places, are hospitable and friendly."

But not everyone. One day, Tom took a side trail and walked for an hour or more without seeing any human habitation. Finally, he came to a rambling log house with some gray-boarded outbuildings. A moment later, a man appeared, a big black hat pulled down over his forehead. His black eyes and his face carried no expression. He hefted a rifle across his arm. To show that he was unarmed, Tom hung his hands over the fence as he asked his way. The man pointed with his thumb, saying nothing. Slowly and deliberately, Tom marched up the trail, not turning around, though he could feel the man's eyes boring into his back.

The oddest adventure occurred when he was hiking along the banks of the White River. One day, after several hours of hard walking, hauling his heavy knapsack, he came to a crossing; the fishing resort where he hoped to stay was several miles upriver, on the opposite side. To his dismay, the ferryman, a plump, stolid man with a face like a pillow and small, squinty eyes, refused to take him across. Pillow-face just puttered around the boat, never looking in his direction. Eventually a team and wagon came down the road and boarded, and Tom hopped on before the sullen ferryman could

Thomas Hart Benton, Lonesome Road, *egg tempera and oil on canvas mounted on panel, 1927. Benton made the first sketch for* Lonesome Road *from a train window during his travels through Arkansas in 1926. The sad mood, the ungainly proportions, and the jerky rhythm of the painting all reflect his efforts to find a visual analogue to black blues music.*

137

raise the plank. The man could be heard muttering, "I know a clever guy when I see him, even in overalls."

On the other side of the river, Benton asked the ferryman for directions. The man pointed him toward a little path that headed off into the woods. "That's shorter," he commented. Still puzzled by the man's unfriendliness, Tom set off. After he had marched into the woods a few miles, the path disappeared.

For hours, Tom stumbled along. Shortly after dark, he reached the place he had been told of. A lean old man with a white beard was sitting on the steps. When Tom asked if he could stay for the night, the man looked him over doubtfully and replied, "There's no place here." At every house he passed, the people were unwilling to put him up. Finally, after midnight, he staggered into Forsyth, the county seat, woke up the hotelkeeper, and got to bed. The next morning, he learned that an Ozark bank robbery had taken place three days before and that warnings against strangers had spread across the hills. After he described his wanderings to the hotelkeeper, he learned that he had walked over fifty-two miles the previous day.

From Forsyth, Tom went on to Springfield, Missouri, where he stayed with his brother Nat. There he met up with his uncle Frank Miller, in whose company he headed southwest in a Model T Ford, traveling through the oil towns of the Texas panhandle. In Amarillo, he looked up his cousin Patty Oles, whose husband, Larry, was in the oil business.

The most important stop was Borger, Texas, where a rapid chain of events had spawned a sprawling city on desolate ranch land. On Monday, January 11, 1926, the Dixon Creek Oil and Refinery Company hit a gusher, which produced five thousand barrels of oil a day, ushering in a frantic search for more. Shortly afterward, a real estate promoter from Missouri, "Ace" Borger, purchased from a local rancher two hundred forty acres just to the west of this spot. Within ninety days, the population had grown from zero to thirty thousand. "Ace" Borger went on to create the Borger State Bank and to found four other boomtowns, in Texas and Oklahoma. His career ended abruptly when, in 1934, a disgruntled county clerk gunned him down in the Borger post office, in front of a crowd of spectators.

When Benton got there, Borger was still a town of rough shacks and oil rigs, with just a single street, about a mile in length, along which buildings had been thrown together in a completely haphazard fashion. Dust blew over everything. The hotels

Main Street, Borger, Texas, circa 1926. This photograph, which is contemporary with Benton's drawing, shows swarms of cars and a forest of advertising billboards. Mac's Studio, which took the photograph, was located just to the right of the Nyal Drugs building in the Oil Town *drawing.*

Thomas Hart Benton, Oil Town, *pencil, ink, and wash on paper, 1926. A sketch made from the second-floor window of Dilley's American Beauty Bakery. "I made many drawings of the western oil industry and the rough life accompanying it," Benton recalled. "One of these, a street scene in the then wild town of Borger, became the subject of one of my best-known 'Regionalist' pictures,* Boomtown.*"

that had bathtubs advertised the fact and charged as much for a bathtub as for a room. Out on the open plain beyond the town, a great column of black smoke rose from a carbon mill that burned thousands of cubic feet of gas every minute—an astonishing waste of natural resources for quick profit. The place was filled with devious-looking real estate men, shoddy preachers, muscular oil workers, and buxom, brightly painted whores, who served plates of tough steak in the restaurants. Several of the rough board hotels carried suggestive appeals: "Nice girls wanted here as helpers."

During his visit, Tom made a sketch, "Oil Town," which provided the basis for *Boomtown*, his first masterpiece of Regionalism. His vantage point was the second-floor window of Don Dilley's apartment at 518 Jackson—just above Dilley's American Beauty Bakery. "I can still remember Benton standing at the window sketching," Mrs. Dilley told a journalist in 1977. "He was an interesting person but I didn't know that he was to become so famous. He dressed very casually and his cousin, Patty Oles, did not approve of his attire. Larry, Patty, and Thomas Hart Benton were our guests for lunch. Then Benton did his sketching, while we talked about Kansas."

After Borger, Tom headed on to Taos, New Mexico, where there was a sizable artist's colony. From Taos, he seems to have taken the train to New York. He got back to the city at some point in the fall, probably September or October.

He apparently set off again in the summer of 1927, for he did not visit Martha's Vineyard that year. Rita told Polly Burroughs: "I lived in the barn alone that summer after T.P. was born. Tom was off . . . galavanting somewhere—I don't know where he was." Tom later confessed: "The bonds of marriage did not lay very heavily on my back." Curiously, however, no travel sketches can be securely dated to the summer of 1927, and his exact whereabouts at that time remain a mystery.

1928

Western Pennsylvania and West Virginia

Tom's summer sketching trip of 1928 was the longest and most productive of his career. He was working at the time on *The American Historical Epic* and in the course of his travels hoped to collect material for the series. This time, he did not travel alone but took along a student, Bill Hayden. They drove a beat-up Ford station wagon, which they had fixed up as a combined kitchen, bedroom, and workshop. It carried food, some thin mattresses, sketch pads, and other artist's materials. Hayden, who

Thomas Hart Benton, Cattle Loading, West Texas, egg tempera and oil on canvas mounted on panel, 1930. In 1926 and 1928, Benton made many sketches of the Texas panhandle, where the most substantial things in the little towns were the grain elevators and the water tanks by the sides of the railroads. He probably made the sketch for this painting late in the summer of 1928. •

came from a wealthy Chicago family, was young, carefree, very good-looking, and completely inexperienced with rustic character. An easygoing fellow, he accepted Benton for what he was and didn't pester him with questions.

From New York, the two men drove to Pittsburgh, where Benton sketched the steel mills. Somehow he managed to get inside one and draw the running steel amidst the flying sparks and the metallic din of open blast furnaces. They then drove through the coal country of western Pennsylvania. Benton wanted to draw the operations of the mines, but there was labor unrest in the region, and again and again they were turned away by the company police from the places where they stopped.

On the lower edge of West Virginia they found a mountainside mine that offered striking material for sketching. Rather than bothering to ask for permission, they just went to work. By the end of the morning, Benton had almost filled a sketchbook. During the lunch break, however, while he was showing his drawings to the workmen, a guard came up and asked to see them. The man was friendly, but worried about his job. He announced that Benton would have to see the superintendent, and told him to go down the road a quarter of a mile and wait. He would join him in a moment and take him to the office.

Benton and Hayden drove to the spot the guard had pointed out and waited ten minutes, then twenty, then half an hour. Tom took out a new sketchbook and made a drawing. It finally occurred to them that the guard was giving them a chance to make a getaway. So they started up the car, stepped on the gas, and roared past the company offices onto the open road, joking about their narrow escape.

Their confidence proved premature. About three quarters of an hour later, as they rounded a sharp curve, they were stopped by two armed deputies at a bridge just before a town. The sheriff had been informed by telephone of their trespass on mine property and instructed to confiscate all their papers. They were escorted to the courthouse and questioned. Fortunately, the police were not very well informed about the nature of their offense, and Tom harangued them eloquently about the rights of travelers. He explained that the problem was all in the guard's mind and that he had just stopped on the highway to make a drawing. He then took a deputy out to the car and handed him the sketchbook containing the last drawing he had made.

The deputy laughed. "Well, that doesn't look very dangerous," he declared. "I won't hold you boys." Tom reached for his sketchbook. "No, you'll have to leave that here," he was told. Tom started to protest. "Aw, get the hell outta here," said the deputy. "You ought to be glad you ain't put in the cooler."

He argued no longer. Fearful lest another telephone call would reveal the extent of their trespass, the two travelers decided to get out of the state. Studying the map, they found a narrow dirt road that cut across the highway and led into Virginia. Before dark they were beyond the jurisdiction of the West Virginia lawmen.

The Smoky Mountains and the Holy Rollers

The two men then spent several weeks in the Smoky Mountain country, where West Virginia, Virginia, Kentucky, North Carolina, and Tennessee converge. Benton was fascinated by the small farms that dotted this area, and by the simple life-style of the hill people who worked them. Several of his later lithographs were based on drawings he made during this trip. *The Meeting* depicts a meetinghouse in the mountains of West Virginia; *Cradling Wheat* a hill farm in eastern Tennessee; *Haystack* a farm in North Carolina; *Going Home* a wagon that Tom and Bill followed on a North Carolina country road.

Tom made many sketches of men felling timber at a logging camp in the area. One day, Bill, invited to a lumberjacks' breakfast, mistook the thick bacon-grease gravy for oatmeal and poured canned milk and sugar on it. Ashamed of his mistake, he nonetheless manfully ate it, while the boys looked on in wonder at his strange and virile tastes.

Fundamentalist religion was flourishing in the region, and in the mountains of western Virginia, on the edge of the coal pockets, Benton encountered a preacher, a Tennessee man, who was "missionaryin' " with his banjo. The fellow had written the word "Holiness" on his instrument case, and performed with three brethren who

Thomas Hart Benton, Share-cropper's Shack, pencil, ink, and wash on paper, 1928. Benton was one of the first American artists to record the poverty of the Deep South: he preceded the work of the WPA by half a decade. He probably sketched this dilapidated sharecropper's shack in central Georgia.

Thomas Hart Benton, Baptism, pencil, ink and wash on paper, 1928. Benton witnessed a Holy Roller service and baptism in the mountains of West Virginia. This sketch based on the scene was purchased by Frank Jewett Mather, a noted professor of art history at Princeton University.

played guitar. He told Tom that God had visited a black man in a meetinghouse in Los Angeles and had told him to spread the Lord's message around the world. Because of his belief in the black man's tidings, the preacher had been persecuted by his fellow Baptists, but he remained determined to carry on God's work.

Benton attended one of his services, in a deep mountain gully under the dark shade of high and thick timber. The preacher and his musicians gathered on a board platform that had been set up. When the music was at its height, a young girl in a simple white dress and a cheap but stylish little hat moved into the clear space in front of the stage. She began to dance, tapping her feet to the music and twitching her shoulders and hips. Two men began dancing around the girl, shouting, "Amen! Blessed be His Name!" Suddenly the girl cried out piercingly, "Jesus, sweet Jesus!" and flopped onto the ground, her breath coming fast, her hips rising and falling, her breasts quivering. Spit rolled down the chins of the men about her as they cried out, "Holy be His Name! Blessed be the will of God!"

Tom stayed on through a sermon and lunch; that afternoon, he witnessed a baptism in a dammed-up mountain stream. Two preachers waded into the pool, whooping and yelling, as several women and a couple of moronic-looking young men were immersed and came up spluttering and shouting. The final participant was a girl about twenty years of age, who was frightened by a water snake as she was ducked, and came out screaming at the top of her voice, while the bystanders laughed and taunted her.

"Tennessee Belle"

The two men now descended the Appalachians and entered a land of cotton that stretched from Texas through Arkansas, Mississippi, Alabama, and Georgia to the Carolinas. In the middle of Georgia they befriended an overseer. Benton made pictures all morning in the field, and during the lunch break he drew portrait sketches, while the black field hands gathered around him, full of hilarious comment.

By late August, the travelers had gone as far west as New Orleans. After a few days there, they decided to explore the old river towns of the Mississippi and its tributaries. One such river town below Natchez had been stranded seven miles inland. A rough road led from the town through the woods to the riverfront, and Bill and Tom decided to drive down it to see what the banks of the river looked like. Just as they were starting to investigate the river, they were hit by a terrific cloudburst, which

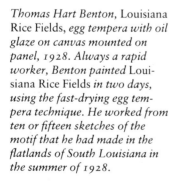

Thomas Hart Benton, Louisiana Rice Fields, *egg tempera with oil glaze on canvas mounted on panel, 1928. Always a rapid worker, Benton painted Loui-*siana Rice Fields *in two days, using the fast-drying egg tempera technique. He worked from ten or fifteen sketches of the motif that he had made in the flatlands of South Louisiana in the summer of 1928.*

turned the dirt road into a wallow of clinging mud. Their car sank in to the axles, and every movement of the wheels submerged them deeper.

They had to camp out four days in the place. While waiting for the mud to dry, they befriended two shanty-boat fishermen, one black, one white, who had been stranded there years before during a great flood. They told of the steamboat *Tennessee Belle*, the last of the old river packets, which would soon be loading cotton at Red River Landing, not far below.

The next day, Tom and Bill borrowed a mule from a nearby settlement and managed to get their car unstuck. Driving downriver, they began to search for Red River Landing. It proved hard to find. They ran up and down two parishes for two days before they found it, an isolated spot below the mouth of the river. It stood about a quarter of a mile from the levee, where the bank slanted abruptly down to the water.

For eight days they camped there, waiting for the boat. The heat was intense. Their butter melted, their bacon turned to rancid grease, and their cornmeal developed a case of worms. The river water—all they could find to drink—was at blood temperature. After three days of this, Bill drove to a town about fifteen miles back of the river

Thomas Hart Benton, Loading the "Tennessee Belle," *pencil, ink, and wash on paper, 1928.*

Thomas Hart Benton, Deck Hands' Crap Game, *pencil, ink, and wash on paper, 1928. Sketched on the deck of the Tennessee Belle. Benton reused the drawing for the* Arts of the South *panel of his Whitney mural.*

143

Thomas Hart Benton, Cotton Loading, *egg tempera and oil on canvas, 1928.* •

and returned with a new store of provisions and three hundred pounds of ice. This alleviated their discomfort but not their boredom.

On the morning of the eighth day, a line of wagons and trucks arrived with cotton. The blacks who lived in nearby cabins came out and sat expectantly on the landing. A lot of cars carrying white men showed up. Finally, around ten o'clock, the *Tennessee Belle* came down the river. For a moment it looked as though she were going to pass by, but after running past the landing a little, she turned, headed upstream, and eased gently in. Lines were put out and made fast. The black men began rolling the cotton down to the boat with grabhooks, and the two artists immediately went to work.

After they had made several drawings, they introduced themselves to the captain, who invited them aboard. He was much pleased by their story of waiting more than a week to make pictures of his boat. "Ah'm the last carryin' packet on the lower river," he boasted. Tom made his portrait, and the captain invited them both to dinner, which turned out to be a celebration in honor of the planters of the parish, a feast of rich, hot, spicy Cajun cooking. Tall glasses of what seemed to be iced tea were set before the guests, and Tom reached for the sugar. "Hold on, son," said an old gentleman sitting next to him. "You'd better taste it fust. It's sweet enough."

Benton tried it and discovered that it was not tea but wine. With a laugh, he exclaimed, "Doesn't the captain know that alcoholic liquor is under prohibition in this country?" "Son," replied the old man, "we live undah the Code Napoleon down heah. That code does not attack ouah digestions."

Eight years later, Tom read in a St. Louis paper that the *Tennessee Belle* had been wrecked and had gone down below Vicksburg.

Texas and New Mexico

It was early September, but the travelers continued to head west. When they reached the southwest corner of New Mexico, they decided to take a rest; they had driven eight thousand miles. Stocking up on groceries at one of the mining towns, they set off into the forest to find a cabin where they had been told they could make a camp.

Autumn had come, and it was cold. When night fell, they had not reached the cabin, so they threw down their mattresses by a stream that ran through a narrow canyon. They were just drifting off to sleep when they were wakened by a horrible screeching. They had no rifle to defend themselves against a savage creature, nothing at hand except a short-handled ax and a shovel. They got up, threw their stuff into the car, and turned on the lights. Tom began chopping brushwood and made a fire. They began to notice an irregular clickety-click sound, and in ten or fifteen minutes, two horsemen came galloping down the canyon, screaming like lunatics. "Here come the mountain lions," Tom said.

The newcomers were two cowboys, named Lem and Slim—both of them very drunk. Tom and Bill went to visit them the next day and found quite a bunch of characters crowded into a small cabin in the mountains—not only Lem and Slim but

Thomas Hart Benton, Slim, pencil, ink, and wash on paper, 1928.

Thomas Hart Benton, Lem, pencil, ink, and wash on paper, 1928.

145

a girl named Minnie, a boy named Jim, a drunken soldier, and a gray-haired man named Shack, who stank of whiskey. For two days, Tom joined the party and sketched them, but by the second afternoon he and Bill had had all they could take and decided to pull out. Rather than go back the way they had come, they decided to push onward, first through the forest, then through sheep land, to the road. On the third day they reached the highway. They were ready to make their way back to New York.

New York, 1926–29

In 1926, when their first child, Thomas Piacenza Benton, was born, Tom and Rita were so poor that they couldn't afford a cradle. Rita tucked the child in a bureau drawer. In the fall of that year, through Mike Robinson, Benton got a job teaching at the Art Students League in New York. This gave him $103 a month, his first significant salary. Rita was earning some money designing hats and producing sewing columns for ladies' magazines, and rent was only $45 a month, so for the first time they were able to get by without too much difficulty.

Finances remained tight, however, for many years. In 1929, when he received an invitation to lecture at Dartmouth College, Benton still had only one presentable suit, and that needed mending. Rita took it to a tailor, but when she went to pick it up she found a locked door and drawn blinds: a Brooklyn relative had died, and the tailor was paying his respects. As a consequence, Tom delivered his first college lecture on aesthetics in an overcoat buttoned to the chin. He evidently did a good job despite his attire, for the next year Smith College and the Art Students League also invited him to lecture.

At first Benton's classes at the League were extremely small, but they contained some very interesting people, including some who would later be famous. Reginald Marsh attended, and Anne Baxter, Frank Lloyd Wright's granddaughter, who became a well-known actress and movie star. So did "Sandy" Calder, who later commented: "Benton's motto was 'Even if it's wrong you make it definite'—[this] might have been his *malheur*."

Charles Pollock began to study with Benton in 1926, and he was soon followed by his brothers Frank, Sande, and Jackson. Rita mothered them all and they became virtually part of the Benton family. Frank Pollock recalls that when he got to New York in the fall of 1928, he took a cab to his brother Charles's apartment on Eighth Avenue but found that he didn't have enough money to pay the fare. Charles didn't either, so he ran up two flights to the Bentons' apartment and borrowed the money from them—although they were nearly as poor as Charles. Frank recalls: "Rita took care of the Pollocks, see; she really loved us all."

Jackson Pollock often baby-sat for the Bentons. "Benton tried his damnedest to work with Pollock," Manuel Tolegian once remarked, "and he was very happy that Pollock was baby-sitting because Benton worked at home and could personally instruct him. I remember Benton making corrections on Pollock's works. It may have been one of those that years after, when Benton was looking at a new book of Pollock illustrations, made him suddenly shout, 'I did that! That's not Pollock's work.' You'd have thought that the Bentons would have worried about having such an undependable guy around, but Pollock behaved himself around Benton and had great respect for him."

Stanley William Hayter recalls that Jackson "never mentioned his own father" but "had found a substitute one in Benton." Philip Pavia reminisces, "We used to laugh. . . . Benton and all those Leonardo poses—poor Jackson was all wrapped up in wop culture then." According to George McNail, Pollock modeled himself on Tom completely. "There was a rhythm, a flow, between them from the beginning to the end

Thomas Hart Benton, Abstract Screen with Sea Motif, *oil on canvas with aluminum and painted wood frame, 1925–26. In the late twenties, Benton joined a collective of artists organized by Ralph Pearson who produced one-of-a-kind designs for hooked rugs. The group created the decor for the Garden City, Long Island, residence of Albert M. Briggs, an ardent fisherman. The living room featured stuffed fish, fish rugs, and this decorative screen by Benton, which opened up to reveal Mr. Briggs's fishing snapshots and fishing trophies. Benton's wave design for the piece reveals his continuing interest in Japanese prints, which he had discovered as an art student in Chicago. With the proceeds from this decorative commission, Benton financed his first sketching trip to the Ozarks.* •

of their lives. It was a physical, gestural rhythm; teacher and student were *bonded,* you might say."

"It was obvious from the very beginning," Benton told the columnist Leonard Lyons in 1965, "that Pollock was a born artist. The only thing I taught him was how to drink a fifth a day."

Since Tom had seldom been able to afford a model on his own, he felt impelled to sketch from the model in his painting class, right alongside his students. Rather than putting on airs, he liked to become one of them—to be accepted by them as a fellow workman. After class, he often invited his students home for a party or a spaghetti dinner.

Reggie Wilson recalls that Benton was only interested when a student worked his way. Once Wilson came back from Ohio with forty or fifty watercolors, and Benton said: "Well, these are pretty good, but they're not what I would have suggested you should be doing, so there is nothing I can say about them."

Mervin Jules recalls that Benton was hard on women. "He would blast the women," Jules states, "using vulgar language, so that they would dwindle away by the end of the month. Then, to keep Benton on as our teacher, we'd have to browbeat new women into joining the class—sometimes people we knew wouldn't last more than a week with this treatment." Elizabeth Pollock, Charles's first wife, remembers

148

Benton with distaste: "I was always ill at ease with [him] because he was such a cold person—a very small man and feisty like a bulldog. He was what I call 'juiced,' the kind of person who sips at something all day long; it made him gruff."

Benton's teaching method at the Art Students League was most unusual for the time, although it has since become standard. The traditional French academic method progressed from simple to more complicated subject matter but hardly analyzed the manner of artistic approach. The goal was not to achieve mental understanding but simply to reproduce reality as accurately as possible. The student began by drawing plaster casts, then moved to the live model, and finally, almost as an afterthought, attempted to create finished compositions.

Benton taught very differently, showing his students how to break down and analyze artistic issues. Alex Horn recalls his method: "Other art students in the other classes were attempting to solve numbers of artistic problems concurrently; learning how to manipulate paint, how to express a form, how to draw, how to compose a picture—all on one canvas. We, on the other hand, seemed to be the kind of people who needed to break down the total complex problem of creating a work of art into its smaller components and solve each of these by itself, one after the other. Benton taught this way."

A phrase that Tom constantly invoked was "the hollow and the bump," which he had adapted from the Synchromists. Stanton Macdonald-Wright had discovered this principle while studying Michelangelo; Willard Wright, in his book *Modern Painting,* applied it to the creations of Cézanne. Alex Horn recalls: "The pursuit of 'the hollow and the bump' was one of these problems that we had separated out as one separates a mustang from the rest of the herd, and we were out to break it to our bidding. 'The hollow and the bump' had a symbolic significance like 'yin and yang.' It expressed for us the polarity from negative, recessive softness to positive, solid, projecting forcefulness."

Critical Responses, 1927

Benton began to shift his artistic allegiances in 1927, breaking his ties with the modernist painters and allying himself instead with modernist architects. Critics writing about his work began to move their focus of attention from his handling of form to his subject matter—in particular, his concern with the contemporary American scene.

The mastermind behind this shift was not Thomas Craven but Lewis Mumford, a

Benton on front page of New York American, *1927.*

writer on architecture and an editor of *The Dial*—and, incidentally, Tom's neighbor on Martha's Vineyard. It was he who built up Benton's reputation as a mural painter, recognized the significance of his colorful renderings of American characters, and first articulated the concept of Regionalism.

The American Historical Epic had never won much favor from modernist painters, but from the beginning it had attracted the attention of architects, for its combination of figuration with strongly geometricized shapes harmonized well with the current popularity of Art Deco architectural ornament. Benton first exhibited his epic at the Architectural League through the support of the architect Ely Kahn, and it won some warm reviews, including one from Virgil Barker, who termed it "the most notable exhibit of the entire exposition."

In 1927 Benton showed both chapters of his epic, along with four designs he had produced on speculation for a space in the New York Public Library, at the New Gallery at 600 Madison Avenue. At this point, Lewis Mumford jumped into the fray, writing both a stirring introduction to the catalogue and an essay for the influential liberal magazine the *New Republic*. "Mr. Benton," Mumford declared, "has rescued the picture with a subject from the banality of the academies, with their lay figures that represent, always in the same garments and the same tedious postures, Blind Justice, Majestic Law, Honest Labor." Instead Benton had gone to real life for his subject matter: "He draws people out of their soil, like potatoes, with the earth still clinging to them." Mumford closed his piece with a vigorous plea that architects find a place for Tom's work. "These panels are a summons to the architect. . . . I do not believe that paintings of this order will long go a-begging."

Up to this time, Thomas Craven had presented Benton as a modernist, albeit one fascinated by the formal accomplishments of the past. He had placed primary stress on the painter's sculptural manipulation of form. In 1927, however, in a note on

"American Month in the Galleries," Craven adopted a new approach—one that would characterize virtually all the criticism of Benton's work thereafter. For the first time, he presented Benton's achievement as a direct challenge to the French modernist school. Benton, Craven noted, had deliberately rejected the modernist pursuit of non-representational form, a direction, he argued, that had become mechanical and sterile. More, Benton brought to his painting a vigorously chauvinistic nationalism—"an Americanism which has challenged the modern European tradition with belligerent confidence." According to Craven, it proclaimed, in unequivocal language, "the emancipation of the American artist from the French tradition."

Shortly afteward, this conclusion was echoed in a brief anonymous note on Benton's work in *Survey* magazine, which reproduced several of his paintings of American characters. It introduced the series with the simple words: "Here are Americans."

The Delphic Exhibitions

Benton consolidated his position as a painter of American life in October and November 1929, when he staged a show titled "The South" at the Delphic Galleries, 9 East 57th Street. All 109 pieces in the show were based on his 1928 trip. About five were oils, the remainder watercolors and drawings. They were divided into four main groups: "King Cotton" (sketches of south Georgia, Mississippi, Alabama, and Louisiana), "The Lumber Camp" (West Virginia, Tennessee, and Kentucky), "Holy Roller Camp Meeting" (Cumberland Mountains), and "Coal Mines" (West Virginia).

The show was covered by all the New York papers and was even praised in the Chicago *Tribune*. Frank Jewett Mather, a noted professor of art history at Princeton University, purchased one of the Holy Roller drawings, and Thomas Beer, author of *The Mauve Decade*, purchased the painting *Slow Train*, a representation of a steam engine halted by cows on the track. Lloyd Goodrich wrote two glowing reviews, one in the *New York Times,* the other in *Arts*. "His pictures of river traffic are particularly stirring," Goodrich commented, "with some of the sweep of Mark Twain's *Life on the Mississippi;* they actually achieve the epic quality for which he has strenuously aimed in the past."

Lewis Mumford. As an editor of The Dial, *he was a strong supporter of Benton's early work. The support ended after Benton became famous.*

The most important painting in the show was *Boomtown*, Tom's evocation of Borger, Texas. Tawdry but romantic boomtowns occupied a major place in popular Western fiction, beginning with Owen Wister's *The Virginian* of 1902. The most popular writer of such thrillers was Zane Grey, a dentist from Ohio, who in the years between 1917 and 1926 placed at least one of his novels on every annual best-seller list. Appropriately, the boomtown in Grey's 1918 novel *The U.P. Trail* is named Benton, after the painter's senatorial ancestor.

It's interesting to compare the painting with photographs of Borger taken the same year. The photos confirm many of the main elements of the painting: the bleakness of Main Street, the humped roofs of the swarms of cars, the forest of advertising billboards. Benton, however, exaggerated the vertical elements of the composition— the telephone poles, the oil derricks, and the great plume of black smoke in the distance. By increasing the vertical markers, he transformed the town from one lost in the spatial vastness to one that seems to prance and gallop downward from the horizon. In his account of Borger, he described the town as an "exultant . . . exploitative whoopee party," and in his painting the buildings seem to dance in a jubilant, syncopated frenzy.

Indeed, the vulgarity of the painting is obvious—Tom was deliberately thumbing his nose at the hermetic integrity of modernism. Lettering, as it happens, was one of the favorite gimmicks of the Cubists (and of Stuart Davis), so Benton cheerfully splashed it everywhere on his canvas. But his signs contain not cute French phrases like "Ma Jolie" but crudely American messages like "Rooms," "Drugs," and "Lunch."

Thomas Hart Benton, Boom-town, oil on canvas, 1927–28. After oil was discovered there, Borger grew in population from zero to ninety thousand in just three months. The place swarmed with real estate men, preachers, cowboys, oil workers, painted women, and Texas Rangers. On the outskirts, a carbon mill burned thousands of cubic feet of gas each minute, raising a huge black column of smoke. The hotels that had bathtubs advertised the fact. •

The sign "Mother Holl's, Bed and Board, Baths 50 cents, Girls Wanted" suggests the sleazy immorality of the place and alludes with raw directness to the great American world of commerce. "Midway Dance" in the painting closely resembles the actual "Ma's Dance Hall" in Borger, which the Amarillo *Daily News* described in 1926: "There are 200 ladies of the kind known as 'dance hall girls.' [They] will challenge you to a dance, at 25 cents a dance. Of this sum each girl gets a dime."

Benton's most important alteration was his replacement of "Nyal Drugs" of his on-the-spot drawing with the fictitious "Red Star Theatre" (the main movie palace in Borger, The Rig, was located a bit farther down Main Street). Thus a movie theater stands at the pictorial heart of *Boomtown*, at the center of both the surging space and the iconographical message of the scene. Tom, of course, had himself worked in the movie trade, and his later claims for the significance of mural painting as an art parallel Rex Ingram's claim for the importance of film: its accessibility to the masses and its contemporary point of view. The stage flats he designed were his first work of mural scale. The flimsiness of the buildings in *Boomtown*, in fact, suggests that they are no more than stage sets.

Reality and art mingled in the world of film. William S. Hart had been an actual cowboy and counted among his friends Wyatt Earp, Bat Masterson, and range detective Charles Siringo. Al Jennings, a Western badman pardoned by Theodore Roosevelt, went on to star in a film about his exploits, which was directed by William Matthew Tilghman, the U.S. marshal who had sent him to prison. *The Bank Robbery* (1908) was filmed on the street in Cache, Wyoming, where Jennings's holdup had occurred. Filmmakers scouted out actual boomtowns as locations; E. Mason Hopper went to Jerome, Arizona, in 1917, when it was in the midst of a mining boom, to film a cowboy movie titled *The Hidden Spring*.

Non-panchromatic film did not register clouds, and left the sky a featureless blur at the top of the screen. Consequently, early movies tended to display high horizons and a strong vertical tilt. Film stock improved, but the eccentric tip of the camera remained. John Ford's horizons, for example, while sometimes high and sometimes low, are consistently eccentric in their placement. This vertical tip may well have been the inspiration for the tilted space of *Boomtown*.

Moviemakers such as Ford also developed an effective shorthand for conveying character. A tall Stetson and a bandanna make a cowboy; a fedora and a suit coat make a speculator; a vest makes a saloonkeeper. Benton made use of this typological shorthand. In the foreground of *Boomtown*, for example, two men are shaking hands on a deal. One, wearing a Stetson and a red bandanna, is clearly a cowboy; the other, wearing a dark suit, is probably a fast-talking city slicker. The fight in the foreground also presents a less romantic version of the duel on Main Street that concluded the standard Western movie. It features some cowboys, a flapper, and a Texas ranger coming in to break it up. From the cast of characters, we can easily guess the motivation for the battle—a girl—as well as its pathetic outcome. Thus modernism meets the movies in Benton's Borger—in a boomtown based on extravagant fantasies, a crossroads at the juncture of crude reality and fabulous Western myths.

Southern Identity

In the summer of 1925, William Jennings Bryan, whose spirited 1896 presidential campaign had swept Tom's father into Congress, died ignominiously in Tennessee, five days after he successfully prosecuted a young high school teacher, John Thomas Scopes, for teaching the theory of evolution. In the course of the trial, the lawyer for the defense, Clarence Darrow, had made Bryan look ridiculous as he questioned him about the literal accuracy of the Bible. Yes, Bryan believed that Joshua made the sun stand still. Yes, he believed that God made Eve from one of Adam's ribs. Yes. Yes.

The trial turned the attention of the nation toward the strange fundamentalist practices of the Bible Belt. H. L. Mencken, for example, sent a lengthy dispatch to the Baltimore *Evening Sun* describing a Holy Roller revival meeting he witnessed in a mountain glade near Dayton, Tennessee—the site of the Scopes trial. Mencken's description of this service forms a striking parallel with Benton's drawings of Holy Rollers, made just a few years later. At the same time, the comparison with Mencken suggests the curious ambivalence of Tom's approach. The writer approached Southern life as an East Coast outsider, appalled by the primitivism of American society outside the big cities. The painter, on the other hand, looked at it with a certain sympathy, as a relic of the rural Southern culture he had known as a boy. William Jennings Bryan, after all, had been a crony of his father. A freethinker himself, Benton could not honestly participate in the wildly emotional practices of the Holy Rollers or the other fundamentalist sects of the South. But his emotions were stirred. Sometimes, when he witnessed these services, "My sides would split with suppressed laughter." But not always. "There were times when its Dionysiac madness moved me deeply," he later confessed.

Thomas Hart Benton has come to be viewed as a spokesman for a Midwestern viewpoint; by the mid-1930s, he was invariably grouped with two other Midwestern artists, John Steuart Curry and Grant Wood. Significantly, however, when he first began to paint the American scene, the region he focused on was not the Midwest but the South. Indeed, in 1929, when he exhibited the sketches and paintings from his cross-country trip of 1928 at the Delphic Galleries, he titled the show "The South." To a large degree, in fact, the attitudes that generated his first Regionalist works were not Midwestern but Southern; and many of the peculiar and distinctive features of his work are bound up with the issue of Southern identity.

Wood and Curry were both Northerners—Wood was from Iowa and Curry from

Kansas, a state settled by Northern abolitionists. Benton, on the other hand, was from Missouri, a border state placed at the intersection of the South and the Midwest. His father had fought with the Confederates and was an advocate of the Populist movement, which gained political dominance only in the former Confederate states.

Curiously enough, while Benton traveled widely and painted scenery stretching from Georgia to Texas, the one region he hardly touched on was the northern belt of the Midwest—Ohio, Illinois, Iowa, Kansas, Nebraska, and Minnesota. Throughout his career, he expressed a renegade Southern viewpoint, and this fact provides a key to understanding both his sensibility and the extraordinary controversy that he stirred up.

Though his viewpoint was Southern, it differed fundamentally from that of the central states of the Confederacy, such as Virginia, South Carolina, and Georgia—the old strongholds of the tidewater aristocracy. His cultural heritage was that of the hill people of Missouri, Arkansas, and Tennessee. These folk had been unable to compete with the large slave-driven cotton and tobacco plantations of the tidewater and moved back into the less desirable land of the hills. Parochial and isolated, they clung to their old-fashioned ways and looked at the outside world with suspicion.

Benton's drawings of the South appeared at just the time that a renaissance in Southern literature was taking place. The very term "Regionalism," which came to be applied to the Midwestern painters, was initially developed in the 1920s by a group of Southern writers, poets, and essayists. Reacting against the urban, mechanized, commercial world of the large cities of the Northeast, they promoted a regional and agrarian point of view. Lewis Mumford, who in the twenties strongly supported Benton's work, popularized a wider extension of this term through an essay on "The Theory and Practice of Regionalism," which he published in the *Sociological Review* in April 1928.

The Civil War, of course, constitutes the experience that has most strongly marked off the South from the rest of the country, but this military defeat was followed by long decades of subjugation in the economic, social, and political spheres. In the postwar period, the South developed a distinctive set of cultural features, many of them pernicious, such as the one-horse farmer, one-crop agriculture, one-party politics, the sharecropper, the poll tax, the white primary, the Jim Crow car, and the lynching bee. Throughout the 1930s, the 1940s, and even the 1950s, the South remained agricultural and rural. What C. Vann Woodward has christened "The Bulldozer Revolution" did not hit the Southern states until the 1960s.

One of the most conspicuous traits of the American way of life has been its prosperity, but to a large degree the South has not shared in this abundance. Since the Civil War, it has lagged dramatically behind the Northern states. In 1880, for example, the per capita wealth of the South was less than a third that of other regions of the country—the same differential as that between the per capita wealth of agricultural Russia and industrialized Germany in the same period.

Therefore, to be Southern and self-aware entails a double burden of criticism toward American life: a sense of guilt toward the Southern past and a sense of distance, of alienation, from the American mainstream. It engenders resentment over one's exclusion from the American feast. Tom Benton's paintings of the 1930s, in fact, were filled with brutal criticism of American society. Unlike the paintings of the Marxists or the Social Content School, however, his criticism was turned in upon itself and did not offer the viewer a simple solution to society's ills. His attitude bears more resemblance to that of one of the Southern writers, such as William Faulkner, who did not write reformist tracts but instead sympathetically explored the life of social deviants.

The South has also developed a distinctive consciousness both of history and of place. In the last volume of his ten-volume study of history, Arnold Toynbee advanced the theory that "the vividness of historical impressions is apt to be proportionate to their violence and painfulness" and speculated that "a child who had lived through the American Civil War in the territory of the Southern Confederacy would be likely to grow up more historical-minded than one who had lived through the same experience in the North."

Thus Southern writers who emerged around 1930 presented a significantly different perspective on American life than the Midwesterners who had dominated American literature in the twenties. The latter—such as Theodore Dreiser, Sherwood Anderson, and Sinclair Lewis—had almost completely lacked an interest in history. As Woodward has noted:

"The characters in the novels of Dreiser, Anderson, and Lewis appear on the scene from nowhere, trailing no clouds of history, dissociated from the past. In the works of some later writers the historical perspective is even more flat. Hemingway's characters appear to live completely in the present. To emphasize their historical rootlessness they are invariably pictured as expatriates, as wanderers, as soldiers or adventurers. They are temporarily in Italy or Spain, in France or Africa, in Cuba or the Florida Keys. A Hemingway hero with a grandfather is inconceivable, and he is apparently quite as bereft of uncles, aunts, cousins, and in-laws, not to mention neighbors and poor relations."

By contrast, the Southern fiction produced in the 1930s by such writers as William Faulkner, Eudora Welty, Robert Penn Warren, and Allen Tate presented a different imaginative vision. Tate has written that the distinguishing feature of this school is "the peculiar historical consciousness of the Southern writer." The Southern literary renaissance, he maintained, was "a literature conscious of the past in the present." Indeed, the haunting persistence of the past is perhaps the major theme of Southern fiction. As Faulkner's Gavin Stevens says in *Intruder in the Dust*, "The past is never dead. It's not even past."

It would be going too far, of course, to maintain that Benton's paintings reflected a viewpoint strictly parallel to that of the Southern writers. His great mural cycles, however, reveal a consciousness of time and history that stands out as unique in American art. Both *A Social History of Indiana* and *A Social History of Missouri* unfold through time in a great historical panorama.

The Southern writers, in addition, tend to convey a powerful sense of the significance of place. On the whole, Americans have not been bound to a particular location. According to Thornton Wilder, "Americans are abstract. They are disconnected. They have a relation, but it is to everywhere, to everybody, and to always. . . . Americans can find in environment no confirmation of their identity, try as they may." C. Vann Woodward, however, has argued that place and locality have played a larger role in the South than in the rest of America. The Mississippian Eudora Welty wrote: "I am myself touched off by place. The place where I am and the place I know, and other places that familiarity with and love for my own make strange and lovely and enlightening to look into, are what set me to writing my stories. . . . Place opens a door in the mind."

Chapter Eight
The New School Murals

José Clemente Orozco. Benton always got on well with the Mexican muralist but clashed with his paramour and dealer, Alma Reed.

"Here's a man who took the whole face of America and tried to make a work of art out of it."

The Commission

Alma Reed, who ran the Delphic Galleries, was blond and buxom, a very good-looking woman. Before becoming an art dealer, she had worked for the Hearst papers in San Francisco and had been sent to Mexico to cover the revolution. There she became involved with the governor of the Yucatán, who left his Indian wife and was about to marry her when he was shot. Despite this setback, she stayed on in Mexico, and shortly afterward met José Clemente Orozco, the mural painter, who also left an Indian wife to run away with her.

In 1927 Alma Reed brought Orozco to New York and established the Delphic Galleries to promote his work. Funding was provided by a woman who wanted to reinstitute the Delphic mysteries in the Western world. This was too deep for Tom Benton, but Reed could not sustain a gallery with just one artist, and Orozco liked his work, so he was signed on. He then brought in his friend Mike Robinson (who a bit earlier had helped him with a job at the Art Students League). Orozco did not want any of the other major Mexican muralists, such as Rivera or Siqueiros, who represented direct competition, to be part of his gallery, but he was willing to have Miguel Covarrubias, a cartoonist from Mérida. These four—Orozco, Benton, Robinson, and Covarrubias—became the stable of the gallery, although Reed also included the work of a few young artists in her temporary exhibitions.

The Delphic Galleries lasted about a year and a half, until the money ran out. Reed always put most of her effort into promoting Orozco, but nonetheless, Benton established a national reputation during the relatively brief period in which she handled his work.

Reed's principal mission after she arrived in New York was to find a mural commission for Orozco. In 1930, when she heard that a new building was being constructed for the New School for Social Research, she went to Alvin Johnson, the director, and offered Orozco's services as a muralist free of charge. Johnson accepted; the two agreed that Orozco would paint a mural for the school's top-floor cafeteria, in exchange for the expenses of execution.

Word of the commission got out to Benton's friend Ralph Pearson, a well-known artist, teacher, and writer on art, who had founded a rug-designing collective to which Tom belonged. The six-foot-six Pearson made an imposing figure when he came to Johnson in indignation. He hotly complained that an "alien" had been commissioned to do a mural, when Tom Benton, an authentic American, whose ancestor had dueled with Andrew Jackson and caused him to limp for life, was unable to find a wall and had to live off what he made from his easel paintings—about five hundred dollars a year.

"Ralph," Johnson replied, "come down off your high horse. I know something of Tom Benton. I could give him just as good a room as I'm giving Orozco. But on the same terms. No pay. And he can't afford it."

Soon afterward, Lewis Mumford, who was still vigorously supporting Tom's work, introduced Rita to Alvin Johnson at a Greenwich Village gathering. She had been well briefed about the whole situation and promptly offered her husband's services. Johnson, of course, was delighted to get paintings by two well-known artists rather than just one. He agreed to supply the materials and offered Tom a space for an egg-tempera mural in the New School's boardroom. The next day, Tom came over to the New School. "Sure," Tom told Johnson. "I'll paint you the mural if you'll give me the eggs."

Unfortunately, Alma Reed responded very negatively to the news, feeling that Benton had taken advantage of Orozco's opportunity to gain one for himself. This was, in fact, precisely what had occurred, although Tom, for his part, could protest that as his dealer she had not done much to further his interests. But she found a number of people who were receptive to her complaints, so once again, as at the Forum Exhibition, Benton found himself saddled with the title of opportunist.

The situation, happily, did not affect his friendly relationship with Orozco. In 1930 Benton arranged for a show of Orozco's work at the Art Students League. But he had less and less to do with Alma Reed and the Delphic Galleries, and had severed his relationship altogether by the time the gallery folded.

Both Benton and Orozco asked Johnson to set the theme for their murals. Johnson asked them each to treat what he considered the most powerful living movement of his time. Orozco fixed on the revolutionary movement; Benton on the development of new technology. He titled his scheme *America Today*.

Execution

Benton painted *America Today* with remarkable speed: he took only nine months for the entire project. He had already accumulated huge numbers of sketches from his

Thomas Hart Benton, America Today: Instruments of Power. *Benton combined symbols of power to show how modern technology has transformed human life.*

trips around the United States, particularly from his long journey of 1928, and consequently he needed to do very little research. The great challenge was to organize the material. It took two thirds of his time, six months, to devise the scheme and construct a clay model for study purposes. He completed the actual painting in a mere three months, spending just a little more than a week on each of the nine large panels, which cover about seventy-five square feet of wall space apiece.

Though Alvin Johnson provided no pay, he proved the ideal patron. It was he who supplied the loft where Benton executed the panels, and he skillfully used his influence to help the artist in other ways. "I have to get into a modern steel mill," Tom told Johnson. "Steel is the very focus of my picture. But those babies won't let me get near steel. 'An artist! What the hell does an artist want with steel? Out with him; must be a communist.' " One of Johnson's good friends on Wall Street obtained permission for Benton to visit the Sparrow's Point plant in Maryland. He featured the hot center of the plant on the New School wall.

Johnson got in the habit of dropping by nearly every day to observe the progress of the paintings, and he was impressed by how systematically Benton worked. He later recalled: "[Benton] had a color table, black at one end, white at the other; red was such and such a percentage of white. With the right relation of darks and lights, plastic form is inevitable."

Clemente Orozco painted his murals in fresco directly on the New School walls, but Benton chose not to tie the fate of his works to that of the building. He constructed special wall panels for his paintings, using plywood wallboard reinforced with one-by-three-inch cradling. This created a surface as heavy and as solid in its own right as a wall of light construction. He glued heavy linen to these panels and coated them with three coats of a gesso made of glue, water, and whiting, to build up a plasterlike surface, about one-eighth inch thick.

For the underpainting he used distemper (a mixture of the pigments with water and a glue or casein binder). The final coat was egg tempera—dry pigment mixed with a half-and-half mixture of egg and water. The pigment contained no oil, although on some of the dark areas he completed the effect with transparent glazes of oil paint. He topped the finished painting with a coating of wax, to protect the surface and produce an eggshell gloss.

Reginald Marsh, who met Benton at this time, later recalled: "When I first got acquainted with him, I called upon him frequently, apparently always in time to help

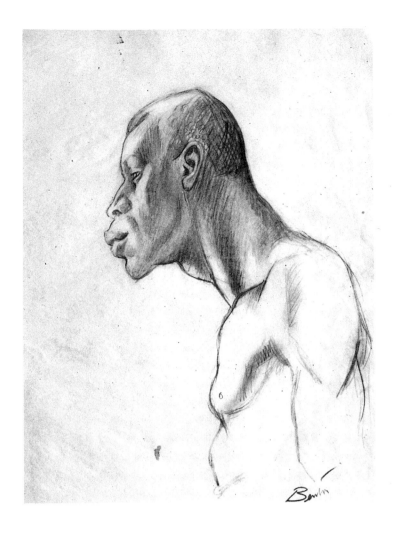

him carry about the studio his 400 lb. murals which he was painting for the New School of Social Research. (I posed for the negro with the drill and learned egg-tempera as a reward.) The time was summer and it was amusing to watch Benton, muscular in his underwear, sit low in an armchair, survey the mural, suddenly load his brush with a lot of tempera goo, crouch like a cat, spring across the room in a flying tackle, scrub the brush around in great circles, catch his breath, and then resume his place in the chair." Marsh noted that Benton was "a little, swarthy and cocky man . . . a colorful, scrappy, uncouth person," and noted that he "resembles a well-nourished Sicilian bootblack rather than a mid-west oldstock American."

Transporting the heavy panels to the New School was a major enterprise. Some were bent while being lowered the twelve stories from the loft to the ground; the resultant stresses in the paint layer caused flaking and cracking in later years. By late December, the large panels had been set in place, and on January 15, 1931, Benton and Orozco held a reception for the formal unveiling of their murals.

Contemporary Criticism

Benton later maintained that his New School murals stirred up a storm of criticism—that they were called "tabloid art," "cheap nationalism," and "modernist effrontery." No doubt all these epithets were eventually hurled at them, but not until later on in the 1930s, when his political position had hardened and the Depression had set in more deeply. The phrase "tabloid art," for example, was thrown at Benton's work in 1934 by Stuart Davis. But the initial press attention was overwhelmingly positive.

The works were reproduced in all the major art magazines; they were featured in the *New York Times* even before they were completed. In the two months after the unveiling, twenty thousand people came to see them. The most important review was Lloyd Goodrich's essay in *Arts*, "The Murals of the New School." Goodrich welcomed Benton's repudiation of the "lifeless productions" of "anaemic graduates of the American Academy at Rome" and his wholehearted avoidance of "the pallid attenuation of the Puvis de Chavannes school." With delight, he noted that Benton's work displayed a "restless vitality" and that "everything in his pictures is concrete and definite, can be touched and grasped." The rich strain of caricature brought to mind Nast, Frost, Kemble, and some of the comic-strip artists; his flamboyant strain of Western humor recalled Mark Twain.

Without exception, this burst of publicity was strongly favorable. But there were some significant omissions in the flood of praise. Notably silent was Lewis Mumford, who had long been an ardent supporter of Benton's work. Behind the scenes, moreover, it appears that the murals stirred up violent controversy.

Lloyd Goodrich recalls that shortly after he submitted his long piece on the murals, Forbes Watson, the editor of the magazine, came up to him at a dinner party at the Whitney Museum and said, "I'd like to talk to you about that article." Watson took him into another room and began attacking what he had written. "I don't want to use that article!" he exclaimed. "Benton is a very poor artist, very pretentious, and I don't want to use it." This was the first time that Goodrich had ever been turned down by the magazine, and he was very disturbed. He stayed up late rewriting what he had said, cutting it down considerably. The next day, he called Watson, who in the interim had changed his mind. "I'm using it the way you submitted it," Watson told him.

"America Today"

In this cycle, Benton finally found a means of reconciling the language of modernism with the narrative themes that had excited him as a child. He showed a complete cross-section of American life, particularly in its working aspects. Lloyd Goodrich commented in 1986: "Here's a man who took the whole face of America and tried to make a work of art out of it. . . . It was a new technique completely in mural painting, of actually taking reality and making mural art directly out of it."

As Emily Braun has rightly noted, these works were painted before the effects of the 1929 crash had become fully apparent, before it was clear that the Depression would be a long-lasting one. In spirit, the paintings mark the end of the Roaring Twenties, the Jazz Age.

Benton did not present a smooth flow of narrative but employed abrupt, restless juxtapositions of different scenes. The panels have no single reading. They can be followed sequentially, crosswise, or in a zigzag pattern across the room. These different juxtapositions evoke complex contrasts of meaning. Thus, for example, the black cotton picker in the panel of *Deep South* contrasts with the white sharecropper who stands across from him in the same panel, but also complements the black driller in the panel of *City Building* on the other side of the room. As Emily Braun wrote: "Like a Gershwin tune, the murals evoke a jazzy rhythm syncopated visually by the jaunty silver bolts of the moldings."

Instruments of Power

In *Instruments of Power*, a gigantic bolt of lightning, which echoes the nervous lines of the silver molding, announces the overall theme of the panel—the control of energy. Benton gathered within the assemblage the various forms of industrial power. Electricity is symbolized by a metal power tower and a hydroelectric dam constructed of the new miracle material reinforced concrete; steam by a rushing locomotive; internal combustion by a cross-section of an engine.

Benton was particularly fascinated by the wonders of modern transportation: a rushing black iron locomotive, spouting purple clouds of smoke; a red airplane with blurred propeller; and a serenely floating white dirigible. Throughout the mural cycle, the train remains the central symbol of the energy of modern industry. There are nine of them in the pictorial ensemble (not counting a view of the interior of a subway), with one in each panel except *Steel* and *City Activities with Dance Hall*.

Through the juxtaposition of the different forms of power, Benton suggested the issue he would explore in his other panels: the manner in which society is transformed through work and technology. For as Charles Beard, one of the founders of the New School, pointed out, a machine civilization is a dynamic one, which continually transforms itself: "The order of steam is hardly established before electricity invades it; electricity hardly gains a fair start before the internal combustion engine overtakes it."

Deep South

On the right wall, three panels—*Deep South*, *Midwest*, and *Changing West*—depicted the Western and agricultural regions of the country. Since this was the west wall of the room, the scenes symbolically transformed the wall into a picture window, which revealed the vistas that lay a thousand miles beyond it.

Unlike Grant Wood, who presented idealized farm scenes, Benton frankly depicted the hardships of rural life in the years preceding the Great Depression. In the foreground, he juxtaposed the poor white and the poor black: on the left, a lean, stooped, sunburned white tenant farmer preparing the soil for seeding with his harrow; and on the right, a black worker emptying bags of cotton. A chain gang of black prisoners watched by a gun-toting guard stands between these two figures, hinting at the racial tensions of the South, which Benton feared would someday explode into violence.

In the distance, he laid out the different sorts of machinery used in the South, most of it relatively antiquated. The middle ground shows a scene that might belong

Deep South. *Benton did not overlook the racial tensions of the region. In the foreground, a poor black cotton picker faces a lean, sunburned white tenant farmer; in the middle distance, a white guard holds a gun on a chain gang of black prisoners.*

to the remote past: black stevedores roll jute-wrapped bales of cotton onto the *Tennessee Belle,* just as he had seen them do at Red River Landing, Louisiana, in September 1928. At the upper left are a rice thresher and a tractor, more modern forms of machinery, although still not truly up-to-date, for the tractor operates with steam rather than internal combustion. Farther off, we see a windmill, a train, and a green sea of sugarcane.

Midwest

Like *Deep South, Midwest* focuses mostly on hard and antiquated forms of work, and it likewise was based largely on sketches made in 1928. About half the panel is occupied by lumberjacks, who fell trees that are then hauled away by a team of horses and a logging train in the distance. The time is the present, but Benton probably intended to evoke the enormous effort that went into clearing the frontier. The remainder of the panel is devoted to farming. To the left, a small, impoverished farmer cares for his withered ears of corn, while a coiled rattlesnake threatens to strike. In the background, a vast field of wheat is harvested by a modern fuel-driven tractor pulling a harvester and a thresher. The juxtaposition suggests that the small farmer is economically doomed, and that modern machinery and huge farming cooperatives will take his place.

Changing West

Changing West is based on the sketches Benton made in Borger and the Texas panhandle. The composition juxtaposes the new West, built on oil and other modern forms of energy, with the old West, based on cattle. Airplanes crowd the sky like a swarm of bumblebees, while in the distance, a lonely cowboy and his herd are silhouetted against purple mesas and the salmon pink of the evening sky. Pumps and turbines, oil rigs, tanks, and other metallic emblems of the modern age litter the landscape, contrasting

162

Midwest. *Muscular lumberjacks and sad-eyed farmers struggle to eke out a living in this sober presentation.*

Changing West. *Benton juxtaposed the new West, built on oil and other modern forms of energy, with the old West, based on cattle. Airplanes, oil rigs, and welders in the foreground contrast with shantytowns, lonely cowboys, and drunken Indians in the distance.*

with the tired shantytown and the weatherworn wooden windmill and water tank in the middle distance. Even here, change has made itself felt, for the modern gas pump has replaced the old-fashioned hitching post. In the left foreground, a surveyor and a red-shirted welder, workers of the new age, contrast with a prostitute and a tired Indian in a barroom just below them to the right, derelict leftovers of the past.

Viewed as an entirety, the west wall showed a progression toward ever more modern forms of technology. In *Deep South,* a rice thresher and a steam tractor occupy only a small part of the panel; in *Midwest,* about a third of the image is taken up by modern methods of farming; and in *Changing West,* new technology takes up most of the design.

Coal

On the east wall of the room, Benton presented the industrial world of the East Coast. *Coal* and *Steel* provide the energy and materials for *City Building. Coal,* the most powerful social critique in the mural cycle, shows a tired miner against slag heaps and a jerry-built coal town, perched precariously on a mountainside. The man's stooped posture and shrunken physique suggest that Benton had observed black lung disease at first hand. Coal was a socially troubled industry in the 1920s, for overproduction, a decrease in demand, and shrinking wages created violent and sometimes murderous confrontations between management and labor. At the left can be seen coal cars, a train, and a ship, means for transporting coal, as well as a modern electric plant, the final use to which coal is put.

Steel

Steel depicts successive stages in the processing of ore, based on sketches Benton had made in 1928 near Pittsburgh and his more intensive study in the Sparrow's Point mill while he was planning the mural. In the center distance we see the exterior of a steel

Steel. *The various stages of the Bessemer process are shown. With the help of Alvin Johnson, Benton visited a Maryland steel mill to make his preparatory studies for the composition.*

mill, with hoists that lift ore up to the blast furnace. In the left background, air flows through a Bessemer converter, which burns away impurities to produce a fine grade of steel. In front, at the left, a giant ladle releases molten metal into molds for ingots. At the right, workers tap the base of the furnace.

City Building

City Building was based on sketches of New York construction sites that Tom had been making since about 1923. On the left are three men shoring up foundation walls, the first step in skyscraper construction. With considerable boldness for the time, Benton showed a black worker with a jackhammer taking his place as an equal on the construction team (Building Common Laborers was one of the few unions of the time that accepted black members). In the right foreground, an architect studies his sketch. Cleverly, Benton placed the architect beside his traditional attribute in Renaissance painting, a column, here represented in the form of a concrete pile.

In the distance are both a completed skyscraper and one in progress, its metal armature silhouetted against the clouds. Two distant figures in dark fedoras probably represent racketeers, alluding to the graft that plagued the construction business.

City Activities with Subway

On the north wall, flanking the entrance, were two panels of urban amusements, *City Activities with Subway* and *City Activities with Dance Hall,* the most crowded paintings of the series. *Subway* contains forty-one people; *Dance Hall* contains thirty-seven, not counting a face on a poster and two figures on the silver screen. (By contrast, *Steel* includes only six figures.)

Urban society had created special profit-making, mass-oriented, machine-age amusements—easily standardized and easily digested, and often appealing to the low-

City Building. *With considerable boldness for the time, Benton showed a black construction worker with a jackhammer laboring beside whites.*

est common denominator of taste. By 1928 Americans expended one quarter of their national income on recreation and play.

On the far right of the left panel, Benton showed his handsome Marxist friend Max Eastman, editor of *The Masses,* sitting in the subway. Eastman, a notorious womanizer, ogles pretty Peggy Reynolds, a well-known stripper of the time, but is unwilling to give up his seat. She wears a cloche hat, the latest sleeveless knee-length dress, and rolled rayon hose. In front of Eastman, a bookie scans a tabloid, whose typical scandalous headlines advertise a "love nest," recalling the Peaches and Daddy Browning scandal of 1926.

Above these figures, two boxers bash away at each other, while the crowd yells for blood and a knockout. The boxers, like Peggy Reynolds, were probably drawn in the Eighth Avenue Burlesque Theatre, which was turned over to boxing matches once a week. A reporter said of Benton in 1935: "He used to go to the Friday night prizefight at the old Eighth Avenue burlesque and he would sit up in the gallery and make sketches. In the middle of a sketch he would drop his pencil and yell at the pugs. He would throw his drawing into the air and yell, 'Kill that guy!' "

To the left, the structure of the elevated rises above some Salvation Army singers; illuminated signs read "Heat," "Burlesque 50 Girls," and "God is Love." In the far distance one can just make out a sign of giant eyeglasses, an icon immortalized in F. Scott Fitzgerald's *The Great Gatsby* of 1925 and employed later in a canvas by Reginald Marsh, titled *Eyes Examined.*

Near them, an abandoned hussy of a burlesque dancer toes it perilously close to a wickedly caricatured soapbox revivalist, while sad-eyed clowns with barrel staves look on. The soapbox speaker brings to mind the famous evangelists of the period, such as Aimee Semple McPherson and Manhattan's own Reverend John Roach Straton. At the far left, a man and a girl are necking on a park bench in a corner of an amusement park.

City Activities with Dance Hall

On the right panel, a couple undulate amorously to the music of a jazz orchestra in a cheap dance hall. She is probably a "taxi dancer," ready to dance with anyone for ten cents a spin. Beside the couple is a still, symbol of the product and the activities of thousands of bootleggers who supplied liquor to a country that was constitutionally "dry." Above them, hands grab at liquor bottles, while a broker casts frantic eyes over a ticker tape, which presumably records a falling market. In the center of the panel, in a darkened cinema, a Hollywood pair are shown in the inevitable "clinch." Elizabeth Pollock sits in the audience, wearing a red hat. Above and to the right, we see a circus, with flying acrobats.

Sandwiched tightly between the movie house, the speakeasy, and the circus is a domestic vignette: a portrait of the artist's wife and son, posed like a Renaissance

City Activities with Dance Hall. On the left, a broker frantically clutches a ticker tape; a couple dance in front of an illegal still for bootleg liquor; and two pretty women sneak off to the movies. On the right, Benton included portraits of his wife and son, and also a likeness of himself clinking glasses with Alvin Johnson.

City Activities with Subway. A juxtaposition of a bizarre variety of urban activities: boxers bash away at each other; Salvation Army lasses sing beneath a sign for the burlesque; and Benton's friend Max Eastman ogles the stripper Peggy Reynolds in the subway.

madonna with child. Beside them Benton placed an elderly, androgynous figure, with a profile curiously like his own in later life. This was Caroline Pratt, one of the foremost progressive educators of the time and the founder of the City and Country School, which Benton enthusiastically supported. The multiplication problem on the blackboard behind these figures, "6 × 7," alludes to his age at the time he completed the mural, forty-two.

Behind these figures is a political poster with a likeness of Judge Sturgis, M. E. Benton's old law partner, and the words "Fearless, Honest, Able." Just to the right of the soda fountain is a shelf of books, one of them inscribed "S. S. Van D . . . Myste . . . " "S. S. Van Dine" was the pen name of the painter's friend Willard Wright, who after a nervous breakdown in 1925 had shifted from art criticism to detective stories. (By 1930 three of his novels had been adapted for the movies, and he was able to write a cheerful short book entitled *I Used to Be a Highbrow but Look at Me Now*.) Benton portrayed himself on the far right, paintbrush in one hand and highball in the other, clinking glasses with Alvin Johnson, director of the New School.

Outreaching Hands

As the Depression worsened, Benton began to reconsider the meaning of his paintings, which had stressed the boom psychology of the 1920s. A little after the unveiling of the murals, he installed a final panel, *Outreaching Hands*, between the two city scenes. "It wasn't clear there was a Depression until I was almost finished," Tom later recalled. "So I put in that breadline over the door."

Social Content

In the 1930s, Benton came under strong attack from Stuart Davis and other Communists, and as a consequence his paintings have come to be viewed as politically conservative. At the time the New School murals were completed, however, while they were sometimes criticized for the vulgarity of their subject matter or their crowded forms, their political viewpoint did not come under fire. Indeed, in the context of its time, the imagery of *America Today* was strongly leftist, both in its organizing principles, which were based on Marxist theory, and in its visual sources, which lay in leftist and Marxist magazines.

In the early twenties, Benton was a Marxist who voted for the Socialist ticket. While not a member of the Communist party, he was friendly with Mike Gold, its

Outreaching Hands.

founder, and once arranged for the outlawed organization to hold a meeting in his apartment. To be sure, in the late twenties, Benton, like his friends Caroline Pratt, Max Eastman, and Sidney Hook, became disenchanted with orthodox Marxism, particularly with the notion of the dictatorship of the proletariat. But he remained strongly under the influence of Marxist and Socialist ideas.

In fact, the "Regionalist" approach that he adopted was a direct outgrowth of the Marxist interpretation of American history, which looked for the cause of events in social and economic factors rather than in political rhetoric and national ideals. This becomes clear when we examine the illustrations that Benton completed, just after the New School cycle, for Leo Huberman's *We, the People,* a Marxist history of the United States which was widely praised in liberal circles and was nominated for the Pulitzer Prize. Many of these illustrations relate closely to his paintings of the twenties and to the New School murals; they show that all these works function quite effortlessly as Marxist portrayals of American life. *We, the People,* in fact, serves well as a guidebook to the social message of Benton's paintings of this period.

Huberman focused not on the doings of a few "great men," as in traditional histories, but on social and economic changes and the activities of the people. Apparently effortlessly, Benton translated his economic and geographical concepts into visual terms, moving with ease from diagrams to illustrations. Huberman stressed three major themes, all of which Benton incorporated into his art:

First was the emancipation of the United States from Europe, to express which Benton showed a map of the United States with the countries of Europe placed over it —leaving a good deal of room to spare. For him, this drawing probably possessed not only economic but cultural import. Why should the United States, which had declared its political independence in the eighteenth century, continue to remain in colonial fiefdom to Europe with regard to cultural affairs? Why should not the United States set forth an artistic declaration of independence?

Huberman's second theme was the development of four distinct regions in the United States—regions that possessed dissimilar economic frameworks and varieties of thought and behavior. These were: the South (with its heritage of slavery and one-crop agriculture), the North (which became economically diverse), the Frontier (which favored independence and democratic forms of government), and the Far West (where new forms of land use and settlement were necessary to cope with the challenges of the Great Plains).

Leo Huberman. The Marxist historian was a close friend of Benton's at the time of the New School murals. Not long after, they fell out over political doctrine and ceased to speak to each other.

Not only did Benton illustrate this concept in Huberman's book, but at the New School he had divided the country up in just such a fashion, exploring the relationship between the means of economic production and social forms. Although he was later accused of narrow-minded and even racist chauvinism, one of the fundamental purposes of his work was to demonstrate the cultural and racial diversity of America. As he told a writer for the social-minded publication *Survey* in 1930: "I realized that the supposed and much-harped-upon standardization of America was a neat descriptive formula which bore only a surface relation to fact. My experience had brought out infinite varieties of ways of living and doing which the formula did not fit."

Huberman's third theme was the worker's struggle against economic injustice, which acquired new urgency when the growth of factories and industry encouraged the exploitation of the worker and the concentration of capital in a few hands. Though strongly biased toward the worker, Huberman did not romanticize his motives. In his account of the growth of labor unions, for example, he clearly showed how the idealistic program of the Knights of Labor, which sought to gather together all the workers of the world in one association, was replaced by the more pragmatic program of the American Federation of Labor, which excluded unskilled workers, who could not battle effectively for higher wages.

Benton made the American worker the hero of his mural. While many of his preliminary sketches concentrate on machinery, in the final mural he enlarged the figures to make them the central element in the design. The closest precedents for these images come from the paintings of the 14th Street School, or the illustrations of political periodicals, in particular those of the Socialist *New Masses*. *New Masses* had published many drawings of similar subjects, including vignettes of pneumatic drillers, construction workers, prizefighters, burlesque dancers, the subway, and Coney Island.

 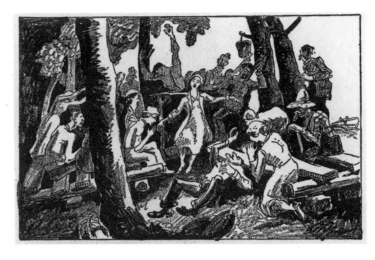

Unlike some Marxist realists, Benton did not sentimentalize his figures. His workers seem to strain with the effort of real labor, and he honestly recorded prostitutes, drunken Indians, racketeers, and other social misfits. As a native Midwesterner and the son of a Populist politician, he naturally felt a strong sympathy for the farmer. Curiously, however, in the New School murals, his presentation of the farmlands of the South and the Midwest was less heroic, less enthusiastic, than that of such urban activities as steelmaking and high-rise construction.

Thomas Hart Benton, Illustrations for "We, the People," *1932.*

Composition

From the standpoint of composition, the difficulty Benton faced at the New School was in organizing disparate scenes so that they would interrelate in a unified pictorial form. To achieve unity, he left parts of the periphery of each design open so that it could flow into and connect with the forms on the edge of the adjoining units. Many of the units differed strongly not only in subject matter but in their forms, the agricultural scenes, for example, containing fundamentally different shapes than those filled with industrial machinery. To compensate, the painter boldly introduced a unifying formal element—he injected sections of the molding right into the mural design. This technique had been employed in the illustrated pages of nineteenth-century magazines and books, as well as in newspaper rotogravure sections. The way Benton abruptly broke off these inner moldings, however, was extremely radical—closer to the abruptly dislocated spaces of Analytical Cubism than to nineteenth-century illustrations.

Expressively, these broken moldings gave an increased intensity to the design, for they conflated the interior of the painting with its edges. In addition, Benton created inner compositional units that were dense and compressed. Nothing like this had ever been seen before in American painting of large scale, and the jumble of the effect was bitterly criticized. Stuart Davis, in a viciously worded attack, denounced both the confusion of the design and the use of inner moldings. Even Lloyd Goodrich, Benton's strongest defender, felt the composition was "too crowded—no question." He wrote: "Every object is uncompromisingly hard and tangible, even those supposed to be far away; there is a lack of deep space or distance. . . . Similarly, the design is overcrowded with dynamic forms, which, for lack of contrast with static, reposeful elements, lose much of their power. The artist is never satisfied to let the large terms speak for themselves, but exaggerates each twist and curve to secure the maximum emphasis, with the result that the moving force of his forms is dissipated in countless minor rhythms, which nullify one another, and the movement of the whole seems forced and arrested."

With the benefit of hindsight, it has become evident that Benton's detractors were incorrect. The *America Today* murals remain the best known and most widely reproduced of all his paintings, and it is precisely their crowded character that gives them their dramatic impact. They represent, in fact, one of those dramatic moments in the history of art when the desire to give expression to a new subject gave rise to a new technique in the organization of form. Benton's innovation has come to be termed the "all-over" composition, and *America Today* marks its first use in American painting —at least its first use with deliberate intent and on a grand scale.

Thomas Hart Benton, Illustrations for "We, the People," 1932.

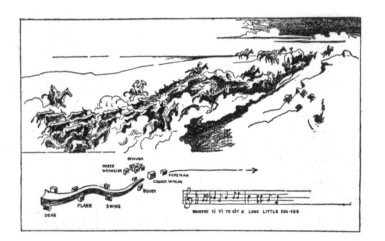

In his desire to express the whole pulse and energy of America, rather than any single part of it, Benton devised a form of composition that differs from that of traditional Western paintings, which concentrate the glance on a few central forms and organize these in simple pyramidal groupings. Benton's design, by contrast, has no single center of focus or impact. Each shape flows uninterruptedly into the next, spreading out toward the edges in a unified field of energy. This tendency is particularly striking in the last two paintings of the cycle, depicting urban activities.

Perhaps the closest precedent for such a compositional approach lay in the work of the Cubists; clearly Benton's composition was deeply affected by their devices of collage and multiple viewpoints. Even the Cubists, however, seem to have feared the loss of the central focus of traditional painting, and while their stylistic innovations tended to lead to fragmentation, they fought this tendency by limiting their subject matter—a newspaper, an absinthe bottle, a guitar. Benton, in his reckless compulsion to seize the whole of America, in his hunger to explore an enormous range of subject matter, exploded the hermetic and tightly sealed world of the Cubists into something quite new—a form of pictorial organization that would reshape the destiny of American painting.

For with the coming of Abstract Expressionism, "all-over" design became the dominant compositional mode—and the most original contribution to compositional form that America has yet made to the pictorial arts. Benton was a decade or two

Stuart Davis, New York–Paris, No. 2, *oil on canvas, 1931. Davis tried to adapt the techniques of French Cubism to American subjects. A number of his paintings of the thirties present a pastiche of buildings from Paris and New York.*

ahead of Davis in this regard, although Davis himself eventually adopted something roughly resembling the "all-over" composition in a few of his major late works, such as *Ultra Marine* or *The Mellow Pad*.

It was undoubtedly at least in part through Benton's example that the Abstract Expressionists developed this manner of composing, for his ideas about the mechanics of form passed directly to his pupil Jackson Pollock, the first of the Abstract Expressionists to recognize the expressive potential of this new scheme. Even Benton's use of silver leaf anticipates Pollock, who introduced metallic paints into his designs.

Because Stuart Davis worked within a fairly conventional and recognizable vocabulary of modernist art, directly lifted from Synthetic Cubism, some recent writers have argued that in his work of the 1930s he composed scenes with multiple viewpoints more successfully than Benton. Davis, indeed, was a remarkably skillful designer; but simply because his work looks flatter than Benton's and is more closely linked with the School of Paris, it would be a mistake to view it as more modern. Indisputably, Davis had little to offer to the Abstract Expressionists and was largely unable to appreciate their work. His art represented a tributary branch of the modernist stream that flowed into the desert and ran dry.

Tom Benton's mode of painting contained old-fashioned elements drawn directly from the Italian Renaissance: three-dimensional space, recognizable subject matter, and narrative progression. These elements have prevented most writers from noting his skill at abstract organization. In fact, his compositions are more original than those of Stuart Davis and had greater influence on the future of abstract painting.

Davis, whose artistic vocabulary was more limited and derivative, could create multiple viewpoints of a single object, in traditional Cubist fashion, but he never found a successful technique for visually combining successive moments in time. His early efforts at realistically rendered multiple views seem thoroughly naive in their simplification of the principles of Cubism; and even his mature attempts, such as his *Paris, New York* paintings, count among his weakest efforts, for he simply placed objects side by side, without overall principles of visual unity.

Davis never successfully incorporated the human figure into his painting; nor did he seek to express the passage of time. He worked by dismembering reality rather than by constructing it; and his art is essentially an art of cut-out shapes, an art of forms that have been cut out of reality and then rearranged—admittedly with great sensitivity to color and the interlocking of edges.

Benton's artistic world possesses a richness that Davis's completely lacks. Time, moment, action, and rhythm, all banished from Davis's art, are fundamental factors in Benton's. As Lloyd Goodrich wrote of *America Today:* "These paintings give one a sensation like that of looking out of the window of a train speeding through cities, past factories and mines, through farmland and woods, over prairies, across rivers. They convey a sense of the restless, teeming, tumultuous life of this country, its wide range of contrasts, and its epic proportions. . . . His design is as insistent as jazz or the beat of machinery, seeming in tune with the speed and emphasis of modern American life."

"I think MGM played a bigger role in those paintings than has ever been acknowledged," Hilton Kramer has commented, and while his remark was not intended to be flattering, it lays bare some of the essential aspects of Benton's unique visual contribution; for Benton drew not only from American life but from the one indisputably American art form.

In its imagery, *America Today* relates closely to the movies. The scenes of park-bench kissing, boxing matches, and Coney Island amusements refer directly to the very earliest Edison films, which included such titles as *Coney Island, The Corbett and Courtney Knock-Out Fight,* and *The Widow Jones* (featuring the first on-screen kiss). Benton's use of unusual vantage points also brings to mind the movies, though ones of a later date than the early Edison loops—the inventive camera angles that Hollywood discovered in the 1930s, which appear in such films as King Vidor's *Street Scene.*

The placement of vignettes in *America Today,* as Emily Braun has noted, often suggests the succession of moments in a movie. In *City Activities with Subway,* for example, a subway ride provides a linking narrative element, associatively connecting the different images. We begin on the right in the interior of the subway car, continue in the middle with the "el," under which the Salvation Army band plays, and end at Coney Island, which became accessible by subway in 1921.

Tom Benton was a bit too much of an oddball to be neatly characterized as a modernist painter; but his contribution to modern art, while more unorthodox than that of Stuart Davis, in the end proved more consequential, because it was based on more significant issues. His utilization of multiple viewpoints, while more literal than that of the Cubists, was also more forceful—and reflected itself even more boldly in the shape of the composition as a whole. He believed that modern subject matter would give rise to modern forms, and in fact his synthesis of Cubist painting, the movies, and American life created exactly that. He gave birth to a new mode of composition, which proved America's most influential contribution to pictorial form.

Chapter Nine
The Whitney Mural

"It is extremely embarrassing for me," Juliana Force wrote, *"to remind you how deeply grateful you were for my help at the time. I am sure you understand my reference to it is made only in justice to myself and because of your evident misunderstanding."*

An Emotional Slump

Despite the pressure he was under to complete the New School murals, Benton found time in the summer of 1930 for a trip to the West with his student Glen Rounds, who was from the Dakotas. The most memorable event of the excursion was a Fourth of July rodeo in Saratoga, Wyoming. Tom told the men in charge of the event that he was a reporter from the Denver *Post,* and they allowed him to roam freely making sketches. He and Glen skipped town before the hoax was discovered.

At the time Benton was working on his New School project, Alvin Johnson arranged for a smaller project to supplement his income—a mural depicting *The History of Water* for Drugs, Inc., located on Fourteenth Street in Washington, D.C. As in his paintings for the New School, he created a multipart composition, broken by jagged moldings, in which he contrasted old-fashioned ways of doing things with modern ones. When the store closed, the mural was put in storage, not to be rediscovered until the 1970s.

Benton's extraordinary energy gave way soon after he finished *America Today.* During the final stages of work, he had labored sixteen hours a day; the completion of the project brought him a sense of letdown. He fell into an emotional slump and for weeks was completely unable to paint.

To get away from New York, he spent Christmas of 1930 on Martha's Vineyard with Rita and some friends, although all they had for heat was a two-burner coal stove in the kitchen. Six weeks later, Benton returned to the island alone. Unfortunately, he arrived with a bad cold, and in the damp, dark, unheated house it rapidly worsened. His friends Bill and Rachel Scott took him in, and he lay on the sofa in their big kitchen, sweating profusely. At nine o'clock at night, they finally obtained a thermometer; his temperature showed his condition to be serious. They bundled him into a Model A Ford and drove him to the hospital. He lay there for three weeks, drenching his bedding with sweat, while the doctors tried unsuccessfully to diagnose his illness. His symptoms resembled malaria, but all the tests were negative. Eventually he recovered on his own, and it was decided that he had just had a severe case of flu, aggravated by nervous exhaustion.

In the midst of his despondency, he developed a new interest. One day he picked up a child's harmonica that someone had given his son, T.P., and began to make noises. After some experimentation, he learned to play a scale. He was so excited that he ran home from his studio to show his new skill to Rita, who had some musical knowledge (she sang and strummed the guitar). She took the instrument from him and

Thomas Hart Benton, Lassoing Horses, *watercolor on paper, 1931.*

Thomas Hart Benton, Wyoming Rodeo, *pencil on paper, 1930. On the Fourth of July, 1930, Benton sketched a rodeo in Saratoga, Wyoming. He told the organizers that he was a reporter from the Denver Post and skipped town before the ruse was discovered.*

Tom, Rita, and T.P. making music together.

Benton transcribing music for harmonica.

played a tune. Other people came in and demonstrated their facility, including his friend M. A. Jagendorf, known as "Jagey," a literary dentist who recited poems to his helpless patients. "If that literary nut can play on that thing, I can too," Tom decided.

Tunes were too much for him, however, so he went out and purchased some music books. For weeks, he did nothing but practice children's songs and elementary folk tunes. Becoming pretty expert, he purchased a more expensive harmonica, which allowed half notes and key changes. He and Rita began playing the guitar and the harmonica together in the evenings.

For a while, he was more interested in the harmonica than in painting. Thanks to his enthusiasm, some of his students got interested also, and began meeting at his home on Monday evenings for musicales. First they tried playing in unison; then they moved on to playing in parts. Their repertoire was mixed. Benton enjoyed such early American folk tunes as "Old Joe Clark," "My Horses Ain't Hungry," and "Buffalo Gals." But he also began arranging classical compositions by Mozart, Bach, Purcell, Couperin, Thomas Farmer, Josquin Desprez, and others.

To make it easier for the novice, he devised a new form of musical notation, which was later picked up by music publishers and is still used by them. Instead of the traditional scale, this system used numbers to refer to holes, and an up or down arrow to indicate whether to blow in or out. For five years, playing the harmonica occupied a good part of Tom's time. He began taking it with him on his summer travels and would perform in farmhouses and at country dances.

Juliana Force

The New School murals enhanced Benton's reputation, and the prices of his paintings jumped to a new level. His income went up as the American economy went down. Though he had a dealer, Fred Price, it was Rita who did most of the selling; she managed to dispose of most of his piled-up stock of paintings, and the family was able to move to a large apartment on Thirteenth Street just off Fifth Avenue. The decor was dominated by the huge fragments of his unfinished *American Historical Epic*. They enlarged their Martha's Vineyard home and constructed a studio there. They even purchased their first automobile, a great lumbering Stutz, from a broker friend who had lost his money in the crash. Tom taught himself to drive but gave it up after he ran into the back of a beer truck, sending kegs rolling all over Seventh Avenue.

The Bentons improved their brand of whiskey. They gave lavish parties and served eggnog to their guests. The gatherings soon grew so popular that they became a Frankenstein's monster. At the 1931 Christmas party, the guests consumed twenty-four quarts of milk and countless ancillary eggs. When Tom and Rita took stock of their inebriated guests the next morning, they realized that they had never met any of them before. They cut down on the parties.

The burst of prosperity proved short-lived. Tom's reputation began to fade, and Rita started to run out of paintings to sell. One day, Tom realized that he was broke and had to make a $3,000 payment on his Martha's Vineyard mortgage. This financial crisis led to his next major mural project, *The Arts of Life in America,* for the Whitney Museum of American Art. It also led to an acrimonious dispute over payment. While

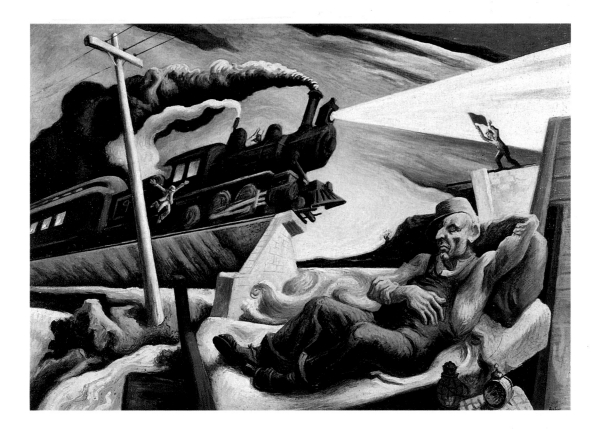

Thomas Hart Benton, The Engineer's Dream, *oil and tempera on canvas mounted on panel, 1931. About the time that he took up the harmonica, Benton began to paint subjects from country music, such as this scene of bridge collapse and train wreck.* •

Thomas Hart Benton, Wreck of the Ole '97, *egg tempera and oil on canvas mounted on panel, 1943. Benton made the initial sketch of this subject in 1927, just after Vernon Dalhart made "The Wreck of the Old 97" into the first million-selling country music hit. The painting wasn't executed, however, until sixteen years later. As a consequence, while the design is similar to* The Engineer's Dream, *the technique is much more polished.*

Gertrude Vanderbilt Whitney.

the particulars of this dispute are often rather technical, it is worth examining them carefully, for the affair vividly highlights some of the less pleasant sides of Benton's personality.

Gertrude Vanderbilt Whitney had turned to art because she was bored with society and with her husband. She worked hard and achieved real proficiency as a sculptor, but her greatest impact was as a patron. In 1914 she started the Whitney Studio Club, at 147 West Fourth Street; the founding members included Tom Benton and Stuart Davis. Dues were prescribed but never collected. By 1931 the club had expanded into the Whitney Museum of American Art, four renovated houses on Eighth Street with eleven galleries, devoted to the display of contemporary American paintings.

While Mrs. Whitney provided the money, the club and its successor museum were largely managed by her secretary, Juliana Force. Juliana was the opposite of stuffy, she had a touch of whimsy, and she made things fun. She glued a fabric with primroses to the floor of the hallway leading to her office, so that on the way to work she could walk down a primrose path. She organized uproarious parties. At one of these, she and the artist Gerald Kelly sat in a bathtub drinking champagne while the guests cavorted around them. Even Tom Benton complimented her on the power of her cocktails. Unintimidated by the usual standards of good taste, she impulsively and unhesitatingly backed the artists she liked and believed in. "If you love a woman, marry her," she once advised. "If you like a painting, buy it."

The Whitney had always been a generous patron of Benton's work. After he completed the New School murals, Mrs. Force purchased fourteen of the related drawings for $840—a very good price for the time. Consequently, in May 1932, when Rita needed $3,000, the first thing she did was to visit Juliana Force. She proposed that the museum provide the sum in exchange for four mural studies that Tom had painted a few years before for a space in the New York Public Library.

Mrs. Force demurred, for she felt that any mural the museum acquired should be designed specifically for it. However, she wrote out a check for $3,000 from her own account. She later insisted that this was a purely personal loan. The Bentons, however, decided that it should be treated as a down payment on a mural, which Tom would design for the museum's library. Shortly after Rita's visit, Tom called on Mrs. Force and pressed her to award him such a library commission, explaining that the "psychological moment" had arrived for him to undertake another mural.

At the end of May, while vacationing in England, she wrote to Tom, agreeing to commission a mural. The $3,000 would be treated as a down payment. The Whitney Museum would cover the cost of materials and pay an additional $1,000 for the work. Somewhat grumpily (for he was eager to be better paid), he agreed to her terms. "I shall accept the proposition contained in your letter," he wrote.

Juliana Force.

Benton painted the murals during the summer of 1932, and the Whitney picked up all his costs, which came not to $600, as he had promised, but to $1,676.25. The museum also printed an illustrated brochure, with a descriptive essay by the artist. At a party on December 7 to celebrate the unveiling of the cycle, Juliana Force handed Benton a check for $1,000. He was very drunk, which helps to explain the events that followed. He later recalled:

"Parties at the Whitney Museum are thoroughly taken care of. Before this one was half started I was thoroughly taken care of myself. I was tight as a jay bird in blackberry season. Mrs. Force came over to me. I recognized her even though she had several heads and seemed to be dancing some kind of shimmy. She held out a slip of paper. I knew it was a check and took it. I couldn't make it out for sure but it looked like ten thousand dollars. I nearly fell over. I controlled my impulse to shout and sticking the paper in my pocket proceeded to get as tight as I could.

"Somebody was giving a party for me that night. I discovered when I started out to it that I couldn't make the grade. I went into a drugstore, got a zinc emetic, and spilt my mural party in the gutter. When I could see clearly I looked at my check again. The check was for one thousand dollars. The sight of it ruined my supper party."

The next morning, he returned the check with a letter asking for more adequate payment. The letter is filled with obvious inaccuracies, but all the odd features of Benton's ingenious methods of bookkeeping need not detain us here. Basically, Tom maintained that he had painted the murals in the belief that "you would some time in the future pay me for what you thought the finished job to be really worth." He then went on to concoct reasons why he should have been paid more. The money he had been paid, he maintained, "in no way accounts for the gathering of the representative material which gives to the work its reality. . . . the cost of these trips I must deduct from the apparent profit in a final reckoning. . . . Looking at the work in this way I have done this work for the Museum as I did the work for the New School—for nothing."

Benton once stated to Richard Beer that he made "three trips into the West" gathering material for the Whitney murals, but in fact the only trip he took in 1932 was a brief sketching trip to Georgia. The three trips west seem to have been the excursions of 1926, 1928, and 1930. By no stretch of the imagination could the museum be held liable for these expenses.

No doubt aware that he was on thin ice—despite his best efforts to stretch the account in his own favor—he shifted the argument away from the contract or his expenses. Instead he proposed an entirely new arrangement. He wrote: "The conventional decorators I understand work on a $35 to $40 per square foot basis. If you want to pay me over and above your legal obligation I would be willing to arbitrate the question of final payment on such a basis—and you would find me lenient and perfectly willing to postpone a complete reckoning. I have no exaggerated notions about the worth of my productions. I have never been able to get the prices my contemporaries seem to command. Nevertheless after 27 years of work I should like to set up some measure of value that would give a little practical sense to the energy I expend."

Even Benton was forced to conclude that he did not have a solid case: "In this letter I am making no demands. Legally you are clear after paying me the $1,000 agreed to in our correspondence of last spring. . . . Mrs. Force, I cannot accept $1,000 as a final payment on the job. This may make you hate the sight of the murals but I must tell you just the same. I feel more at ease in letting the murals stand as a gift to the Museum which has helped so many young artists. A gift to the Museum which you have helped to make possible but nevertheless a gift."

Mrs. Force replied on December 8, returning the check for $1,000: "The Museum does not look upon these murals as a gift from you, although I agree with you that the price we have paid is very small. I am sorry you feel you cannot accept the $1,000 which I offer you in addition to the price agreed upon. May I take this opportunity to remind you that the $3,000 which I gave your wife last spring was not given as a payment on the murals. It was given, at great sacrifice to myself, because at that moment you needed the money to save your $12,000 house. It later became a part payment on the murals, at your suggestion, and I, in good faith, feeling that I understood your gesture, allowed it. It is extremely embarrassing for me to remind you how deeply grateful you were for my help at the time. I am sure you understand my reference to it is made only in justice to myself and because of your evident misunderstanding. That your attitude is so unfair and unjust, and that your letter is obviously a misstatement of facts, can only be the source of amazement to me."

Benton replied on December 9, acknowledging the check, which he deposited the same day. The museum still has the canceled check. "Try to get something out of the murals," he wrote, "and in return I'll forget I even did them or had any illusions about what they might be worth to me."

The record makes it plain that he had no reasonable grounds for protest; Juliana Force and the Whitney Museum had more than fulfilled the terms of their contract. Benton was undoubtedly truthful, however, in maintaining that he had made no profit from the murals. As he stated in his letter to Mrs. Force: "A work like this decoration of yours is not done without getting tired. But as things stand now there is no such thing as rest to be thought of. I must call immediately on every resource at my command to meet my responsibilities. Of course, this is an artist's life."

He concluded with the declaration: "I entered this particular situation with my eyes open," and: "I don't bellyache about it." In fact, he did "bellyache about it," to the press. In January 1933, he complained to the reporter Anita Brenner that the Whitney had not paid him properly; she published his claim in an article in *The Nation*.

Juliana Force got a copy of the article before the issue hit the newsstands, and she wrote to the board of editors, protesting that their statement was libelous. After a flurry of correspondence, she arranged to meet with Miss Brenner and obtained a verbal apology from her. Tom was in Indianapolis, working on a new mural commission, but he soon got word of Juliana's activities. On February 26, 1933, he wrote to her from the Hotel Harrison in Indianapolis, offering halfheartedly to make amends. He declared: "Now, Mrs. Force I say, habitually, what I think and yet in this case I want to be fair to you. You did leave me alone when I was working—you let me have my way completely—and that is something for an artist worthy of appreciation, if only because it sets a precedent. . . . I wish you would let Mrs. Benton talk to you about the whole business. I am sending Mrs. Benton a copy of this letter with instructions to call you."

His evasiveness here was almost worthy of Alfred Stieglitz, but Juliana Force did not fall for it. On March 8, she replied: "My talk with Miss Brenner was definite and plain. She said that you claimed I had not paid a bill for models and for your travelling expenses West. I answered that I had not seen any such bills nor had you spoken to me about such bills. Miss Brenner then agreed with me that the only thing to do was for you to come and explain what you mean by the statement that you had incurred expenses in doing this work for the Museum which had not been paid, or show me these 'unpaid' bills.

"This is a matter to settle between you and me and not between Mrs. Benton and me. My contract was with you and all my promises were made to you. I have fulfilled my contract and have kept my promises. If you have any bills, in accordance with our

contract which are unpaid, I insist that you send them to me, or better still, come and see me yourself. This matter, I am afraid, is getting beyond your control now and the only honest and square thing to do is for you to come and see me as soon as you can conveniently do so."

Benton never did call on Mrs. Force, as she requested. Two years later, however, in 1935, he wrote her a remarkable letter: "Enough time has passed since the installation of the Whitney Library mural for some sort of judgement to be passed as to its worth. I can ask the questions—Has its existence been of value to the museum? Has it continued to wag the tongues of and interest the minds of those young artists, aesthetes, amateur sociologists etc. who keep the ball of art rolling along?

"If the mural has proved itself (even as a stimulant) I think we should take up again the matter of its monetary value. The Federal Government has established a square foot price for the execution of murals. Would you consider that price as a basis for adjusting the little difficulty that arose between us when the mural was finished?"

Mrs. Force did not reply to this curious epistle, evidently feeling that it was better to let the matter rest. Benton, for his part, was still not quite finished with the dispute.

Thomas Hart Benton, Dudley Vance, Fiddler, Bluff City, Tennessee, pencil, pen, and ink on paper, 1930–32. The Tennessee fiddler told Benton that the records "never wuz right." "Wuz a time," he said, "when I'd cross bows with any fiddler from here to Florida." •

Thomas Hart Benton, Wilbur Leverett, Galena, Missouri, pencil, pen and ink on paper, 1931. Benton's brother Nat introduced him to the Leverett brothers, who wore striped overalls and carried their instruments in flour sacks. Wilbur picked the guitar, sang, and yodeled.

In his 1937 autobiography, *An Artist in America,* in which he presented an audaciously misleading account of the affair, he concluded with an account of his flamboyant gesture of returning the check to the museum. He did not note that Mrs. Force sent it back to him and that he cashed it. The Whitney Museum obtained proofs of the book shortly before it appeared, and Lloyd Goodrich, who worked for Juliana Force, tried to persuade her to sue for libel.

Although she had a solid case, Mrs. Force decided to let the matter rest. In the end, Benton's greedy attempt to get more money backfired badly, alienating him from one of his most vigorous supporters. After 1932 the Whitney purchased no further paintings from him, and his work seems to have been pretty much dropped from their exhibitions. The dispute also lost him the support of Goodrich, one of the finest writers and art historians of his generation, who up to that time had been among the most eloquent defenders of Benton's work.

Goodrich had been the first to recognize the significance of the "In Missoura" watercolors; he had praised the drawings Benton made during his travels around the United States; and he had written a glowing tribute to the *America Today* murals, against the strong resistance of Forbes Watson and other "sophisticated" critics. Goodrich also helped get Benton's essays into print. He edited them for *Arts* and even redrew Tom's pencil diagrams in pen and ink, to make them suitable for publication. He edited and arranged the publication of Benton's essay on his Whitney Museum murals. But after his piece in *Arts* about the New School murals, Goodrich did not write again about Tom until 1957, eight years after the death of Juliana Force.

In his letter of 1935, Benton had proposed that his murals for the Whitney had appreciated in value and that he should be paid some sort of bonus. In 1954, however, when the museum moved to new quarters, it was decided that there was no space for these paintings, and they were sold to the New Britain Museum of Art for five hundred dollars, significantly less than had been paid in 1932 simply for materials. The last laugh was on the Whitney. Today the murals in New Britain are worth several million dollars.

"The Arts of Life in America"

"The arts which today have most vitality for the average person are things he does not take to be arts: for instance, the movie, jazzed music, the comic strip, and too frequently, newspaper accounts of love nests, murders, and exploits of bandits."
—*John Dewey*

The library of the Whitney Museum was a small space with sloping ceilings on the third floor, squeezed up above the picture galleries. The slender windows looked out onto the neighboring rooflines; the books were stored in old-fashioned cupboards. As a setting for murals, the place presented unusually difficult problems. It was small, making it impossible to step back from the paintings; it was broken up by bookshelves and other architectural elements; and it was poorly lit, with thin, deep windows that produced a harsh glare.

Perhaps because of these difficulties, the Whitney cycle seems less successful than Benton's other decorative programs of the thirties. In contrast to the New School murals, all the figures were presented within a single coherent spatial framework. Because large-scale composition of this type was new to him, Benton employed it a bit awkwardly, and the units, such as the group of bronco busters in *Arts of the West,* seem to break away from the composition as a whole, as if they want to float out of the design.

The awkwardness of the Whitney cycle was certainly not due to lack of time.

From the date when he received the commission (and he had probably begun planning several months earlier), Benton took about seven months to execute the Whitney program. This is only one month less than he needed for the much bigger project at the New School, which contained ten panels rather than six and included nearly twice as many figures—149 as opposed to 83. Except for the murals for Jefferson City, Missouri, in 1936, he spent more time on the Whitney project than he did for any other project of the 1930s.

More probably, Benton's compositional difficulties came about as a consequence of the way he planned the design. For even before he received the commission, he had begun creating semi-independent vignettes of two, three, or four figures. These formed compositional building blocks, which he was ready to adjust to virtually any space that a patron handed over to him.

In his program for the New School, he had shown America at work; for the Whitney Museum, he showed the country at play. He titled his project *The Arts of Life in America*, and he described his subject matter as follows:

"The 'arts of life' are the popular arts and are generally undisciplined. They run into pure, unreflective play. People indulge in personal display; they drink, sing, dance, pitch horseshoes, get religion, and even set up opinions as the spirit moves them.

"These popular outpourings have a sort of pulse, a go and come, a rhythm; and all are expressions—indirectly, assertions of value. They are undisciplined, uncritical, and generally deficient in technical means; but they are arts just the same.

"The real subject of this work is, in the final analysis, a conglomerate of things experienced in America: the subject is a pair of pants, a hand, a face, a gesture, some physical revelation of intention, a sound, even a song. The real subject is what an individual has known and felt about things encountered in a real world of real people and actual doings.

"This mural, 'The Arts of Life in America,' is certainly not a pure work. . . . No plastic device is used for itself. Practically every form is bound up with implications which take the attention away from purely plastic values. This is deliberate.

*Thomas Hart Benton,
The Arts of Life in America,
Arts of the West. Murals for
the library of the Whitney
Museum of American Art, egg
tempera and oil on linen
mounted on panel, 1932. •*

"The things represented were known in real life and found significant enough to call for representation long before the complete form of the mural was considered. The final form here shown is then an attempt to integrate units each of which has in itself its own separate value as a thing, as a true thing, with a meaning of its own.

"The conception of perfect sequence is constantly assaulted by the recalcitrance of these units. They can be modified only just so much without losing their representational values."

In *Indian Arts*, Benton showed Indians dancing, weaving, preparing skins, invoking the "Great Spirit," and hunting buffalo. He frankly confessed that he had never seen an Indian sticking a buffalo and that the design as a whole was an "instance of romantic indulgence" based on "Cooper, Buffalo Bill, and the dime novels." *Arts of the West* pictured horse roping, poker playing, shooting, horseshoe pitching, music making, and dancing. *Arts of the South* featured a Holy Roller service, black singers, crapshooters, a mother feeding a baby, and a mule driver outside a church.

Arts of the City progressed from right to left, in a series of vignettes: a taxi dancer smearing on lipstick; small boys reading the comics; a jazz orchestra with dancers; a woman pulling on her stockings; a plump diva singing on the radio; a woman shaking cocktails; a beauty contest; and men rummaging for food and queueing up for a handout.

Arts of the City. •

Indian Arts. •

186

Each panel contained figures originally sketched in many different places. In *Arts of the South,* for example, the farmer resting on his wagon in front of a church was based on a sketch Benton made in Arkansas in 1926, during his first walking trip through the Ozarks. He also included three black crapshooters whom he sketched on the deck of the *Tennessee Belle* at Red River Landing, Louisiana, in September of 1928. The group of Holy Rollers at the upper right was based on the sketches he made in West Virginia in 1928, although he seems to have restudied most of the figures from live models.

In *Arts of the West,* the cardplayer on the left is Tex, a professional rodeo performer from Fort Worth, whom Benton sketched in 1930 in Saratoga, Wyoming. The bucking horses in the background were also sketched at the Saratoga rodeo. The figure across the table from Tex is Slim, one of the drunken cowboys Tom met in New Mexico in 1928 during his cross-country tour with Bill Hayden.

The figure playing the guitar over on the left is Wilbur Leverett, a hillbilly musician whom he met while visiting his brother Nat in Springfield and sketched in Galena, Missouri, in the summer of 1931. The fiddler is based on Dudley Vance, a country fiddler whom Benton sketched in Bluff City, Tennessee, in the early 1930s. The boy playing the harmonica beside him was Tom's new pupil from California, Jackson Pollock.

In his subject matter, Benton seems to have done his best to be shocking. Among others things, in his panel of *Arts of the South* he presented what must surely be the first trash pile in the entire history of mural painting. Indeed, it may well be the first painting of a garbage heap in American art, for the artists of the Ashcan School, despite their sobriquet, never actually made paintings of garbage cans.

New York critics of the time were less disturbed by this pile of rubbish than by a strain of social and political cynicism that runs through the paintings. In his ceiling panel, *Strike, Parade, Speed,* Benton included a jeep, an airplane, and a locomotive

(symbols of speed); a parade of chorus girls; and a group of strikers, one of whom carries a sign reading "Work for Wages," who are being shot at by a group of guards on a rooftop. Most of these elements belong to the standardized imagery of leftist painting, but he presented them in such a way that they did not convey a clear social message. He did not seek to enlist the viewer's sympathy; he simply reported.

The most shocking panel was *Political Business and Intellectual Ballyhoo,* in which he thumbed his nose at his old leftist friends—and indeed at the political world as a whole. On the right, one sees "Political Business" in the form of a top-hatted broomstick labeled "The Representative of the People," who says, "We nominate Ed," and stands on a podium with the idiotic advertising slogan: "Don't be a trilium / They call it halitosis / 5 out of 6 have it!"

On the left is the "Intellectual Ballyhoo" of Benton's old leftist friends. At the top, a group of cartoon characters, including Mickey Mouse and Mutt and Jeff, stand beside a sign that advertises the "Greenwich Village Proletarian Costume Dance." Jeff holds a placard reading: "Literary Playboys League for Social Consciousness." Behind him the New York *Post* blares the headlines: "Love Nest Murder," "Greater Circulation," and "Arrest!"

Below these figures appears an equally cartoonlike group of readers of leftist magazines. A reader of the *New Republic* utters, "Really, merely quantitative"; one of *The Nation,* "You don't know the half of it, dearie"; and of the *New Masses,* "The Hour is at hand." Underneath the panel is the slogan: "Oh the eagles they fly high in Mobile." This alluded to a current obscene song:

> Oh, the eagles they fly high in Mobile.
> Oh, the eagles they fly high in Mobile.
> Oh, the eagles they fly high,
> They will shit right in your eye.
> Oh, the eagles they fly high in Mobile.

Art historians today recognize this lunette as the most original panel in the series, for it directly introduced cartoon characters into large-scale painting, demolishing the usual barriers between "high" and "popular" art. The effect looks forward to 1960s Pop Art, in which cartoon figures were used by Andy Warhol and Roy Lichtenstein. When the murals were unveiled, however, many of Benton's contemporaries, particularly his old leftist friends, did not find his joke the least bit funny. Indeed, his *New Masses* reader (with his curly hair, sloping forehead, prominent nose, and recessive chin) was widely viewed as a tasteless anti-Semitic caricature.

Critical Reactions

Critical reactions to Benton's work began to polarize at the time he completed the Whitney commission. Lloyd Goodrich got a foretaste of this at the party for the murals' unveiling in December 1932. There he became engaged in a heated discussion with Guy Pène du Bois, a fine painter and an articulate, sophisticated art critic, who told him the paintings were terrible. Goodrich recommended an open mind, to which his friend retorted: "Don't keep *your* mind so open that your brains run out."

The new work got a very mixed press, ranging from strongly enthusiastic to violently hostile. Edward Alden Jewell, the *New York Times* critic, wrote a series of pieces praising the murals, which he thought superior to those in the New School. Jewell felt that Benton's technique had "mellowed" and that the effect was akin to chamber music. Everyone else found the series loud and jarring. Some enjoyed that fact; others didn't. Ralph Flint, in *Art News,* described the project as "a brilliant bit of bedlam." Louis Kalonyme, in a piece on "The Arts in New York" in *Arts and Decoration,* termed the Whitney program "immeasurably superior" to the work at the New School but was otherwise not particularly flattering. He likened the work to "cartoons" and felt it lacked real bite or variety. Henry McBride of the New York *Sun*

Thomas Hart Benton, The Arts of Life in America, Political Business and Intellectual Ballyhoo, egg tempera and oil on canvas, 1932. •

189

Thomas Hart Benton, Arts of the City.

complained: "There isn't a single reference to the rewards of virtue or the charm of ordered living. . . . The painting of these murals is quite as raw and uncouth as the subject matter. Any one who has been educated to what has heretofore been considered 'style' in painting must shudder at Mr. Benton's cheap colors and the unnice manner in which they have been banged upon canvas."

The most hostile review—the *first* entirely negative assessment of Benton's work —was written by Paul Rosenfeld for the *New Republic.* "Ex–Reading Room" condemned the murals as an offense to their location, to social decency, and to artistic good taste. In the best novelistic fashion, he began by describing how the Whitney's reading room had once been a cozy, "quiet little place"; after Tom got through with it, "the frightened visitor" was confronted by "super-life-size Michelangelesque figures . . . squirming forward and up and making as if to spring out and land full force upon him."

This terrifying experience, Rosenfeld argued, could have been avoided if Benton had properly studied Puvis de Chavannes and learned to make his paintings shrink back into the wall. Instead the painter had created a " 'pseudo' plasticity," which "smells of formula." Benton's color, Rosenfeld declared, "does almost nothing"; and "as for contrasting textures, he does not seem to be aware of their existence." Thus the eye moved monotonously from one form to another, unable to find more than "another tiresome expression of the childish lack of respect for the identity of things."

But what was most shocking was that Benton lacked "fine, true feeling." According to Rosenfeld, his thesis was "that the arts of life in America are thoroughly crude, gross and ungracious. And to illustrate it he has presented us with dancing, carousing, murdering types drawn from the primitive fringe of American life, from among Indians, city racketeers and burlesque-show entertainers, hillbillies and cornfield Negroes; and exhibited them now humorously, now nastily, violently, hysterically expressing the national insensibility. . . .

"We have lost more than we gained," Rosenfeld commented, and then added, just to rub the painter's nose a bit deeper into the dirt, that it was "indisputable" that the paintings represented "an advance" over his "fresco" in the New School.

To Benton's discomfort, shortly after Rosenfeld's piece appeared, a group of teachers and students at the Art Students League, apparently led by Stuart Davis, passed around a petition urging that the murals be destroyed. The main reason for this stand was the alleged racism of his portrayal of black people. Around this time, Benton lost all the black students in his classes, as well as a good many of the Jews and other liberals. Mervin Jules, for example, later stated: "[Benton] and I broke up over his portrayal of the Negroes in the mural he did for the Whitney. There was a basic antihumanist approach that was reflected in all his people."

Despite this controversy, Benton's work continued to receive high praise. *The Nation* singled him out for their "Honor Roll" of Americans who had made an important contribution to art or literature over the course of the year. The Architectural League awarded him its gold medal for mural painting.

In November 1934, the Whitney murals again became the subject of dispute, this time in the trial for custody of ten-year-old Gloria Vanderbilt, whose mother sought to wrest her from her aunt, Gertrude Whitney. The Vanderbilt lawyer claimed that the

Whitney Museum housed immoral art, and that consequently Mrs. Whitney was unfit to retain custody of the child. John Sloan's rooftop love scenes were mentioned in the indictment, but the paintings that got most attention were Thomas Benton's "Communistic" murals, with their cast of gamblers, bootleggers, gangsters, chorus girls, and women of easy virtue. Photographs of the murals were taken by court order and shown to the jury, and curious crowds began to gather outside the museum. The director of the galleries closed the library to the public.

The New York *Evening Journal* noted that Benton spoke "the plain language of the Midwest" in defending his work. He told their reporter: "It is true my murals include the synthesis of the color and tempo of the jazz age as represented by racketeers, fast women, gunmen, booze hounds and so on. Merely viewing these subjects would hardly debauch or harm anyone. Censorship is damnable. My subjects portray American life in the 20th century realistically. It may be life that should be criticized; but not my painting of it. . . . The Vanderbilt child would see much more of life in the raw on the streets of New York than in any museum."

Despite his dispute with Juliana Force, he ended with words of high praise for what the Whitney Museum had accomplished: "Mrs. Whitney deserves no censure for her museum. The results she has accomplished there have greatly advanced American art in the discovery of new talent as a constructive contribution to the aesthetic growth of the nation."

Chapter Ten
The Indiana Mural

Richard Lieber. An ardent conservationist, he pushed through a bill to have Benton paint the Indiana mural, against strong political opposition.

"This mural . . . is the outstanding and most significant painting in the history of American art."

"[This work] should offend the sensibilities of every Hoosier who has respect for the hardy pioneers from the East, West, North, and South that came to form the melting pot now known as Indiana."

"A Social History of Indiana"

Just at the height of his feud with Juliana Force, in December 1932, Benton fell unexpectedly into the largest commission of his career—a mural several hundred feet long for the State of Indiana. On its completion, a newspaper described the project as "possibly the longest unbroken and continuous mural composition ever painted."

In 1929 the Indiana legislature had appointed a committee to draw up plans for the state's contribution to the '33 Chicago World's Fair. After considerable bickering, it was decided that Indiana should send something more exciting than the usual display of pumpkins, ears of corn, and photographs of pigs. Instead it should send a mural. But seven months before the opening day, the committee was still deadlocked in choosing an artist. Aware that something had to be done in a hurry, they threw the problem into the hands of their chairman, Richard Lieber, an energetic conservationist of the Theodore Roosevelt/Gifford Pinchot persuasion, who had been running Indiana's state parks.

A few interviews convinced him that no Indiana artist had the technical know-how to perform the task, so he asked Thomas Hibben for advice. Hibben, the state architect for park improvements, recommended Tom Benton, whom he had met a few years before at the New York apartment of his brother Paxton Hibben, a writer and poet. He had also seen Benton's early mural experiments at the Architectural League and had vigorously approved of them.

At first Benton was appalled by the size of the task and the limited time for its execution. The painting was to be 14 feet high and 230 feet long—about the size of a city block. It had to be ready for installation in Chicago by June 3, now six months away. However, the state was offering substantial pay for the job, ten thousand dollars, far more than Benton had ever earned and a sizable sum for the middle of the Depression.

After his name was announced in the newspapers, a storm of protest broke out. Many representatives wanted to have a native son create the scheme. They pointed out that no one in Indiana owned a Benton. Some of the legislators read the New York *Sun* and remembered that Henry McBride, in a review of the Whitney murals, had labeled Benton a Communist. Photographs of the murals were circulated to the legislators, accompanied by the question: "Do you want this artist, already judged incompetent by New York, to represent our State at the World's Fair?"

A Hoosier History (World's Fair booklet cover), 1933. Benton's largest mural was the one he painted in six months for the State of Indiana. It was shown at the 1933 Chicago World's Fair.

A STORY IN FORM AND WORD

INDIANA

A HOOSIER HISTORY
by
DAVID LAURANCE CHAMBERS
· BASED ON THE MURAL PAINTINGS OF ·
THOMAS HART BENTON
1 ⊠ 9 ⊠ 3 ⊠ 3

Thomas Hibben. The architect for the state of Indiana recommended Benton for the Indiana mural commission.

The opponents, however, did not present a clear alternative. When questioned, none of them could come up with the name of an Indiana muralist. Richard Lieber, moreover, gave a persuasive presentation of Benton's family background. He explained at length that this artist was the son of a Missouri congressman and U.S. district attorney, and was the grandnephew of the great Missouri senator whose name he bore. Thus Benton's Midwestern credentials were established for the first time. After some controversy, the contract was approved, and the artist signed it late in December 1932.

Even then, feelings still ran high in the Indiana art community, for because of the Depression, the plight of painters was unusually desperate. One Indianapolis artist, Elmer Taflinger, was so upset at not having been awarded the commission that he sued for a "change of nativity" in the Marion County Circuit Court, arguing that he might have had a better chance to sell his work to the state if he had not been born in Indiana.

Just after the legislature's vote had finally been taken, one old gentleman demanded the floor. Facing about, with his hands upraised in solemn admonition, he addressed the chamber. "Gentlemen," said he, "you have chosen Mr. Benton. So be it. But there is one thing more which I would like to know. It has been brought out that Mr. Benton will use crates of eggs in doing this job. What I want to know is this. Will Mr. Benton buy his eggs in Indiana or New York?"

Tom got off to a slow start, for just after his arrival in Indiana he came down with a bad cold, which laid him up for a week. While lying in bed in an Indianapolis hotel, he worked out preliminary plans and read whatever local history he could get hold of. After three weeks of reading and making sketches, he set out with a very able park department employee, H. K. Roberts, to drive around the state and gather impressions. They covered some three thousand miles, visiting places with names like Turkey Run and Nashville, and although it was winter, and cold and windy, Benton collected a great deal of material. He and Roberts would come into a small town or city, look up the mayor and civic leaders, and explain their purpose. Invariably, they received a warm welcome.

Indiana is a great state for historical hoarding, and they located all kinds of costumes and implements from the early days of the region's history. Benton also sketched Indians, local characters, and old buildings, and analyzed the color schemes of the landscape. At night they visited the pool halls and bowling alleys, and often, on Wednesdays, the churches.

After completing his tour of the state, Tom moved into an abandoned beer hall in Indianapolis, the Germania, at 37 South Delaware Street. The Hall was approximately forty by one hundred feet, with a twenty-foot ceiling and a balcony that extended about fifteen feet from one of the end walls. This amount of space made it possible temporarily to arrange the panels he painted in approximately the same position they would occupy in the World's Fair building in Chicago.

He received his first payment in January, but it didn't last long. Ross Teckemeyer, who acted as agent and auditor of the mural project for the Indiana World's Fair Commission, later recalled: "When Mr. Benton received his first $1,000.00 he immediately attempted to take care of the needs of every deserving artist and art student in sight. He gave a rather elaborate party for all. The result was that Mr. Benton had received the first $1,000 for his painting and had no money for the Benton family in New York. Hearing of this party Mrs. Benton immediately came to Indianapolis and arrangements were made, that in addition to my being Auditor for the commission I was to be the financial agent for Mr. Benton, so that from January until he completed his work partial payments were made to Mr. Benton and 50% immediately sent to Mrs. Benton, the balance being used to pay Benton's hotel bills and other necessary living expenses. . . . Under this arrangement a stop was put to many of the extravagant parties. And for the time my popularity with the artists and Mr. Benton dropped to zero, and although I was with Mr. Benton as much as any other person during the time he completed the mural I am not one of those lucky enough to have his portrait appear."

Construction of the wall panels, which were very similar to those Benton made for the New School, was handled by the state World's Fair Commission; the carpentry was carried on in Germania Hall side by side with his artistic activity. The commission had great difficulty finding canvas large enough for the panels, but it eventually obtained five rolls directly from the manufacturer, sixty feet long and twelve feet four inches wide. These rolls were more than sufficient in length, but allowed only two inches to wrap around top and bottom, and to make the canvas secure.

The usual custom was to employ white lead to glue the canvas to its support, but it soon became apparent that this did not dry quickly enough because of the vast picture surface. After some experiment, Roberts found that boat glue made an excellent quick-drying substitute, but a thorough search of Indianapolis turned up only about half a gallon of boat glue. Luckily more could be obtained from the manufacturer. The white lead was used to paint the backs of the panels, which fortuitously helped prevent them from warping the next year when they were stored in a damp horse barn.

Once the canvas had been fastened down, it was covered with three coats of gesso, producing a surface like a plaster wall. Each of the twenty-two completed panels weighed approximately a ton.

Among the difficulties connected with the ordering of materials, Teckemeyer noted that "One other problem . . . came about through authority given to Mr. Benton to purchase all supplies necessary at state expense. This authority was handled by him about the same as if authority had been given a six or seven year old child to purchase any or all of the toys he could find, without any regard to cost.

Thomas Hart Benton, Studies for the Indiana Mural, 1933. "If my murals come to have an enduring life," Benton wrote in 1933, "it will be wholly because their form was directed by little drawings like these made in the heat of direct experience."

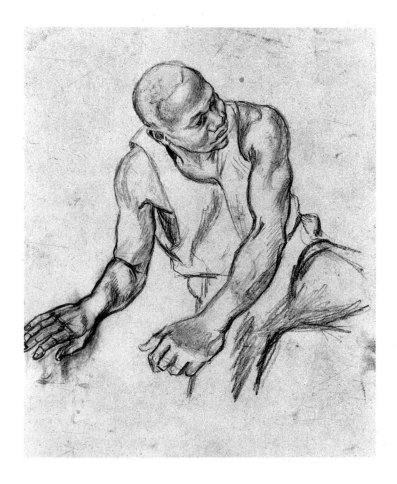

Thomas Hart Benton, Studies
for "A Social History of Indiana," *pencil on paper, 1933.
Benton logged thousands of
miles traveling through the state
of Indiana, making on-the spot
sketches of Indiana people.*

196

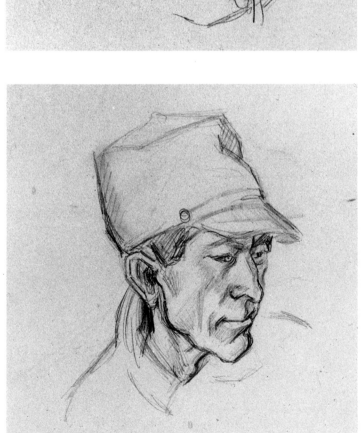

"Mr. Benton had been rather hard put for materials before he took this contract. . . . The purchases were all selected from catalogues of H. Lieber and Company and after considerable correspondence between H. Lieber and Company and the brush manufacturers, they were able to deliver approximately 50% of Mr. Benton's original order because the balance of the brushes selected by him were either out of stock or were no longer manufactured. It developed later that the 50% of the order delivered was sufficient to complete the entire painting of the murals."

He continued: "One item in particular which caused us considerable trouble was Mr. Benton's request that he have not less than two dozen fresh eggs each day. By fresh eggs he meant eggs that were not more than 24 hours old. . . . One of the assistants who was helping with the construction work lived in Whiteland, Indiana and since he commuted each day he was given the additional task of securing the . . . eggs."

Benton made the first sketch of the mural composition in pen and ink on a strip of paper that was four inches high and proportionally long. Once this was complete, he modeled each compositional unit of the mural in clay and photographed the sculptures, lit from a precise angle, in order to study the distribution of light and shade. He painted the model in color (previously, he had painted his models in black and white).

Once the model was complete, he enlarged the composition up to scale in two stages, referring as he did so to the drawings he had made during his tour of Indiana, as well as to other sketches, mostly portraits, that he did later. (During the course of the project, he made more than six hundred drawings, over one hundred fifty of which were portraits of local people.)

The final black-and-white full-scale cartoon was executed by referring to the three types of preparatory studies—life drawings, compositional sketches, and the clay model. The last step was to make a full-scale cartoon in color. Benton generally worked steadily through the day, got drunk for an hour or so in the evening to relax, jerked himself sober by a walk outdoors, and then worked on into the night.

In March 1933, just as he was completing the cartoon, the John Herron Art Institute in Indianapolis put on an exhibition of his work. Although he had begun to be described in the press as a "Midwestern" artist, this was Benton's first one-man show to be held west of New York.

In the catalogue, he stated: "These drawings are not only objective records, but carry a full train of personal association which enables me to return in imagination to the place and people they represent and live over my experience. If my murals come to

Thomas Hart Benton, Working Drawings for "Colleges and City Life," *pencil on paper, 1933.*

have an enduring life, it will be wholly because their form was directly by little drawings like these made in the heat of direct experience."

Until past the middle of March, the large panels lay untouched while Benton worked on his sketches, the clay model, and the cartoon. Then, with the help of some students and friendly artists, he squared up the cartoons and transferred the design to the mural panels. Only at this stage—having already rigorously analyzed the initial life experience, the overall composition, the sculptural arrangement of volumes, the balance of light and shade, and the distribution of color—was he ready to begin painting.

Thanks to his painstaking preparations, he was able to work with almost incredible rapidity. In a reminiscence about this project, he later wrote: "The very thought of large spaces puts me in an exalted state of mind, strings up my energies, and heightens the color of the world. After I have gone through with my practical preparations, which are elaborate and occupy the major part of the time spent on any job, a certain kind of thoughtless freedom comes over me. I don't give a damn about anything. Once on the wall, I paint with downright sensual pleasure. The colors I use make my mouth water. The sweep of my brushes, after I get really started, becomes precise and somehow or other beyond error. I get cocksure of mind and temperamentally youthful. I run easily into childish egomania or adolescent emotionalism."

Once he began painting, he worked from morning until dinnertime without a break, and frequently went back to work at night. He made no changes or corrections after he had finished a passage. In an almost unbelievable feat of stamina, he painted the entire mural, totaling some 2,600 square feet of canvas, in sixty-three days. He later boasted to Richard Beer: "I guess that beats Rivera's time."

Like hobbyists who construct cement boats in their basement, Benton had made an impractical creation, too large for the door and the stairs. To get the paintings out, workmen broke through the wall of Germania Hall, making a space about twenty feet high and two feet wide. A derrick then lowered the two-thousand-pound panels to the ground, three stories below. Because of the delicacy of the panels, all the workers who touched them wore white cotton gloves; they had attended a special session on proper handling.

Capital Transport Company of Indianapolis shipped the mural to Chicago, in a trailer that had been specially constructed. Unable to travel flat without damage, the panels needed to be packed in a vertical position along their shortest dimension. Consequently the interior of the trailer was slightly over twelve feet high. Since the roof could rise no more than thirteen feet, in order to fit under the elevated railways on the route, the floor of the trailer was set less than twelve inches above the roadbed.

Things went well until the truck reached the outskirts of Chicago, where it was discovered that Illinois required only a twelve-foot clearance on overhead tracks.

The Fur Traders and Pioneers. *To the left, George Rogers Clark crosses the swamps of the Wabash River to capture the English fort at Vincennes. To the right, American pioneers push into the wilderness, despite some Indians who lie in ambush.*

Women's Place and the Old Time Doctor and the Grange. *The brilliant but unstable bluestocking Frances Wright, an agitator for women's rights, lectures to a group of middle-aged women. Two amused boys look on, and others strip off their clothes and cavort naked around a swimming hole. Behind her, paying no heed to her words, a couple kiss in a side-bar buggy.*

Because the truck would not fit under the bridges, a hundred-thirty-five-mile detour was made to Evanston, north of the city. There the truckers found a route to the fairgrounds, running through Northwestern University, that did not pass under any overhead bridge. In order to get through the campus, however, it was necessary to tear down and then re-erect a college gateway. The paintings got to the fairgrounds twelve hours late.

Benton came to Chicago to supervise installation in the Indiana pavilion, where it completely encircled a room thirty-eight feet wide and seventy-eight feet long. He had left one panel unpainted, feeling that he could finish it better in Chicago, where he could see just how it would be lit. Ross Teckemeyer has recorded the difficulties this created: "After working two or three days, between night life in Chicago and an ulcerated tooth, Mr. Benton decided that it would be impossible for him to complete this panel in time for the opening. So after a rather heated argument I told Mr. Benton that I would obtain a sign painter friend of mine in Indianapolis who I was sure could complete the panel before the opening day. Mr. Benton immediately arranged to visit a dentist, have the ulcerated tooth treated, and return to his task, and did complete the panel in plenty of time for the opening."

The opening proved, quite literally, to be a stormy one. Because of a misunderstanding about meeting places, the governor of Indiana, Paul McNutt, dressed in formal attire, walked in heavy rain from the Twelfth Street entrance to the fairgrounds to the Twenty-third Street gate—a distance of about a mile and a half. As Teckemeyer commented, "You can imagine his mental attitude toward the entire affair when he discovered that the reception committee was at another entrance."

The governor's annoyance was mild compared to that of some of those who attended the Indiana Day celebration, which had been set inauspiciously on July 13. There Charles O. Grafton, a dissident member of the state's World's Fair Commission, backed by the directors of the Hoosier Salon, publicly complained once more that the mural commission had not been awarded to a native of Indiana. A journalist covering the affair nicely summarized the views of this group: "By the adverse critics [the mural] is declared to be entirely misrepresentative of the spirit of Indiana and its figures are

The Mound Builders. *The sequence of "Cultural Progress" began with a scene of the prehistoric mound builders of Indiana.*

The Indians. *Benton started the sequence of "Industrial Progress" with a scene of the Algonquian Indians of Indiana, hunters who possessed only a few simple crafts.*

Home Industry and Internal Improvements. *The pioneers clear the land and construct houses and gristmills.*

Frontier Life and The French. *The French were the first settlers in Indiana. Benton showed Jesuits working to convert the Indians, and high-spirited settlers dancing and fighting.*

Reformers and Squatters and Early Schools and Communities. *In the foreground is Abraham Lincoln, who spent his first fourteen years in Indiana. Behind him stands a printer, with a poster for a runaway slave; and a country "blab" school, so called because the pupils conned their lessons out loud. In the distance on the right, Benton showed the New Harmony community, led by Father Rapp, who claimed to receive divine guidance from an angel. The angel hovers overhead. In the right foreground is the English idealist Robert Owen, who bought out the Rappite Community.*

Indiana Puts Her Trust in Work. *Benton ended his industrial saga with a view of the vast limestone quarries of the Bedford-Bloomington district. In the background are an oil storage tank and factory smokestacks. Above the doorway, to the right, is a bank closed at the start of the Depression. A construction worker rivets together a new building in the foreground. The future seems hopeful but uncertain.*

The Civil War and Expansion. *After the Civil War came a burst of growth and prosperity. Railroad building takes place in the foreground; farming with a new-fangled tractor and thresher in the background.*

Indiana Puts Her Trust in Thought. *Above the doorway, a scientist works in his laboratory, and Governor Paul McNutt, a Democratic reformer, campaigns in front of headlines broadcasting unemployment and social discontent. Just to the right, three tough-looking characters stand in line for relief beside a sign reading "No Help Wanted." To the far right, basketball players compete and cars race around the Indianapolis Speedway. In the lower part of the panel, Benton showed himself painting a portrait of Thomas Hibben, the architect of the Indiana World's Fair pavilion.*

The Farmer, Up and Down *and* Coal, Gas, Oil, Brick. *Benton's mural included a typical farm of the Depression era, as well as an unsightly strip-mining scene, based on his travels through the Terre Haute district of southern Indiana. The mining panel showed Eugene Debs addressing mineworkers and an angry striker preparing to throw a rock at a soldier.*

Colleges and City Life and Leisure and Literature. *A parade marches through the center of Indianapolis, briefly halting two cyclists and a mule-drawn streetcar. To the right, a professorial figure in his mortarboard and academic gown stands in front of emblems of his learnedness—books, diplomas, and a globe.*

Electric Power, Motor-Cars, Steel. *This panel portrayed the heavily industrialized Calumet district of Indiana, with its steel mills, oil refineries, and electric plants. In the foreground, Benton showed the plan of the first gasoline-powered car constructed in America, the "Pioneer," developed by Elwood Haynes of Kokomo. This marvel achieved a speed of eight miles per hour.*

Parks, the Circus, the Klan, the Press. *A number of disconnected vignettes suggest the variety of Indiana life. A typesetter prints a newspaper while a reporter taps out a story; firemen douse the flames of a burning building; airplanes soar in the sky; the Ku Klux Klan stages a "Klavalcade"; a young black girl gets free hospital care; a circus girl rides a horse bareback; and two state park employees plant a tree.*

declared to be grim and forbidding. Only a Hoosier artist, they say, could have done justice to this work and Benton is not a Hoosier artist."

Subject Matter and Social Content

Because of the opposition of local artists, the mural had made strong enemies before it was even begun. Benton did what he could to ingratiate himself with the Indiana legislators. After work every day, he met with local politicians for a hotel-room drinking party—which they whimsically christened the "Children's Hour." Benton and his friend Tom Hibben footed the bill for the bootleg liquor but were well repaid in goodwill.

To his surprise, Benton found that he could air his political views far more freely than had been possible in New York. His supposed communism had already come up before the Indiana legislature, and the allegation that he was still a "fellow traveler" had thrown a real scare into Richard Lieber. At a time when even Franklin Roosevelt was widely viewed as a dangerous radical, any serious allegation of communism might have caused a political scandal.

In these "Children's Hour" gatherings, the painter would discuss his leftist affiliations quite openly. He told of his friendship with Bob Minor and of how, during the early twenties, he had helped find meeting places for the outlawed Communist party —on one occasion inviting them to his own apartment. He also detailed his disillusionment with communism and how he had lost faith in its applicability after his travels around the United States. Much of what he told them could have been damaging if repeated out of context, but no further allegations reached the newspapers, even though a number of reporters attended the drinking sessions.

Though well-read and liberal-minded about artistic experiment, Richard Lieber retained a strong sense of social propriety. He conceived the mural as a depiction of a chain of high achievements little different from the conventional statehouse or public library performance. With Tom Hibben's help, however, Benton was able to persuade Lieber to put subject matter as well as style entirely into the artist's hands. Once Lieber had decided to do so, he made only one sustained protest—when Benton included a representation of the Ku Klux Klan. Here the painter outmaneuvered him, however. With the complicity of an Indiana legislator named Bob, he invited Colonel Lieber to a "Children's Hour."

Once the group was together, Bob, according to plan, asked Tom whether he thought the Klan episode was of any importance to the state's history. Tom replied that he was unsure about the matter and appealed to the assembled politicians. These men were all newly elected Democrats, who took some pleasure in the fact that the growth of the Klan had occurred under a Republican administration. They promptly informed him that the subject was of immense importance, that it had nearly ruined the state, and that on no account should he leave it out. When Colonel Lieber left the party, he winked at Tom and told him, "You win."

Later, when Benton included a striker throwing a rock at a soldier, Lieber feared that Governor McNutt would take offense. The governor was undisturbed by it, however, and was further mollified when Tom put in a portrait of him campaigning, in the culminating panel of the mural. Indeed, he flattered many of the Indiana politicians by including their likenesses in the design.

Like the Whitney murals, the Indiana project presents the figures in a single, unified space—more successfully this time. Whereas the Whitney design breaks apart visually into independent vignettes, the Indiana one presents a unified flow of forms. As Thomas Craven observed, Benton's arrangement was established by abstract considerations of harmony and balance: "He sets one movement, or unit, of block-forms against another—a few large blocks against many small ones, a dominant rhythm balancing several minor strains—and all circulating around poles or centers of interest."

What was new about this mural was that it treated history and the passage of time—something Benton had not undertaken since his *American Historical Epic*. Space became time as history flowed onward like a great river. In the brief piece he wrote on the mural for a booklet circulated at the world's fair, he noted that the Indiana commission represented "a dream fulfilled," an opportunity to complete the social history he had attempted in his *Historical Epic*.

His treatment of history, however, was now considerably more vivid. Several of the panels focus on specific regions of Indiana: the Terre Haute district with its strip mines, the Calumet district with its steel mills and electric plants, and the Bedford-Bloomington district with its limestone quarries. A circus scene pays tribute to Peru, the winter home of the circus. A scene of automobile manufacture honors Elwood Haynes of Kokomo, who designed the first gasoline-powered car ever constructed in America, the "Pioneer," which achieved a speed of eight miles an hour.

Benton divided his general theme, *A Social History of Indiana*, into two series, "Industrial Progress" and "Cultural Progress," which balanced each other on opposite sides of the room. The two were not neatly distinct, for industrial developments had cultural consequences and vice versa. Indeed, some events, such as the carnage of the Civil War, appeared in both sets of panels.

"Industrial Progress" opens with a scene of Indians, with their primitive tools. They are displaced by the French fur trappers; and the trappers, in turn, are displaced by the pioneer settlers, who clear the land, plant crops, build houses, and construct gristmills. The panel titled *Internal Improvements* shows the rise of modern methods of transportation: a raft with a muscular boatman, a barge being pulled by a mule, a steamboat puffing upriver, and a steam locomotive. Overshadowed by this rush of activity, a tragic event occurs in the background: an Indian woman and her child are expelled from their land by armed men, to be sent to Kansas, on a death trail.

At the center of the Industrial Progress sequence Benton placed the Civil War. On the left, we look over a row of tombstones toward two corpses lying on a battlefield. In the center, a line of soldiers in blue uniforms marches into the black smoke funnel of war. On the right, Indiana's war governor, Morton, exhorts the troops forward on their march, while a woman behind him bursts into tears.

From this point onward, Benton showed the rise of modern industry, not without indicating its devastating social effects. New farm machinery, for example, brought increased production but also a dramatic drop in prices. The dilapidated farm conveys the effects of the recent vicious cycle of overproduction, mortgaged land, debt, and taxes (by 1933 farm property had dropped to half its 1920 value). Similarly, the strip mining scene portrays not only the unsightly detritus of modern mining methods but recent labor unrest as well. A leftist agitator (possibly Eugene Debs) addresses striking mineworkers, one of whom carries a placard reading: "Workers, why vote the rich man's ticket?" Farther to the right, an angry striker prepares to hurl a rock at a soldier. And the industrial saga ends, above the doorway to the right, with a foreclosed bank.

"Cultural Progress" begins with scenes of the prehistoric mound builders and the French settlers, and moves on to vignettes treating such cultural themes as *Early Schools*, *The Old-Time Doctor*, and *Colleges and City Life*. Several of the panels concentrate on the state's most notable figures, such as Abraham Lincoln, who spent his first fourteen years in Indiana; Robert Owen, who established a utopian community in the state; and Fanny Wright, the brilliant but emotionally unstable campaigner for women's rights. Most of the scenes contain outrageous juxtapositions. In one, Indiana's first statehouse is juxtaposed with its first lunatic asylum; another contrasts the cultivated painters and poets of Indiana with unrefined amusements such as a "Snake Lady," a horse race, and a trained pig. One particularly odd and crowded scene combines firemen putting out a fire, newspapermen setting up a paper, two park employees planting a tree, a circus girl riding bareback, a young black girl getting free hospital care, and the Ku Klux Klan burning a cross.

Once again, the sequence moves toward its close on a cautionary note. The recently elected Governor is seen campaigning in front of headlines that blare "State Reorganization" and "Unemployment." Below, three tough-looking characters stand in line beneath a sign reading "County Employment Relief"; another sign reads "No Help Wanted."

The last panel features basketball players and the Indianapolis Speedway. At the bottom, Benton can be seen painting the portrait of Tom Hibben, while Hibben designs the pavilion in which the mural was to be placed.

The two halves of the mural joined with a scene of the dunes country of Indiana, showing a strip of sand, a lake, and the black trunk of a dead tree. Sadly, this panel was never photographed and was lost or destroyed after the World's Fair. Its significance was explained by Wallace Richards, superintendent of the Indiana pavilion: "The history of the world shows that, despite all this progress, we will return to the land, symbolized by the lonely dunes and the desolate tree."

Afterward

As with *America Today* and *The Arts of Life in America*, *A Social History of Indiana* was widely reproduced. Sections from it appeared in such publications as the New York *Herald Tribune*, *Art News*, *Arts and Decoration*, and *Design*. Thomas Craven considered it Benton's finest work and wrote effusively: "This mural . . . is the outstanding and most significant painting in the history of American art." For once, Tom's work stirred up little controversy in the New York press. Indiana was probably too far away to seem significant.

In Indiana, the mural was much discussed. Zora Askew, president of the Lawrence County Historical Society, was particularly incensed by Benton's treatment of Indiana's early settlers. He declared that the work "should offend the sensibilities of every Hoosier who has respect for the hardy pioneers from the East, West, North, and South that came to form the melting pot now known as Indiana."

Lucille Morehouse, art reviewer for the Indianapolis *Star,* took issue with the unheroic depiction of Abraham Lincoln. "But methinks," she wrote pompously, "that the quite out of proportion head is so small that it hardly indicates the brain capacity of Lincoln." Other Hoosiers objected to the woman with scandalously large bare feet and a pink see-through dress in the *Home Industry* panel. In addition, they complained that the farmer's mule was standing still. Benton later recalled that a breeder of prize hogs objected to the common run of Indiana pigs that he had depicted.

The reactions of most viewers were apparently less heated. One reporter sat for a morning in the Indiana pavilion and recorded the interested but slightly puzzled responses of several visitors.

"It seems sort of odd for Indiana," one middle-aged woman in a summer dress commented to her friend. "But I feel sure it's very artistic. All but that old stump of a pine tree."

"Well, it's modern enough, all right," another amply proportioned woman declared.

In June 1933, Wallace Richards issued a statement denying that Tom was a Communist. "He has not injected propaganda into this mural, which was paid for by the state. But in showing the unrest in the southern mines, and displaying a sample of the propaganda displayed there, he gave that part of the history of the times."

Controversy about the paintings continued until the end of the fair and complicated efforts to find a home for them afterward. The Indiana art groups that had criticized the murals proposed that they should be sold or destroyed after the fair ended, on November 12, 1933. Fortunately, the state did not bow to their pressure but dismantled the twenty-two panels and shipped them to Indianapolis. Because of their size, a section of the wall of the pavilion was knocked down to remove them. This time, however, it did not prove necessary to go through Evanston. The truckers discovered that by using a private driveway through the South Chicago Gas Plant, they could eliminate several hours of travel.

In Indianapolis, the paintings were stored in the Capital Transfer Company's garage on East Washington Street. After a year, to save storage fees, they were moved to the Manufacturers Building at the State Fair Ground in Indianapolis, a structure used as a stable most of the year. Soon state fair officials began to complain that the paintings were taking up "valuable space." In 1938 Governor M. Clifford Townsend donated the mural to Indiana University, and it was transferred there the next year.

In 1941 most of the panels were installed in the new university auditorium, and on March 22 of that year Benton attended the dedication of the building. The architects had placed large urns containing spotlights atop the marble pilasters on each staircase, and Tom exploded when he saw them, for they blocked the view of his paintings. "Who put those god-damned spittoons in the way?" he shouted.

The next day, the St. Louis *Post-Dispatch* and the Indianapolis papers carried the story. Betty Foster, art critic for the Indianapolis *News,* commented snidely that the architects had not placed the "spittoons" on the pilasters until they saw the murals. Today the urns sit on the floor, although no one seems to know exactly when or how they got there.

Chapter Eleven
Hitting the Big Time

"The Modernist movement has come and gone," Craven wrote hopefully. "It went over in a remarkably short time."

Return to New York, 1934

The years 1934 and 1935 marked a watershed in Benton's life, a turning point after which his existence was never the same. On December 24, 1934, he was featured on the cover of *Time* magazine and achieved the stardom he had always dreamed of—the sort of fame to which business leaders, statesmen, and movie stars aspire, but that no previous American painter had ever realized.

This notoriety did not prove entirely a blessing. Benton's outspokenness, his political viewpoints, and the egotistical directness with which he had pushed his way to the top inspired bitter hatred and jealousies. By the spring of 1935, he had become embroiled in bitter disputes with Alfred Stieglitz, with Stuart Davis, with his old leftist and Communist allies, and even, odd as it may sound, with diehard defenders of the Deep South. New York became increasingly unpleasant for him; he could not give a lecture without being shouted down. In April 1935, he fled the conflicts he had stirred up, to return to his native state of Missouri.

By the time he completed his Indiana mural, Tom felt like an empty sack; returning to Martha's Vineyard, he found it hard to do much more than toot on his harmonica. After six weeks on the island, he went back to New York City, but the atmosphere there was cold and inhospitable. Leo Huberman and the rest of the Marxists were openly unfriendly to him, and so were his fellow teachers at the Art Students League. In search of some local color, he went to the Tammany Club in his Greenwich Village neighborhood, but the poker-playing, dice-throwing politicos assumed that he was looking for a soft spot on the WPA, and they ridiculed him and his work. He quickly fled back to the art world; his only real companionship came from his young students.

Fortunately, late in September 1933, he received a note from his friend Carl Ruggles, the composer, suggesting a visit to his place in Vermont, where the autumn foliage was just beginning to burst into color. Benton and Ruggles were kindred spirits. Rowdy and impractical, Carl was fond of ribald stories, which his wife did her best to suppress, and was, as Tom recalled, "one of my favorite masters of 'cussing.' " Like Tom, he was unimpressed by high society. As the musician Charles Seeger recalled: "He is just as likely to be having for dinner the local traffic cop or the village house-painter as a distinguished writer, artist, capitalist or scientist." Carl composed his music on old pieces of wrapping paper of varying colors and sizes—ruling his staff lines about an inch apart and marking in the notes with a crayon.

Having nothing better to do, Benton made the trip up to Arlington, assuming that a walk through the autumn hills would recharge his empty spirits. He got recharged, all right, though it was not the scenery that did it but Carl Ruggles himself. Not more

Thomas Hart Benton, Self-Portrait, *oil on canvas, 1925. The artist wields his paintbrush like a club.* •

Thomas Hart Benton, The Sun-Treader (Portrait of Carl Ruggles), *egg tempera on canvas mounted on panel, 1934.* •

than an hour after he arrived, while Carl was banging out Wagnerian chords on the piano, Tom started making drawings of him.

After he returned to New York, Benton composed his sketches into a painting, *The Sun-Treader,* a portrait of the composer at his piano. Ruggles liked to work in nondifferentiated secundal counterpoint—a form that stresses the inharmonious seconds and sevenths. His music, consequently, had a continuously dissonant, grainy texture, which he emphasized by the use of all-string or all-brass instrumentation. In one piece, for example, he set six horns in unison against an orchestra. Tom tried to capture this impulsive, dissonant spirit in his painting.

The title comes from Ruggles's best-known composition, named after a line from "Pauline," Robert Browning's 1833 elegy to Percy Bysshe Shelley: "Sun-treader, life and light be thine forever."

Shortly after completing the portrait, Benton wrote to the composer: "The portrait I made of you came off fairly well though Charlie [Seeger] says (in fun) that the piano looks like its going to take flight. . . . As a picture it is the best thing I've done this winter." Later in life, he commented: "I have always thought this to be one of the best portrait compositions I ever made."

Paintings of Blacks and Hillbillies

After the demise of the Delphic Galleries, Benton moved to the Ferargil Galleries at 63 East 57th Street, run by Frederic Newlin Price. Tom later remembered him as "a pretty good fellow," but added: "He was a regular dealer; like all the rest of them he was working for himself rather than for the artist." And: "He had a lot of fake Ryders. He had the only Ryders that didn't have cracks. So he probably had them made by somebody."

In April 1934, Ferargil exhibited Benton's recent paintings and drawings, including several studies for the Indiana mural—the first New York showing of his work in four years. His continuing interest in controversial social themes was demonstrated by such titles as *Milk and Mortgages, Strike,* and *Kidnappers.* There was one abstraction, painted within the year, *Twelve Planes and a Silver Egg.*

Edward Alden Jewell of the *Times* loved the show; Royal Cortissoz of the *Tribune* had mixed feelings. Genteel Henry McBride of the *Sun* declared: "The drawing is rough and unsensitive, the color is crude, and the wit is the kind that passes, possibly, in a logging camp, but is not apt to have success elsewhere." Despite the mixed reviews, the paintings were beginning to sell. In November 1933, the Metropolitan Museum acquired *The Cotton Pickers,* which had been exhibited at the Chicago World's Fair; and in the spring of 1934, the Addison Gallery of American Art at Phillips Andover Academy purchased *Cattle Loading, West Texas.* In December 1934, Marshall Field III purchased *Cotton Town,* a painting based on Benton's 1932 trip through Georgia.

At this time, Benton's subject matter increasingly emphasized the blacks and poor whites of the rural South. He virtually ceased to paint urban scenes. His new focus on blacks and hillbillies signaled his growing estrangement from the New York art world, his disenchantment with "ideas" and the mouthings of intellectuals.

During the summer of 1934, Benton returned to the South. This time, he visited a small country seat in West Virginia, on the outer rim of the Blue Ridge where it breaks into the Cumberlands. At the only theater in town, he found a sign announcing that that evening at eight, "Five Famous Colored Artists and Entertainers" would perform. He entered the pool hall next door and asked what the show was. "Ah don't reckon they'll be no show," one of the loafers declared. "It's a bunch of uppity niggers and we don't 'low no niggers in here."

The performance went on without incident. The black performers somehow sensed the unfriendly atmosphere and put on an exaggerated pantomime of fear, rolling their eyes and working their thick, painted lips. The audience applauded and laughed uproariously, and during the night the troupe slipped away unharmed. The next morning, a boy in the hotel told Benton, "Them niggers was all right." Tom's

sketch of the performance later served as the basis for his painting *Minstrel Show*. In
it, he grotesquely exaggerated the large ears and protruding elbows of the poor white
audience, the eyes and lips of the black performers.

In December 1934, Benton and Bill Hayden made a brief excursion into the
Smoky Mountains. Their expenses were covered by an Italian newspaper correspondent, who wanted to verify the social conditions described in Erskine Caldwell's *Tobacco Road*. He was a man of luxurious habits who took great pride in his cultivation.
Tom and Bill drove him from one disreputable dump to another, trying their damnedest to offend his sensitivities. As he was looking for *Tobacco Road* color, he should
have been delighted, but instead he was generally in a dyspeptic mood.

One day, a bit west of Greenville, South Carolina, they came upon a strange
caravan of holiness people, all tired and bedraggled. After a stint of "missionaryin' "
up in the mountains, this troop had walked for two days on their way home. In
exchange for a lift, they allowed Tom and his friends to witness their service the next
day. A woman preacher prayed for the healing of a child with rickets, but her performance was interrupted by a stabbing outside, which emptied half the benches.

The experience led to one of Benton's most ambitious paintings of 1934, *Lord,
Heal the Child*, which incorporated the preacher, the child, and a lanky banjo player
named Red. Benton also added elements as they were needed for the design, such as,
in the orchestra, Homer Leverett of Galena, Missouri, and "Uncle Lawrence," an aged
mountain fiddler from Tennessee.

Starting in the late 1920s, Benton began to make musicians and country ballads a
central theme of his work, particularly his easel paintings. Many of his most memorable paintings of the period derive their titles from country music, including *Country
Dance* of 1928, *The Engineer's Dream* of 1930, and *Missouri Musicians* of 1931.

Country music, in fact, had come to national attention at almost exactly the
moment that Benton turned from painting modernistic "figure organizations" to depicting American subject matter. In 1923, just shortly before Tom went to visit his
dying father in Missouri, Vernon Dalhart released the first million-selling country

music hit, a railroad song on which Tom based a painting in the 1940s, *The Wreck of the Old 97*. His interest in musical themes reached its peak in 1933–34, for his four most significant paintings of that year—*Minstrel Show, Lord, Heal the Child, The Sun-Treader,* and *The Ballad of the Jealous Lover of Lone Green Valley*—all deal, in one way or another, with music.

Perhaps the most remarkable of these was *The Jealous Lover of Lone Green Valley*. At the lower right, a group of musicians plays the song that gives its title to the piece, while the words of the song materialize up above them to the left, where the jealous lover is shown stabbing his unfortunate girlfriend. Green, the color of jealousy and envy, predominates in the color scheme.

In addition to sight, the painting evokes each of the other four senses. It conjures up smell through the flowers (and the outhouse in the distance!); touch through the woman being stabbed (and the blood she feels with her hand as it oozes from her body); and taste through the jug of liquor on the table. Sound, of course, is the main subject of the painting and is evoked by the swirling band of color superimposed with musical notes and designed in an ear-like shape.

Throughout the painting one finds references to Benton's study of abstract art: the rainbow of color, representing the violinist's music, derives directly from Synchromist effects; the tipped-up tabletop at the lower right recalls Picasso's *Les Demoiselles d'Avignon*, where a very similar element appears in the same portion of the design. Indeed, the design exemplifies those principles that Benton passed on to Jackson Pollock, who posed for the moronic-looking figure on the left, humming on a Jew's harp.

Thomas Hart Benton, Lord, Heal the Child, *egg tempera and oil on canvas, 1934.* •

Thomas Hart Benton, The Ballad of the Jealous Lover of Lone Green Valley, *egg tempera and oil on canvas, 1934.* •

Ravin' Craven

From their direct contact with modernism, Tom Benton and Thomas Craven had learned a lot about the power of language—had learned that successful art movements need strong words quite as much as strong paintings. Synchromism, for example, the creation of their good friend Macdonald-Wright, was nearly as much a manifesto as a school of painting. The first Synchromist exhibition in Munich stirred up a sensation thanks to the flier that accompanied it, five thousand of which were distributed in a few hours. The Synchromists, in their turn, had learned from the Futurists; a year or so before the first Synchromist show Morgan Russell had pasted the Futurist Manifesto into his scrapbook.

Starting in 1919, as we have seen, Craven and Benton formed an alliance of art and art criticism. Benton provided Craven with theories and opinions; Craven promoted Benton's work. From that time on, they moved forward like two mountain climbers roped together. Until 1926, Craven wrote mostly for *The Dial,* which reached an audience of adventurous sophisticates to whom he presented Benton as a figure in the vanguard of modern art. After 1926, however, just as Benton was turning toward American subject matter, Craven began to write for mass-circulation tabloids. He shifted to picturing Benton as a foe of French modernist influences and as the leader of a native American school. About 1929, Craven launched a frontal attack on French influence, in articles with such titles as "The Curse of French Culture."

214

In the spring of 1931, just after Benton had completed his *America Today* murals, Craven published *Men of Art,* a survey of Western painting from Giotto to modern times. The book was packed with racy anecdotes and colorful invective; the Book-of-the-Month Club made it one of its main selections, and it became the best-selling artbook of the decade. For the first time, an American writer on art broke through to a popular audience on a grand scale. Most of the book dealt with the old masters, but one chapter was a condemnation of the French modernists, and a final seven-page coda described the author's "Hopes and Fears for America." Here Craven praised "the growing desire to throw off the European yoke" and expressed his belief that "It is in North America, or Russia, or perhaps in combination of the two, that we must plant our hopes for the significant expression of the new age."

Men of Art was followed with *Modern Art: The Men, the Movements, the Meaning,* in the summer of 1934. This was a direct assault on the modernist movement. "Thomas Craven Embalms Modern Art and Buries It on the Left Bank," one headline announced; Virgil Barker described the tract as "a piece of modernist-baiting to make a Babbitt's holiday." "The Modernist movement has come and gone," Craven wrote hopefully. "It went over in a remarkably short time."

The essay on Matisse in *Modern Art* typifies those qualities of Craven's writing that recent scholars have found offensive. He began by comparing the French painter to a prosperous Jew and then denounced him and his "Negro-maniacs and would-be Persians" for his "infantile draftsmanship" and for worshipping "Congo sculpture, the descriptive scratches of the Bushman, Peruvian pottery, and everything else that was savage and undisciplined." Matisse's chief contribution was that of "deflecting the Modernist current into the sleazy boudoir tradition of France." By no means all of Craven's targets lived on the other side of the Atlantic. He ridiculed the "preposterous theories" of Alfred Stieglitz, "a Hoboken Jew without knowledge of, or interest in, the historical American background."

Two factors seem to account for the heated tenor of these assaults—which, it should be noted, often run directly counter to Craven's earlier statements in *The Dial.* The first of these was his move from intellectual to mass-circulation magazines. Somewhere between lay H. L. Mencken's *American Mercury,* and it was probably in part from Mencken that Craven developed a fondness for flamboyant invective. (It stands as a tribute to the power of Craven's prose that many reviewers of his books did not attempt to summarize them but simply quoted long passages.) The second factor was Craven's strong identification with Benton, whose critics had initiated the game of name-calling in their mosquito-bite reviews, such as Paul Rosenfeld's vigorous attack in the *New Republic.* Craven retaliated with hundreds of pages of vituperation. These attacks came at a time of severe hardship for many artists, and they undoubtedly won Benton as many enemies as friends.

Because Craven cudgeled the modernist movement so vigorously, it has not been noted that his plea for a cultural nationalism was largely drawn from the modernist precursors. The conservative American painters, the denizens of the National Academy of Design, were quite comfortable with a conformist sort of painting that resembled the academic productions of the French. The American modernists, however, felt very differently. Even before the First World War, journals such as *The Dial,* the *New Republic,* and *The Seven Arts* made a conscious effort to invigorate the American spirit. After the Armory Show, Stieglitz ceased to promote the work of Europeans and sought to cultivate American forms of expression; Francis Picabia told journalists in 1913 that Europe was outplayed and the Modern Age would flower in the United States.

For all the force and power of his criticism, Craven failed to take the final step necessary to bring Benton's work to national attention. From the late 1920s up to autumn 1933, both he and the other writers sympathetic to Benton's work spoke of him primarily as a mural painter, as an American counterpart and rival of the Mexican Diego Rivera. What brought Benton to national fame was not the partisan support of Thomas Craven but less idealistic motives: the desire to market paintings and to sell magazines. In the autumn of 1933, his work was linked for the first time with that of two other Midwestern artists, John Steuart Curry and and Grant Wood. This linkage began as a promotional ploy, a sales gimmick initiated by an art dealer; but the notion of a Midwestern school proved captivating, and was picked up by the national press. Before long, it not only dramatically shifted public perceptions of Benton's art but brought about a major shift in the nature of the art.

TIME Magazine and "The U.S. Scene"

Maynard Walker has never been discussed in histories of American painting and has never been mentioned in the books on Thomas Hart Benton. Yet it was he who made Benton famous and created the art movement now known as Regionalism.

Walker was born in Garnett, Kansas. He studied painting, worked briefly as a journalist in Kansas City, and by the early 1930s had landed at the Ferargil Galleries, as the partner of Frederic Newlin Price. Despite his move to New York, he remained in touch with his friends in the Midwest, and in 1933 he organized a small exhibition of thirty-five American paintings at the Kansas City Art Institute. Most of the canvases came from the Ferargil's stock. In this show, Walker brought together, for the first time, the work of Benton, Curry, and Wood—who were to become the "big three" of the Regionalist movement.

They had all burst into public attention only a short while before. Thomas Hart Benton had begun to get attention when he exhibited *Boomtown* at the Delphic Galleries in New York in 1929, and he became famous a year later when he completed his *America Today* murals. John Steuart Curry had first received acclaim in 1928 when he exhibited *Baptism in Kansas* at the Corcoran Gallery in Washington; it was praised by Edward Alden Jewell in the *New York Times*, was widely reproduced, and was purchased by the Whitney Museum of American Art.

By a curious irony, it was during one of his few trips to Europe that Grant Wood conceived the style of Midwestern painting for which he is remembered. In 1928 he went to Munich to supervise the construction of a stained-glass window, and encountered the paintings of Memling, Holbein, and Dürer in the *Alte Pinakothek*. After his return to Cedar Rapids, he began a series of neo-Flemish paintings that have since become famous. The first of these, *Woman with Plants*, passed by with modest recognition, but the second, *American Gothic*, a portrait of his sister and his dentist, became an immediate and a lasting popular hit.

Although they all painted American subject matter, the three men came from very different artistic backgrounds. Curry began as a commercial illustrator, working under Harvey Dunn; Wood began as an Iowa Impressionist, painting postcard views of France. Of the three, only Benton had been actively involved with the modernist movement and had seriously experimented with abstract painting. As Craven noted: "In approach and accomplishment, they are totally dissimilar."

In 1933 even Walker seems to have sensed only vaguely the promotional possibilities of linking together the three painters, as is shown by the unpolemical title he gave the Kansas City exhibition, "American Painting Since Whistler." In a statement to *Art Digest*, however, he mentioned only Benton, Curry, and Wood, and not the thirty other artists he had included. With impressive panache, he presented the works of these three men as a Midwestern art movement and contrasted their sturdy realism with the bizarre eccentricities of the French modernists. Walker's fundamental plea for

Maynard Walker, *circa 1933. Art dealer Maynard Walker first brought together the work of Benton, Curry, and Wood in a small show at the Kansas City Art Institute. Within a year he had made celebrities of all three.*

216

an indigenous form of American art was an old one. What was new was his belief that this art would be created in the Midwest.

Walker cleverly appealed to cultural stereotypes, many of which had been pressed into service a generation before for the Populist political movement. He played on the notion that Europe and the East Coast were effete and overcultivated, and that the Midwestern mentality was fundamentally solid, trustworthy, and pragmatic. At the same time, he challenged deep-rooted cultural conceptions, for the Midwest had always been written about as an artistic backwater. Whatever one may think of the movement he invented, he most ingeniously tied the art of painting to larger cultural issues. His statement is worth quoting in full, for it has provided the framework for all subsequent thinking about Benton's work, right up to the present day:

> One of the most significant things in the art world today is the increasing importance of real American art. I mean an art which really springs from American soil and seeks to interpret American life. Not only are American artists forgoing Europe to stay at home and produce works that demand worldwide attention, but American collectors and art patrons are staying home to buy them.
>
> And very noticeably much of the most vital modern art in America is coming out of our long backward Middle West. Largely through the creative output of a few sincere and vital painters, the East is learning that there is an America west of the Alleghenies and that it is worth being put on canvas.
>
> In Chicago, perhaps the most stirring thing I found in the whole World's Fair were the murals which Thomas Benton, Missouri born, has made for the Indiana State building. I understand that Indianans are enraged because a Missourian instead of a native son was selected to paint the murals, but they will all be pointing with mighty pride before long. In my opinion, they are not only Benton's greatest achievement, but are the finest murals in America. Why should the Mexican Rivera make a laughing stock of us when we have men like Benton?
>
> Another high spot in the Chicago show is the painting "Baptism in Kansas," by John Steuart Curry, a native of Kansas. This painting is probably more famous in

John Steuart Curry, Baptism in Kansas, *oil on canvas, 1928. Curry burst into public attention with this work, which he exhibited at the Corcoran Gallery in the fall of 1928. Edward Alden Jewell of the* New York Times *hailed it as "a gorgeous piece of satire."*

Europe than it is in America, and Curry, still in his early thirties, is generally spoken of in the East as one of the leaders in American art. . . . Curry's themes have been mainly of the Middle Western scene, and in such subjects as "Kansas Tornado," "Hogs Killing a Rattlesnake," and "Kansas Pastures" he has created immortal epics from homely scenes hitherto wholly neglected.

Grant Wood is another Middle Westerner who has made the world sit up and take notice by his thoroughly American paintings. He became famous overnight through his painting, "American Gothic."

The sad part of it is that the West has been so slow in recognizing and fostering these famous sons of hers. Too often, when they have done a masterpiece as Benton has done for Indiana, all they get is anger and boos. If we could have more institutions like the Whitney Museum of American Art, which has done so much good in supporting the real American artists like Curry and Benton and Wood and others like them, it would not be long before America would have an indigenous art expression.

The depression has actually been instrumental in opening the eyes of many American art patrons to the worthwhile art that is being produced in this country. The complexity and ultra-sophistication of the era just preceding the crash led many to seek only the bizarre and the sensational in art. Unless some absolutely incomprehensible creation was put forth, it failed to be noticed. If in addition the painting was the work of a madman or a drug addict or a carpenter, and could therefore be tagged with the alluring term "naive," it had all the possibilities of success.

But with the crash of 1929 everyone began to look around to see if there were any realities left in the world. The shiploads of rubbish that had just been imported from the School of Paris were found to be just rubbish. The freaks and the interesting boys with so much "naivete" have lost caste. There have been pictures which gained great fame when it became noised about that their author bit another man's ear off [Van Gogh, who cut off his own ear]. But the balloon is "bust," those days are no more. People have begun to look at pictures with their eyes instead of with their ears.

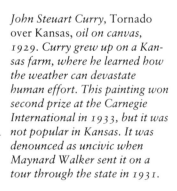

John Steuart Curry, Tornado over Kansas, *oil on canvas, 1929. Curry grew up on a Kansas farm, where he learned how the weather can devastate human effort. This painting won second prize at the Carnegie International in 1933, but it was not popular in Kansas. It was denounced as uncivic when Maynard Walker sent it on a tour through the state in 1931.*

Walker linked together a number of pressing cultural and artistic concerns: desire to support an indigenously American form of art, bewilderment with the strangeness of European modernism, anxiety over the Depression, distrust of the East Coast because of the stock market crash, concern over the plight of the farmer, belief that the Midwest represented American's heartland, and hope that the nation would return to simpler and more virtuous ways.

The ingenuity of Walker's scheme is not lessened by the fact that his motivations for devising it were largely commercial. It seems likely, in fact, that he stressed the Midwestern painters because he was hoping to develop Midwestern clients for his gallery. He had attempted this once before. In 1931 he had arranged to tour John Steuart Curry's paintings through Kansas, but despite the energetic support of the journalist William Allen White, the citizens of the state did not care for them. Similarly, the show at the Kansas City Art Institute seems to have resulted in no sales and to have had little local impact. Thus, in terms of his immediate goals, Walker's sales pitch was a failure. It proved successful, however, in a way that he could never have anticipated—it was picked up as a cover story for *Time* magazine.

This came about through a series of odd coincidences. Improvements in printing techniques made it possible for *Time* to illustrate an inside story in color. In order to show off this new feature as dramatically as possible, the magazine decided to publish a feature on art. Since the piece was scheduled for the Christmas Eve issue, *Time* wanted something uplifting and patriotic, in keeping with the holiday season. Someone on the magazine evidently went to Fifty-seventh Street and had a chat with Maynard Walker. The result was "The U.S. Scene," which appeared on December 24, 1934, and circulated to more than 485,000 Americans.

The essay singled out Benton, Curry, and Wood as the leading painters of the American scene. Further, it praised Charles Burchfield as a kind of "elder statesman" who had anticipated the artistic program of the Midwesterners, spoke of Edward Hopper as a sturdy American realist, and cited Reginald Marsh as a painter of urban scenes whose healthy emphasis on American qualities resembled that of the Midwestern figures.

Taking its lead from Maynard Walker, *Time* deplored the inroads of French modernist painting, which had led to canvases "so deliberately unintelligible that it was no longer news when a picture was hung upside down." It went on: "In the U.S. opposition to such outlandish art first took root in the Midwest. . . . Of these earthy Midwesterners, none represents the objectivity and purpose of their school more clearly than Missouri's *Thomas Hart Benton*."

Time described Benton as the leader of this new Midwestern group; it placed his

Dr. McKeeby and Nan Wood beside American Gothic, 1942. *Grant Wood's* American Gothic *of 1930, a tongue-in-cheek double portrait of his sister and his dentist, made him famous overnight. When he exhibited it in Chicago, requests for photographs of the painting began pouring in from newspapers and magazines all over the country. Within a few years, the piece was as familiar to the public as that of Whistler's mother.*

John Steuart Curry and Grant Wood. The two met for the first time in 1933, at Wood's art colony in Stone City, Iowa. They hammed it up in farmers' overalls for a local photographer.

1925 self-portrait on the magazine's cover. This was the first time an artist had appeared there; it was the first time the magazine had reproduced paintings in color; it was the first time a major American periodical had given as much attention to artists as to leaders of politics and industry. In addition to being featured on the cover, Benton was given significantly more space inside the magazine than the other painters: seven long paragraphs at the beginning of the article as opposed to one devoted to Burchfield, one to Marsh, two to Curry, and four to Wood.

The piece observed that Benton's fame rested chiefly on his murals for the New School, the Whitney, and the State of Indiana. Noting that all these works had stirred up controversy, the article stated: "To critics who have complained that his murals were loud and disturbing, Artist Benton answers: 'They represent the U.S. which is also loud and not in "good taste."'"

Actually the whole notion of the Midwestern trio of painters was somewhat farfetched. Of the three, only Wood actually lived in the Midwest: Curry lived in the artists' colony of Westport, Connecticut, and Benton lived in New York. In 1933, at the time that Walker began to promote them, Benton and Wood had never even met.

Significantly, when they were first exhibited, the paintings of Curry, Wood, and Benton were generally viewed as satirical, not nationalistic. Midwestern farmers wrote letters of outrage about Wood's *American Gothic,* and Gertrude Stein expressed her pleasure at the caricatures in his *Daughters of Revolution.* Benton's *A Social History of Indiana* was denounced by many of the state's citizens. Curry's *Baptism in Kansas* was described by Edward Alden Jewell as "a gorgeous piece of satire," and when a show of Curry's paintings toured through Kansas, one offended viewer wrote to William Allen White: "To be sure, we have cyclones, gospel trains, the medicine man, and the man hunt, and we have had an automobile tip over a bank and kill a man, as he portrayed in his canvas 'The Death of Ray Goddard.' But why paint outstanding friekish [sic] subjects and call them the 'spirit' of Kansas?"

The extent to which this effect was intended raises complex issues. Curry, Wood, and Benton all employed satire differently, and their barbs were tempered by their affection for aspects of the Midwest. Wood, in particular, tended to deny the satirical elements of his paintings, out of a fear that confessing them would disturb his neighbors and encourage adverse commentary. Yet all these artists looked on Midwestern life critically. After the piece in *Time,* however, they came to be regarded as champions of the American way of life. In addition, they all gradually softened the satirical elements in their work in order to fulfill this view of their cultural role.

Although Thomas Craven has widely been credited with creating the Regionalist Group, in actual fact he was relatively slow to discover the work of Curry and Wood. As late as the summer of 1934, in *Modern Art,* he did not once mention Wood and spoke of Curry only briefly, although he devoted a whole chapter to his friend Tom Benton. His first discussion of the three Midwestern painters occurred nine months after the article in *Time,* in a piece titled "Our Art Becomes American: We Draw Up Our Declaration of Independence," which was published in the September 1935 issue of *Harper's Monthly.*

What was soon to become known as "Regionalism" was, in fact, the creation of neither the art press nor the art critics. It was the creation of the art dealer Maynard Walker. The article in *Time* had no real precedent other than Walker's statements. Indeed, when the work of Benton, Wood, and Curry was finally exhibited in New York at the newly established Walker Galleries in November 1935, the critical response was harsh. Even Jewell, who had been a strong supporter of Benton, described Regionalism as an "overnight facade of time-serving, back-scratching, cheap surface display and general quackery." By this time, however, the protests of the critics were

Benton on the cover of Time, *1934.*

too late—the Midwestern triumvirate was already a part of the popular consciousness. *Time,* with its huge readership across the country, had created an artistic movement.

Somewhat accidentally, Benton had stumbled on a new success strategy for the American artist—one he would exploit with considerable skill over the remainder of his career. Before him, artists pushed ahead by developing alliances with critics, dealers, and collectors. The lucky ones acquired patrons, who bought their works and in some cases even gave subsidies (such as those awarded to the artists in the Stieglitz stable). Even Stuart Davis, for all his Marxist critiques of capitalism, was happy to rely on patrons such as Abby Aldrich Rockefeller and Juliana Force, who provided him with regular support. Tom, however, never had any single long-term patron; nor any dealer (except Rita) who manipulated the prices of his work over a long period. Instead he got ahead through publicity. As his colleague the painter Vincent Campanella has commented: "Once the front page was taken over by Regionalism, which was a political thing, he knew how to get back onto the front page. In other words, it's better to be called a louse, anything, than not to be mentioned at all. He became public news—not on the art page, on the front page."

Even Benton later expressed some bewilderment about the sudden emergence of Regionalism. "How or why this first occurred is hard to say," he later wrote. "A play was written and a stage erected for us. Grant Wood became the typical Iowa small towner, John Curry the typical Kansas farmer, and I just an Ozark hillbilly. We accepted our roles." None of them accepted his fame more readily than Tom. As he later boasted: "Like movie stars, baseball players and loquacious senators, I was soon a figure recognizable in Pullman cars, hotel lobbies, and night clubs. I became a regular public character."

Not all the painters featured in *Time* accepted their roles gladly. Burchfield, in 1935, wrote his dealer, Frank Rehn: "I notice of late my name has not been used so much with the Benton-Wood-Curry idea. If this is due to your efforts, a thousand thanks to you. You would think that nothing original ever came out of America until youngsters in the middle-west started painting." Three years later, in another letter to Rehn, he put the matter even more bluntly. " 'Regionalism,' " he stated. "It makes me sick!" Similarly, Hopper, late in life, declared to an interviewer: "The thing that makes me so mad is the American Scene business. I never tried to do that American Scene as Benton and Curry and the Midwestern painters did. I think the American Scene painters caricatured America." Marsh was even more direct: "It was Tom Benton who made the enemies of American realism."

Chapter Twelve
Stieglitz, Davis, and the Communist Front

Dorothy Norman, Alfred Stieglitz, *1933. "He talked all the time," Benton recalled of Stieglitz. "I thought he was a pain in the neck."*

"I have not read your letter as yet but expect to tomorrow if I get any chance," Stieglitz wrote. "I have the intuitive feeling that your letter is an amicable one. . . . I did read the first half a page to be accurate. It showed me that you certainly had me all wrong."

Goodbye, Stieglitz

After the *Time* article appeared, Benton, in an almost ritualistic assertion of his own independence, severed his principal links with the modernist movement. His first step was publicly to criticize Alfred Stieglitz, with whom he had maintained an off-again-on-again relationship for years. In 1934, in honor of Stieglitz's seventieth birthday, his friends and admirers published a fat collection of tributes—essays, poems, stories, and reproductions of paintings and photographs. Pretentiously, the editors titled the volume *America and Alfred Stieglitz,* as if they intended to challenge the uniqueness of Tom's claim to be the one who had found a true form of artistic expression for America and the American spirit. Its appearance exactly coincided with the issue of *Time* that featured Benton on the cover and heralded his leadership of the "American Scene" movement.

In January 1935, Benton published a piece sarcastically titled "America and/or Alfred Stieglitz" in *Common Sense,* a leftist magazine. In it, he bluntly attacked Stieglitz's "mania for self aggrandisement" and declared that his influence, once potent in American art, had been destroyed by the advent of Regionalism. Somewhat crudely, he suggested that the morbid self-reflection that Stieglitz encouraged was mental masturbation. "This man and his confreres are like boys addicted to bad habits whose imaginative constructions have so defined the qualities of 'life' that they are impotent before the fact." To his way of thinking, Stieglitz had lost his sense of humor; he had become too preoccupied with playing the role of "prophet." "Stieglitz is touchy. He cannot be criticized. He never laughs at himself as we common Americans do. He never finds himself funny. . . . Humor and the role of seer do not go together."

Benton's central complaint was that Stieglitz claimed to represent the forces of American life. At the end of his essay, he attempted to demolish this claim. Most Americans, he noted, had no use for the intellectual obscurity of the artists whom Stieglitz supported. Nonetheless, "In the conception of himself as 'seer' and 'prophet' lies Stieglitz' real tie to the ways of our country. America produces more of these than any land in the world. The place is full of cults led by individuals who have found the measure of all things within themselves. They have not heretofore made the 'Literary Guild'; and I think it is a little unfair that Stieglitz's contemporaries, Father Divine and Aimee McPherson, who have such large followings, should be slighted, while he, with such a small band, should be enthroned."

To his credit, Benton did not dismiss Stieglitz's contribution entirely. Although he shunned Stieglitz's support of nonrepresentational art, he gave him credit for his idealism and for his genius as a photographer: "This Stieglitz is likeable. More than that, as this book plainly indicates, lovable, capable of arousing a genuine devotion. . . . Though Stieglitz's influence on Art has vanished, let me make it clear that he has done things of a substantial nature. His work outlives his talk. Stieglitz reached a high mark in the development of photography."

Not surprisingly, however, Stieglitz was not ready to take this lying down. On December 29, even before the issue of *Common Sense* that contained Benton's article was on the newsstands, Stieglitz sent him a note defending himself against the attack. First he pretended that the slings and arrows had not hurt. "And ye Gods didn't I chuckle," he wrote, "as . . . I shared the good time you had while writing it." He then compared Benton's logic to the "contortions" in his murals and implied that he was simply jealous at being excluded from the inner sanctum of the Stieglitz circle. Not so long before, "I listened to your pleas to have your work shown at 291." With obvious hypocrisy, he claimed that he felt "real pleasure" now that Tom was basking in the light of the "American Sun" (a punning allusion to The American Scene). He then wound things up with what was probably a dig at Benton's height: in his view, Tom had not "grown any in stature in the last 17 years."

Two days later, on the first of January, Benton wrote Stieglitz an explosive reply. He began by pointing out that he had never asked Stieglitz for support: "Don't let your imagination run away with your memory about my relations with you at 291. Of course I would have liked to show my pictures there but never did I ask you to allow me to do so. It is possible that some of my friends did, but not I. No Stieglitz, probe again. I would have used you if I could but I knew my situation there too well to take any steps about it."

Tom boasted that he himself did not get tied in knots by abstract ideas but involved himself directly with real life and real situations. He ranted: "To go into painting, in all of its aspects, and with all your heart is to live really a life. You're always in a battle royal. You work away full of steam and genius and all of a sudden something pops up in your picture you never figured on and you stand back, full of

John Marin, Movement No. 2, Related to Downtown New York (The Black Sun), *watercolor on paper, 1926. Stieglitz looked at art in mystical terms and favored intensely personal forms of expression. One of his favorite painters was John Marin, whose watercolors present the world in broken forms surrounded by radiating lines of energy.*

223

Georgia O'Keeffe. Stieglitz ardently promoted O'Keeffe's work and married her in 1924.

Freud, Jung, Holt and Hart and you say to that something, 'You son-of-a-bitch, where did you come from? Git out of my way.' And you sail in to put that something out of the works and when you do get rid of it, it turns out to be just what you needed and you have to set to and coax it back again. And, believe me, that coaxing exercises your ingenuity and enlarges your acquaintance of many, many things that you'll never read about. It's one 'desperate situation' after another, but, by God, let me live desperately —I'll let the literary gigolos do the 'thinking' if I can keep tangled up in situations. I'm an American and when I have a theory it's a tool and not a God.

"You ask old Marin about this. And tell him, for me, that he also was 'just in the way' and that, even though I do think I make better pictures than he does, I'm his friend and salute him. One brother to another in the stew.

'Well Stieglitz—twenty-one years is quite a time—words are just words—only fools take them for stones.

"When am I going to make that drawing of your face to put in some future picture of New York? There I *ask* you for something.

"Happy New Year to all of you, even Paul Rosenfeld.

"P.S. Tell Lewis Mumford, for me, that barns are made of wood and of course don't know when they are hit. (This in answer to his note telling that I had not hit even the side of the barn.)"

Determined to have the last word, Stieglitz wrote back the next day with a lengthy piece of double-talk, in which he declared that he had not read Tom's letter and then went on to answer its accusations at great length. He began with a whining appeal for sympathy: "Do you know what it means to see about 4 or 5 thousand people at least in 21 days. And to see them single handed. And want nothing from any of them and to be ready to answer any or every one of them if within my power to give an answer to the myriads of foolish questions and some very, but rare, intelligent ones. Have you any idea what it means to be daily at the Place on an average of ten hours without going out to lunch and doing this week in and week out for eight-and-a-half months a year."

Having established his sainthood, Stieglitz then slid rather deviously into the matter at hand. "I have not read your letter as yet but expect to tomorrow if I get any chance. I am writing now, it is nearly ten o'clock for I have the intuitive feeling that your letter is an amicable one." Even Stieglitz seems to have realized that this was a whopper, so he pulled back a bit and added: "I did read the first half a page to be accurate. It showed me that you certainly had me all wrong."

He went on to pretend that he was a complete innocent, who had nothing to do with the creation of the recently published tribute and had never schemed or plotted to build up a group of admirers. "What have I to do with the literary people? . . . Now I had as little to do with the idea of a book as you have had. Don't for one moment believe that I have been *engineering* anything or have been building up a machine or a group or a political party or a gang. . . . I am still very alive in spite of your thinking the contrary. What I can't understand is the animus which prompted you to pour your slops over my head. Just because some people insisted on writing a book about me because I happened to be seventy years old and in service for fifty years without ever having received any remuneration personally in any form for all this service."

After making it clear that he had no interest in promoting himself, Stieglitz spoke of his cultural contribution: "I think I'll have to be judged by my own photographic work, by *Camera Work,* by the way I've lived and by the way I have conducted a series of interdependent demonstrations in the shape of exhibitions covering forty years. I know that neither you nor Craven have the slightest idea what I have been doing. I know that Craven in a way is as blind as a bat and as prejudiced as any man I have ever met. That may be his strength. Nevertheless I have recommended everybody to read his books. A great deal of his blindness and prejudice I ascribe, maybe erroneously, to your hypnotic influence over him when it comes to the question of painting, art, etc. I somehow feel that you read me according to your actions and I know that we are very different. That may be your luck."

In referring to Benton's "hypnotic influence," Stieglitz was lifting words from Craven's hostile piece in *Modern Art*, in which he had accused Stieglitz of hypnotizing his followers. Stieglitz then went on to allude to Tom's love of money—obviously he had heard about the Whitney controversy in detail—and to congratulate him for his skill at stirring up publicity. "What I do hope," he wrote sarcastically, "is that your 'backers,' the Common Sense people, reap a harvest through the advertisement of your article. I'm always glad if somebody, I don't care who it may be, makes goodly money out of using my name even if vilifying me without rhyme or reason. I don't know the gentlemen who are running *Common Sense* but . . . they undoubtedly have plenty of money to blow and I hope they have paid you damn well. If not just tell them to get busy and give you a bonus."

Having scored a direct hit, Stieglitz was now ready to wrap things up by returning to the pretense that he had not been wounded and that, indeed, he had not even gotten around to reading Tom's "conciliatory" letter. "I'd love to be able to work myself into a white heat about what you've written and what they've done but for the life of me I can't be anything but gently amused. Every time I think of the article and the ad I have to laugh. And there have been plenty of people who have come to ask me what I had to say on the subject. And I've really had nothing to say. I repeat I'll read your letter tomorrow. Thanks for writing it whatever it may contain." Rather charmingly, he ended his long epistle on a note of friendship: "When O'Keeffe is well enough I wonder whether you and your wife won't come to supper some night. I know the ladies would like it and I know you and I will have a good laugh over what you have done in public." It's fairly clear that this was not a true invitation—just a rhetorical device to smooth things over. Needless to say, the four never got around to sharing a meal.

This time, Benton did not bother to reply, doubtless aware that Stieglitz would keep flooding him with words until he cried quit. In 1937, however, in *An Artist in America*, he paid tribute to Stieglitz's 291 as "New York's high temple of aesthetic pose and lunatic conviction." For all Stieglitz's affectations, Tom clearly felt a sneaking fondness for him and for his genuine devotion to artistic creativity. He wrote nostalgically: "Now that it is well in the past and its troublesome effects on my youth forever gone, I think sometimes of the 291 crowd with a sort of regret."

Diego Rivera and the John Reed Club

The bitterest dispute in which Benton became involved during the 1930s was the one with the Communists of the John Reed Club and his old rival, Stuart Davis. This was really two separate quarrels, the first a debate with the John Reed people (which coincided in date with the destruction of Diego Rivera's mural for Rockefeller Center), the second an exchange with Davis, kicked off by his annoyance that Tom's self-portrait had been featured on the cover of *Time*. By the spring of 1935, however, these fights had got mixed together in a most confusing and acrimonious fashion.

Benton had always detested Davis, but in the twenties he counted many leftists and Communists among his friends. One of his closest companions in the early twenties was Boardman Robinson, who had traveled with John Reed in Russia; he was also very friendly with Bob Minor, the radical cartoonist, who was the founder of the American Communist Party. "I used to vote the Communist ticket," Benton told a reporter in 1935, "more as a protest vote than anything else." And as we have seen, he had once permitted the outlawed party to meet in his apartment. In 1933 he participated in an exhibition at the John Reed Club devoted to art and social meaning.

Diego Rivera. *The Mexican artist used mural painting as a vehicle for Communist propaganda.* "Art is propaganda," *he once wrote,* "or it is not art."

225

As early as 1928, however, Benton had begun to criticize the excesses of Marxism, and his battle with its adherents began in earnest on February 11, 1934, when he spoke to the John Reed Club in New York.

Both artists and Marxists were in an angry mood because of the recent uproar over the Diego Rivera mural in Radio City. The artist had refused to remove a likeness of Lenin, so the landlord destroyed the painting. Nelson Rockefeller was indirectly involved, as an intermediary; the leftists generally viewed the destruction of the work as an action of the Rockefeller family.

Although Benton has come to be associated with chauvinistic nationalism, this speech began with a critique of the concept of "national will," which he labeled "a dangerous fiction." In a clever inversion of orthodox Marxism, which argued that economic forces determined human behavior, Tom argued that it was chiefly because of such intellectual fictions, not economic realities, that men became dangerous: "Men are adaptable and flexible in their practical behavior. It is through their ideas and their emotional attachment thereto that they are dangerous, inflammable, and a menace to the world."

He then extended this generalization from the realm of politics to that of art. He proposed that art should not be based on theories, whether artistic or political, but rather be built from concrete, lived experiences. As an alternative to nationalism in art, he spoke in favor of localism—art that was tied to specific regions and modes of living. So-called Marxist art was a joke, he argued, because it imposed meanings on life rather than drawing meanings from it. He noted that the John Reed Club had recently invited artists to make art about miners based on photographic materials they had collected. The very nature of the program demonstrated that they were not interested in making contact with real life but wanted only a secondhand record of appearances, with a predetermined message. The result might please the John Reed Club, but

Diego Rivera, RCA Building Mural, 1933. Rivera stirred up a front-page controversy when he refused to remove a portrait of Lenin from his mural. When the owners of the building destroyed the painting, leftist artists rose up in protest.

a real miner would be able to spot that the result was phony. "Do you think the miners will do anything but laugh at such junk?" he bluntly commented.

His essential argument—hardly a very shocking one—was that artists should study reality rather than the ideas superimposed on it. Unfortunately, he resorted to two tactics in his presentation that were later turned against him with a vengeance. One was to mention the names of his opponents—something he would never do again. In passing, he disparaged such academics as Ezra Winter, Paul Manship, José Sert, and Frank Brangwyn, and such modernists as Max Weber, Hugo Gelhert, and Louis Lozowick. Brief as these mentions were, they established a precedent for making personal attacks rather than dealing only with issues.

He also made use of some sexual innuendos. He spoke of the modernist painters as "hothouse flowers"—a phrase that surely carried with it the implication that they were "pansies." Continuing, even more rudely, the implicit metaphor that modernists had become artistic transvestites, he said: "The field of art today is like a costume ball; those who enter must come dressed up." Further on, he resorted to another sexual pun to support his belief that artistic forms should be based not on what Picasso or some other fellow did in Paris but on experiences that were specific and local. "What makes the Flemish, the German, the Italian virgins of Christian representative art so different?" he asked. "The difference is made by the life experience of the creative artist who made his forms from his intercourse with the local virgins." It was through such "substantial contacts," he declared, that the real artist found his "driving motifs." In short, an engagement with concrete experience resulted in a manly art rather than an effeminate one. Such use of sexual metaphors proved tactically unwise; it set the stage for the crude insults and scatology of Stuart Davis.

What caused most offense, however, was Benton's indifference to the destruction of the Rivera mural. Here he did not express himself tactfully; it is hard not to feel that he was motivated chiefly by a sense of competition, by his conviction that his own art deserved the sort of attention that Rivera's was receiving. He also contradicted himself by invoking, at least indirectly, the very concept of "national will" that he had attacked in the first paragraph of his presentation. He concluded:

"In answer to some persistent questioning—I have not joined those who have been protesting the indignity put upon Diego Rivera's work in Rockefeller Center because I do not feel, in view of the seriously decadent condition of our own art, that what happens to a Mexican art is of great importance. I respect Rivera as an artist, as a great one, but I have no time to enter into affairs concerning him, because I am intensely interested in the development of an art which is of, and adequately represents, the United States—my own art."

These words were amazingly inflammatory. One of Benton's lectures in this period ended in a chair-throwing brawl. The Rivera speech was delivered at an unusually sensitive time. Although Roosevelt had been in office for a year, the Depression was at its worst. Most artists were out of work, and many Marxists believed that the time was ripe for the destruction of the capitalist system and a Communist takeover.

The Controversy with Stuart Davis

Benton's controversy with the leftists grew even more bitter after Stuart Davis entered the battle. Davis had returned to New York from Paris in 1929. For a brief time things went well for him: he had several shows at the Downtown Gallery, and in 1931 and 1932 he taught at the Art Students League. Then his luck started to slip. He lost his job at the League, where he had engaged in a number of nasty disputes with Benton. In addition, he experienced tragedy in his private life. In June 1932, his wife went to an abortionist, who bungled the operation; she died of peritonitis.

In December 1933, pressed by financial hardship, Davis joined the newly formed Public Works Art Project, later reorganized as the Works Progress Administration Federal Art Project. Until 1939 he devoted most of his time to politics rather than painting. He became president of the American Artists Union, editor of the union's propaganda sheet, *Art Front*, and secretary of the American Artists Congress. Davis's political viewpoints were passionately Marxist, and until the Hitler-Stalin pact he was a hard-line supporter of Stalin's policies. He was a signer, for example, of a group statement declaring that the notorious Moscow trials, through which Stalin liquidated his political opponents, were morally justified.

Time's eulogistic piece on Benton and the Regionalists came out on December 24. A week later, Davis wrote a savage attack on the group in *Art Front*, running one by one through the artists singled out by *Time* and landing a few unflattering remarks on each of them. He saved his harshest comments for Benton, whom he accused of racist bigotry. "Are the gross caricatures of Negroes by Benton to be passed off as 'direct representation'? The only thing they directly represent is a third-rate vaudeville character cliché with the humor omitted. Had they a little more wit, they would automatically take their place in the body of propaganda which is constantly being utilized to disfranchise the Negro politically, socially and economically. The same can be said of all people he paints including the portrait of himself which is reproduced on the cover of *Time*. We must at least give him credit for not making any exceptions in his general under-estimation of the human race."

Davis then went on to attack Thomas Craven, whose ideas, he claimed, had managed "to bring art values to the plane of a Rotarian luncheon." Though editorial standards at the time forbade the specific mention of excrement, Davis indulged in thinly disguised "toilet talk." He described Craven's art criticism as something soft and squishy to the step, and he ended his piece with a metaphor of bodily functions bordering on gross bathroom humor: "The slight burp which this school of the U.S. scene in art has made may not indicate the stomach ulcer of Fascism. I am not a political doctor, but I have heard the burp and as a fellow artist I would advise those concerned to submit themselves to a qualified diagnostician, other than witch doctor Craven, just to be on the safe side." Doubtless, censorship required that Davis substitute burping for farting. The reference to bad doctors may have reflected unconsciously his recent experience with the abortionist.

As it happened, Davis's attack almost exactly coincided with a new statement by Benton, who on February 8, 1935, reported to the *New York Times* that his just-completed tour of the Midwest had demonstrated to him that the young artists there were growing increasingly radical. He stated: "None of us can as yet exactly define this radicalism, nor can I say exactly where it is leading. The young artists of the Middle West, however, have roughly accepted collectivist ideals." He went on to declare that these Midwesterners had not been swayed by the doctrines of orthodox communism, which "regards art as merely a form of propaganda, as merely a vehicle for the expression of communistic doctrine. These young Middle Western artists, however, as is characteristic of American temperament, are more interested in things than in ideas; and it is just here that I see a battle brewing. I believe that the communistic idea of art as propaganda leads to the death of art, because it denies experience, and experience is the only thing that changes form. Communistic art sets up symbols, such as the working man and the capitalist, and attempts to produce art by combination of these symbols."

The references to "radicalism" and "collectivist ideals" make it clear that Benton's political thinking was quite far to the left—not conservative or "fascist," as has been widely maintained. His quarrel was not with liberalism but with the rigidity of the Stalinist brand of communism. In retrospect, particularly with our knowledge of Soviet

Realism as proof of the banality of Communist propaganda, this statement sounds perfectly sensible. At the time, it created a furor. As a result of this statement and Davis's assaults, Benton became persona non grata among the New York leftists.

Just after his return, the directors of the Art Students League asked him if he would repeat his Midwestern lectures for their student body. The event was so well publicized that it had to be transferred from the League's quarters to a nearby building on Fifty-seventh Street, Vanderbilt Hall. As he arrived in the crowded room, however, Benton recognized a whole battalion of Communists and fellow travelers from the John Reed Club, including some well-known left-wing lecture-baiters.

He had hardly started his talk, which dealt with the relationship between art and culture, when four young men, led by a former student of his, marched up the steps to the stage and demanded to be heard. When Benton asked why, they said, "This is a forum. We have the same right to be heard as you." Tom pointed out that he had not been invited to participate in a forum but to deliver a lecture. He spoke loudly, so that the audience could hear, and received a solid round of applause. But the would-be forumists refused to budge. They stood on the stage, grim and sure in their self-righteousness, and Benton stood waiting for them to leave. Finally, Cliff, the League's maintenance man, walked up with a couple of burly janitors and escorted them off the stage. As they passed in front of Tom, his former student leaned toward him. "I always knew you were a dirty anti-Semite, Benton," he said. This crude slur threw Benton completely off balance. When he turned to the audience, he could see nothing but the twisted bitterness in the boy's face.

His previous acquaintance with the young man had been slight. Three or four years before, as a student in Benton's class, the boy had sat apart from the other students, with two young Jewish girls who held him in obvious adoration. He would make spindly lines on his drawing pad with colored pencils, paying little or no attention to the model. After he made each line, he would pause and contemplate it before making another. The girls imitated him.

Benton attended the class twice a week to look over the students' work but made no criticism unless he was asked to. As the new student and his girlfriends seemed to be satisfied with themselves, he just ignored them. At the end of their second week in class, the young man called out to Tom: "You haven't said anything about my work." "How can I?" Benton replied, and then added, with his characteristic lack of tact: "You're not studying the model. I can't see any way to help you."

"I didn't ask for help," he said. "It's just that, as a teacher, you should notice me."

"I've already done that," Benton replied sarcastically. At this, the young man took the pad off his easel, put his box of colored pencils in his pocket, and walked out of the class, followed by his girlfriends. This was Tom's sole personal contact with the fellow, although he saw him later at the John Reed Club, when he gave a lecture there after finishing the Whitney mural.

With the stage cleared, Benton attempted to start his lecture again, but he was interrupted by an outburst of boos and the chant, "We want to be heard. We want to be heard." He yelled out: "Well, you're being heard, all right. It's like the zoo at feed time in here. What is it you want us to hear besides your howling and stomping?" A young man stood up and waved a clenched fist. "They want these people to know there is a different way for American art than the Fascist one you stand for," he shouted. This provoked sustained cheering and clapping from the Communist sympathizers, while the rest of the audience began shouting, "Shut up!" and "Keep quiet!"

By now infuriated, Benton began to shout about the ignorance of America and American meanings that prevailed in the artistic and intellectual ghettos of New York. The John Reed Club boys calmed down, delighted to have Tom's "fascist" views so

Stuart Davis. Davis never forgave Benton for telling him to study in Paris. After Benton was featured on the cover of Time, *Davis led the Communist attack on his work and sought to brand him as a racist and a bigot.*

openly exposed. The lecture had got completely sidetracked, and he couldn't pick up the lost thread. After his diatribe, he asked for questions and improvised for half an hour. The applause at the end indicated that he had the sympathy of a good part of the audience; after this, however, he gave no further lectures in New York. It was probably around this time that Fred Price of the Ferargil Galleries took him aside to tell him: "Tom, for God's sake shut up. You are not only making the Commies mad, you're making everybody mad."

Despite his decision to lecture no more, Benton's difficulties with the Communists were far from over. Stuart Davis had devoted more hostile remarks toward him than toward any of the other artists singled out by *Time*. Shortly after the lecture show-down, a delegation from *Art Front* came to visit and invited Tom to reply. They did not tell him that Davis, who had written the hostile article and had been sniping at Tom's successes for nearly twenty years, was the magazine's editor.

Nonetheless, he smelled a rat. On February 14, he wrote a letter declining the offer, questioning whether the delegation was sincerely interested in intellectual dia-logue. The next day, however, against his better judgment, he telephoned *Art Front*, offering to answer any ten questions posed to him. They were sent and he responded, but then he telephoned again. Would he be answered in the next issue? When told yes, he asked for five hundred more words of rebuttal. This *Art Front* refused to promise, with the hypocritical declaration that the magazine was "limited for space." Realizing that he was being set up, Tom then sent his answers to *Art Digest,* so they appeared in two publications rather than one. Doubtless he hoped that this would guarantee that his views would be presented accurately, but in many ways it just added to the confusion. Rather than fighting a battle on one front, he did so on two.

Most of the questions *Art Front* posed were distinctly loaded. "Is provincial isolation compatible with modern civilization?" the magazine asked, an implicit attack on the whole concept of Regionalism. "Is there any revolutionary tradition for the American artist?" was a challenge to Benton to dispute the belief that art should promote revolutionary dogma.

With surprising pedantry, Benton devoted much of his reply to questions of definition. His phraseology often recalls the writings of John Dewey and William James. He confessed that he had been influenced by French art. When questioned about his political beliefs, he advocated some form of collective ownership. "I believe in the collective control of essential productive means and resources," he wrote, "but as a pragmatist I believe actual, not theoretical, interests do check and test the field of social change." With regard to social understanding, he made the perfectly reasonable comment: "Belief, when it becomes dogma, has been historically detrimental to the evolution of artistic practice." Rather unflatteringly, although certainly accurately, he declared: "The Communist Party at present is an isolated mental area in the United States."

Did a revolutionary tradition exist for American artists? "In the current Commu-nist sense," he argued, "there is no revolutionary tradition for the American artist." In a larger historical sense, however, he proposed that such a tradition existed. Briefly paraphrasing the argument of Frederick Jackson Turner, he observed that revolution-ary change had existed in America since colonial times, wherever the frontier environ-ment remolded old traditions. A revolutionary tradition "began with the first effects of the frontier upon provincial forms in the East and South and continues to this day in the actual moves of conflicting interest. . . . The answer is 'Yes' if you *know* your America." He concluded by declaring his belief that the future of American art lay in the Middle West: "In that area the direct perception of things, since it is less weighted with intellectual conceptions of meaning, purpose, and rational progression, has a better chance to modify ways of doing in an unstereotyped and uncategorical manner.

. . . Unlike the East, as a whole, it has never had a colonial psychology."

Art Front placed Benton's answers beside an equally long article by Jacob Burck, whom the magazine described, with an irony that presumably was not intended, as "one of the outstanding revolutionary artists." According to Burck, Tom had turned traitor to the Communist movement, for after associating with Mike Robinson, Bob Minor, and other revolutionary cartoonists, he had betrayed them by painting social themes without a revolutionary message. As Burck heatedly declared, in a delightfully confusing metaphor: "He put away in his knapsack chunks of artistic ore which he stole from the natives in the form of innumerable sketches, only to return to 'smelt' the stuff down in New York for appraisal by the art dealers."

Burck imagined Benton and Craven as the generals of a hostile army, planning to encircle and destroy the forces of Marxist ideology. "These two have mapped their 'campaigns' with a keen sense of strategy, almost military in conception (probably in preparation for a future esthetic 'putsch' to save America from its coastal 'oppressors.') The set-up so far is: Benton—Missouri, Grant Wood—Iowa, John Steuart Curry—Kansas. Thomas Craven is recruiting sergeant. The rest of the Middle West remains to be divided among the new talents whom Craven expects to entice with his honeyed pen. For the sake of gaining a common objective—the impending federal jobs—an alliance has been consummated with an eastern power—the National Academy. The hostilities, which had existed between the two camps for more than a year, have ceased. The fat federal money bags are about to be surrounded."

No doubt Burck had somehow picked up the rumor that Benton had been approached to undertake a federal mural project. But his conjecture that Tom wished to gain control of the Federal Art Program was an instance of unfounded paranoia. Benton never lobbied for government work, never joined the WPA, and abandoned his work on the federal mural—for the Postal Department—after he found the government's restrictions on subject matter too confining. Burck's accusations apply much better to Stuart Davis, who politicked aggressively for control of government patronage and completed several large mural projects for the WPA. Unlike Benton, Davis had no difficulty tailoring his work to federal requirements.

With twisted logic, Burck accused Benton of creating "tabloid art," because his juxtaposition of episodes was rich and ambiguous and did not carry clear and definite social meanings. What Burck clearly wanted was Communist propaganda. "Revolutionary art has already created artistic giants in our time. And among them cannot be numbered Thomas Hart Benton." To his credit, Burck made it clear that Benton's art was only an incidental element in his indictment. "His attitude toward the destruction of Rivera's works by the Rockefellers is answer enough."

Benton's five-hundred-word reply in *Art Front* was remarkably conciliatory, given the nastiness of Burck's remarks. He said that he wished to withdraw from the field of battle, which had degenerated from a discussion of issues to a series of personal attacks. He pointed out, however, that he had been misrepresented as a social conservative: "I wish to correct him by simply saying that with five of his six points, which he supposes are antithetical to my views, I am in complete accord, and that my objection to the sixth is a tactical one. I still believe that collectivization may result from democratic procedures without the violent disruption of our social services, and without the need of armed forces installing and protecting a dictatorship."

Burck's diatribe in *Art Front*—a rather comical exercise, in retrospect—was not the only attack on Benton's position. *Art Digest*, eager to stir up excitement, invited Stuart Davis to reply to the statement, and needless to say, he made the most of the opportunity. Hypocritically, Davis began by stating that he did not intend "a personal feud" with Tom but sought only to respond to the way he had answered the ten questions. In fact, he brushed past the replies in a brief paragraph, then devoted ten much longer paragraphs to personal accusations. Apparently undisturbed by any qualms about fair play, Davis reduced Benton's carefully phrased statements to such ridiculous positions as: "Social understanding usually hurts the artist."

Most of his piece consists of a laundry list of insults, unconnected by any logical thread other than that they all purport to show Benton's art and personality in a negative light. Davis called almost anything into evidence to fuel his remarkable thesis that Benton, in every aspect of his life and work, was "cracked." He stated: "The compositional enigma of the applied picture moldings to his murals in the New School for Social Research is an outstanding example of his inability to think logically in terms of materials. Another example is his persistence in the use of some painting surface which cracks badly. Witness the murals in the New School and the Whitney Museum. These irresponsibilities are characteristic of Benton's public acts as an artist and one has to allow oneself the bad taste to call attention to them. A cracked surface is of relatively little importance, but cracked thinking may have disastrous effects on American art and artists when indulged in by an aggressive man."

According to Davis, Benton's work was just the thing for "Fascist or semi-Fascist" patrons. "On past performance Benton should have no trouble in selling his wares to any Fascist or semi-Fascist type of government that might set itself up." And Davis stated: "His qualifications would be in general, his social cynicism which allows him to depict social events without regard to their meaning. Specifically he could point to his lunette in the library of the Whitney Museum of American Art where his opinion of radical and liberal thought is clearly symbolized. It shows a Jew in vicious caricature holding the *New Masses* and saying 'the hour is at hand.' Hitler would love that. For Huey Long he can point to his Puck and Judge caricatures of crap shooting and barefoot shuffling negroes. No danger of these negroes demanding a right to vote even if the poll-tax has been taken off."

Davis was probably justified in asserting that Benton's satire was not always in good taste. What he omitted to mention was that Tom attacked the extremes of the right as well as those of the left. His claim that Benton's art appealed to political reactionaries was obviously and blatantly untrue. Indeed, the Indiana murals (and the later ones for the state of Missouri) stirred up the most heated opposition from political conservatives, who disliked both their "vulgarity" and their unflattering treatment of capitalism.

The issues, as Davis stated them, involved political values more than artistic ones. Rather than judging a work of art on aesthetic grounds, he proposed to assess it as an illustration of doctrine. Moreover, he and Benton held directly opposing notions of how these ideas should be generated. Benton believed that actual living experience should generate form; Davis believed in an art that fulfilled a specific political program —a communism modeled on the Russian communism of Joseph Stalin.

As with Jacob Burck, Tom chose to withdraw from a quarrel that had become one of personalities rather than issues. "Benton Cries Quits," *Art Digest* announced in the April 15 issue, as the headline to a letter from Tom withdrawing from the controversy. "I considered *The Art Front*'s questions thoughtfully and without personal reference," Benton asserted. His opponents, on the other hand, "dropped back to the level of a personal attack." He concluded: "I am no more interested. The controversy in so far as I am concerned is closed."

His public reaction to his attackers remained surprisingly mellow. Just before the closing of his Ferargil show in April 1935, he was interviewed by a reporter for the New York *Herald Tribune*. Once again he carefully set forth his political views: "Don't get the idea that I have any hatred for Communists—I used to be one of them myself ten years ago, and I am still a collectivist. But they are annoying, like a mosquito, and they keep me talking too much for my own good. I'm sick of them, their

talk and their views, which are not based on anything except reports. My main quarrel with this New York group of radical intellectuals is not their social objectives so much as their dogmatic, irrational beliefs. They twist reality for the sake of their beliefs.

"They want to take the Marxist slant at everything. Why, gol ding it, the Marxian idea was built up in 1848. How can it be valid in every gol dinged detail today? If the radical movement is to get anywhere in this country it has got to drop Marxism as an outworn historical and economic notion and rely wholly on a pragmatic observance of developing facts. You can't impose imported ideologies on people. The point I wish to make is that social revolution has got to come from the grass-roots. But the way the Communist intellectuals are going about it—never! Communismn is a joke everywhere in the United States except New York. . . .

"Sure, I know that they call me a Fascist for this kind of talk. They go around calling names and think they have said something, explained something. . . . They even called me a Fascist the other day because I dared say that Huey Long is interesting. Well, gol ding it, he is interesting!

"The point is that they are really not proletarian. Most of them are the sons of small tradesmen. They want to act big and tough because that's the way they think a proletarian acts. It's put on."

For the next few years, he continued to fire salvos against the Marxists. In the winter of 1935, the *University of Kansas City Review* published his "Reply to Rivera" (probably written earlier). In July 1937, he published "Confessions of an American" in *Common Sense*—the magazine in which he had made his attack on Stieglitz. The subheadings to the three-part article convey its substance. "Why I Don't Like Marxism," "Marx and the Jeffersonian Ideal," and "Class Rule Versus Democracy." Benton compared communism to fascism, noting that however much they diverged in theory, in practice they both return to "the primitive leader principle" and move away from legal procedures. And he noted, quite sensibly: "With political control of business, monopoly is not escaped. Its growth is, as a matter of fact, accelerated."

Stuart Davis, House and Street, *oil on canvas, 1930. Despite Davis's deep commitment to Marxism, his paintings of the 1930s generally contained no figures and were devoid of political content.*

Stuart Davis also continued to vent his opinions. He played a central role in organizing the First American Artists Congress in 1936, which was titled "Artists Against War and Fascism." His distinctive voice is clearly recognizable in a statement issued by the Congress: "In the field of criticism, Thomas Craven, the most vociferous champion and apologist of the American Scene group, has gone even farther in his muddled thinking. He has made statements which in their nationalistic tendency show him to be congenial to fascism."

The Congress (i.e., Davis once again) also published similar statements by Hitler and Craven, to prove the point that the latter's thinking was reactionary:

"Hitler: Art must not only be good but it must be popularly grounded. Only that art which draws its inspiration from the body of people can be good art in the last analysis and mean something to the people for whom it has been created.

"Craven: Again and again, with all the temper at my command, I have exhorted our artists to remain at home in a familiar land, to enter emotionally into strong native tendencies, to have done with alien cultural fetishes."

Here Davis's reasoning was far more "cracked" than any ideas Tom Benton ever advanced. No one seems to have noted that Hitler's statement might easily have been made by Robert Henri, whose contribution to American art was generally appreciated and recognized. One might just as well have quoted Hitler saying, "It's a nice day," and called Craven a Fascist because he once said the same thing.

Despite Davis's politicking, however, the most heated opposition to Benton's beliefs had died away by the spring of 1935. When an attempt was made at this time by a few Communist diehards to picket an exhibition of Benton's paintings, there were not enough participants to make it worthwhile. By this time, owing in part to disillusionment with Stalin, American social realist art had begun to change from out-and-out support of world communism to a more realistic presentation of the less fortunate members of American society. In its visual form it became remarkably similar to Tom's own paintings.

Throughout their debate, the political styles of Benton and Davis formed a striking contrast. Benton always advanced his ideas as an individual. Davis, on the other hand, maneuvered much more deviously. He worked through confederates, committees, and congresses; through dummy organizations and through magazines in which his own role was carefully concealed.

Tragically, Davis's assumption that Benton's work was right-wing and conservative has been adopted even by Benton's supposed advocates. Yet it was Davis who defended totalitarian forms of rule, Benton who spoke up for democratic differences of opinion. To be sure, in retrospect it has become clear that Benton was wrong in significant ways—his faith in the artistic future of the Midwest was certainly misplaced. It was not his mistakes, however, that earned him his enemies on the left—it was his outspoken denunciation of Communist tactics.

"South's Pride Is Sorely Hurt"

During this period of battles with the leftists, Benton was fending off conservative attacks as well. On January 20, 1935, the *New York Times* reported a fuss he had stirred up during a speaking engagement in Richmond, Virginia. "Civil War Murals Assailed," it trumpeted. "South's Pride Is Sorely Hurt." At the end of his lecture, the artist had been questioned about the Civil War murals Charles Hoffbauer had painted for Battle Abbey in Richmond. He had begun by deploring the selection of a French artist to execute the program, declaring that "hundreds of artists born and bred in the South could have done a better job." Then he had confessed that he himself found the murals "flat, dull and lifeless," and commented: "It's probably a good piece of pictorial work, but so are a lot of three-for-a-nickel postcards."

234

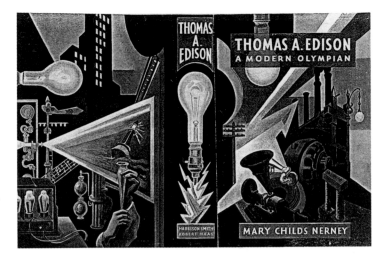

Thomas Hart Benton, book jacket for Thomas A. Edison: A Modern Olympian, *1934. Some of Benton's smaller works look surprisingly similar to the paintings of Stuart Davis. Benton showed Edison's first generator, the "long-waisted Mary Ann," next to a modern generator, and his first cylinder phonograph next to a modern disk phonograph. When he was through, Benton commented that he would rather cover fifty feet of wall space than work again within book-jacket dimensions.*

Southern voices immediately rose up in protest. The Richmond *News Leader* attacked his "arrogant tirade." F. William Sievers, a well-known local sculptor, declared that "no amount of slanderous swill" would ever damage the reputation of Hoffbauer's work in the minds of the discriminating. He added that Benton's own work "is to true art what jazz is to classic music, or 'a rose is a rose, is a rose, is a rose, &c.' is to poetry." Julia Sully, a Richmond art critic, pronounced the Hoffbauer murals "the truest most vivid picture of the war between the States, the most matchless portrayal of the men of the South." The Charlottesville *Progress* declared that they are "beyond question the greatest war paintings in the world." Even a few Northern voices joined the chorus of protest. Carl Blenner, a conservative New York painter, labeled Benton's comments "bosh."

As the *New York Times* perceptively pointed out, the essence of Benton's criticism was that Hoffbauer's murals were done in the conventional manner and "are not modernistically rendered." Hoffbauer's defenders, on the other hand, regarded his conventionality as an asset. The article noted: "Certainly whether Mr. Benton is right or wrong in his estimate of the murals, his judgements concerning them have been as a bombshell to Richmonders, the great majority of whom had assumed that Hoffbauer's work, like Robert E. Lee's character, was beyond criticism."

Chapter Thirteen
Farewell to New York

"If young gentlemen, or old ones either, wish to wear women's underwear and cultivate extraordinary manners it is all right with me. But it is not all right with the art which they affect and cultivate."

The Midwestern Lecture Tour

From reading about himself in *Time*, Tom had discovered that he was the leader of a Midwestern art movement. Although the conception was new to him, he promptly threw all his energy into the promotion of this cause. At the same time that he broke his ties with his old modernist and leftist associates, he forged a new alliance with John Curry and Grant Wood. Publicly they managed to present a united front. Privately they discovered that they were very different in their temperaments, politics, and approaches to art.

Benton had first met Curry in 1926, at an exhibition at the National Academy of Design. They did not become friendly until after Tom returned from Indiana, by which time Curry had befriended Thomas Craven, who had also grown up in Kansas. The Bentons began inviting Curry to their spaghetti dinners, and although he was a slow and clumsy talker, they both warmed to him. Curry was a Kansas Republican, whereas Tom was a vociferous New Deal Democrat. "We were not always in political harmony," Tom noted.

When the *Time* piece was published, Benton had met Grant Wood only once, in October 1934, when Wood made a whirlwind visit to New York City. The fact that he actually lived and painted in the Midwest made him the most convincing spokesman for a Midwestern school of art. Tom wanted to become a true Midwesterner too, and Wood's ideas about the growth of regional art centers had an influence on him quite out of proportion to their intellectual merit.

Even before the *Time* article, Benton had arranged to give a lecture tour of the Midwest. Early in 1935, he obtained a six-week leave of absence from his classes at the Art Students League and set out on a circuit that extended from Pittsburgh to Lubbock, Texas. At the beginning he delivered a prepared speech, but he soon grew bored with that and took to answering questions from the floor. During this journey he made the arrangements necessary to exchange his East Coast identity for a Midwestern one: to leave New York for Kansas City.

On Janaury 20, in Iowa City, he had his first substantial meeting with Grant Wood, which resulted in a long friendship. After lecturing at the University of Iowa, Benton was the first guest of the newly established Society for the Prevention of Cruelty to Speakers, whose clubroom Wood had lovingly decorated with Victorian antiques. The eccentric decor included hair wreaths, blue plush chairs with horn arms and backs, and a stuffed canary under a bell-glass cover. Wearing false whiskers, Tom posed with Wood for a photograph and then played "Frankie and Johnnie" on the harmonica for the assembled club members; Wood performed a clog dance. Benton later described

Thomas Hart Benton, Preparing the Bill, oil on canvas, 1934. In this portrayal of the hotel party where Benton's Missouri mural was first proposed, State Senator Ed Barbour, in a snappy hat and light suit, is flanked by two of his constituents, O. E. Jennings and "Dig" Chinn. Benton later wrote that he showed Senator Barbour "engaged seriously in his legislative business with all the proper paraphernalia of his trade." Nonetheless, Barbour was not pleased by his portrait, and at his insistence, Benton withheld it from exhibition for fifteen years. •

Grant Wood and Thomas Hart Benton. In January 1935, after speaking at the University of Iowa, Benton posed with Grant Wood in Victorian clothing, wearing a false beard.

Wood as "a middle-western character devoid of the usual paraphernalia of sophistication."

These two most famous artists in America disposed of any rivalry in humorous fashion. In a letter to Tom Yoseloff, the president of the Times Club, the organization that had brought Benton to the campus to speak, Wood wrote: "As you know I am modest to the point of being frail and therefore look to you to see that I am not embarrassed by excessive praise, no matter how true it may be. If you feel obliged to mention something about me, it might not be out of place to point out the well-known fact that American Gothic is *the* outstanding American painting today.

"On second thought, perhaps that is too strong. Dinner for Threshers also is a superb painting. As for Thomas Benton's paintings, you should bring out that he has a mustache, a beautiful wife and comes from Missouri."

Benton's rejoinder went: "I should tip you off that America's most celebrated examples of rural painting were, by a strange coincidence, painted by me. My murals in the Whitney Museum and the Museum of Modern Art are simply staggering. My murals in the Indiana Building at the World's Fair are knockouts. This is the straight stuff. As for Grant Wood, I refer you to *Time* magazine in which I am quoted as saying: 'I know an ass and the dust of his kicking when I come across it.' "

In the course of their meeting, Wood planted the notion that Tom should return to the Midwest. "Why don't you come out here and live where you belong?" he asked.

On January 28, Benton lectured in Kansas City. During his visit, Ross Howard offered him a teaching position at the Art Institute. In addition, Tom made the connections that shortly afterward led to his commission to paint a mural for the state capitol in Jefferson City.

In *An Artist in America,* Benton suggested that he was pushed into the capitol mural project by happenstance: "I gave a lecture in Kansas City and my brother, Nat, then prosecutor in Green County, Missouri, came up and induced me to take the trip to Jefferson City, the capital, to meet some of the Democratic boys. In Jefferson City I ran into some old Missouri acquaintances and we had one of those regular hotel room parties where you pour liquids down you and stories out of you until the world begins to spin. When the world was spinning pretty well for me, Ed Barbour, the senatorial incumbent from Greene County and an old friend, said with his good Missouri drawl: " 'Say-ay, Tom, you did a picture there for Indiana. Why don't you do one for your home state?'

". . . Now the world was spinning for me and I took Ed's proposition just to be a part of the spinning and forgot about it. I went back to New York and fell into a lot of wordy controversies again. But it seems that Ed and my brother Nat had talked over the business of a Missouri mural before the hotel party, that they had made rather extensive plans which I knew nothing about, and that Ed's question to me was no mere party question but one that had substance to back it up."

Vincent Campanella tells a slightly different story—one he heard from Tom himself: "As a politician he knew how to go about it. While I was painting his portrait, you know, he was talking about the way he got his mural. He was with some of the politicians and it was at a party and they were drunk. And he just slipped it to them: 'What you need is a mural by Benton.' They said, 'Yes, yes, yes, yes.' The next day he showed up and said, 'Where's the contract?' And they said, 'What contract?' They had forgotten. But he put it over and he got the contract. He made the mural. He made the connection. They didn't come looking for him."

The Speaker of the House of the Missouri legislature in 1935, John G. Christy, recalls that it took some negotiation to settle the price. The morning after the party, one of the group, probably State Senator Barbour, called up the governor. As Christy recalled: "Guy B. Park was Governor and they called him sometime early in the morning with the suggestion. I think the figure, if I recall correctly, that they talked about was $50,000. . . . The Governor was rather pithy in his statements and with a few oaths he said, 'Don't you know there's a Depression goin' on? Can't you do it for less than that?' And Thomas Hart Benton said, 'Yes, I *could* do it for nothing.' "

On March 5, Senator Barbour introduced Concurrent Resolution Six, describing Tom as "one of the greatest living painters" and proposing that he create a mural for the state capitol. A similar measure was introduced into the House by Roy Hamlin of Hannibal, who probably supported the project because Benton planned to devote much of his mural to characters from the writings of Mark Twain, Hannibal's favorite son. Both resolutions were approved, and shortly afterward the money for the mural was allocated in a bill introduced by Senator James Rollins, whose father had been the closest friend of Missouri's great nineteenth-century painter, George Caleb Bingham.

By May 28, the appropriation bill had been passed in both chambers. Benton was to be paid $16,000, considerably less than the $50,000 he had requested. Though all his expenses were to come out of this fee, it was still a substantial amount for the period—more than the governor's annual salary. Benton later estimated that he kept about one third of this amount as profit. The job was to be completed by January 1937.

Nat and Thomas Hart Benton.

Benton subsequently recalled that he received approval for his Missouri mural and the Kansas City Art Institute teaching position on the same day. "I made up my mind suddenly to leave New York and go home to Missouri for good."

When the mural contract arrived, he got an unpleasant surprise: a brief clause stated that he was to work with a supervising commission. He feared—rightly, as it turned out—that his mural would contain "subjects too unconventional to submit to the timorous judgements of any official art commission." Screwing up his courage, he returned the contract to Senator Barbour with a note saying that he could not undertake the work unless this clause was deleted. A week later, the revised contract was returned to him, and he was completely free. The contract stated only that the mural should be a social history of Missouri that would include a comprehensive presentation of the evolution of the life and customs of the people of the state. Thus he did not submit a preliminary design to the Board of the Permanent Seat of Government, overseers of the state capitol. Nor did he, like the earlier muralists in the building, have to work under the Capitol Decoration Commission.

Shortly after the commission had been approved, Senator Barbour billed Benton five hundred dollars for "legal services." Tom complained to his brother, but on Nat's advice he paid it. Later in life, he commented to one of his friends: "I paid off a politician five hundred dollars and that did it."

His acceptance of the Missouri commission led Benton to abandon his sole unhappy attempt to work for the federal government. A few days after he returned to New York from his Midwestern lecture tour, he had been asked by Forbes Watson, Edward Rowan, and Ned Bruce to paint two six-by-ten-foot panels in the lobby of the new Postal and Justice Department building in Washington. All three expressed concern about the social content of Tom's work and urged him to tone it down in his design. They required that he submit his designs to a committee for approval and make such changes as it deemed necessary; moreover, they wanted any statements he made to the press about the project to be screened by the committee. Unfavorable publicity, they noted, might jeopardize the entire Federal Arts Project.

Most of the designs for the Postal Department featured fascinating and dramatic ways of moving the mail. Benton's were no exception: they showed a modern mail carrier and one in colonial times. But he was obviously not very interested in mail carriers, and neither design has much to recommend it. He eventually rescinded his contract in an undated letter to Rowan, posted from Jefferson City, Missouri, probably in late autumn of 1936, when he was working on his mural project there. He said: "The subject matter of the Post Office was just a bore to me. I only undertook it because I wanted to be in on something which I believe has genuinely significant cultural prospects for the country."

"Preparing the Bill"

While Benton was lobbying for a mural commission, he flattered Senator Barbour by sketching him at his work. He told the Senator he intended to develop this into a painting, to be entitled "A Western Senator and a Lobbyist." Soon Barbour was telling his colleagues, "Benton knows real Missourians. He's an honest-to-God Missourian himself. Why he'd rather sit in a store window and talk houn' dog stories and drink whiskey than do anything else."

The legislator was not pleased, however, by the finished work, *Preparing the Bill,* which shows two of his constituents, O. E. Jennings and "Dig" Chinn, plying him with liquor while they discuss senatorial business. In *An Artist in America,* Benton obliquely alluded to the resulting flap: "I once made a careful and accurate portrait of one of my brother's friends, a state senator of Missouri. I pictured him engaged seriously in his legislative business with all the proper paraphernalia of his trade. He was an interesting man and I flattered myself that I had presented him not only as interesting but with all the nobility becoming his character as a statesman. To my great surprise I heard that his family regarded my realism as a libelous slur and as a thing which 'would do him no good.' "

The leftist press, on the other hand, seems to have particularly liked this work, and praised the painter for getting "below the surface to more significant meanings."

Apparently bowing to pressure from Barbour, Benton ceased sending the painting to exhibitions. Years later, when the curator at Randolph-Macon Women's College queried him about the identity of the figures, it was still a sensitive subject. He replied testily: "What difference does it make who the law makers were? No law makers after Lycurgus are important. These aint. . . . P.S. These fellows have kids and grand kids—leave 'em alone. Has nothing to do with 'Art' anyhow. T.H.B."

Despite the controversy the picture aroused, it seems unlikely that Benton painted it as a social critique. He liked the sort of "good ol' boys" it portrayed and found them more trustworthy than liberal idealists.

"Farewell to New York"

In 1912 Benton had fled Kansas City, where he had planned to teach at the Art Institute, because of the disgust and embarrassment he felt after attending a rowdy party filled with homosexuals, some of whom were wearing dresses. In 1935, by a curious cast of fate, he returned to Kansas City to head the painting department at the very institute he had quit before. In 1912 he had been a graceful, long-haired, almost girlish-looking boy of twenty-three, who sported the elegant attire of a Parisian artist; in 1935 he was a rough-hewn man of forty-six, who dressed like a workman, in plaid shirt and blue jeans. Once again, however, he was making a getaway; once again, in his own mind at least, he was escaping the homosexuals.

The decision to leave New York was made with considerable public fanfare. For about a month beforehand, both the New York and the Kansas City press reported the rumors; on April Fool's Day, when he made public his decision, the story was broadcast as far as California. Benton boasted that the Midwest "has never had a colonial psychology," and went on to predict: "The Middle West is going to dominate the social changes due in this country and will thereby determine the nature of the phenomena to which the artist *must* react if he is to make forms which are not imitations of other forms. . . . You've got the manpower, the vote, and you raise the groceries for the rest of the country. . . . I want to be here to see what happens, not just to hear about it."

W. Rickert Fillmore, a Kansas City grain merchant, who served as president of the Art Institute, stressed that Benton's coming signaled a new age of culture for the Midwest. As he told the Kansas City *Times:* "The Midwest has been calling the strongest men in the art field, one after another, and I am satisfied that the influence of Thomas Craven, noted critic and author, has been brought to bear upon his favorite painters, among them Benton and Curry, with the idea of inducing them to join Grant Wood in the Middle West. With Benton at Kansas City, Curry at Manhattan, Kansas, and Grant Wood already painting in Iowa, the strategic points are well covered. We should be able to make a strong stand."

Benton followed his announcement with several attacks on the degeneracy of New York. On April 12, the New York *Sun* reported that "Mr. Benton Will Leave Us Flat —Is Sick of New York and Explains Why." His explanation: "Since the depression it has lost its dynamic quality. On the upswing New York is grand—when it is building buildings, tearing down buildings, making and spending money, its life is irresistible, and in its drive it's a grand show. But when it is on the downswing it gets feeble and querulous and touchy. The place has lost all masculinity. Even the burlesque shows, which to my mind are the best barometers of the public state of mind, have lost all their uproarious vulgarity. . . .

"The zest for real life has gone out of thinking. It is no longer experimental or observant, but it has gone scholastic, monkish and medieval. . . . You can't go to any cocktail party or sidle up to any bar without having somebody grab you by the coat lapel and deliver you a body of principles. Principles . . . That's what the town has come to. It don't act any more, it talks. The place has gone completely verbal and people are getting the idea that if they can make a sentence that is logical they have demonstrated a truth.

"Even the pretty young ladies who ought to have their attention concentrated on their legs address you with a, 'Do you or do you not believe?' and look at you contemptuously when they discover you don't believe anything. It's a hell of a note when women who can generally be counted upon to hold on to some human sense and not be fooled by language, begin to go the way of Harvard graduates. . . .

"I'm leaving New York to see what can be done for art in a fairly clean field less ridden with verbal stupidities. . . . I've been here twenty-one years and that's too long for any American to stay in one place. Do I think I am going to escape stupidity in the Middle West? Of course not. Wherever people talk idiocy thrives."

The following September, as the movers were packing up his household goods, Benton penned his notorious "Farewell to New York," which was included in his 1937 autobiography. He declared that "The great cities are outworn," and that New York, when "stacked up against the rest of America, is a highly provincial place." New Yorkers "have a tendency to mistake their interests, wishes, and hopes for those of the whole country." In addition, they, more than people of any other place in the country, treasured "the attenuated political, artistic, and economic ideas of Europe." People of extreme views, both radical and conservative, dominated the city's intellectual life. For both extremes, "borrowed ideas are a mark of distinction."

He dismissed the followers of Karl Marx as "dogmatic, self-righteous, and humorless," and accused them of trying to force the art of the young "into the stereotypes of propagandist pattern." They belonged to "the same psychological class" as those who were "intent on ridding art of all meaning in favor of pure abstraction." Similarly, he deplored the "conservative academicians," who touted "the negative refinements of conformity" and advocated "outmoded practices and a narrow naturalism."

Curiously, however, the New York Marxists and conservatives were not his prin-

MR. BENTON WILL LEAVE US FLAT

Is Sick of New York and Explains Why.

PLACE HAS GONE INSIPID

He's Going West to Escape 'Principles' and Talk.

Thomas H. Benton, the American mural painter and one of the leading indigenous artists of this country, is sick of New York and in a few months will pull up stakes for the great open spaces. Fresco Tom, as Mr. Benton is sometimes indelicately referred to, is a nephew of the first Senator from Missouri, and has decorated the walls of more public and private buildings in his time than you can swing a cat in or shake a stick at, or whatever you want to do in private or public buildings.

Mr. Benton has been living in New York for twenty-one years, where he has been doing some, if not all, of his best work. He is a Missourian by birth and homing instinct, and when he leaves these parts this coming summer he will head for Kansas City to take up his new duties as Director of Fine Arts of the Kansas City Art Institute. It is difficult for a layman to describe Mr. Benton's work, but it is generally realistic, vivid, bright with color and shows how people look on Riverside Drive, Union Square, in subways, elevators and on the tops of tall buildings under construction.

Mr. Benton was asked to elaborate on his clews, and he sat down and wrote a little essay in pencil. Herewith is printed the bulk of it. In total it ran a little long for the limited space available in a daily news paper.

Why Am I Tired of New York?

"Because since the depression it has lost its dynamic quality. On the upswing New York is grand—when it is building buildings, tearing down buildings, making and spending money, its life is irresistible, and in its drive it's a grand show. But when it is on the downswing it gets feeble and querulous and touchy. The place has lost all masculinity.

"Even the burlesque shows, which to my mind are the best barometers of the public state of mind, have lost all their uproarious vulgarity.

"The zest for real life has gone out of thinking. It is no longer experimental or observant, but has gone scholastic—monkish and medieval. Of course that has come out of Europe. New York has always had a little touch of the colonial spirit because of its large unassimilated, immigrant population, and partly because of the snobbishness of the rich and cultivated who gather here, and who have no way of manifesting their assumed superiorities except by adopting European manners and things which seem smart because they are unfamiliar.

"When the town is on the go, the roar and push of its activity swamps all this, but when, as now, the trade wheels don't turn or show any promise of turning, New York loses confidence and begins to rationalize and explain itself. And God knows when a town or a person gets to that point you can count 'em as dead. New York is a trading town and a trading town to keep alive has to trade. It can't depend on the mouthings of economists who act as if their art was a science; on philosophers who've turned prophets; and on eight or ten thousand amateur sociologists—for its vitality. Did I say eight or ten thousand? That don't begin to hit the number. You can't go to any cocktail party or sidle up to any bar without having somebody grab you by the coat lapel and deliver you a body of principles.

"Principles . . . that's what the town has come to. It don't act any more, it talks. The place has gone completely verbal and people are getting the idea that if they can make a sentence that is logical they have demonstrated a truth.

"Even the pretty young ladies who ought to have their attention concentrated on their legs address you with a 'Do you or do you not believe?—' and look at you contemptuously when they discover you don't believe anything.

"It's a hell of a note when women who can generally be counted upon to hold on to some human sense and not be fooled by language, begin to go the way of Harvard graduates.

'Belief Patterns' Everywhere.

"The PWA work in this town has shown that no progress in the socialization of creative and experimental art can be made in New York because of the grip of entrenched conventions on the machinery of action. The two dominant art forces in this town, the National Academy representing officialdom, and the Communist groups representing the propagandist view of art, are in the grip of frozen and static belief patterns. They are unable to turn out anything but dead conventions.

"The Middle West has no inhibiting cultural patterns wrapped up in a lot of verbal logic, or tied to practice habits that stop action.

"I'm leaving New York to see what can be done for art in a fairly clean field less ridden with verbal stupidities. . . . Then I've been here twenty-one years, and that's too long for any American to stay in one place. Do I think I am going to escape stupidity in the Middle West? Of course not. Wherever people talk idiocy thrives."

SAYS NEW YORK HAS LOST ITS DYNAMIC QUALITY

Sun Staff Photo.

Thomas H. Benton, mural painter

cipal targets. His chief phobia was homosexuality. During his twenty years in New York, he had not publicly attacked homosexuals, except for a coy allusion to "hot-house flowers" in his 1934 speech to the John Reed Club. Starting in September 1935, however, they became the central butt of his attacks. "Tom did a lot of quite unnec-essary talking about fairies taking over the art world," his sister Mildred recalls. "He had this violent hatred of homosexuals. There must have been some terrible urge in him that made him do it. His hatred wasn't natural."

The New York art world, Benton stated in his essay, suffered from "the concen-trated flow of aesthetic-minded homosexuals into the various fields of artistic practice. . . . Far be it from me to raise my hands in any moral horror over the ways and taste of individuals. If young gentlemen, or old ones either, wish to wear women's under-wear and cultivate extraordinary manners it is all right with me. But it is not all right with the art which they affect and cultivate. It is not all right when, by ingratiation or subtle connivance, precious fairies get into positions of power and judge, buy, and exhibit American pictures on a base of nervous whim and under the sway of those overdelicate refinements of taste characteristic of their kind."

Homosexuals, he declared, had attached themselves to powerful institutions. In an apparent dig at the Fogg Art Museum at Harvard University, at the time the chief training ground for American museum directors, he declared: "In an important train-ing school of taste, appended to one of the great eastern universities, they have made deep inroads, and potential directors of museums emerge from the sanctums of this institution with a lisping voice and mincing ways."

But such mannerisms and sexual deviancies, he boasted, could not find root in the Midwest. "The people of the West are highly intolerant of aberration. In the smaller cities there are no isolating walls of busy indifference where odd manners and cults can reach positions of eminence and power. Power, in smaller places, is promptly known and subject to the scrutiny of strong prejudice."

To be sure, the culture of the Midwest had been constrained by commercialism and greed—by a disdain for the higher goals of life. But he expressed hope that a new form of American art, based on real experiences, would emerge in Midwestern centers: "It is in the drama of *things that are* that art must take its first original steps. In those outlying places of the great rivers and fields which, in the self-satisfied vanities of the great cities, are regarded as the abodes of hicks and stuffed shirts, the promise of an artistic future seems to lie. The great cities are dead. They offer nothing but coffins for living and thinking."

Though today this diatribe sounds zany, its attack on urban life represented at the time an intellectual position that many considered viable. Where did Benton get his ideas? While his attacks on homosexuals form a distinctive feature of his presen-tation, his endorsement of a regional, Midwestern school of art was for the most part borrowed from Grant Wood.

"Regionalism"

Grant Wood made an unlikely prophet. Chubby, soft-spoken, and painfully shy, he blushed and swayed back and forth while he talked, and emitted his words so slowly that, his biographer Darrel Garwood noted, "He spoke like a schoolboy reading in bad light." His formal education had ended with high school. Nonetheless, *Time* anointed him as "the chief philosopher and greatest teacher" of the "U.S. Scene" movement and as the chief spokesman for "Regional art." It was he who turned the U.S. Scene movement into what has become known as Regionalism.

Wood's sole experience with "regional art centers" derived from his involvement with the Art Colony in Stone City, Iowa, a few miles from Cedar Rapids. This school lasted only two summers and folded at the very moment that the U.S. Scene movement

Title Page of Revolt Against the City, *1935.*

was featured in *Time.* For the purposes of the magazine, this flimsy, half-baked experiment was enough. "No man in the U.S.," it announced, "is a more fervid believer in developing 'regional' art than Grant Wood. Long before the Public Works Art Project . . . , Wood had established his own Iowa art colony." At about the same time that Benton penned his "Farewell to New York," Wood published a long essay, "Revolt Against the City," which presented a very similar position. In it, he condemned the corrupting cultural influence of the cities of the East Coast, particularly New York, and called for the development of Midwestern regional art centers.

Like most of Wood's pronouncements, "Revolt Against the City" was ghostwritten for him. The journalist Frank Luther Mott, a teacher at the University of Iowa, spliced together statements Wood had made in lectures and interviews. Tom's essay, for all its crackpot flavor, makes entertaining reading. By contrast, the Wood/Mott manifesto is as cliché-ridden as a presidential address, stuffed with pompously academic words such as "validation," "utilization," and "educative process," and such trite turns of phrase as "blowing of trumpets," "literary flowering," and "old frontier values." More clearly than Benton's essay, however, the Wood/Mott production elucidates the manner in which the so-called Regionalist movement came to take on a nostalgic and reactionary character. It lauds isolationist and agrarian political theories of a most unworkable and retrograde sort and uses them to justify the Regionalist artistic program.

"Wood" began by speaking positively of the tariff barriers and political isolationism which, we now recognize, were among the chief causes of the Great Depression. Then he argued for an extension of this policy in cultural terms.

In the final section of the essay he introduced the term "regionalism" with reference to literature and art, and spoke of "the regional movement." This may have been the first time that these words had been specifically applied to the work of Benton, Wood, and Curry. Noting that "each section has a personality of its own," it concluded: "When different regions develop characteristics of their own, they will come into competition with each other; and out of this competition a rich American culture will grow. It was in some such manner that Gothic architecture grew out of competition between different French towns as to which could build the largest and finest cathedrals. . . . I am willing to go so far as to say that I believe the hope of a native American art lies in the development of regional art centers and the competition between them."

Not only does this essay reveal the intellectual weaknesses of the Regionalist movement, it also suggests how the artistic direction of Benton, Wood, and Curry was subverted after they became famous. All three had begun by painting strongly critical satires of Midwestern life. Success transformed them into boosters, and their paintings shifted from social commentary to nostalgia.

Benton was a sucker for Grant Wood's dubious theories both because he wanted to get out of New York, which the leftists had made most uncomfortable for him, and because in certain respects Wood's ideas echoed his own thinking. In one sense, Benton had been a "Regionalist" painter for a long time. From Marxist writers, such as his friend Leo Huberman, he had developed an interest in the different regions of the United States and had attempted to portray them in his art. He loved to paint the isolated, rural areas of the South and the Midwest.

Until 1934, however, he had never identified himself with a specific region. His approach was that of a roving reporter; he wandered freely over the face of America. When he ran up against local chauvinism in Indiana, he vigorously repudiated it. After 1934, owing in large part to Grant Wood's influence, Benton made a significant about-face of artistic purpose. He began to identify himself with a specific region, southwest

Missouri. He embraced provincialism; he encouraged distrust of outsiders. He ceased to be the painter of all America and became the painter of the Ozarks.

History has not been kind to Benton's predictions of a Midwestern cultural renaissance. Unfortunately, he chose to embrace agrarian life just when it ceased to play a dominant role in the American economy; to attack New York at the moment when its economic dominance began to resurge; and to disparage the art of New York just as the city started to produce the first American art to attract international attention. While he pictured the Middle West as masculine rather than effeminate, he soon found that even in his own chosen hometown of Kansas City, the affected "pretty boys" he despised played a controlling role in cultural life. His imprudent effort to dislodge them created a conflict quite as bitter as anything he had ever experienced in New York. As a further ironic twist, his Regionalist allies did not prove the manly fellows he had supposed them to be. It seems likely, as Benton himself later came to believe, that his closest associate in the Regionalist movement, Grant Wood, was a closet homosexual.

Because of these shortcomings, Tom's "Farewell to New York" has not held up well as a contribution to social theory. As a document of his own psychology, however, and of the issues that seemed most central to him, it should not be overlooked. The hysterical attacks on homosexuals touch on traumas that scarred his adolescence, when he struggled to find a place for himself, and a manly one, in the highly feminized milieu of the visual arts. Moreover, the essay sets the stage for the public conflicts that would dominate his life for the next five years. In his attacks on socialites and homosexuals, he singled out the very figures who would bring about his downfall.

Benton's conversion to "Regionalism" was primarily a publicity stunt and an act of political opportunism. But he would not have made the shift if it had not corresponded to emotional needs that were both powerful and authentic. As a spark for artistic creation, these new doctrines brought positive benefits. They allowed him to come back home. They encouraged him to paint the kind of subject matter he knew best and felt about most deeply. While his art became less broad, it became more personal—more closely tied to his father and to the world of his childhood. Tom's return to Missouri allowed him to confront his past.

Exhibitions in New York

Benton held his last show before leaving New York at the Ferargil Galleries in April 1935. As usual, the most positive reviewer was Edward Alden Jewell of the *Times*, who proposed that the viewer try to overlook the ballyhoo and look at the paintings. Royal Cortissoz of the *Tribune* was hesitantly affirmative: "In the upshot Mr. Benton may not achieve beauty, but at least he secures the vitality of truth attacked at first hand. . . . There is no disputing the impact of his forthright brush." Henry McBride of the *Sun* was upset, as usual, that Benton's work was not genteel, but concluded: "You can take it or leave it, but you cannot deny that it is native."

Perhaps the most touching review was Lewis Mumford's in *The New Yorker*—the last piece he ever wrote on Benton. He had become a caricature of his real self, Mumford lamented: "his real talents as a painter begin at the point where his ballyhoo gestures and his sentimental rhetoric leave off."

To Mumford, the Ferargil show revealed three sides of Benton's complex personality. One was the man with "a great appetite for facts," the creator of the direct sketches of life, studies of places and characters, mostly done in ink and wash—the expression of "the man who swaps stories at the roadside and plays a harmonica in the kitchen after supper." Mumford asserted: "To find Benton's equal in this department one must go back to Winslow Homer in his best days after the Civil War."

Second came Benton the mural painter—"the ambitious fellow who wants to become the Great National Painter by leaving his mark on vast expanses of public wall." This ambition, in Mumford's opinion, "has had a depressing effect on Benton's work. . . . In order to do a big canvas, it is not enough to have big figures. One must also embody significant ideas. Benton's symbols have not usually been equal to his task, because he has deliberately suppressed important aspects of life. Afraid of being highbrow, he takes refuge in puerility. . . . The fact is that much of Benton's larger studies of the American scene, like 'Lord, Heal the Child' and 'Preparing the Bill,' belong to the level of journalism. Benton is like a newspaper reporter who spends a week polishing a news story that should have gone into the first edition. The result is not imaginative literature but bad reporting, which has not even the merit of its own kind of quickness and directness."

Finally, Mumford discerned a third Benton—the poetic recorder of intimate scenes. "This is the Benton who carries over into his smaller oil paintings a sense of the peace and beauty and lonely wistfulness of man facing the earth. He shows us the tired farmer at his plough, or a solitary figure and a water tank and a freight car under the moonlight—'Waiting.' Here he is not preaching Americana, in the fashion of the Hearsts. . . . In these smaller paintings, there is no fake hardness, no fake anti-intellectualism, no silly jingoism. . . . After the Riptail Roarer and Peck's Bad Boy have had their fling, there may still be a handful of his paintings that one will not be ashamed to house in the same gallery that holds a Ryder."

As usual, Mumford expressed his thoughts beautifully, but in his review he confused his feelings about Tom Benton the man with his evaluation of Tom Benton the artist. No doubt the sensitive student of nature was easier to live with than the brash, self-conscious recorder of the American scene. But it is hard to agree that his work as a pure landscapist had the same power as his later mural programs. Mumford wrote the piece not so much as an art critic but as an estranged former friend.

Benton seems to have done his best to disregard the critics by losing himself in music. "Now I must tell you about last night," he wrote to his friend Carl Ruggles, just after the Ferargil show closed. "A big public farewell party was given us at the Gallery where my pictures are hung. Everybody including the press was invited and we had such a crowd as you seldom see in New York—a crowd that threw away all its presumptions and pretensions and sat on the floor and had a good time. I drilled my harmonica players for four hours a day all last week till they could play our part stuff as clean and neat as a whistle. We stood out in front of your portrait and played that first thing you wrote us with 4 harmonies and we got such a hand that we swelled up as if we were regular performers. We had to play it four times before we could go on. The reception we got for that gave us enough confidence to play through our other stuff without slip. . . . We are going to play once more on the 27th at a benefit dance for the Art Students League, and I'd give anything to have a modern thing of yours about the length of the *Ave, Verum* corpus—something to make people sit up as your first one did. We are not afraid of chromatic changes of tone, of time or key changes. . . . Write me one more thing and I'll not bother you any more. And we must have it so that we can get several days practice before the 27th April. If I impose too much Carl, tell me to go to Hell."

Later that month, Benton told a reporter that his main regret in leaving New York was that it would break up his harmonica quartet.

Was Benton a Racist?
Stuart Davis's contention that Benton was a bigot has colored critical reactions to his work up to this day. Is there any truth to this? Benton himself always maintained that the charge was a cynical smear, devised by Davis to win the support of the John Reed

Club, many of whose members were Jewish. These individuals were eager, indeed almost determined, to interpret opposition to their viewpoints as motivated by racial prejudice.

On the whole, Davis's accusations were vigorously contradicted both by Benton's statements and by his personal behavior. He actively supported organizations that defended minority groups, such as the NAACP and the American Civil Liberties Union. In 1940, he specifically disavowed racism of any sort. "We in this country," he wrote, "put no stock in racial genius. We do not believe that, because a man comes from one racial strain rather than another, he starts with superior equipment. We do not believe this is true in any field; but particularly in the field of creative endeavor do we repudiate it."

In his personal behavior, Benton undoubtedly followed these precepts. It is hard to believe that he was hostile to foreigners, for he married an Italian immigrant—one whose foreign accent always remained noticeable. Nor does the claim that he was anti-Semitic hold up to serious examination. In Paris, his first close friend was Abe Warshawsky, a Jew, and during the period when he was being attacked by Stuart Davis he had a Jewish lawyer, Hymie Cohen, and a number of close Jewish friends, such as Dr. Raabe. After he moved to Kansas City, he was actively supported by Jewish patrons, many of whom were excluded from the social group affiliated with the Nelson-Atkins Museum of Art. Lester Siegel provided him with a major mural commission; Samuel Sosland purchased his paintings; and at the end of his life, Bernie Hoffman was one of his three closest friends.

Unfortunately, Benton's quest for an American form of art—one drawn from the native environment—slipped easily into a form of chauvinism. The article in *Time*, with its strong nationalistic slant, encouraged this tendency. When Benton had first turned to American subject matter, he stressed the diversity of the country. After 1934, however, he identified himself with the Midwest, and blasted the degeneracy of the East Coast, particularly New York. So far as is recorded, Benton never slipped into racist name-calling—not even when he was drunk. But this cannot be said of his friend Thomas Craven, whom the art historian Matthew Baigell recently labeled "a xenophobe and anti-Semite."

Oddly, one of Craven's best early short stories, "Love in Smoky Hill," which was published in *The Dial*, presents an assault on bigotry: a homely farm girl falls in love with a Bohemian farmhand and arranges to marry him in secret; but her family so violently oppose her association with a "bohunk" that they drive him from their homestead with horsewhips.

In his art criticism, however, Craven often slipped into racist epithets—and Benton was associated with these apparent slurs. The best that can be said in defense of Craven's mouthings is that they seem to reflect a pattern of invective rather than a pattern of belief. In his descriptions of figures like Matisse and Stieglitz, Craven's use of the word "Jew" sounds pejorative. Yet he used the same word to describe artists whom he endorsed. Thus he wrote approvingly of "Pascin, a wandering Jew, who, with his curious irregular line, is capable of turning any motif into living form." "Craven never minced words," Benton later recalled, "and often in the interests of strong statement would go clear overboard." Benton's reputation got dragged overboard as well.

Craven's ethnic and racial attacks had notable precedents. Royal Cortissoz, for example, attacked the modernist artists in the Armory Show, declaring: "The United States is invaded by aliens . . . types not yet fitted for their first papers in aesthetic naturalization—the makers of true Ellis Island art." And Craven may have picked up his fondness for inflammatory language from H. L. Mencken, who subscribed, somewhat eccentrically, to nineteenth-century pseudoscience concerning heredity and race.

Significantly, Craven's first attempt to separate out the "good Americans" in a list of painters appeared in Mencken's *American Mercury,* in an essay "Men of Art: American Style," published in 1925. Craven's rhetoric in this piece sounds alarming, but in fact his list of "good Americans" contained two Jewish figures, one of whom was born in Bulgaria. If he intended to divide the art world up according to racial categories, he did not do so with any coherence.

Benton was undoubtedly tarnished by his association with Craven. In addition, the dangers of his nationalist position were well summed up by Malcolm Cowley, in a review of *An Artist in America:* "The trouble is that Benton's nationalism shows a tendency to become exclusive. He defines the real America to suit himself; he puts everything and everybody else outside the pale. New York, for example, is not American, nor are the New York intellectuals, nor are the ideas that they import from Europe. . . .

"There is nothing to guarantee that someone among his pupils or associates won't carry his theories toward their logical limit; all theories move in that direction. In this case, the logical limit would seem to be a sort of anti-foreign, anti-red, anti-Jewish, anti-intellectual ku-kluxery, a homespun and hayseed fascism advanced under the pretense of fighting fascism and communism and all un-American doctrines. There are vague signs that such a movement is beginning among the artists. But if it gets to be dangerous, I hope and believe that Benton will be among the first to fight it."

Fortunately, whatever the "vague signs" were that Cowley witnessed among Midwestern artists, they remained extremely nebulous—so hazy that they seem to have left no trace. Benton never had to fight them after all.

Benton's Paintings of Blacks

To make paintings of black people, even today, is to touch on some of the most distressing issues of American history—slavery, poverty, racial discrimination, and the place of the South in American life. Benton's paintings of black subjects touch on all these issues, and they still have great power to stir up either enthusiasm or anger. The first step toward understanding these works is to recognize that he did not portray blacks as they live today but as they lived in the 1920s and '30s. Even the language used to describe Americans of African descent has changed. The terms "Negro" and "colored," then judged to be polite, are now considered insulting.

Despite the abolition of slavery, in the 1920s and '30s the plight of most Southern blacks had changed little since antebellum days. They remained tied to their small plots of land, confined to farming with simple hand tools, in a state of never-ending debt to store owners and landlords. Benton's canvases record this primitive, almost feudal way of life. He told Paul Cummings: "I made them not as gentlemen but as workers. . . . What they were doing—it was all you ever saw. It was fascinating. . . . Cotton picking and tobacco work and all that stuff—corn, sugar cane. I did a lot of paintings of them." In 1926, when he began his travels, no other American painter was engaged in this task. He preceded by nearly a decade the work of the WPA artists and photographers.

Many black people liked these images. During a book-signing in St. Louis in 1937, for example, a young man told Tom of the local reaction to a Benton lithograph that he had sent home to his father, a doctor in rural Arkansas. The print showed a poor black sharecropper guiding a single plow across a field; and when the boy's father hung it up in his office, patients, particularly the blacks, gathered around the image in groups to discuss and admire it. In fact, they "got so excited about it," and created so much disturbance, that the doctor decided to take the print back home.

Starting about 1928, Benton had a number of black students who were interested in his treatment of Southern life. "They were my friends and they came because I was

248

249

painting the Negro," he later recalled. In the 1930s, his records of the hard lot of the Southern black earned him many favorable reviews; as late as 1938, the Marxist historian Charles Beard praised them in his volume *America in Midpassage.*

Benton lost his black pupils after his satire of the leftists in the Whitney mural brought him under attack as a reactionary. His student Mervin Jules, who left at the same time, later remembered: "He and I broke up over his portrayal of the negroes in the mural he did for the Whitney. There was a basic antihumanist approach that was reflected in all his people."

In 1973, when he was interviewed by Paul Cummings, Benton confessed that blacks had become hostile to his early paintings of black workers. "I don't know whether we should record this or not," he commented. "But I don't dare show any of my Negro paintings today—paintings of Negroes working in the fields or anything like that. The museums have put theirs aside. The Metropolitan has great thick plexiglass on the Negro paintings that I did. Because of vandalism. The Negroes don't like to be shown as workers in the fields. So when they get a chance they'll scratch it up. . . . Now this is something I don't know whether you should put on publicly now because the Negroes will sooner or later get over that."

Two factors have made these images of blacks controversial: their social viewpoint and their sense of caricature. That Benton deplored Southern racism is demonstrated by his chapter "The South" in *An Artist in America.* Malcolm Cowley considered this the best section of the book. "The southern temper is a strange thing," Tom wrote. "In spite of its readiness to flare, there is a kind of frigidity about it. It is the outcome not of hot blood but of a kind of fury of pride."

Yet although he was strongly opposed to racism, he suspended his feelings to observe firsthand how it operated. He wrote sympathetically, for example, of an overseer of black cotton workers in the middle of Georgia whom he befriended. And he wrote critically of those Marxist ideologues who advocated bloody race war in the South from their comfortable vantage point in New York.

Benton created a few paintings of the heroic black worker, such as the construction worker in *America Today*. And he made at least one image of a black being oppressed, *The Lynching* (which originally bore the magnificently cynical title *Century of Progress*). But works such as these are the exception; more typical are images that point to no easy moral, such as *Minstrel Show*, which presents an uncomfortable moment of racial confrontation. In works such as these, he seems almost deliberately to have created images that would satisfy neither the bigot nor the social reformer. Rather than making bigotry pleasant or social reform easy, they suggest the naïveté of quick moral judgments. Even one of his most direct representations of simple poverty, *Ploughing*, was later retitled *Ploughing It Under*, to suggest the foolishness of reform, however well meant, that was imposed from above.

Equally disturbing to some viewers is Benton's sense of caricature. He exaggerated the features of everyone he painted, and this always evoked varied reactions. In 1934, for example, when he showed his portrait of Carl Ruggles at the Ferargil Galleries, Karl Freund described the painting as a "strange and unflattering likeness of a friend"; and Henry McBride dismissed Benton as a "caricaturist" who pleased the "very vulgar." Edward Alden Jewell, on the other hand, hailed the work as "exceptionally well painted and brilliantly successful in its reading of the sitter's character."

Many viewers have felt that whatever Benton said about his intentions, his manner of caricaturing black people reveals an implicit condescension and racism. Undoubtedly he caricatured them—endowing them with thick lips, rolling eyes, and sloping foreheads. Often his paintings recall the cartoons of his friend Miguel Covarrubias, whose renderings of blacks were collected into a book, *Negro Drawings*. Ironically, however, Benton's use of such exaggeration derived from the very modernist movement he has been condemned for abandoning. It recalls the work of Henri Matisse, whom Benton greatly admired during the 1920s. Whereas Matisse distorted the symmetry of gorgeous odalisques, making their eyes, noses, and other anatomical features out of joint, Benton gleefully applied the same sort of willful exaggeration to the features of poor of Southern whites and black sharecroppers.

Benton always denied that he intended to ridicule his subjects. He wrote his friend Seth Low: "I've seen America with a humorous eye at times (what sensible person could do otherwise), and I have occasionally . . . tried to work in the vein of caricature, but the body of my work is primarily realistic in intent and I would like it to be taken as such. . . . I am not a dignified man but I would like to have my past presented with a measure of seriousness because it has been, for all my clowning, a serious piece of business."

In *An Artist in America*, he tells of a time when he was sitting on the curb of a broken-down street in the South, drawing a ramshackle house. Some black people sitting on the porch went inside when they saw him. Soon a tall man wearing much-patched but clean overalls came out of the shack and walked toward him hesitantly. "Sir," he said, "I beg your pardon, but my mother thinks you are making fun of her house and wants you to please go away."

Tom went.

Thomas Hart Benton, A Lynching, 1934. Benton contributed this painting to an exhibition organized by the NAACP, "An Art Commentary on Lynching." As the result of conservative protests, the Jacques Seligmann Galleries canceled the exhibition, but it was restaged at the Arthur U. Newton Galleries in February 1935. The show included a painting by John Steuart Curry of a black man pursued by bloodhounds, and a drawing by Reginald Marsh titled "This Is Her First Lynching," which showed a little girl being held up by her mother to see over a lynch mob. Benton's painting, one of his few statements of pure social protest, was ruined by water damage after he stored it in a leaky shed on Martha's Vineyard.

Chapter Fourteen
Shame on You, Mr. Benton!

"If I have any right to make judgments, I would say that the Missouri mural was my best work."

Kansas City

Benton arrived in Kansas City on September 23, 1935, and took up residence at 905 East 47th Street. George O'Maley recalls meeting him shortly after he got to town: "I saw these people that looked like they were yard men out just beyond our property line and I thought, well, I'll go over and negotiate for them to cut [my mother's] grass. So I walked up to what I thought was a strange and unique-looking person. He needed a haircut, and he had holes in the sleeves of his tweed coat. He had on old pants and high shoes. So I said, 'Are you the new gardener?' He took off on me. He said, 'I am like hell!' He said, 'I'm Thomas Hart Benton, the new head of the painting department at the Art Institute.'"

Bill McKim, who was a young student at the Art Institute, recalls that he was surprised to discover how short the new teacher was. "I had pictured a man of some real physical stature, but I found, of course, he was only five feet two inches." His disappointment disappeared, however, when he engaged Benton in conversation: "After talking with him a short time, I never again really gave any thought to his height. Except one time. . . . We were down visiting his brother in Springfield and had to stay the night, and the next morning I got up a little before Tom and I saw his pants draped down over the chair. My shirt was on another chair, next to it. I noticed that his pant legs were shorter than my sleeves."

Benton always spoke of his return as a homecoming, but from the beginning his goals differed significantly from those of many of the social leaders of the town, who emulated the culture of Europe and the East Coast. When he first arrived he was much feted. At one afternoon affair, he was sitting conversing when the double doors from the pantry swung open and a butler marched into the room with a tray of frosty glasses. Tom's eyes lit up. "Oh good!" he said. "I was afraid this was one of those damned lemonade parties." The glasses held lemonade.

East Coast people often imagine Kansas City as flat, but in fact dramatic two-hundred-foot bluffs rise up steeply from the river bottoms, and the general landscape is rolling, with frequent rock outcroppings. The city originated as the starting point of the Santa Fe and Oregon trails. Its frontier character did not last long. In 1869 the first railroad bridge across the Missouri River was constructed at Kansas City, and not long afterward, Charles Francis Adams, Jr., the Boston Brahmin descendant of two American presidents, gained control of the local stockyards. Kansas City rapidly converted itself from a cow town, the home of Wyatt Earp, Bat Masterson, Doc Holliday, and "Wild Bill" Hickok, to a respectable banking and commercial center.

In 1881, just two years after Adams took over the stockyards, an anti-gambling law was passed, a first step toward cleaning up the place. In despair, one noted faro dealer, Bob Potee, put on his best silk hat and walked into the river. He left a note for Charlie Basset, owner of the Marble Hall gambling den, asking him to "plant me decent." In 1882 Jesse James, the Baptist minister's son who robbed trains and banks, was shot by the cowardly Robert Ford; and later that same year, Jesse's brother Frank strode into the Missouri governor's office, unstrapped his six-gun, and surrendered.

The push for cultural improvement was spearheaded by William Rockhill Nelson, a three-hundred-pound newspaper baron from Indiana. An impetuous reformer, he once recalled that when he arrived, "Kansas City was incredibly ugly. I decided that if I were to live here the town must be made over." During his lifetime, Nelson campaigned for parks and boulevards; upon his death, he left the bulk of his enormous estate to create an art gallery. Shortly afterward, Howard Huselton brashly predicted in *The American Magazine of Art* that Kansas City would soon become famous for its collections of art—"a great art center."

In September 1933, Paul Gardner was appointed the museum's first director. He had been a dancer in Anna Pavlova's ballet company, had a degree in architecture from MIT, and had done some work toward a doctorate in fine arts at the Fogg Art Museum at Harvard. William T. Kemper, Jr., recalls Gardner as "a pompous man." His genteel taste is documented by a speech he gave in Lincoln, Nebraska, in 1936, in which he inveighed against the sordidness of most modern painting: "What must foreigners think when they come to our galleries and see displayed pictures of bread lines, of squalid tenement scenes. . . . Why should [our artists] persist in painting the uglier side of existence and calling it the 'American scene'?"

Gardner's two principal deputies had also been trained at the Fogg. His consultant for European paintings was Harold Woodbury Parsons, whom Thomas Hoving, former director of the Metropolitan Museum of Art, recalls as "courtly, soft-spoken, witty—and charmingly dishonest." In appearance, he seemed to have "stepped right out of an elegant portrait of the turn of the century, perhaps by John Singer Sargent. . . . I had never run into anything like *him* in my life. The man's *accent* . . . an efferves-

Thomas Hart Benton, A Social History of Missouri: Pioneer Days and Early Settlers. *On the left side, a trader exchanges beads and whiskey for furs with an Osage Indian. Settlers compete in a turkey shoot; a pioneer plows the soil; and pioneers transport goods by boat, mule, and covered wagon. On the right side, a black man and a white work side by side to construct a house in front of a slave auction. Just behind a river baptism, in the middle distance, stand early monuments of church and state: the basilica of St. Louis, a typical Protestant church, a log cabin in St. Charles that served as the first state capitol, and the nineteenth-century state capitol at Jefferson City. Above the door, Huck Finn admires the fish that Jim has caught, as the steamer* Sam Clemens *steams by in a shower of sparks.*

Downtown Kansas City from the War Memorial. In the 1930s, over 300 trains stopped daily at Kansas City's Union Station, the largest railroad depot west of Chicago. Boss Tom Pendergast ruled the city from his office a few blocks behind the station, at 1908 Main Street.

cent combination of Boston and Oxford, cadenced in a never-ending chain of skillful pleasantries."

The most impressive figure of the group was Laurence Sickman, a handsome unmarried young Orientalist, who was living with his mother in Peking when he joined the staff of the Nelson. A brilliant scholar and connoisseur, Sickman rapidly put together one of the world's great collections of Chinese art. John Russell, art critic of the *New York Times,* has described Sickman's contribution as "one of the finest single curatorial achievements in museum history."

Whatever the actual ability of its members, however, the staff of the Nelson epitomized the tone of pretentious refinement that Benton had blasted in his "Farewell to New York." His young friend Dan James recalls: "[Tom] felt they had a bunch of fakes there. He was very harsh on what he called the 'limp-wrist crowd.' Actually made it rather tough for them. Some of them were a bit lacking in talent, but others were very, very important and excellent curators, it turned out. It wasn't the best aspect of Tom that he would take out after that."

Planning the Jeff City Mural

Benton had originally thought he would do a Huck Finn mural, as a tribute to Mark Twain. When he learned the size of the space set aside for him in the state capitol, he decided to alter his program. "But don't worry," he assured a reporter, "Huck will be in it and so will the King and the Duke and their raft." From the first, he envisaged a social history and resolved "not to emphasize heroic figures or epic events." The mural would be "Missouri from start to finish."

He put down his first thoughts in a small notebook: jottings about such matters as bull boats, early coinage, and the French method of dividing up fields, as well as references to "Houck's History" and other notable texts. He had already begun to think in terms of subject groupings: the annual bonnet show at Big Shoal Church in Liberty; dueling; the organization and building of churches; the Mormon wars; banditry, with Jesse James and the Youngers. Only a few of these ideas found their way into the mural.

Soon he began traveling the state, looking for different types of Missourians: "I met all kinds of people. I played the harmonica and wore a pink shirt to country dances. I went on hunting and fishing parties. I attended an uproarious three-day, old settler's drunk, in the depths of the Ozarks. I went to political barbecues and church picnics. I took in the honky-tonks of the country and the night clubs of Kansas City and St. Louis. I went to businessmen's parties and to meetings of art lovers' associations. I went down in the mines and out in the cornfields. I chased Missouri society up and down from the shacks of the Ozark hillbillies to the country club firesides of the ultimately respectable."

Matthew Baigell has commented: "Many of his trips through the Southeast and Southwest and throughout Appalachia took on the aura of a political tour . . . , as if he were his father visiting his constituents around America, stepping into their lives, talking to them."

In July 1935, Benton had spent several days in Springfield, visiting his brother Nat, and was amazed that the courtrooms were crowded with spectators. It occurred to him to paint a Missouri courtroom scene. "It may be in the state capitol but I don't know," he told a reporter. "Anyway, I shall paint it somewhere, for nothing is more typical of Missouri than the average courtroom audience."

In June 1936, he made his first visit in twenty-four years to Neosho, his hometown. He attended a political rally that featured Nat as the main speaker, and the brothers were honored guests at a chicken dinner at the inn at Big Spring Park. A number of old friends were there, some of whom hadn't seen Tom in thirty years. One described him as "the shiftiest left-end the town football team ever had"; another remembered him as "a bearcat with his fists."

The next morning, Benton sought out his father's former law partner, Horace Roark, but failed to find him on the town square, where Horace usually sat to greet the farmers coming into town. So the painter went over to nearby Pineville to visit with the Oklahoma short-story writer George Milburn. Later in the day he found Horace, who denied that he had been hiding.

"Tom, I just went fishing for trout out Big Sugar way. I'm willing to pose for you. Maybe I owe it to you, Tom. The other day a writer for some magazine was here and asked me about your boyhood days in Neosho. 'The only thing I can remember about Tom Benton,' I told him, 'is that he always was being brought up in court and fined $1 and costs for fist fighting.' Remember the time I paid your fine so your father wouldn't find out you had been at it again?"

William Rockhill Nelson.

The next day, Benton took his sketch pad to Rube Rose's farm near Springfield to draw a mule, which was held for him in the barnyard by Mrs. Rose and her son. That afternoon, on the way back to Kansas City, he suddenly stopped the car. "Those heifers," he exclaimed. "Just the age and kind I want." The journalist accompanying him noted: "The portrait of Sooky went into the sketchbook, along with Lawyer Roark, Rube Rose's mule, a typical Missouri silo and a coal mine. For just the right man, just the right mule and cow, Mr. Benton traveled more than 500 miles through Southern Missouri. This summer he will continue traveling and searching."

Duard Marshall recalls that Benton sold three large paintings during his first year in Kansas City (one of these was *Lonesome Road,* which was bought by the Nebraska Art Association in Lincoln). With the proceeds, he purchased a house on Valentine Road; but as it lacked a studio, he worked on the Jefferson City clay model up at the painting studio of the Art Institute. "Tom's tracings and drawings were just scattered all over the floor. I had a tracing of the sorghum mill right out of the waste-paper basket. Somebody stole it from me later up at Colorado Springs."

"You can't change your mind up on the scaffold without the risk of everything going awry," Benton once commented. In the design of a mural, "Every inch of it must be planned beforehand." The Missouri mural was the most rigorously planned of all his paintings. His plastilene model was fifteen feet long and twenty inches high; it took two months to build. The model was built on a basic plane tipped back at a forty-five-degree angle. Benton had the clay models photographed by Ed Hense, who worked for the Kansas City *Star,* and used the photographs to check the accuracy of his values.

Students at the Institute often served as his models. Jackson Lee Nesbitt posed for most of the figures in the courtroom scene. Benton placed different heads on most of the bodies, but kept Nesbitt's on the man seated at a table in front of the judge with his back to the viewer. "That's all of me," Nesbitt has commented, "needin' a haircut and everything else." Benton generally sketched very quickly, but Rossiter Howard remembered him spending an entire afternoon studying the hand and forearm of a model.

Unlike all Benton's earlier murals, the one at Jeff City was painted in the room in which it was placed—the House Lounge. As he had for his previous projects, he constructed a secondary wall of five-ply wood in front of the brick and masonry building wall. He covered this with Belgian linen attached with casein glue, and covered the linen with a gesso created from white chalk mixed with glue and egg yolk. Most of the outlining of the drawings was done by Lawrence Adams, a teacher at the University of Missouri, who marked off the surface into three-foot squares and transferred the design unit by unit.

Benton himself did all the painting, working in egg tempera with some glazes of oil. He began in the second week of July, working from a large rolling scaffold on which he kept about fifteen jars of hand-mixed paint, nearly a hundred brushes, and a pipe. He also kept a diminishing glass handy, so that he could guess what the figures would look like from below. Despite all his planning, the work moved forward slowly. His small figure was dwarfed by the scale of the great wall; the reporter Paz vanMatre, who visited the House Lounge during the first week of work, compared the painter to "a fly on a window pane—industriously moving toward some great unfathomable, mysterious future, oblivious to time and speed."

Execution

The summer of 1936 was a scorcher; the heat killed over four hundred people in Missouri. Through most of July and August, the temperature rose to 100 degrees or more. Though Benton kept all the doors and windows of the lounge open, the heat was intense, and the eggs he used for pigment rotted quickly, filling the room with a sulfurous smell. Mary Humphrey, then a young secretary in the Capitol, recalls: "It was awful, because the paints would get all runny and sometimes he would have to work with them to cool them down. Sometimes he'd stick them in a bucket of ice water, the tubes, before he'd start bringing them out on the palette."

Since his days as an art student in Chicago, Benton had always enjoyed painting in public. He had the option of closing off the House Lounge while he worked, but he chose instead to turn his project into a public performance. He posted a letter in front of his movable scaffolding:

TO THE VISITORS

Friends:

Many of you who come in here to watch the progress of this painting have questions to ask. Others know things about Missouri which they feel I should include in this painted history of the State.

I would like to answer the questions and I am appreciative of all information but I cannot give time to the first and it is too late for the second to operate on this work.

Later on some kind of comment will be prepared to explain in detail what is here. For the present let one just say that the theme of the painting is the evolution of society in the State of Missouri.

This theme does not demand the representation of specific characters or events emphasized in historic record. It calls simply for a depiction of the ways people lived and the changes they effected in their environment as Missouri developed. I

have been as inclusive as possible with my subject matter but although these are big walls there is much significant and interesting matter I have had to leave out.

I have spent a year planning this affair, comparing, weighing, choosing and discarding aggregations of facts. My first choice of any particular group of historic facts has been determined by two things. First, by its similarity and near relationsip to facts which I have experienced myself, directly. This is because things intimately and directly known by the artist can be made to appear more lifelike in his work than things he only gets by hearsay, however well they are documented. The second thing that determined my choice was the manageability of facts in the logic of this pictorial scheme.

I think any of you can see that the objects painted on these walls are not just slapped on arbitrarily. The filling of every square quarter inch of space in this room has been planned and worked out so that the shapes, volumes and colors of things shall stand out and carry the eye over and in and out of the picture space. When you look at this painting a man's body or a tree trunk may be just a body or a tree trunk to you but they are also functioning parts of a geometrical pattern which insures that your eye shall travel easily from one place to another on these walls and get a sense of unity from what is on them. The "realness" of this work depends on a lot of abstract adjustments of lines and planes and gradations of color. These adjustments cannot be disturbed without causing me a lot of work, without, in fact, making me do this thing all over.

Write me all the information you have. I may need it some day, but do not ask me to inject more subject matter into this plan. Mail to me at Room 100, State Capitol.

I am very appreciative of the interest that is being shown in this mural and I

Thomas Hart Benton, clay models for A Social History of Missouri, *1935–36. This was the largest clay model Benton ever produced—12 feet wide and about 2½ feet high.*

hope people, seeing the work I have yet to do, will pardon my refusal to consider things that interest them.

Sincerely yours,

THOMAS HART BENTON

Mary Humphrey, a secretary in the building, got in the habit of going into the lounge during her lunch hour. Benton started work around six in the morning and worked steadily until about five in the afternoon. Some days he worked quickly, others more slowly, depending on "how much he had to drink the night before." He painted on as he ate his lunch, munching cheese and crackers, and drinking beer or Coke out of a bottle with a straw. As Mary Humphrey recalls: "He always painted during the noon hour because he said that was the quiet time for him. No interruptions. He didn't care for too many people talking at one time. I started by going in, taking my lunch, sitting in a chair, not saying a word to him. I asked for his approval—did he mind if I kept my mouth shut and just sat and watched?—and he said no, he'd be delighted to have me. And that's how our friendship arose."

After a while, they began talking and teasing each other. "When you got to know him he was a really a very delightful person. . . . And he would laugh, bless his heart. He was never really attractive to me as far as looks were concerned. . . . But . . . he had a great sense of humor . . . and he had many, many good stories to tell. Funny as they could be, and they weren't always clean, I can tell you. He was an intelligent man, but people never gave him credit for being. They thought he was a nut."

Benton responded to busybodies, however, with frigid silence. One day, a woman broke away from her friends and went over to where the artist stood on the scaffold, to complain about some figures. He paid no attention, completely ignoring her comments. "He doesn't understand the English language," she reported to her companions. Sam Blair, who later became a prominent judge, visited the House Lounge one day with a lawyer friend; they began to fool around with some of the paints on the table. Benton silently climbed down from his scaffold, walked over to them, and scribbled a note saying, "God damn it, keep your fucking hands off my stuff." He gave it to them without saying a word and then stalked back to the scaffold and his work.

Despite the letter he had posted, he often willingly corrected mistakes in his representations. One day, a tall, lean, elderly farmer asked, "Is that there a new fangled kind of plow?" He was pointing to the plow hitched to the mule near the main door. Tom asked what was wrong with it and received a detailed answer: 'O' course I don't know nothin' erbout hand paintin', but I kin tell the hind part o' that plow is too short for the man you got a-usin' it. Why it ain't no more'n a child's plow. And the handles ain't got enough turn to give enybody a real grip on 'em. That big mule a-pullin' it would yank the blade right up outen the ground most every step or so." The painter enthusiastically thanked his adviser and promised to correct the matter as soon as he could.

Photographs of Benton at work on the mural show that he proceeded in the manner of the old masters, from top to bottom, from background to foreground. Generally he worked down the major lines of construction of his design and then filled in the intervening areas. Scrivener recalls that "Sometimes he would skip and one day you would find him working in one section and the next time he would be over somewhere else."

The drawing on the wall conveyed only the outer contour of the figures—not their facial features or any interior elements. Thus it allowed Benton considerable freedom to improvise as he moved along. No doubt he had sketched many of the heads before he began work, but often he would stop painting, round up a model, make a drawing, and immediately transfer his sketch to the wall.

As he worked, he added the portraits of all kinds of people: a supreme court judge, the governor, a dairy farmer, a postmaster, an insurance agent, and the warden of the state prison. Dan James posed as his illustrious ancestor Jesse in the train robbery scene. "He stuck me in one of his damn baroque positions," he recalled, "where I had to stand forever with my knees bent holding this giant Colt revolver."

When Otto Feuerbringer of the St. Louis *Post-Dispatch* visited on July 18, Benton had painted most of the Huck Finn panel but wasn't satisfied with the face of Huck. He had sent a friend to find a suitable eleven-year-old boy in Jefferson City. In addition, he had several friends out fishing for a Missouri River catfish for Nigger Jim to hold. "But so far they haven't brought him any," Feuerbringer reported.

"Popeye" Williams, a janitor in the capitol, posed for Jim: "One morning Mr. Benton called me over and said, 'When you're through, come on up to the mural room. I'd like to talk to you.' I said, 'Why?' He said, 'Well, for two or three reasons, but first let me say there's a catch.' I said, 'What's that, Mr. Benton?' He said, 'You're going to be in Huckleberry Finn.' But he said, 'Now get set because I'm going to say something to you and you might not like it.' I said, 'What's that, Mr. Benton?'

"He said, 'Let me tell you first what the character's going to be.' I said, 'All right.' He said, 'You're going to be—wait a minute now, I'm pretty near scared to say this to you.' I said, 'Mr. Benton, you won't make me mad, I don't believe you will.' He said, 'Well, the character's going to be Nigger Jim.' His face bloomed up and he looked at me funny. But I told him it would be quite an honor to have my picture on that wall."

Tom then quickly sketched Popeye on a small sheet of paper. "It seemed like he just made three or four marks and then he said, 'Come back here in a while, I'll have your picture on the wall shortly.'" Around two-thirty, he called Popeye up from the janitor's room. "So I went up there and there I was," Popeye recalled. "Only I was holding two fish."

One of the most controversial vignettes showed a woman wiping a baby's bottom. The child was Harold Brown, Jr., son of the state adjutant general, whom Tom had sketched for the courtroom scene. While he was visiting the family, he noticed the year-old-infant. "I like that baby," he commented. "I need to get that baby into the

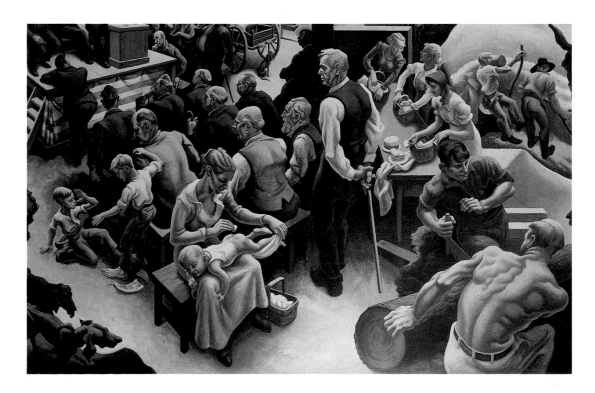

Detail, East Wall, Politics, Farming and Law in Missouri. *To critics of the diapering scene, Benton replied: "There couldn't have been any military history if there weren't any babies to put diapers on."*

259

Thomas Hart Benton painting the murals in the Missouri State Capitol, 1936.

mural." Mary Tunnell, who worked in the State Highway Department, was invited to pose as the child's mother. When she agreed, Benton said: "Wait 'till I tell you what I want." He explained that she would be seen diapering a baby, and Mary replied, "That's all right with me. I don't mind at all." She and Harold Brown, Jr., posed separately; they met for the first time forty-six years later.

While Benton was working on the political scene, a black politician from St. Louis complained to Governor Park about the vignette depicting the whipping of black slaves by the overseer of the lead mine. He wanted that part of the mural removed. The governor replied that he found nothing in the scene "reflecting on the negroes," but privately he pulled Tom aside and advised him that he'd "be smart" to take the section out. "These St. Louis blacks are very important to our organization in the eastern part of the state for the coming election. It was our organization that gave you this 'muriel' job and you can do it a little favor like I'm asking for in return. Be good for your future anyway."

Benton arranged to meet with the objector, who had never actually seen the painting. He explained that he hoped to show the progress Missouri's blacks had made from their unhappy beginnings to their present position of political importance. He then added that he was looking for a prominent black politician to place in the political scene, leaning against a tree. "How about my putting your face on that figure?" he asked. "Why, Mr. Artist," the man replied, "I think that would be all right." Tom had his face up on the wall that afternoon.

The next day, the politician and his friends came in and whispered and chuckled about the image. That afternoon, Governor Park invited Benton into his office for a highball. "They say you are an artist, Tom," he commented, "but you're a better politician."

One of the last figures Benton filled in was Tom Pendergast, the political boss of Kansas City. "I told him that this was to be a mural of contemporary Missouri, and what the hell, it can't be complete without you, and he agreed that that was true. So he posed for me in his Kansas City office. He wanted to be in it or he wouldn't have posed. There wasn't any trouble at all." The *Post-Dispatch* rhapsodized about this addition in a tongue-in-cheek editorial on December 9: "If the Benton murals are to symbolize our twentieth-century Missouri, the figure, one might say the transfigure of Pendergast, must, in veraciousness, contribute to the pictorial writing on the wall."

On December 19, 1936, the Jefferson City *Daily Capital News* reported that Benton had applied the last brush stroke. He and workmen were sealing the mural with a coat of shellac, alcohol, and clear varnish, and then covering it with a coat of wax.

Form

A Social History of Missouri is the only one of Benton's mural programs of the 1930s that still remains perfectly intact, in the same room for which it was painted and in its original arrangement. It is also his greatest single artistic statement of the decade. He worked on it significantly longer than he had on any of his previous mural projects—the planning took him eighteen months, the execution an additional six—and later declared that this cycle "completed the last phase of my development as an artist." Shortly before his death, he said: "If I have any right to make judgments, I would say that the Missouri mural was my best work."

Benton's genius as a composer, as a manipulator of form, in many ways ran against the main tendency of American painting in the thirties. Most of the greatest canvases of the period, the Regionalists' or those of rival artistic camps, function as icons, presenting flat shapes overlaid one on another rather than rhythmic sequences of receding shapes. Three of the most famous paintings of the decade can serve as a

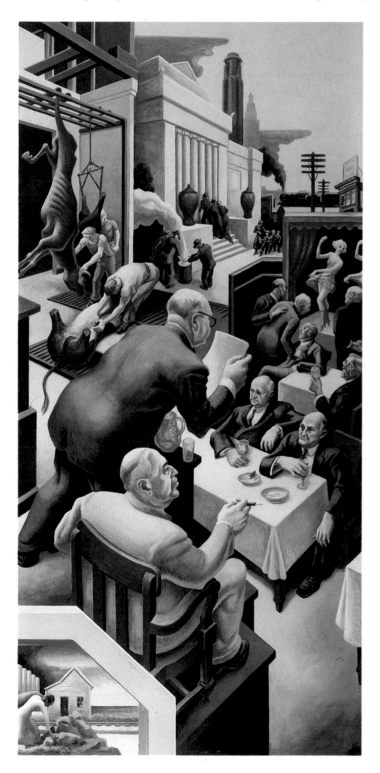

Detail, Pioneer Days and Early Settlers. *In the early eighteenth century, blacks were imported from Santo Domingo to work the lead mines of St. Francis County.*

Detail, St. Louis and Kansas City. *In his Kansas City panel, Benton suggested the close ties between machine politics and the Kansas City business world. Boss Tom Pendergast, in the foreground, listens to a speech by Bryson Jones, a local businessman. Seated in the audience are banker W. T. Kemper and real estate developer J.C. Nichols. When questioned about the scantily clad dancer, Benton replied: "I've been to many business men's parties here and in St. Louis and I want to tell you I put considerable clothes on her."*

sample: Grant Wood's *American Gothic,* Edward Hopper's *House by the Railroad Track,* and Georgia O'Keeffe's *Cow Skull with Red, White and Blue.* Usually these works are considered to be in disparate stylistic categories, but in fact they all rely on essentially similar visual strategies. They present mundane, familiar elements from American life in large scale, isolated from the surroundings, much as billboards do with commercial products. These paintings endow their subjects with new and enigmatic meanings. Flat, iconic, and frozen, they are moved from the ordinary world into the realm of religious contemplation. This approach, which led to simple and powerful effects, made paintings that carry well in reproduction. When we encounter the original canvas, we are often disappointed to discover that the image that has been burned into our heads corresponds to a mere physical reality, an object created by human hands.

Benton's restless compositions function very differently. The eye can never rest on a single object but is always forcefully pushed through the composition, jumping from one object to another, not only racing over the surface but penetrating deeply into the pictorial space. Benton sought to capture the spirit of America not by turning American artifacts into icons but through an analogy with the rhythmic energy of forms—by creating an atmosphere of energy and power that somehow corresponds to the energy of a vast continent.

As Thomas Craven wrote of Benton in 1934: "The form that he has developed is almost a perfect equivalent of the realities of American life. The tumultuous forces of America, its manifold dissonances, and its social anarchy, are perfectly expressed in the restless counterplay of his forms. The common criticism that his work is without poise or serenity is an unwitting affirmation of its truth, its connection with its time and place." Benton himself once wrote of his style: "This realism tried to symbolize the turmoil of America by setting up a turmoil of rhythmic sequences." Such formal energy was out of step with the general spirit of the 1930s, but it returned to American painting in the late 1940s and the 1950s, most notably in the work of Benton's pupil Jackson Pollock.

The House Lounge, Missouri State Capitol. Politics, Farming and Law in Missouri *on the south wall. "They just looked like they was jumpin' out at me,"* State Senator John Christy commented of Benton's murals. *"I thought of these people trying to go in there and sit down and relax and play cards and I was quite concerned about it."*

To a greater degree than any of the other projects, the Missouri mural functions as a unified ensemble. Its panels cannot be easily broken down into self-contained scenes; it works on the spectator as a three-dimensional surround. The figures are designed so that their gestures relate to, their bodies seem to address, not only their immediate neighbors but figures of past and future across the room.

Within the historical flow of events, it is often ambiguous where one scene begins and another breaks off. In addition, particularly in the farmhouse and courtroom scenes, Benton disassembled architecture as if it were a stage set—freely removing ceilings and partitions, and even bending angles, as in an architect's isometric rendering, to make the interior of the space more visible. Many of the details, such as the brick chimney on brackets in the farmhouse kitchen, seem improbable if not impossible; they make sense as visual pathways for the eye, not as constructible entities.

In the New School panels, his spatial handling alluded to Cubism; in the Missouri mural, although he reorganized space with equal freedom, he borrowed not from the Cubists but from the Italian old masters, particularly Annibale Carracci's Farnese Gallery. Caracci, however, strongly distinguished between the supporting figures and those that played a role in the design: he painted the supporting figures in monochrome, to give them the appearance of sculpture. Thus the two levels of reality are neatly divided.

In Benton's mural, the flanking figures are not so distinguished, and thus they are able to move, in a rather disconcerting fashion, from one form of pictorial reality into another. They threaten to step from the narratives in which they belong into the mythology panels; at the same time, they lean out in front of their frames, threatening to emerge into the room and confront the spectator.

The emotional power of the Missouri mural is grounded in the visual pathways that link disparate forms and the violent confrontations of meaning they evoke. Thus the Nelson-Atkins Museum of Art is juxtaposed with the Kansas City stockyards, or a swankily dressed society boy with a low-class gangster. Through the pressure of these juxtapositions Benton forces us to recognize contrasts, affinities, and relationships. Significantly, the meanings of these relationships remain ambiguous—or at least cannot be reduced to a single consistent pattern. Sometimes he stresses a visual affinity or contrast, sometimes one based on moral or social consideratons. Not infrequently he uses visual puns to trigger mental associations. Thus, by juxtaposing a black man leaning against a tree with a black man who has been lynched from a tree, he provokes thoughts about the changing social role of blacks. The excitement of the effect comes partly because these juxtapositions push us through a variety of mental pathways—we may find ourselves exploring a series of protruding and receding noses and chins at the same time that we are comparing and contrasting the social roles of the individuals portrayed.

Significantly, the meanings of these juxtapositions are not fixed, as in the propagandistic art of the social realists. Each image allows a wide variety of interpretations. Rather than fixing his narrative to specific historical episodes, Benton allows the spectator to devise his own interpretation—invites him, in effect, to invent his own story for the picture. As he explained to I. G. Morrison, a guide at the Missouri State Capitol, who gave tours of the mural: "The purpose of a work of art is not so much to tell what the artist's thoughts were as to stimulate thoughts in those who view it. A cartoon tells a specific story and lasts a day—a work of art tells as many stories as there are people to see it. It lasts by that power to continually stimulate as long as its material holds together."

Morrison later testified that Benton's panels effectively accomplished his goal. "Every day," he wrote, "I see visitors to our capitol walk under the dome on the first floor level and look up. There they admire the beauty of that fine dome. They see those thirteen renowned paintings of Frank Brangwyn; some of the finest murals in the world. They will look maybe for three or four minutes and they are through. Not a wheel has turned over in their heads. They will maybe say, 'Well, isn't that pretty?' That is all; 'Isn't it pretty.' The murals do not mean a thing.

"Then these same visitors walk into this room and immediately commence to gesticulate and become vocal. Thomas Hart Benton makes you think something when you step into this room. It may be hard to tell just what you will think, but you will think something."

"A Social History of Missouri"

The Missouri River, the main artery of the state, winds through the background of the mural, completely encircling the room. (The actual river is visible from the windows on the west wall.) Human events take place in front of this backdrop and are presented in a strong vein of social criticism.

The first panel introduces two central themes: the oppression of minorities and the amorality of capitalism. A French fur trader, modeled by Benton's student Glen Rounds, exchanges beads and whiskey for furs with an Osage Indian, behind whose head a wagon wheel, placed like the halo of a medieval saint, suggests both the innocence of the Indian and the forces of progress that will roll over him.

The social critique of the pioneers continues in the next panel, in which white and black laborers construct a house in front of a slave auction. Thus Benton contrasted honest laborers, in close contact with the realities of the physical world, with capitalists willing to translate anything, even their fellowmen, into the abstraction of money. Behind the slave auction we see a river baptism—a juxtaposition of religion and injustice that was surely intended ironically. And below these scenes are smaller panels showing a black slave being whipped and a Mormon being tarred and feathered while his home is burned down behind him.

On the northeast wall, a billowing cloud of smoke represents the destruction wrought by the Civil War. Soldiers fight; a house burns; a woman and child flee. In black silhouette against the flames can be seen a hanged man—perhaps a freed slave who has been lynched, undoubtedly meant to provide a contrast with the well-dressed black man leaning against a tree in the political scene.

On the southeast wall, Benton painted a balancing black column of smoke—this time that of modern air pollution, produced by factory chimneys. The imagery of the wall ends on a menacing note: a miner with sticks of dynamite and a machine-gun-like drill.

The south wall is devoted to contemporary urban life. A St. Louis scene shows workers in the breweries, shoe factories, and sweatshops. One of the brewers swigs beer from a mug, in a gesture to match that of the trader in the first panel. This time, it is the white man, not the Indian, who is intoxicated.

A Kansas City scene shows the butchery of the stockyards, the economic foundation of the town, taking place in front of the Nelson-Atkins Museum of Art. Three bums huddle around a burning trash can, while a man in a top hat strides up the museum's front steps. In the right foreground is an indication of the close alliance between Kansas City politics and business. R. Bryson Jones, an insurance executive, reads a speech, while Tom Pendergast, the political boss of the city, puffs on a cigarette and listens. Seated at a table are two of the community's business leaders, W. T. Kemper, a banker, and J. C. Nichols, a real estate developer and trustee of the Nelson-Atkins Museum of Art. Behind them is a nightclub scene, with a scantily clad dancer.

In the small panels below, a scene of poverty, with blacks lounging and a woman gathering coal along the railroad tracks, contrasts with a scene in an expensive nightclub.

A Painted Autobiography

Against this background of greed and exploitation Benton inserted scenes of a more nostalgic nature which refer back to his own childhood. Indeed, he once referred to the mural as "almost like a painted autobiography." Most of the northeast wall is occupied by a political panorama. Tom's father delivers a speech from an outdoor platform, standing before a poster of Champ Clark, the favorite son of Missouri who lost the presidential nomination to Woodrow Wilson in 1919 after a struggle that extended through forty-four ballots. The hounds in the foreground probably allude to Clark's campaign song—"You've Gotta Quit Kickin' My Dawg Around." In the town behind him, flimsy false facades of wood are just beginning to give way to the brick storefronts of progress.

On the northwest wall, a cutaway view of a farmhouse interior reveals four generations of a Missouri family. The great-grandpa's picture hangs on the wall; grandfather reads; grandma rolls dough; father, just in from the fields, washes his face and neck in a washbasin; and a child munches on a sandwich. Lovingly observed details establish the simple style of living: the basin (running water has not yet been piped in), the handmade quilt on the bed, the towels hanging to dry beside the coal stove, the broken comb next to the bar of homemade soap, and the bare plank floor.

The remaining section of the wall shows a courtroom scene in which Benton's brother Nat addresses a jury before a judge who is half asleep on the bench. The floor beside a spittoon has been stained where someone took faulty aim. In the background stands the red brick courthouse of Neosho, which was torn down the very year the mural was painted.

Significantly, Benton portrayed neither his mother nor his two sisters—of the 235 people in the mural, only 32 are women—but he did include all the male figures of the

Politics, Farming and Law in Missouri. *On the left wall, Benton's father delivers a political speech in front of a poster of Champ Clark. In the center, Missouri farming: an old-fashioned Ozark farm and sorghum mill to the left of the door, and a more up-to-date farm of the thirties to the right. To the right of the cutaway view of the farmhouse interior, Tom's brother Nat addresses a courtroom, before a dozing judge. Behind him rises the courthouse of Benton's hometown of Neosho. To the far right, a miner from the southwest corner of the state hefts a machine-gun-like drill. Above the door in the center, the Jesse James gang robs a bank and holds up the Chicago and Alton train.*

Benton clan: His father orates, his brother addresses a courtroom, his son eats a sandwich, and his brother's two children fight over a watermelon. We see the Colonel at the height of his career, without a hint of the circumstances that dashed his bright ambitions. It is almost as though, in this most ambitious of his murals, Benton sought a final reconciliation with his father.

Although he did not include a self-portrait, he left indirect tokens of his presence. Karal Ann Marling has suggested that the tom turkey strutting through the barnyard between Nat and the Colonel was intended as Tom Benton's surrogate. In addition, Benton included the year of his birth, 1889, in the cornerstone of the brick building behind his father.

Missouri Mythology
Above the doors, Benton represented scenes of "Missouri Mythology"—songs and legends associated with the state. Over the north door, Huck Finn and Jim float on their raft. Huck looks up in admiration at his companion, wishing for a catfish as big as the one Jim has caught. A steamboat named the *Sam Clemens* steams by in the background, puffing white steam and black coal smoke and raining orange sparks.

Above the east door, the James Gang is hard at work, carrying out both a bank job and a train robbery. And over the south door, Frankie blasts away at Johnnie. As in the other two scenes, the action takes place at night; the sky behind the swinging doors of the saloon has darkened to a deep velvet blue. There are many humorous details, such as the man whose suspender has snapped as he rushes out the door. Benton here paid tribute to an image that inspired many of his earliest artistic efforts: on the barroom wall hangs the Anheuser-Busch print of "Custer's Last Stand."

Controversy
Some years earlier, the energy of Benton's murals had caused great anguish to a few sensitive readers in the library of the Whitney Museum. Fortunately, there were not

266

too many of them, although the paintings were sufficiently disturbing to earn Benton a severe lecture on artistic deportment from the *New Republic,* as well as the permanent enmity of a good part of New York's artistic community. But in Jefferson City, the impact of his work was significantly greater. He upset the peace of mind not simply of a few art-minded readers but of an entire state legislature. The repercussions echoed through the State of Missouri, and soon a good part of the country was embroiled in the controversy.

In the 1920s, H. L. Mencken, with his assaults on the Puritans and the Philistines, had carried out in literature much the same program that Benton pursued in his painting. Critics labeled him "the boy-pervert from Baltimore," "a literary stink-pot," and "a public nuisance." But Mencken was undismayed and actually collected the most vicious invectives in a little book titled *Menckeniana: A Shimpflexikon.* The attacks proved that his writings were having an effect: if people are angry at you, it shows they care.

Benton took a similar approach. "I paint sometimes to get people to criticize my work," he told Forrest Scrivener. As early as January 17, 1937, the Kansas City *Star* reported that the Jefferson City mural was "replacing the duke of Windsor and Mrs. Simpson as the popular topic of conversation in Kansas City." An editorial noted breathlessly: "Our first impulse was to duck. The great scale on which the pictures are made, together with the apparent smallness of the room and the vividness of the colorings, the impression of distorted proportions in some of the larger figures, sort of combine to make the spectator feel he is about to be overwhelmed and crushed, perhaps, in an avalanche that somehow seems very threatening and imminent."

A desire to duck was also the first instinct of many of the legislators. One of them, John Christy, recalls going into the House Lounge shortly after the murals were completed: "And they just looked like they was jumpin' out at me, and I thought of these people trying to go in there and sit down and relax and play cards and I was quite concerned about it."

"It's like a symphony," Benton later explained, defending his work. "You're not expected to live with a symphony. You hear it occasionally. Nobody will be with this mural all the time. But those who do see it will know they're seeing something."

To many people, the symphony was too loud. On January 14, the *Daily Capital News* reported that the intensity of the mural—and the increasing flood of visitors coming to see it—had driven card players out of the lounge to the House floor, where they used the press table. "It's just not comfortable in there," one representative complained. "How can you keep your mind on playing pitch with Jesse James jumping off the wall at you?" Representative Max Asotsky commented: "They'd go swell in a lot of Kansas City barrooms." The state engineer, Matt Murray, told a reporter: "I wouldn't hang a Benton on my shithouse wall."

A neatly printed handbill was circulated throughout the capitol, signed by "A Bum Art Critic." The writer commented that while Benton's portrait of Kansas City was accurate, it left out some important things—"an overstuffed ballot box, a $40,000 underworld funeral, a Union Station massacre, a bandit golf course, and a kidnapper's retreat." But it concluded: "Shucks, art is art."

On May 6, the *Star* reported that members of the House had completely abandoned their efforts to seek relaxation in the lounge; Majority Leader Roy Hamlin had introduced a resolution to fix up another room as a retreat for his colleagues.

The morning of the first session of the legislature, John Christy was eating breakfast at the Missouri Hotel, where he was joined by Hamlin. He had seen the mural for the first time the night before, and he was furious. "Roy," he said, "have you seen those damnable things on the walls in the House Lounge?" Hamlin tried to quiet him, but Christy went on impetuously. "Roy, that's terrible. We can't have those. You . . . get a resolution prepared and introduced to have those walls redone and let's get rid of those things." By this time, Hamlin was pushing at Christy's face and saying, "That's Mr. Benton. That's Mr. Benton."

Tom was seated at the next table, glowering. He got up just as a young lady rushed over to him and gushed: "Oh, Mr. Benton, I've seen your murals and how beautiful they are. May I have your autograph?" He didn't acknowledge her but stood up and addressed Christy. "I have," he said, "just heard some remarks from one who knows nothing about art—and should he study it the remainder of his life would know less." With that, he strode out of the restaurant.

On January 8, Walter Heren reported in the Kansas City *Journal-Post* that among the people he polled, there was no middle ground in opinions of the murals. "You either like 'em or you want the wall painted a deep black," he reported. Heren observed, however, that the portrait of Pendergast "helps keep down some criticism . . . because many of the Solons believe he'd never have permitted his picture to be painted into something that wasn't just right."

On March 10, Representative T. E. Roberts introduced a resolution to put up a railing to protect the mural from being damaged by the many onlookers. He described it as "magnificent" and declared that "posterity will point with pride instead of shame to this superior work of art." This effort backfired. Representative C. P. Turley of Carter County drew noisy applause from fellow House members when he amended the resolution the next day to whitewash the paintings. Although the band of whitewash would be "a monstrosity," it "would fit in well with the monstrosity out there on the walls." Roberts hastily withdrew his resolution.

On March 19, however, the mural won the qualified support of the new governor, Lloyd Stark. He had won his office with the endorsement of Boss Pendergast, who produced for him a vote total in Kansas City that was greater by two hundred thousand than the population recorded by the federal census. But unlike the previous governor, Stark did not remain loyal to the machine. Benton later recalled his nervousness when he showed the new governor his handiwork. Stark walked directly over to the figure of Pendergast, which dominated the Kansas City panel. Looking as deadpan as possible, Benton said to him, "That is a fact of Missouri's social history."

"That *was* a fact," Stark rejoined.

Soon afterward, he issued a statement in defense of the work: "I do not think it is a beautiful piece of art. But the murals are skillfully done and depict significant occurrences in the life of Missouri in the early days."

Stark's appreciation was not shared by his wife. When she was told a year later that an artist had been found to paint her portrait for the governor's mansion, she reacted with concern: "I hope it is not Mr. Benton, because I do want to look like a lady."

Newspaper Reviews

The first few reviews were favorable. On December 21, 1936, the Kansas City *Star* editorialized: "The artist has interpreted his facts with subtlety and force. His humor is eminently good-natured." On Christmas Day, the *Journal-Post* described the House Lounge as "the most interesting room in Missouri." Many readers of these papers disagreed.

Lou E. Holland, the president of an engraving company and the former executive manager of the Kansas City Chamber of Commerce, told a reporter for the *Star* that the murals were in poor taste: "They do not show Missouri in a proper light. Missouri is not proud of hangings and Negro honky-tonks. She is not proud of the whipping of slaves, the slave block and Jesse James holdups. The figures, themselves, in the paintings, and the execution in general are terrible and not in taste."

T. G. Field of Kansas City complained that the murals were not true art, but just cartoons which "got more laughs than Popeye."

Cyrus Williams of Turney, Missouri, who claimed to have "been raised in a Missouri feed lot," protested against the stockyard scene: "If a Missouri cattle feeder had a tubercular-looking calf on his farm like the one pictured, he would at once take it to the woods, shoot it, and bury it to keep it from his dogs."

And Kansas City realtor Howard Huselton, a former president of the Kansas City Art Institute, described the effect as "a low type of painting" and predicted: "A time will come when Missouri will find the murals so odious its executives will order they be blacked out."

Detail, Politics, Farming and Law in Missouri. *"I've lived here 40 years and I never saw a cow like that before,"* one critic commented.

In late January, several papers reported that the mural had required $2,751 worth of fresh eggs. Benton denied this, stating that he used only about 35 dozen eggs in all, a total expense of $10.50.

The Independence *Examiner* viewed the mural unfavorably, complaining: "Missouri is not a houn' dog state. The whole thing is sordid and rather disgusting and it's more like a cartoon which picks out and emphasizes the weaknesses and extravagance of early Missouri life and leaves out the mighty purposes, the strong characters, the ideals of men and women who built Missouri." Ed Watson, the editor of the Columbia *Daily Tribune*, vigorously concurred: "It is generally agreed that the applause would be general and deafening should Gov. Stark order this whole 'realistic' mess obliterated."

The most scathing indictment appeared in the Tulsa *Tribune*, which said in part:

> "Shame on you, Thomas Hart Benton, shame on you, and shame on whoever, representing Missouri's government, paid $16,000 to buy this picture of infamy. Shame upon the people's representatives in the capitol from Governor Stark to every member of the state's legislature who will allow such a picture to remain brazenly exhibited on Missouri's capitol wall.
> "Mr. Benton has lied about Missouri. He has desecrated its capitol walls declaring that Missouri's social history is one of utter depravity. That is a lie— Missouri's social history is a story of growing refinement and nobility."

Benton later noted with contempt that the *Tribune* was a Republican paper.

The controversy only stirred up more publicity. *Art Digest* carried the headline: "Thomas H. Benton Paints the History of Missouri—Starts a Civil War." *Life* magazine sent its photographer Alfred Eisenstaedt and three other staff members to photograph both the mural and some "original Benton types" that they visited in the Ozarks. A richly illustrated story on the painting appeared on March 1.

Question-and-Answer Sessions

Benton did not accept the criticism passively but went out to confront his foes in a series of public forums. On January 15, in a question-and-answer session at the Art Institute, he described his brand of realism in some detail. His painting, he declared, portrayed "the conditions under which history is made rather than history itself. . . . Had I treated the theme as a succession of events I would have had to receive my impressions at second hand. I never put anybody in a picture of this kind unless I have had an opportunity to become acquainted with him or to sketch him from life."

Curiously, he noted that many visitors liked the portrayal of Champ Clark in the political banner, although in this likeness he had deliberately parodied the mechanical deadness of photography. "It is the only 'portrait' people tell me I have not caricatured. That is something that puzzles me. . . . Champ Clark was a friend of my father. I knew him. Had I painted my own idea of him it would have been something quite different from the photograph, which is so obviously a pale and lifeless reproduction of a retouched likeness. . . . It was not a good photograph for it had been retouched. I can only conclude that people have gradually come to base their ideas of the appearance of political candidates and others in the public eye upon photographs rather than upon the testimony of their eyes."

He had taken great care, he averred, to represent activities accurately. "I think it is important that details be right because if a visitor sees two young men wielding a crosscut saw in a manner that will result in the binding of the saw, he won't believe anything else is right in the picture."

What about his figures' large hands and feet? Surely they weren't accurate. "I like the hands of working people," he commented. "They are beautiful. I like to have them large enough to be seen. The feet must correspond in size, of course. The fact is that most of the hands and feet you have seen in the pictures have been painted too small."

When one critic charged that there was neither "beauty nor refinement" in the mural, Tom replied: "There is truth. Besides, all that I have put into the picture is beautiful—to me." Someone asked him how he designed the mural. "Well, I sat down and monkeyed with a pencil."

On January 24, he answered questions again, at a luncheon of the American Legion in a private dining room at the Hotel Phillips in Kansas City. Some of the members complained that he had shortchanged the military history of Missouri, others complained about the diaper scene. He replied: "First, there couldn't have been any military history if there weren't any babies to put diapers on. Second, if I'd had more space I would have done it—that is, put in more military history. But Missouri's military affairs were mostly skirmishes when we consider the entire budget of time."

To the comment that he had made people "funny looking," he replied: "No individual who is painted there on the murals likes it, but most of his friends do." Someone asked if he worried whether he would get any more state jobs after putting in Tom Pendergast. "I never considered it. I don't care very much," was the answer. Was he depicting Pendergast as a statesman, a boss, or what? Chuckling, he replied, "I just put him in there."

A more heated confrontation occurred on February 3, at a luncheon with 250 members of the Kansas City Chamber of Commerce. "I left a lot more out of the murals than I put in," Benton told his audience. "Before I painted them, I read most of the histories of Missouri I could find. I read a lot about Missouri idealism. But it is not what people think but what they do that makes history. I tried to paint the average life of Missouri." Asked if he treated early fur trading in St. Louis, he replied, "Oh, yes. I showed early day St. Louisans giving whiskey to the Indians and taking their furs away from them."

The most vigorous criticism came from one Thomas Dods, a dry cleaner, who objected to the presence of Jesse James: "If Illinois had a mural painted on the walls of the capitol, that state wouldn't show Al Capone. The inclusion of Jesse James in the Missouri mural is a disgrace to the state." He added, acidly: "If I had my way, I'd get a lot of whitewash and cover the murals. If I had enough whitewash left over, I'd use it on those responsible for the paintings."

"If Illinois had any regard for truth," Benton replied, "it would have to include Al Capone in the mural."

One individual asked him about the slaughterhouse scene. "I've lived here 40 years and I never saw a cow like that before."

"That's because you never saw a cow with my eyes. Everyone sees things differently. Naturally, I am forced to paint things as I see them, and I believe my work has sharpened my eyes considerably." He went on to explain that some distortion was necessary to create a pattern and to set up sequential relationships. A mural is not reality but a reflection of the human mind.

"I think they picture the mind of the man who put them there," Mr. Dods interjected angrily. "That's right, they do," Tom snapped, and blew a cloud of tobacco smoke.

Toward the end, the questions turned to technique—the egg-tempera medium and how it was shellacked, waxed, and polished. "Wouldn't that be hard to take off?" someone called out, amid general laughter. "Rather hard," Benton replied. "I'd white-wash it out, that's what," Mr. Dods shouted.

The artist confronted his critics again on the evening of February 28 at the Community Church in Kansas City. The irrepressible Mr. Dods was featured on the panel, along with the man who would become the most dedicated of all Benton's many opponents, Howard Huselton. Dods opened the questioning with a long statement,

St. Louis and Kansas City. *Detail. To the left, Benton showed the breweries, shoe factories, and clothing sweatshops of St. Louis. To the right, he portrayed the stockyards of Kansas City, the Nelson-Atkins Museum of Art, and a Kansas City business gathering, presided over by Boss Pendergast. Above the door, in one of the less reputable parts of St. Louis, Frankie blasts away at Johnnie in a saloon because "he done her wrong."*

and concluded, predictably: "Not only would I whitewash the murals, but I would whitewash the heads of the men responsible for them." Tom spoke for the first time: "I alone am responsible for them." "No wonder then," said Dods, and sat down.

Howard Huselton was a neatly dressed, elderly man with wire-rimmed glasses, his hair parted exactly in the middle. He asked Benton to speak loudly, because he was hard of hearing. "I was born in Missouri and you were too," Huselton began. "Are you proud of your native state?"

"I don't know," Benton replied. "I only know I'm interested in it." This got a big laugh from the audience.

Huselton then asked for an explanation of the subjects included in the murals. "Why did you not do as the public at large and your employers expected you would do, choose as subjects for your murals the important and finer things from the colorful history of this great state and include something with regard to its many famous men and women, including Senator Thomas Hart Benton?"

"In the development of Missouri," Tom answered, "General Pershing was not as important as an ordinary old bucksaw and my granduncle, Senator Benton, was of far less importance than a common Missouri mule." He explained that Jesse James was a Missouri institution; he had learned from reading letters of early settlers that James and his brothers were regarded with veneration.

"Why Frankie and Johnnie?" Huselton inquired.

"They are a legend, just as Huck Finn and the James boys have become a legend. After all I have to have my people doing something. I can't have them just sitting around long tables reading the latest news about the Constitution."

"How about that scantily clad dancer?"

"Well," Benton countered, "I've been to many business men's parties here and in St. Louis and I want to tell you I put considerable clothes on her."

"Why did you make Missourians all of the hick type?"

"There you have it. You suggest there is something wrong with the hick. I found him more interesting and more intelligent."

On March 8, Benton took a trip to St. Louis to defend his murals to the Junior League. He told a reporter: "I've been called many things by many people. Good Communists say I'm a Fascist and conservatives say I'm a 'damn Red.' But I'm trying to make an objective picture of American society. I know, of course, I bring an attitude to my work. But I am not using my stuff as propaganda for a predetermined conception of what society ought to be."

On March 11, he was back in Kansas City, in bed with a cold, announcing that henceforth he was going to charge one hundred dollars and expenses for his public appearances. If a man talks his throat sore, he told a reporter from the *Star*, he should at least be rewarded with a fee to cover the cost of healing.

But on April 14 he was back on the rostrum. To the charge that his mural did not portray ideals, he answered: "The fact that Frankie shot Johnnie because he done her wrong is proof she had ideals the most respectable church people could approve. I don't take ideals seriously unless they have idealistic results. It's what ideals do, their actual performance, that must be judged. You people in Jefferson City ought to know that the high ideals people express usually cover up social acts that are anything but ideal."

When asked if his opponents knew why they opposed his murals, Tom replied: "I can't tell you. But I've sometimes thought I should have painted those jackasses in the murals with open mouths."

The controversy raged on month after month. On April 14, a woman wrote to the *Star*: "I . . . have a decided dislike for the Benton murals. . . . To me they are repulsive. I believe the crudeness and lack of feeling portrayed in these murals sets a bad example. On the other hand, I desire to thank the *Star* for the sensitive and constructive article, 'Calling All Dogs,' written by Albert Payson Terhune."

But by spring it looked as though Benton was winning the battle. On March 3, the *Journal-Post* opined that the painter was "as skillful in debate as he is with the brush. He has definitely come out on top in his argument with the buttercup school of art criticism." On April 19, Leo Spaulding, who had watched Benton paint part of the mural, wrote to the *Star* that "with his flashing, witty mind, [he] successfully has defended his brain child against all comers. He has routed his adversaries. . . . Perhaps someone will have to paint silencers on the James boys' six-shooters, a diaper on the baby, and a lid on the famous bucket, but it won't be Benton."

Lawrence Adams, who had helped Benton transfer his design to the walls, declared: "There's nothing the matter with being a houn' dog state. Missouri should be proud of its Ozarks. And who can deny the existence of slavery in Missouri? Or have they forgotten about a certain 'Dred Scott' case?" Adams claimed that the people "who stayed and absorbed the story being laid out" were the rural people. "It was the so-called 'educated' person, with enough sophistry and study of painting to corrupt his artistic taste, who left in a huff and claimed to be 'shocked.' "

Despite all the controversy, the mural did not inspire political or ideological debate. As Benton later noted: "The incident of the St. Louis negro protest could have been worked into such a debate had it not been privately settled, but I did not, as in Indiana, once have to justify or explain away, or even acknowledge, any kind of political beliefs. . . . A few artists and writers in St. Louis, 'provincial' members of the New York Artists and Writers Congress, did once try to inveigle me into a discussion in St. Louis, but that would have been so out of place in a Missouri context that I easily brushed it aside. Later when the mural drew its extreme conservative criticism, these fellows were all on my side anyway."

On March 6, KMBC reporter Neal Keehn interviewed the painter at the Beaux-Arts ball at the Hotel Muehlebach. "How did you get away with it?", he asked Benton, who was garbed as a Spanish gypsy. "I don't think I got away with anything," Tom replied. "I wasn't commissioned to paint the ideal side of Missouri."

What Makes an Interesting Face?

Benton's ability to capture faces reached its peak in the 235 portraits in the Missouri mural. "He had ambitions to be a cartoonist at one time," Bill McKim has commented. "With a few quick strokes of either pen, pencil or brush he could get a face that you knew you had seen somewhere before. Not just another face. They were individuals."

Benton confessed to a reporter in 1935: "What I am doing now is just about what I did back in Joplin—picturing people as they are at work and play, in their background and environment. I used to go out and make sketches for the paper of the business men in their shops. About the only difference now is that my work is more informed."

In November 1936, just as Benton was completing the Jeff City mural, he was interviewed for the *Journal-Post* about "What makes an interesting face?" Tom's replies reveal how he struggled to grasp the meaning of what he drew. Naturally, his remarks were off the cuff, the words of a painter practicing his craft and looking for handles to grasp it, rather than a scholar looking for an explanation or a theory. Yet it is precisely this informality that makes his remarks so fascinating. His answers show off his intelligence but also freely disclose his odd quirks and prejudices—for example, his loathing of the pomposity of businessmen and intellectuals, and his simultaneous fondness for the charades of lawyers and politicians.

What sort of people have the most interesting faces?

Men and women who have lived fully—and struggled hard. The average businessman has an absolutely uninteresting face. Why? Because he has dealt with abstractions for so long that he has ceased to be a realist. The only time when he is at all realistic is when he is flat under his car, tinkering with its parts, or when he is out on the golf course whacking a ball around. On these occasions he must face actual existence.

The most interesting faces I have seen do not belong to notables, to people who are much publicized. They just chance to be owned by the unknown. . . . Your garage man, your coal man, your farmer—they are men with physiognomies which attract and hold attention. When sketching you differentiate a business man, say, from a farmer. The farmer is more weatherbeaten, it is true, but this does not necessarily give him a more rugged face. The main difference between the farmer and the business man is that the farmer is dealing with solid things and the other with abstractions, with money which, in the last analysis, has no actual existence. This is all reflected in their faces.

Where in your wanderings have you encountered faces you found more interesting than others?

In the steel mills. . . . The faces of these steel workers are more marked than others. About the steel worker there is always a certain amount of drama—tenseness. The unexpected, you see, can always happen in his life. That is what makes him so interesting.

Is the criminal face an interesting one, and if so, why?

No, I have never found the true criminal type to have an interesting face. The criminal is so flat-eyed you can make nothing of him. You know, as an artist sketches a man, he grows more and more interested. At first he may feel that the face he is doing has nothing behind it but gradually it lights up from within. The owner of it reveals himself gradually, comes out of his shell. You get flashes and glimpses into that inner life which most of us shield and keep concealed from others.

Well, with the criminal one gets nothing whatever from his face because of that flat or opaque eye of his. The cat's eye is opaque but not as opaque as a criminal's. There is nothing behind the criminal eye, no depth, nothing but a blankness.

Has the politician a striking type of face?

Yes, your politician, who handles men, is also thus dealing with things—this time living things, tractable things, pliant things. He molds them. He pulls the strings. He is the stage manager, the showman; they, often as not, the puppets. He usually, as a result, develops an interesting kind of face. I have drawn a couple of our aldermen and ward leaders. They all develop a definite kind of physiognomy. A ward leader in Kansas City is not greatly different from one in New York. . . .

The college girl, or better, I might say, society girl, has the most vapid face of all. The working girl's face is more interesting, even though it belongs to a girl who does nothing more exciting than answering the telephone. She, at least, is in the midst of life. You have got to get next to life and away from the cloistered existence to develop an interesting face.

Do domestic duties give to women an interesting cast of countenance or quite the contrary? Are they too humdrum to etch interesting lines in a face?

Not at all. A wife, a mother, a homemaker is a worker. Surely she is about as close to life as anyone can get. She creates it. And she, too, deals with things—not with symbols. You have got to get right close up to life to develop an interesting face.

What about the intellectual, the scholar?

The process of thinking varies in the way it affects physiognomy. The more genuine, the more profound thinkers develop interesting faces. And even in the intellectual life . . . it is the fundamental life struggle of the man which makes his face interesting or the contrary. The greater ease of accomplishment there exists in a man's life the less likely is he to develop an interestingly expressive face. . . .

Must one necessarily have suffered deeply to develop an interesting face?

Not at all. You do not have to "pass through the fire" to be interesting and to have an interesting face. Children are frequently interesting. They act on their own, spontaneously, with originality. They have not yet learned everything by rote.

To Malcolm Cowley, Benton's attention to faces, rather than to the beauty of the human body, reflected a residual moral rigor. "I could talk for hours," he wrote, "about the heads that Benton has sketched in his travels—miners, plantation over-seers, field hands, old back-country fiddlers, done so that each of them is a complete individual and yet at the same time a representative of his class and section. But apparently Benton takes no such pleasure in drawing the human body. His figures have clubfeet and hands that look as if they were encased in thick Canton-flannel gloves. The torsos, if naked, are shown with strained and tortured muscles, and yet are strangely motionless. Of course it may be that Benton never learned how to draw bodies; he tells us that he rebelled from art school and preferred to work alone. But it seems to me that what he reveals is a sort of Midwestern puritanism that still, subconsciously, finds the body sinful and therefore wants it to be ugly."

Chapter Fifteen
Howard Huselton and His Campaign of Hate

"MR. BENTON'S AMAZING BOOK. *No sane man would dare print of another what Mr. Benton penned and printed about himself. Those of you who have read the book know it to be an amazing, shocking parade of things and incidents vulgar, profane, blasphemous, erotic.*"

1937–38

After his completion of the New School mural, Benton had fallen into an emotional slump; but when the Jeff City project was finished, five years later, his pace did not slacken. He lectured widely. In February he made drawings of the flood-devastated regions of southeastern Missouri, which were published in the Kansas City *Star*. In July he drew for *Life* magazine scenes of supposed labor unrest in Michigan. "I went to see if I could find a revolution there," he commented, "but found that I couldn't." At the end of the summer, he spent a month in Hollywood, on another assignment for *Life*. During the day he sketched in the studios, concentrating not on the stars but on the extras and support people. In the evening he went to parties, where he would draw and drink, until the former gave way to the latter. By the time he returned to Kansas City, he had made eight hundred drawings.

In October 1937, Benton published an autobiography, on which he had been working for several years. He told of his boyhood and his travels in a humorous, down-home, seemingly casual style. He had intended to title it "From Ozark Boy to Mural Painter," but at the behest of his editors, he settled on *An Artist in America*. The volume received excellent reviews and sold extremely well. John Selby called it "the best book on art in recent years" and "the most refreshing literary venture of the week." Bruce Catton commended the "gusto" of the narrative and described the book as "rich, opinionated and gaily colorful." Clifton Fadiman wrote: "His book is like himself, forthright, courageous, full of rural and state patriotism, often mistaken, always crackling and alive. All Missouri and no Compromise."

The book's most vigorous advocate was Sinclair Lewis, who praised it in *Newsweek* and on a lecture tour. "Here is a rare thing," Lewis wrote, "a painter who can write. Here is a rarer—a man who meditates on beauty and has the sanity to recognize it. . . . He has the painter's eye, that perceives the strangeness in everything from the bayous of Louisiana by moonlight to the expert spitting of a Georgia justice of the peace."

Most reviewers were amazed that a painter could write with such literary flair, with such command of diction and rhetoric. Margaret Miller noted that the book demonstrated that Benton was "a writer . . . not just a man who has written a book." The reviewer for the Kansas City *Star,* "J.D.W.," commented: "It is . . . a pleasant surprise to discover with what ease the artist writes, avoiding trick constructions and elaborate effects for direct narration. Benton's handling of dialogue, always difficult and especially trying when different dialects have to be introduced, is agreeable evidence of his ability to suggest character in prose as readily as in his usual medium of expression."

"I think sometimes he was a better writer than he was a painter," his sister Mildred Small has remarked. "Certainly just as good. He wrote extremely well. I never hear it mentioned at all." Even the New York art critic Hilton Kramer—not one of Tom's admirers—has confessed a sneaking admiration for his literary skill: "I think his autobiography is a really splendidly written memoir. Benton missed his vocation. He really should have been a writer rather than a painter."

On October 19, Benton stopped off in Pittsburgh to view the Carnegie International and to give a lecture at Carnegie Tech. First prize at the International had been awarded to George Braque's *The Yellow Cloth,* and Tom commented that the painting had "no more importance than those stitchings ladies do when they have nothing else to do. . . . Anyway, it was a nice gesture to give a man who had worked so long that prize."

On October 23, Benton arrived in New York to celebrate the publication of his autobiography, to preside over a show of Missouri artists that he had sponsored, and to attend the opening of an exhibition of his drawings. Henry McBride, as usual, described the work as "uncouth"; a review in *Art News,* on the other hand, declared that "so much vigor and insight have gone into these drawings that they seem to raise their own characteristic din, obliterating for a moment the roar of city traffic."

A week later, Benton went out to Chicago to open another exhibition of his works, at the Lakeside Gallery. In a rave review, Eleanor Jewett of the *Tribune* wrote: "His characterizations are as pungent as the smell of an old pipe. You will find it very hard to tear yourself away from the 'Ford Trouble,' 'Cotton Pickers,' 'Missouri Town,' and the rest."

When Benton was not on the road, he and Rita entertained lavishly in Kansas City. Bill McKim recalls that Grant Wood, who was deeply unhappy in his marriage and fought bitterly with his colleagues at the University of Iowa, would often visit with the Bentons to escape from things and cool off. On January 3, 1938, he stopped in en route to Texas, where he was to lecture at women's clubs. Both men had just

Thomas Hart Benton, Flood Drawing, *pencil, ink, and wash on paper, 1937.*

signed contracts to produce lithographs for the Associated American Artists; consequently much of their conversation concerned lithography.

"Now here's a trick," Benton commented. "I just take and cover a big chunk of the stone with grease, then scratch it with sandpaper to get light effects. See the sky light coming through the grease cloud? Those grass blades I cut out of the grease with a razor blade."

"I had a cold when I was doing 'Tree Planting Time,' " Wood recalled to Tom, "and part of a big sneeze fell on the stone. I tried to blot it, rub it off, but finally the best I could do was just pencil it over."

Benton had agreed to complete eight stones a year. "Do you get time to paint anymore?" he asked Wood. "I just can't seem to sandwich it in."

On March 5, the "Regionalist Triumvirate"—Benton, Curry, and Wood—gathered at the Hotel Muehlebach in Kansas City to serve on the prize committee of the Beaux-Arts Ball. The party's theme that year was the Arabian Nights—"A Night in Bagdad." The three judges posed, surrounded by a bevy of young cuties, for a *Life* photographer, and to the horror of proper Kansas City, they awarded the first prize for a man's costume (a case of whiskey) to a Mr. Malang, who wore a pair of pajama bottoms. "The affair was an orgy in the true sense of the word," Howard Huselton complained; and Fred Cameron Vincent, the president of the Kansas City Art Institute, expressed his displeasure. Asked if Benton would be the judge at the next year's ball, the affair's organizer spluttered, "I don't think so."

The catalogue of the Lakeside Gallery exhibition contains a brief description of Benton, which demonstrates that he had mellowed from the unsmiling, prematurely aged young man whom Thomas Craven had met years before at the Lincoln Arcade: "He is 49 years old, rather short in stature, and has black hair and a black mustache. There is nothing of the stolidity of the typical businessman about him. Nor is he a dreamer. If he does any dreaming, he does it on the move, for he seems to have unlimited reserves of energy and to feel no contentment unless he is expending them. When he is in a quandary, he thinks out loud, the words coming from deep in his throat. Despite the fact that he spent only six months or so in the navy, he walks with something of the spraddling, rolling gait of the sailor. Among the best of all his traits is his keen wit and his irrepressible sense of humor. When we tried to get him to write this sketch, he demurred. 'No, no. Get someone else to write it. I find that whenever I try to write an autobiography, I never do myself justice.' "

The Huselton Campaign

While most of the reviews were favorable, not everyone liked *An Artist in America*. The most extensive intellectual critique came from the New York Marxist Meyer Schapiro, who dissected Benton's Regionalist program in *Partisan Review*. Schapiro largely passed over the account of the author's childhood and the descriptions of his wanderings, which took up nine-tenths of the text; but he examined microscopically the eight-page "Farewell to New York" and the brief allusions to Benton's social views scattered elsewhere. A champion hairsplitter, Schapiro declared that it was "premature" to label Benton a Fascist, then argued at length that he was one in spirit because of his repudiation of Marxism and modernism. He particularly faulted him for preaching a doctrine of "conciliation" in dealing with racial tensions in the South. To Schapiro, from his comfortable seat in a Columbia University classroom, Benton's desire to move forward through pragmatic compromises represented a betrayal of the class struggle.

Not surprisingly, even a number of the positive reviews took objection to the artist's attacks on New York. Clifton Fadiman asserted: "These sectional generalizations are really not much sounder than racial ones." Forbes Watson deplored the "inaccurate and undignified" attack on the Whitney Museum and described the slurs against New York as a twisted reaction to Benton's many personal feuds in the art world. Only Grant Wood, despite his own somewhat ambiguous sexual preferences, loyally came to Benton's defense. "He has had a good deal to say," Wood observed, "about the parasites and hangers-on of art in general, with their ivory-tower hysterias and frequent homosexuality. . . . He has brought out into the open things that ought to be discussed frankly and sincerely."

Howard Huselton.

The most extensive assault came not from intellectuals in New York but from moralists in Kansas City. Howard Huselton had not forgotten his public humiliation in the forum devoted to the Missouri mural; he was merely waiting for an opportunity to renew his harassment.

The son of a soap company manager, Huselton was born in Kansas City in 1871 and began his career as an editor of the Kansas City *Star*. In 1910 he entered real estate, and he built up a respectable fortune. An amateur pianist, something of a prig, he never married but lived with his sister. He felt a proprietary interest in the Kansas City Art Institute, for he had served as its second director. Indeed, he was president of the struggling young school in 1912, when Benton nearly taught there but was put off by the drag party.

William T. Kemper remembers Huselton as "an odd man." According to an article in the *Star*, he tended to be "a lone eagle," or "lone wolf": "loss of hearing has tended to shut him off by himself, preventing him from working on committees or with large groups." In all his undertakings, however, Huselton revealed remarkable stubbornness and determination. After he had lobbied successfully to have Oak Street widened, a campaign that had taken ten years, the *Star* commented: "He can be halted, but not stopped. Such a persistent chap."

On May 28, 1938, Benton left Kansas City for a sketching tour in the Mississippi valley. He was accompanied by his student James H. Fitzgerald, a large, jovial, hard-drinking Irishman. The two drove first to New Orleans; then to the boomtown of Disney, Oklahoma, where Tom made sketches; and then on toward parts unknown. (Rita and T.P. left Kansas City also, to vacation in Italy.)

Howard Huselton chose this as the moment to strike. On June 16, the *Star* reported that Huselton had purchased six copies of *An Artist in America* and a red pencil, which he used to circle the most offensive passages. "The red pencil tells why Mr. Huselton thinks Mr. Thomas Hart Benton, kin to Missouri's first senator, should no longer be retained as head of the painting classes." According to the *Star*, Huselton "can quote Benton's colorful rejoinders from memory." None of these red-penciled copies can now be located, but undoubtedly Huselton was offended by the sexual frankness of passages in which Benton mentioned masturbation, the loss of his virginity, and his Parisian mistress.

"I have read a lot of books in my time," Huselton remarked earnestly to a friend. "But for sensuality, grossness—why the little gray-haired, alert woman at the bookstand told me of people returning the book, mad about the profanity, the vulgarity. . . . Didn't each of Benton's three mural jobs get him into trouble? . . . I think the art world is tired of this modernistic thing."

During the week of June 16, the Art Institute's board of governors met to review the renewal of teaching contracts, but as the board failed to achieve a quorum, a second meeting was scheduled for June 22. On June 21, Huselton took his six books around to the homes of the board members, to show them the underlined passages. The next day, after a two-hour session, President Vincent revealed that the board had passed favorably on the contracts of the other members of the staff but "no motion was made to renew Benton's contract." While the board did not formally discharge Benton, its bland inaction was tantamount to a dismissal.

Howard Huselton exclaimed, "Glory be," when he heard the news. "The next step should be the removal of the Jefferson City mural," he commented. "Benton's work does not truthfully represent the people of Missouri and for that reason his mural is offensive to them. I see Benton as on the way out. He can't complain, because he dug the pit for his own downfall when he wrote his smutty autobiography."

Fred Vincent, on the other hand, issued a cautiously worded statement of support: "I feel Benton is a splendid instructor in painting and drawing. I do not feel qualified to express an expert opinion, however. I am influenced in my opinion by Rossiter Howard [director of the institute] and several students who had studied at the institute and elsewhere, and who regard Benton highly."

Not so guarded in his response was Benton's painter friend Frederick Shane, who described Tom as "a man of the highest artistic and moral integrity. . . . By coming here to teach, Benton gave Kansas City art a new lease on life, and brought Kansas City's Institute into national prominence."

A June 23 editorial in the Kansas City *Times* described the board's treatment of Benton as "inexcusably shabby" and noted that he "was tried and convicted without a hearing." The piece bluntly characterized the decision as "a mistake."

On June 24 Benton arrived in New York, where he learned what had been happening in Kansas City. He and Fitzgerald had been tracing a leisurely zigzag route through Louisiana, Oklahoma, southern Missouri, Tennessee, and North Carolina. Tracked down in the Brevoort Hotel by an Associated Press reporter, he expressed complete surprise over the attempt to oust him from the Art Institute: "Why, when I left there appeared to be no question whatever about the contract. In fact I had suggested to Mr. Howard that it might be well to have the appointment settled before I got out of the city, but somehow it never seemed possible to get the board together. What happened?"

Informed that the attack upon him centered on passages in *An Artist in America*, Benton pointed out that the work had been published in October, the beginning of the previous school year: "None of the governors said anything about it to me then—at least anything that gave me any hint they objected. Why didn't they bring it up while I was still in the city? They knew me. I'd have thrashed the thing out with them. Why wait till I left town? I like Kansas City. I like the people. I like teaching at the Art Institute. . . . I've turned down several teaching offers because I'd rather be in Kansas City. But if the board isn't going to reappoint me, I've got to know and know right away so that I can make my plans for next winter. And it's got to be understood they're hiring the same Tom Benton. I'm not going to change." When asked to make a comment about Howard Huselton, Benton declined. "I know who he is," was his only reply.

In the meantime, community support was beginning to swing in Benton's favor. Chester Staton, director of the Midwestern Art Institute in Kansas City, Kansas, issued a statement attacking the "small time reformers trying to run Tom Benton out of town. . . . There's a principle involved, that of giving a man his day in court. We can't sit by and let these small time reformers try to run this man out of Kansas City." At the instigation of Fred Shane, the alumni of the Art Institute met and issued a unanimous statement in Tom's support. Kansas City's booksellers also rallied behind him. A petition asking for his reappointment was placed in most of the city's leading bookshops; the stores reported that sales of *An Artist in America* were unusually brisk.

Two days before the next meeting of the board, a local radio broadcast seemed to reveal that the lay public was warm toward Benton and cold toward Huselton. Sample responses included: "How come Huselton never came across *An Artist in America* until Benton left town?" "Is that institute hiring an author or is it hiring an artist?" "Doesn't the Middle West appreciate originality?"

To this, Huselton replied: "Piffle. I didn't tune in on that broadcast. Those agitators across the state line are of recent mushroom growth, artists and their followers who have no past knowledge of the art institute or of those who have built it to where it is today. . . . Do I get letters? Scores, and good reading. Telephone calls, constantly. . . . If the board members should reverse themselves they would find themselves in a 9-hole before a public that fast is becoming familiar with the objectionable contents of Mr. Benton's singular book. It is inevitable that public interest in the off-color parts of Mr. Benton's revelations about himself and his vagabond wanderings gradually will spread far and wide to the detriment of the name of the institute because of the re-employment of Mr. Benton, after a turn-down of his contract."

The incident provided an opportunity for negative comment from outside Kansas City. An editorial in the St. Louis *Post-Dispatch* declared: "It strikes the onlooker as odd that a morality movement in Kansas City should be directed against a distin-

Thomas Hart Benton, Screening Room, *pencil, ink, and wash on paper, 1937. One of the 800 drawings Benton made on his visit to Hollywood.*

Missouri Painter and His Book
(*St. Louis* Post-Dispatch *photograph*), 1938.

guished American painter when the town reeks with far juicier material for those with the reformer's urge. If the youth of Kansas City are to be saved from the 'sensual, gross, profane and vulgar,' a tour of Kansas City honkytonks, clip joints and strip tease dives would supply material enough to make Anthony Comstock turn over in his grave. . . . The Kansas City incident will chiefly serve to reflect upon the taste of those who engineered it."

On June 27, the day of the next meeting, Huselton circulated a seven-page memorandum summarizing his case and deploring the absence from the previous meeting of several board members who opposed Benton's appointment. This document typically proclaims: "MR. BENTON'S AMAZING BOOK. No sane man would dare print of another what Mr. Benton penned and printed about himself. Those of you who have read the book know it to be an amazing, shocking parade of things and incidents vulgar, profane, blasphemous, erotic."

At twelve-fifteen, the board of governors and an advisory committee, consisting of three former presidents of the Institute, gathered at the University Club. Not until shortly after two-thirty did Fred Vincent emerge from the meeting with this statement: "Mr. Benton has been reappointed as instructor. . . . Mr. Benton did not lose his job nor was he dismissed, as has been stated so freely. Action by the board of governors merely was put over until another meeting. No matter what anybody may think of Mr. Benton's book, or of his painting, there has been no question regarding his ability as an instructor."

Benton took the good news calmly. On June 28, he told a reporter: "I knew the board of governors had too much sense to fire me. . . . Of course I will return to Kansas City. . . . The whole affair was simply a joke to me."

A short time later, Frederick Shane got a brief note from Benton: "Dear Fred, thank you for building me up a character. Tom." On the side was a caricature of the artist carrying a stick that bore a placard: "Unfair to disorganized immorality."

Howard Huselton issued a statement the evening of the board's vote. "The right-about-face of the members of the board of governors today smacks of moral cowardice. . . . Not one of the members of the board of governors and the advisory council will say the Benton autobiography is other than obscene and immoral. . . . Mr. Benton played a winning poker hand, but I predict his return to Kansas City will be for a stay not longer than until he can find a comfortable berth elsewhere."

Huselton's private correspondence reveals that Benton retained his job thanks to the real estate developer J. C. Nichols, whom the painter, not very kindly, had shown sitting alongside Boss Pendergast in the Jeff City mural. Nichols was a brilliant businessman, who created the nation's first shopping center, Country Club Plaza in Kansas City. He was also a shrewd politician. Recognizing that "Christian morality" was the central issue of the debate, he enlisted the help of Richard Fillmore, of the Unity School of Christianity, and with his assistance persuaded a number of board members to change their vote in Benton's favor.

Although Huselton's effort failed, his views were shared by many business leaders and their wives, a lot of whom wrote to congratulate him on his firm moral stand. One expressed his horror at "that bizarre party pulled off for the Art Institute last winter," and another offered his "appreciation and gratitude for defending Missouri Youth from the impossibilities in art. . . . Art should represent not only the accumulated culture, but the possibilities of the refinements of tomorrow."

Still another correspondent concerned about Benton's effect on the young wrote: "I do not think anybody in this State should be expected to stand for any man that fails so utterly to emulate the finest things we have but on the contrary revels in the opportunity to degrade them. . . . To continue him in any capacity where the aspirations of the youth of his generation could have been warped and degraded was preposterous." And yet another exclaimed: "How any sane man, especially the father of children, after reading the book in question, could vote to put the Author thereof in the position of instructing youth, is more than I can understand. . . . Recently it was brought to light that female prostitutes in the town have brought their business, practically, to the front door of one of the public schools in Kansas City, without any objection, let or hindrance from either the Council, Mayor, City Manager or the School Board, and now, according to the statements in this book, apparently, a male who confesses and admits the things that are admitted in this book, is inside one of our Institutions undertaking to teach the youth of the city and community."

And a citizen named Paul Patton spoke for many when he told Huselton: "I congratulate you on your efforts and wish I could do something to help you. . . . I see in the papers you are making a fight against the vulgarity and coarseness which masquerades under the name of art."

(It is interesting to note that Huselton's own moral record may not have been spotless. According to Fred Shane, Huselton kept a mistress for twenty years and then dumped her for someone younger. When the first woman attempted to file suit against him, he arranged through a lawyer friend to pay her off. Unlike Benton, however, Huselton did his best to keep his private affairs private.)

In a memo dated November 2, 1939, Huselton stated regretfully that W. T. Kemper, Jr., and Gordon T. Beaham, Jr., both of whom had been reelected to the board of governors, "are ardent followers of Benton, the artist." Two new members had been elected, but they failed to tip the balance. One of them, Mrs. U. S. Epperson, he noted with pleasure, "has been a strong opponent of Benton, the artist." This new recruit for his hate campaign was canceled out by the election of Henry C. Haskell. For Haskell, as Huselton observed, "is a member of the editorial staff of the Kansas City *Star,* writing about art, and a son of Henry J. Haskell, editor of the Kansas City *Star.* . . . Henry C. Haskell, at this time, with the backing of his father and the *Star,* is the most enthusiastic and ardent admirer of Mr. Benton in Kansas City and largely responsible for much of [his] local reputation."

Howard Huselton had lost the first round.

Chapter Sixteen
Two Too-Nude Nudes

A SUGGESTION THAT WILL NEVER COME TO PASS

Cartoon of Benton repainting Susanna, circa 1938.

Thomas Hart Benton, Persephone, *egg tempera and oil on linen over panel, 1939. Benton executed* Persephone *in his advanced painting class at the Kansas City Art Institute, while his students made smaller versions of the subject around him. Technically, the painting represented a breakthrough for Benton—the beginning of a new mastery in the handling of natural textures. The theme gave him an opportunity to confront some of the deepest traumas of his childhood. ▪*

"The nude is stark naked," she protested.

Susanna and Persephone

Benton began dealing with sex in his paintings even before Huselton took the offensive. His first bold venture in this realm was *Hollywood,* his major painting of 1937, which he once described as "the combination of a machine and sex that Hollywood is." The composition revolves around a scantily clad blond sex bomb, in front of whom a man kneels, offering up an ambiguous phallic object. The woman's appearance pays nostalgic tribute to Jean Harlow, from Kansas City, who had died earlier in the year. Various movie scenes take place around her, such as the burning city from *In Old Chicago,* which Benton had watched being filmed. Initially, he hoped to use this design for the lobby of a large movie theater, but he didn't find a backer and consequently executed it as an easel painting. To his disappointment, *Life* considered the effect salacious and declined to publish it. Two years later, it won the "Popular Prize" at the Carnegie International, and the magazine reproduced it in a double-page spread.

Huselton's attack did not halt Benton's new interest in sexual themes. Indeed, far from being intimidated, he painted two works far more provocative than his earlier efforts. One of these updated a biblical story from the Apocrypha, *Susanna and the Elders*—an account of two old hypocrites who attempt to seduce a beautiful young virgin as she bathes. The other, *Persephone,* represented the Greek goddess of spring, who was raped and carried off by the ruler of the underworld.

Susanna and *Persephone* contain essentially the same elements. In each, a nude woman, stripped for bathing in the river, is observed and lusted after by an old man (or men). The same blue river curves away from the lower left, bending around a sturdy oak; the dirty old men are on the right, behind the woman, partially concealed. We see her clothing, suggestive of a striptease—skirt, blouse, and sexy high-heeled shoes. On the horizon are symbolic and narrative supports; in *Susanna,* a church and the mules and Model T that brought the elders to the scene; in *Persephone,* a ripe grain harvest and the mule-drawn chariot that brought Pluto up from the lower world. Despite their similarities, however, the impact of the two canvases is very different.

Benton started *Susanna* in late January 1938 and finished it a month later. His model, he later recalled with pleasure, was a "delightful hillbilly girl (a true *Ozark product, gone wrong*)." "My boy—what a skin, what a blood-pulsing skin," he later rhapsodized. "Just enough yellow in the belly to make the 'tits' look pink." As Karal Ann Marling has pointed out, the inspiration for the painting dates back to the Holy Roller service that the painter had witnessed in West Virginia during his cross-country wanderings of 1928, when he had watched a young woman, in a cheap but stylish cloche hat, writhe on the ground in orgastic religious spasms. Her costume provided the basis for the neat pile of Susanna's garments that rests on the ground to her left;

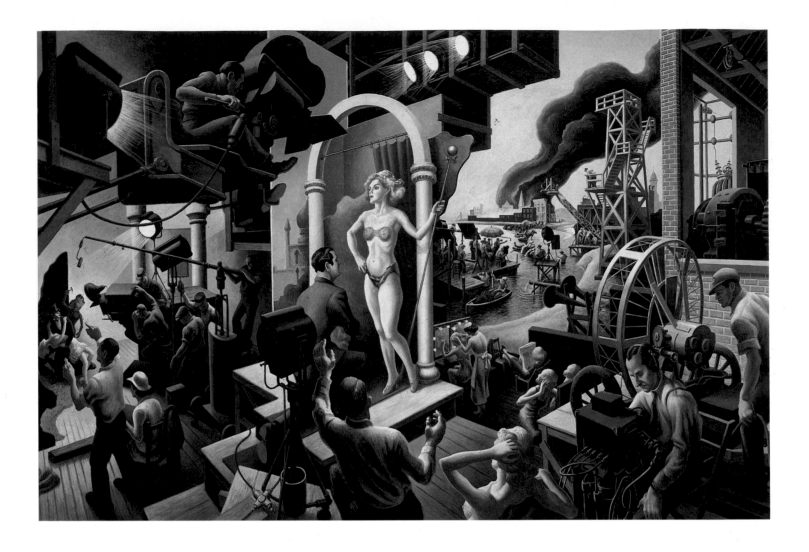

the repressed lust that fundamentalist religion encouraged served as the major theme of the painting.

Two things made *Susanna* seem shocking: its contemporary setting and its unblinking faithfulness to female anatomy. Benton provided his subject with an up-to-date piquancy by giving Susanna red fingernails, a modern hairdo, and high-heeled shoes. The two Missouri farmers have just arrived in a out-of-date roadster. This touch helps suggest the narrowness, frugality, conservatism, and sexual repression of the elders peering out from behind the bushes.

In addition, Benton violated convention by showing pubic hair—which was invariably omitted not only from "artistic" paintings of the time but even from the calendar girls and *Esquire* pinups. (Only in 1970 did *Penthouse* create a revolution in girlie magazines by introducing a shadowy patch of pubic hair.) "I left nothing out which the position of my ladies permitted to be seen," Benton commented. The papers discreetly alluded to his brazenness when they ran such headlines as "Too Nude Girl Irks Art Critics." When Benton's friend Archie Musick described *Susanna*, in a review, as a barroom nude, Tom vehemently objected. "Don't you know," he wrote heatedly, "that bar-room nudes do not have hair on their pussys?"

Benton worked hard on *Susanna*. He later confessed that it took him two months to get the flesh tones right. Nonetheless, the painting seems crude beside *Persephone*. Technically, the work still has the cartoonlike quality of the Jefferson City mural and lacks a convincing presentation of texture. Expressively, it also remains cartoonlike, for the subject serves as the basis for a sniggering satirical statement, rather than for intimate revelations.

Both technically and expressively, *Persephone* enriches and refines the qualities of the earlier work.

"The model was a beautiful girl," Benton later said of Imogene Bruton, the black-haired, ivory-skinned young woman from Independence who posed for *Persephone*. "I saw her the other day and she's more beautiful than ever. She's so beautiful that you go away muttering for the rest of the day." Roger Medearis, who got to know Imogene when he worked as a cashier at Glenn's Grill, recalls that in addition to her modeling, she acted in short film advertisements that were shown in movie theaters before the main feature.

Benton painted *Persephone* in the old greenhouse studio of the Art Institute, in the midst of his painting class, surrounded by students who turned out their own smaller versions beside him. He planned the project as elaborately as a mural—making numerous drawings, a clay model, a small version in grisaille, and another in color. Duard Marshall recalls that "the old duffer with the warts on his nose" was "one of the models we got down at the mission. He was just a lousy—and I mean lousy—dirty old bum. We had to air the studio out when he was posing down there." The last thing Benton worked on was the flowers in the foreground. Charles O'Neill was working alone in the studio one Saturday afternoon when Tom came in with the flowers for Persephone's basket. He painted them in an hour or so then handed them to O'Neill, telling him to give them to his girlfriend.

Karal Ann Marling has described *Persephone* as "one of the great works of American pornography. . . . It's a great experience to walk into some stuffy old art gallery and all of a sudden come into contact with that lady." The basic form of the work was lifted from an old-master painting—Correggio's *Jupiter and Antiope*, in the Louvre. But the woman brings to mind the calendar art of the period, such as that of Tom's old friend Jack Armstrong—the first specialist in girlie calendars—or of George Petty, who made pinups for *Esquire*. Thus the painting exists in an ambiguous realm: it is a homage to the nudes of the old masters at the same time that it pokes fun at the sexual urges that must have inspired them. It is at once a homage to girlie magazines and an attempt to surpass them.

Significantly, Persephone does not make eye contact with either the old man or the viewer, but remains lost in her own thoughts. The viewer intrudes upon the scene visually and psychologically; her reaction remains inscrutable. The drama of the painting centers on the expression of the grizzled hillbilly behind her, with his limp, blue-veined hand. It focuses on his age, his helplessness, and his inadequacy. Indeed, in 1974, when he was given a retrospective at the Nelson-Atkins, Benton jokingly entitled the painting "Twenty Years Too Late."

Benton was approaching fifty when he painted *Persephone*—he was undoubtedly concerned with his mortality. Interestingly, his younger child, Jessie, must have been conceived at the time he conceived of *Persephone*; she was born shortly after the painting was completed, in July 1939. (Thirteen years separated her from her brother, T.P., for Rita had suffered a series of miscarriages.) Roger Medearis recalls that Tom "was proud not only of his daughter but also of this evidence of his enduring masculinity.'"

A major theme that runs through *Persephone* is an equivalence between the fecundity of woman and nature. The body of Persephone swells and undulates in perfect harmony with the landscape. "I see a great deal of Breughel in Benton," Lloyd Goodrich has commented. "I think he must have known *The Seasons* by Breughel in Vienna. He had that feeling for the whole relation of humanity to nature."

Indeed, one contemporary viewer felt that the painting was intended as an environmental statement. According to a review in *Art Digest*, the implication of the painting was "the despoliation of the land by the American farmer. . . . Benton is scoring the greed of those who cultivate the land to exhaustion, to the point of drouths, erosion, and dust storms." This parallel between a raped woman and the ravished

288

Alexander Hogue, Mother Earth Laid Bare, *1936, oil on canvas.*

land was not uncommon in paintings of the thirties. In 1936, just two years before *Persephone,* Alexander Hogue painted *Mother Earth Laid Bare,* which presents the eroded land in the likeness of the prostrate body of a raped woman, who lies with her throat slit and her face bashed in.

The plants in Benton's painting all carry narrative significance. Pluto, the lord of death, stands on unfertile red dirt, behind a dead log. To see Persephone, he must push aside grapevines, a symbol of intoxication. Her basket is filled with daylilies, which allude at once to purity and to the contrast between day and night.

Technically, *Persephone* represents an astonishing advance. Benton had come under the influence of both the Flemish primitives and the work of Grant Wood, and this led him to take a new interest in natural textures. Every plant and flower was based on meticulous preliminary studies. Every portion of the painting contains a complete little landscape or still-life composition, although each is rhythmically integrated with the overall design. The color has a glowing brilliance new to Benton's work; he created it by painstakingly building up translucent glazes of oil over the tempera foundation.

Expressively, Benton transformed the themes of *Susanna* from smug satire to personal confession. As has been noted, the model for Pluto in the painting was a bum from the downtown mission; but this hillbilly "Peeping Tom" bears an unmistakable likeness to Tom Benton. His own son noted the resemblance. "You know, Dad," he commented, "you're getting to look more and more like the bum in that painting." *Persephone,* in short, is a kind of autobiographical statement, "A Portrait of the Artist as a Dirty Old Man." In it, Benton placed himself in the most vulnerable of roles. Despite the jocular character of the painting, and its billboardlike brashness, it serves as the vehicle for personal revelation.

Embedded in the work are a series of allusions to Benton's early sexual traumas and his coming of age. When he painted *Persephone,* it seems likely that he had in the back of his mind the barroom nude he had seen many years before in the House of Lords in Joplin—the canvas that determined his choice of an artistic career. Significantly, that painting, too, depicted an assault, with a young man stabbing a naked woman. What could be more appropriate than that the painter who began his career in a barroom should devote his most ambitious efforts to a barroom nude?

Somewhat obliquely, *Persephone* seems to refer back to Benton's first sexual encounter, with the prostitute he described as "a black-haired young slut who wore a flaming red kimono and did her hair in curls like a little girl." Persephone has curly black hair and lies on a bit of flaming red drapery that loosely resembles a kimono.

At the deepest level, *Persephone* seems to confront one of the artist's earliest emotional traumas, for the contrast between an ugly man and a beautiful woman had

Thomas Hart Benton, Susanna and the Elders, *egg tempera and oil on canvas mounted on panel, 1938. In Benton's version of the biblical theme, Susanna has red fingernails, and one of the elders arrives in a Ford roadster. The painting was nearly banned in St. Louis, where one local moralist described it as "lewd, immoral, obscene, lascivious, degrading, an insult to womanhood and the lowest expression of pure filth."* •

a deep personal resonance for him. His father was an old, fat, ugly man with hillbilly manners; his mother was young and beautiful. The issue of a man forcing himself on an unwilling woman was one of which Tom became conscious at an early age. "As a little toddler," he recalled, "I was more than once frightened by my mother's protesting screams when my father entered her room at night. And I was aware of the anger and sense of outrage she felt for days following." In *Persephone*, he seems to have reen-acted this early trauma, placing himself in his father's role. The original title of the painting, in fact, was *The Rape of Persephone*.

When *Susanna* and *Persephone* were exhibited, they got a great deal of attention in the press, although many of the critics disliked them. Jerome Klein, in the New York *Post*, described the two paintings as "salon nudes" and considered them "dis-mal." He compared them unfavorably with the "wholly disarming exuberance and frankness" of Waldo Pierce. Emily Genauer in the *World-Telegram* called them "cheap and trivial, with the subtlety of a calendar picture." (The paintings seem always to have been particularly offensive to women.) Several writers even complained that the girls were not good-looking. The Indianapolis *Star* noted that "*Susanna* would not be 'Miss America' at Atlantic City. She wouldn't even be 'Miss Missouri.' Her arms are lean. She's a bit raw-boned." Art historian Milton Brown didn't care very much for Persephone. "Altho prettier than 'Susannah,' " he commented, "she is on the whole too reminiscent of those skinny-shanked, sex-starved mid-western school teachers out of the pages of Sherwood Anderson."

On February 7, 1939, the New York *News* reported that Meyric Rogers, the director of the City Art Museum in St. Louis, had described Tom's *Susanna* as "very nude" and intended to bar it from display in the museum's Midwestern exhibition. No doubt Rogers was particularly sensitive because he had just been embroiled in controversy over the nude figures Carl Milles had designed for a foundation in Aloe Plaza in St. Louis. Rogers had defended the piece, but he had been vehemently opposed by Alderman Hubert Hoeflinger, a tailor, who spoke up in favor of clothes. The nude figures, Hoeflinger declared, "would be all right in an art museum," but were unsuit-able for a public setting.

When a reporter called the Benton home to get a comment about Rogers's pru-dery, Rita had difficulty at first understanding his question.

"Who'd you say bought *Susanna*?" she inquired.

"Not 'bought' but 'barred,' Mrs. Benton," the reporter replied. "Mr. Rogers of the St. Louis Art Museum has barred *Susanna*."

"But why?" Rita asked.

"He said it was 'very nude.' Is *Susanna* very nude, Mrs. Benton?"

"I'll say she's nude," Rita replied. "But what's the matter with St. Louis? Can't they take it? I'd think they'd enjoy *Susanna*."

Shortly afterward, the reporter reached Benton at the Art Institute. "Why was it banned?" Tom asked. The reporter explained that Mr. Rogers considered the painting "very nude."

"Is that really the reason?" was the rejoinder. "Well now, that's a nutty thing to do. The picture has been exhibited all over the country, in the major exhibitions of paintings, including those in New York, and the comment has been everywhere that it has been the best in the shows. That's not my comment; it's the comment of others."

Meyric Rogers decided to hang the painting. He put velvet ropes in front of it, however, to keep people at a safe distance. On February 6, Mary Ellis, a sixty-five-year-old, white-haired pastor, announced that she had never seen a nude as naked as Benton's Susanna. She demanded that the painting be removed from the museum. "The nude is stark naked," she protested. "It's lewd, immoral, obscene, lascivious, degrading, an insult to womanhood and the lowest expression of pure filth. It leaves

nothing to the imagination." A reporter relayed these remarks to Benton in Kansas City. "That's funny as hell," he commented.

No one tried to ban *Persephone*, but it also attracted a good deal of attention. Thomas Craven featured the work in *A Treasury of Art Masterpieces*, the first popular artbook with lavish illustrations in color. He described it as "unsurpassed by anything thus far produced in America." To promote the book, Brentano's put the painting in the window of its bookstore on Fifth Avenue, and it drew enormous crowds. One of the store managers commented to a reporter: "I brought my wife down Saturday night to see the window and couldn't get within half a block of it. It ought to help sales if we can get to the books."

In 1941, at the opening of a show of his work at Associated American Artists, Benton shocked the prudish by proposing that his paintings looked better in bars than in art museums. After a man had four drinks under his belt, he said, he would be ready to believe that Persephone was real. After reading these comments, Billy Rose, the theatrical impresario and art collector, picked up a telephone within hearing of a *Times* reporter, put a call through to the artist, and said loudly: "I've got a saloon—perhaps the biggest in the country. You have a great picture, perhaps the greatest in America. Let's get together." They did, and arranged for *Persephone* to hang for a month in Billy Rose's Diamond Horseshoe in New York City.

Some years later, Sid Larson did some restoration work on *Persephone* after it was slightly damaged during an exhibition in Chicago. He vividly recalls its impact on a passerby. "I'd left the lights on in my studio," Sid relates. "There were woods behind my house; it was dusk, and you could, from the street, look right through the hall, right at the doorway and the illuminated painting. Suddenly there was a great screeching of brakes and a crash. . . . Some guy had driven by, had done a double take, had hit the brakes, looked again, and bashed into my neighbor's parked car. When I told

Benton about this and suggested that it was indeed testimony to Benton realism, he said, 'By God, you're right!' "

The Associated American Artists Show, 1939

Until 1939, Associated American Artists sold only prints, but in that year the gallery's director, Reeves Lewenthal, persuaded both Benton and Grant Wood to abandon Maynard Walker. In April, Lewenthal held AAA's first exhibition of paintings—a large Benton retrospective. The earliest painting in the show was *Contre Soleil*, painted in France in 1908, but the selection was heavily slanted toward recent productions, including both *Susanna* and *Persephone;* fourteen of the the forty paintings had been completed in the previous twelve months. It was Benton's first New York show in four years and his first retrospective since 1927.

Challenging all precedents, the show opened not in New York but in Kansas City, at the Nelson-Atkins Museum of Art. There it attracted the largest crowds the museum had seen since the record-breaking Van Gogh exhibition several years before. On weekends the galleries were almost too packed for visitors to see the paintings. "This is a personal triumph for Mr. Benton," Henry Haskell editorialized in the *Star.* "Cer-

Thomas Hart Benton, Pussy-Cat and Roses, *egg tempera and oil on canvas, 1939. Around the time of* Persephone, *Benton began to paint small still-life compositions, in which he worked on the rendering of different textures. The Maltese kitten was a stray adopted by Benton's students at the Art Institute. They would feed it the spoiled eggs they couldn't use to make tempera. •*

Benton looking at weeds, circa 1938.

tainly, no other local artist has ever aroused a comparable interest." The show then moved on to New York, where it opened two days after the artist's fiftieth birthday.

Benton obliged the reporters with one of his characteristic blasts at New York: "As far as I'm concerned, New York is still full of talkative intellectuals and amateur politicians, and it's still boring. . . . I'm sick of ideas and talk. I'm after realities—if there are any to be found." Unbothered by logical consistency, he added: "I'm anti-Fascist, because I like to keep my tongue wagging. I want to be able to sound off when I want to."

He also discussed his new interest in still life and landscape. "When I painted my first nude I didn't have enough grasses, so I began to study them. . . . Human reactions seem much the same as you get older. I am more interested in vegetables and mules than I am in human beings. . . . The mule is a damned dramatic animal. I don't know what it is about a mule, but they are so fascinating."

He ended his tirade on a wistful note. "When I lived here before I had a harmonica quartet and we played all over town. I didn't bring my harmonica along this time, though. There isn't anybody left to play with."

For once, most of the critics raved about Benton, and they all commented on his new mastery of texture. Oddly, to the last man (and woman), they liked the glossy rural landscape better than the early work or the recent nudes and figure paintings. Even Emily Genauer, who condemned the two large nudes as "cheap and trivial," described the little landscapes as "right good stuff." One of the most popular paintings was *Shallow Creek,* which was purchased by the novelist John Marquand. From the commercial standpoint, the show was a triumph: about a third of the paintings were sold.

Even before Benton got back to Kansas City, Rita used the proceeds to purchase a large rambling old stone house at 3616 Belleview Avenue, with a carriage house out back that could be converted to a studio. At this time he finally paid his $300 debt to Macdonald Stanton-Wright, contracted twenty-eight years earlier.

Benton sitting on the swing in front of his house, 1940s.

Thomas Hart Benton, Roasting Ears, *egg tempera and oil on canvas, 1938–39. Benton made the sketch for* Roasting Ears *in the summer of 1938, at the same time that Howard Huselton was campaigning to get him fired.*

On July 9, a reporter from the *Star* paid a visit to the new home and found the artist in blue jeans, stripped to the waist, working on some renovations with the carpenters and plumbers. "Well, I guess I can thank the East for this home," he announced. "I sold thirteen of those pictures, practically all of them in the East. I make my pictures in the West, but the East buys them." Among the paintings that he had sold was *Roasting Ears,* which the Metropolitan Museum of Art purchased for three thousand dollars. "That's good money for these times," Tom ventured. While he puffed on his pipe in satisfaction, Rita winked and added, "Whew, they must have put a beautiful frame around it."

In September 1939, a small group of Benton's paintings, including the controversial *Susanna,* was shown at the Fine Arts Association Gallery in Des Moines. To an interviewer, Tom confessed that he was "fairly obsessed with America—the Mississippi region, the Ozarks, and the places where I can see lonely plowmen, cotton pickers, river boatmen, and ramshackle houses that never were much good. I like to get out in my car and drive. Just drive anywhere so long as I go through the Ozarks and down around Oklahoma and that territory. I like to make drawings. Sometimes I make a hundred a week; sometimes only one."

Around this time, Rita confided to a reporter that her husband was working harder than he ever had before. "In New York, artists would come up to see Tom's work sometimes and say, 'This is not just right,' or 'You didn't get that thing so good,' and Tom would rage and holler and say they didn't know a thing about painting, but after they left he'd tell me he just hadn't learned how to do those certain things. Once he stopped painting for three months and played the harmonica. When somebody asked him about his painting he just laughed and said, 'Oh, I only paint on the side.' Now it's different. I call to him and he says, 'It can't be time to eat. I only just started.' He used to quit work every day at least by 4 o'clock. Now he works until all the light is gone and he comes in saying there ought to be longer days."

Benton as a Teacher

In New York, Benton had inspired very varied reactions from his students, but in Kansas City his pupils, most of them young country boys, universally looked up to and adored him. The reaction of Duard Marshall is typical: "It was more like a big outgrown family than anything else. It was a lovely time. . . . He was always very patient, very kind with me. I had what I would consider a wonderful relationship with Tom."

Benton worked in the class alongside the boys. Roger Medearis recalls: "Benton wanted to be one of the students, one of the workmen. Where other artists might talk about inspiration, Benton would talk about work. He would urge—both he and Rita would always urge us as students—to work, to work hard."

Earl Bennett comments: "When people say we were a bunch of little Bentons? Well, we all were. Tom said to us, 'I'm going to teach you guys the tools of this trade. Then you go out and go on your own way. But while you're here, I'm going to teach you what I know.' "

"I never attempted to eliminate the style of Benton," Roger Medearis says. "This never really concerned me. I believed very much in what we were taught, all of which came out of studies analyzing the old masters, the interlocking curves, the opposing curves, the repetitions of rhythms that you would find in Rubens, in Tintoretto, in El Greco, and so on."

Benton constantly stressed the importance of fundamental structure. He had his students make quick sketches of old-master paintings, which he flashed on the screen at five-minute intervals. To teach them the principles of color organization, he asked them to make color studies from Persian miniatures. In drawing the model, he encouraged them to step up and feel any muscle about which they were unsure. Earl Bennett recalls: "Tom's phrase was 'grand design'—you've got to get the grand design first. Don't get into detail and don't get into this, that, and the other until you've got a grand design. When you've got the grand design you can make a painting."

"A word that he used a lot was 'logic,' " says Roger Medearis. "He was a very logical man. The painting had to work based on the principles that he had determined from the early Renaissance painters. . . . He would talk about the great masters of the Renaissance and he would discuss the way they went about making a picture and then, in the midst of his students, he would do the things he had talked about."

Earl Bennett comments: "He hated phony, he hated posturing, and he liked good honest emotion, good honest painting. There was a guy came into the class one time at the beginning of a semester and he sat down—here's a model and the whole thing—and this guy gets out some purple, and he puts down a big glob of yellow. Tom says, 'That's it!' He said, 'No bughouse art. No bughouse painting in my class. You're out.' The guy lasted about as long as it would take you to put down about four or five blobs of color."

In 1940 Benton sponsored a completely unprecedented exhibition of his students' work at Associated American Artists. Thomas Craven praised the show to the skies and called Bill McKim the best animal painter in the country. Some critics complained that the work lacked originality, but all spoke enthusiastically of the high technical standard.

Along with the technique, Benton worked on building up the will and determination of his students. Earl Bennett recalls that his teacher passed on to him a commission to make a painting for the graduating class at the University of Kansas. But it was spring, and word came back to Benton that his student was spending more time chasing girls than working in the studio. "I got notified to come over to the house," Bennett remembers. "Tom wanted to talk to me. I'd never been called up like that before. It was pretty nerve-racking. Rita called me in first and said a long speech about,

'My Tom is a great man and the reason Tom is a great man is because with the first break of day he's out in that studio working, and he works hard, and he never lets anything interfere.' And so on. 'Tom thinks you've got talent and so he wants to talk to you. Now go on out to the studio.'

"As I approached the studio I heard this harmonica going. When I looked through the screen door, there's Tom perched on a high stool, whanging away on his harmonica. He looked up. He says, 'Come on in, Fuzz. See what I've got. Look at this. By God, I'm trying to get those darks to go as dark as they go and still be red or still be green. How did those Flemish masters do it?' And then he said, 'I'll tell ya—we're all in the same ship.' I didn't know what the hell to say. I sat there and said, 'Yeah, but you're the captain of that ship.' Now this is sort of corny dialogue, but Tom said, 'Yes, I guess you're right.' Then he said, 'Now goddammit, Earl, you show as much talent at your age as I did and more. You can become a damn good painter. But you gotta quit chasing girls.' I walked out of there believing that I was going to be the next Tom Benton or even better because he had said so. Tom fired little country boys or minor talents to where you believed you could do these things, you could actually do

Thomas Hart Benton, Aaron, *egg tempera and oil on canvas, 1941. The model was an eighty-two-year-old black from Independence, Missouri, Ben Nichols, who had been born a slave.* •

some of it! I told this story to another guy, another student, and he says, 'You mean you was called in for that same interview?' "

A Year of Calm

Benton's triumphant New York show seems to have calmed somewhat his restless urge to prove himself, and in 1940 he more or less stayed out of trouble. He was *not* asked to judge the Beaux-Arts Ball, but he did attend it, as was recorded by the Kansas City *Star:* "Artist Thomas Hart Benton, his hair disarrayed as usual, said he combed his hair every morning, when someone asked him if he had brushed it since last year's ball."

In his class at the Art Institute, Benton painted two memorable likenesses of black models, *Aaron* and *Instruction.* Bill McKim turned up the model for *Aaron.* Eighty-two-year-old Ben Nichols had been born a slave, and in his face Benton found a metaphor for the fortitude of black people against injustice. Roger Medearis, who watched Benton paint the work, had written that it "must surely rank among the greatest of American portraits."

Someone else in the class discovered the model for *Instruction,* a fellow selling snake medicine in the pool halls of downtown Kansas City. The man caught rattlesnakes and let them rot and ferment in gallon jars; he then sold the result as an aphrodisiac. He was also a preacher and conducted Sunday school classes. *Introduction* shows him teaching a lad to read the Bible. The props for the picture—an old table and a screen covered with newspapers—were assembled behind the models in the classroom. Unfortunately, the young boy twisted and squirmed, so Benton held his head firmly with his left hand while painting with his right.

With his new interest in textures, Benton was producing pictures somewhat more slowly. Consequently, before his 1940 Associated American Artists show, he wrote to Reeves Lewenthal confirming that he would exhibit only sixteen canvases. "This country out here is full of subject matter," Tom wrote, "and I am constantly stimulated by it. But to get that matter into pictorial form is not easy and can't be rushed at will."

He was also beginning to respond to the repeated criticism that his paintings weren't pretty. He liked to tell of an old Missouri woman who brought a little girl from the Ozarks to see his murals in the state capitol. "I think Mr. Benton's painting

Benton sketching at a farm sale in Independence, Missouri. Benton's pupil Jackson Lee Nesbitt snapped this photograph in April 1940. The sketch he made, now in the Benton Trust, showed Pop and the Boys, *a country music group. Benton later used the sketch for one of his illustrations for* The Grapes of Wrath, *as well as for a painting of 1963.*

is very good," the little girl commented. "But it ain't beautiful." Asked what Mr. Benton ought to paint, she replied: "A cow, a pond, a tree, and a sunset." Taking up her challenge, in 1940 Benton painted *A Cow, a Pond, a Tree and a Sunset.*

Also in 1940, Lewenthal worked out a deal with the film producer Walter Wanger for nine AAA artists to paint scenes during the shooting of Eugene O'Neill's *The Long Voyage Home.* This time, Benton worked rapidly; whereas Grant Wood took nearly a year to complete his canvas, Benton finished in seven days. During this brief period, he would get up at five o'clock in the morning and work without interruption until dark.

Raphael Soyer, one of the artists who went with Benton to Hollywood, described what it was like to watch him work. "The moment he came he got drunk and slept the rest of the day," Soyer recalled. "But the next morning he woke up early in the day and I watched him. Out of clay, of plastilene, I don't know what, he created a little theater, a little street with terrific skill. A street with houses, lamp posts, and the lamp posts were illuminated. Somehow he illuminated them so that there were shadows. From that I understand he painted the scene. It amazed me. He did it with such dexterity, so aptly, so well. I was amazed by his ability, by his talent."

Benton later commented that he had a swell time in Hollywood. He brought home, for T.P., a portrait sketch he made of Edward G. Robinson, which the actor inscribed for the boy. He also made a quick sketch of Marlene Dietrich, who was astonished to find that he drew nothing but her head, her hat, and a huge earring. The legendary Dietrich legs were not there at all. He did not spend all his time with the movie stars but flew up to Bakersfield to study the locale for illustrations he was making for a limited edition of John Steinbeck's *The Grapes of Wrath.*

Rita cutting grass.

The atmosphere of Benton's social life has been described by Roger Medearis, one of the students who was regularly invited over for evenings with spaghetti, green salad, and red wine. The sound of T.P.'s flute wafted down the stairway from the room where he practiced. There were also many Saturday-evening parties, with an assortment of unusual people—Jesuits, teachers from the university, a writer from France, a neighbor, a lawyer, musicians from the Philharmonic, art students, and so forth. There was generally music—everything from hillbilly tunes to Mozart, Bach, and Brahms. Benton's friend Emmet, a strolling minstrel, wandered from group to group, strumming his guitar and singing ribald verses (his favorite, often repeated, was called "Blue Violets"). "We aren't allowed to serve you [kids] hard liquor," Rita said, "so we give you Emmet instead."

Tom, parading with a glass of bourbon and water, would tell stories, in a mix of graceful phrasing and plain Missouri dialect. His talk was punctuated by chuckles and profanity and sometimes gross obscenities. Rita would interrupt to confirm his stories or to add to them in her distinctive Scottish-Italian accent, cigarette bobbing in her lips as she spoke, wisps of smoke drifting upward.

At times she would challenge his facts—or he hers—and she would shout indignant protests while he replied in kind, until finally a sort of compromise would be reached. Tom's vulgarities were always followed, as if on cue, by Rita's reprimands, as if she were constantly surprised by his outrageousness.

On February 16, 1940, the Divorce Reform League chose Benton as one of the country's "best husbands," along with four other celebrities, including President Franklin D. Roosevelt. Tom did not seem the least surprised by the news when a reporter contacted him.

"It's because I've got a system," the artist said.

"What I want to know," Rita interjected, "is how do they know Tom is the best husband?"

"I've got a system," Tom continued. "I leave my wife alone and she leaves me

alone, and I always eat what she puts in front of me. Never kick about your wife's cooking."

"What kick have you got?" Rita commented.

"That's what I say, never kick."

Rita then explained that Tom was not the dish-drying, baby-changing type of husband. She revealed that he spilled ashes from his pipe all over the rugs, never helped with the cooking Thursday nights, and never tried to handle diapers except once. "Tom stuck a pin in Teeps. It was the last time I let him try. Anyway, that's my job, not his."

Tom nodded. "Boy," he said, "let me tell you it takes a system to stay married eighteen years, but reluctantly I have to admit my wife deserves some of the credit."

On November 3, in the course of a lecture at the University of Wisconsin, Benton shocked artistic purists by describing the current popular song "Pistol Packin' Mama" as "true art." He declared that the song had left "a distinct impression" on current American culture: "Perhaps it isn't as good as European art, but it's our own." He also extolled the 1920s tune "Yes, We Have No Bananas." "From a quantity of art forms like 'Mama,' a truly national brand of art will form in the post-war world," he said.

A variety of music experts emphatically disagreed. Roy Shields, music director for NBC, said, " 'Mama'—it's really elemental. I don't quite know what Benton means by art forms." And Al Dexter, the Texan who wrote the ballad, allowed that he was "plain dumbfounded." He commented: "I made the song kind of simple when I wrote it because these simple songs catch on easier. I never figured it was art. I'm a country boy. I don't know much about this art business."

In May 1940, Benton finished up the school year by taking nine of his advanced students to Newton County, Arkansas, for a ten-day sketching expedition. He explained to a reporter that this foray played an integral role in his teaching: "Nature is different from the studio, both because the light comes from many directions and because the motifs are jumbled together, not neatly selected. The problem is to find the real character of objects when they're set in a confusion of light."

"Tom Benton worked fast," Earl Bennett recalls. "He could go out and—almost like Van Gogh—he could do a painting in a day out in the field because he was so excited. He'd get so excited. We were down there in Arkansas and he said, 'Just look at this one, just look at that set up! By God, that just makes the seat of your pants smoky!'

"We had beautiful big Kansas City steaks in the trunk of the car and he had the lid up and was painting. He was about fifty feet from the car and an old razorback sow and her piglets got into that and dragged every steak out. When he came to, the last steak was being shook around in the dirt by this little sow. We had sardines and crackers that day."

On the way home, near Branson, the car skidded on the wet asphalt and went off the road into a ditch. "Tom was a great painter, but he was a lousy driver," Bennett says. "We damn near went off the steep side of the mountain, but he managed to get the car into the ditch on the uphill side. The car went along the side of this carved-out rock wall like a giant nutmeg grater, grinding panels, paint and fenders until it slid to a stop." Tom looked over the back seat and asked, in a hoarse whisper, "Is anybody hurt?"

"It was the first time I ever heard no voice come out of this leader of ours," Bennett recalls. "It was always, 'You guys, get the hell down to the river and take a bath! You smell like a bunch of artists!' I never saw Tom Benton at a loss for words or not able to speak. He was always in command—always in command."

ARTIST THOMAS HART BENTON HEADS CLASS INTO OZARKS TO SKETCH "NATURE IN THE RAW."

Cartoon of Benton's sketching trip with students, Kansas City Star.

Bill McKim, Jackson Lee Nesbitt, and Thomas Hart Benton looking at damage to their car. "Tom was a great painter," Earl Bennett recalls. "But he was a lousy driver."

Thomas Hart Benton, T.P. and Jake, egg tempera and oil on canvas mounted on panel, 1938. When his son's dog died in 1946, Benton wrote a long tribute to him in the Martha's Vineyard Gazette. "Jake had a laughing face. His mouth was so set that, active or in repose, he had a smile. . . . He was named Jake because he was a country dog, a country jake, who hadn't learned city ways." •

Chapter Seventeen
Getting Fired

The Nelson-Atkins Museum of Art. The imposing neoclassical structure opened to the public in 1933.

Paul Gardner (left) and Keith Martin. Martin, the new director of the Kansas City Art Institute, had been manager of the glee club at Harvard. He and Benton clashed from their first meeting.

"In the East I said goodbye to the panty-waists in art. The phoneys. The screwballs. The hot air circuit. . . . And now after six years the Art gang here in Kansas City is after my scalp."

By the end of the 1930s, largely as a result of the Depression, the Kansas City Art Institute had reached a desperate financial state. Benton's supporter, director Ross Howard, believed that the only solution was to merge with the University of Kansas City, but his trustees thought otherwise, and he was pushed gently out to pasture. He resigned in the summer of 1939, and Paul Gardner, the director of the Nelson-Atkins Museum of Art, headed the committee to find a new permanent director.

In October the board of governors announced their choice—a dapper young Hollywood portrait painter named Keith Martin. The youngest director ever appointed to the Art Institute, Martin had studied painting in Europe and was a graduate of Harvard, where he had managed the glee club. He had recently married a blond starlet, Jeanne Maddon. Benton and Martin clashed from their first meeting. Fred Shane recalls Benton's reaction when he came back from his summer on Martha's Vineyard and found Martin's portraits hanging in the school's office. "Tom comes into the office for the first time after his return and sees these pictures and he says, 'What are these things?' And the guy says, 'Well, these are my paintings.' And Tom says, 'Get them out of here. This is an art institute.' "

Aside from his personal conflict with Keith Martin, two specific issues clouded Benton's relationship with the school. First was the matter of grading. Benton did not need grading to motivate his students and was strongly opposed to the practice. Martin, on the other hand, wanted to regularize the inconsistent and often lax procedures that the school had condoned in the past. He insisted on grades. Then there was the question of the sketching excursion to the Ozarks. Word had got back to the governors that during these trips Benton sometimes drank heavily and that the students—both men and women—swam naked in the Ozark streams. They did not feel that this reflected well on the reputation of the Art Institute. For Benton, these expeditions were a fundamental part of his teaching—an introduction to life in the raw; but the governors felt that they should be discontinued.

Keith Martin would not have been human if he had not considered replacing Benton with someone more acquiescent and congenial. In January 1941, he discovered a logical candidate when Fletcher Martin (no relation) came down from the University of Iowa to serve as one of the judges of the Midwestern Artists Exhibition. Roger Medearis, who lived with the Keith Martins that year, recalls that Keith and Fletcher Martin "hit it off very well. . . . If I had been somewhat more mature, I might have detected a small cloud on the horizon of my teacher."

Despite the frictions, however, in 1941 Benton's position at the Art Institute seemed secure. The Huselton affair had blown over. His paintings were being more

and more favorably reviewed. All seemed calm until early April, when he went to New York to prepare for the opening of an exhibition at Associated American Artists.

On the rainy afternoon of April 4, Benton gave an impromptu interview to a few reporters in a small back room of the gallery, which was crowded with his paintings. While he talked, he alternately puffed on his pipe and sipped rye whiskey from a leaky paper cup. Casual though the setting was, his remarks were apparently premeditated. According to his student Herman Cherry, the painter told his friends some time in advance that he planned to stir up a fuss and proposed that they might like to contribute to the debate that he would initiate.

He began by labeling the typical museum "a graveyard run by a pretty boy with delicate wrists and a swing in his gait." He went on: "The pretty boys run the museums because it's a field most living men wouldn't take on. It's a field where you take care of the dead, and nobody wants that. You've got to have a sort of undertaker's psychology to go into the museum business. If it was left to me I wouldn't have any museums. I'd have people buy the paintings and hang 'em anywhere anybody had time to look up at 'em. I'd like to sell mine to saloons, bawdy houses, Kiwanis and Rotary Clubs and chambers of commerce—even women's clubs. . . . Three years from now, when I have my next show, they'll have a bar in here or I won't have anything to do with the place. I can do better than this at home."

These remarks would have been shocking enough had Benton stuck to general accusations. But he included some unmistakable references to the staff of the Nelson-

Thomas Hart Benton, The Hailstorm, *egg tempera and oil on canvas mounted on panel, 1940. In his second exhibition at Associated American Artists, Benton showed mostly landscapes of his native Missouri.* •

Paul Gardner. Gardner was the first director of the Nelson-Atkins Museum of Art.

Atkins. Thus: "Do you want to know what's the matter with the art business in America? It's the third sex and the museums. Even in Missouri we're full of them. We've got an immigration on out there. And the old ladies who've gotten so old that no man will look at 'em think these pretty boys will do. Our musems are full of ballet dancers, retired businessmen, and boys from the Fogg Institute at Harvard, where they train museum directors and artists. They hate my pictures and talk against them. I wouldn't be in the museums except that people demand that I have representation."

No one in Kansas City could have had any doubt about his references. The ballet dancer was Paul Gardner, director of the Nelson-Atkins Museum of Art, who had danced with Pavlova's company; the boys from the Fogg were Harold Parsons, the adviser for European art, and Laurence Sickman, the Orientalist. The "retired businessmen" were the museum's trustees. To call this outburst politically unwise would be an understatement, for Benton directly attacked some of the very individuals who controlled his fate. Gardner, his chief target, served on the board of the Art Institute —the very board that reviewed staff contracts. J. C. Nichols, who had rescued him from being fired two years before, was a trustee of the Nelson-Atkins Museum.

Laurence Sickman recalled that he always got on well with Benton on a personal basis; it was Gardner who inspired the painter's animosity. Gardner sometimes dropped unflattering comments about Benton's work; Mrs. Milton McGreevy, one of the *grandes dames* of Kansas City, recalls that he often said Benton's paintings would fall apart in twenty years because of his incompetent handling of materials. In addition, Gardner had chaired the committee that had selected Keith Martin, and Benton was undoubtedly irked that he, rather than an artist, had decided this appointment.

On April 5, Benton's statements were published in newspapers nationwide. The very next day, negative responses began to appear. Tom Colt, director of the Virginia Museum of Fine Arts, announced that museum directors were not all limp-wristed. Colt had been a flier in the Marine Corps, where he had risen from private to first lieutenant. "I was in the art field before I went into aviation," he said, "and I returned to it." Colt accused Tom of biting the hand that fed him. "I know Tom Benton and I am fond of him. But."

On April 15, Peyton Boswell, generally a defender of Regionalism, complained of

Benton: "He strikes out with all the strength of his pugnacious soul, but too often dogmatically condemns whole groups because of his bitterness against an individual."

On April 18, Barbara Barton countered the artist's remarks in the Kansas City *Times:* "Thomas Hart Benton seems to suffer from a warped viewpoint. Could he possibly wish to imply that children, 6 years old and up, should take up beer drinking in saloons in order to obtain a glimpse of the beauties of art and the world?"

The most thoughtful critique was provided by Henry Haskell of the *Star,* who pointed out that Benton's remarks largely contradicted his own essay in the March *University of Missouri Review.* There he had spoken favorably of art museums as "a constant stimulant to new research" and had praised an exhibition of the Dutch old masters at the Nelson-Atkins Museum of Art. In response to Haskell's piece, on April 25 Tom wrote a letter to the *Star,* confessing that he had been guilty of exaggeration: "I have to do a lot of work with contradictory conceptions. These, however, produce practical truths."

This letter was remarkably close to an apology. By this time, however, events were moving beyond Benton's control. On April 23, during a preliminary meeting of the Art Institute board, strong objections were raised to the renewal of his contract. Four days later, he informed the press that Keith Martin had telephoned him and asked for his resignation. "This thing has been coming a long time," he told a reporter. He insisted, however, that he had no intention of resigning: "Those kids are for me, and I'm going to make a fight for it. I've licked 'em once, and I'll lick 'em again."

He boasted that if he was fired, he wouldn't mind having a bit more spare time: "I've still got a lot to learn. In the art field I'm competing with Rembrandt, and as a harmonica player I'm competing with Larry Adler. When you've got competition like that you're got a job on your hands."

By the next day, he had already become less sanguine about his prospects. He announced to the press that he did not expect his contract to be renewed, and claimed that a "tea-party whispering campaign" had been waged against him since he had made those statements in New York.

On the same day, April 28, John de Martelly, head of the Institute's department of graphic arts and a close friend of Benton's, resigned from the faculty, issuing an angry statement to the press: "I am leaving the Kansas City Art Institute for good. I have found out that the people who are running the place are not only stupid about what is good for them, but underhanded, too. I thought so when they fired Mr. Ross Howard, but I have proof of it now. Keith Martin called me up the night of April 24th and told me that Mr. Benton was leaving the school and he offered to give me his place as director of the painting department. I nearly fell over with surprise. I know Tom Benton well and he had not said anything about leaving the school.

"Some of the students were in my house when Martin called up and they heard my answers to him. I told him he was foolish to give up a big artist now and that he should do all he could to keep Tom Benton in the school. He kept insisting that I take this offer but I refused.

"Martin and those people with him know that Tom has a sharp tongue. They know that he can out-think them 10 to 1. They figured that if I took the job Tom would lay off them because of liking me and would not want to hurt me. I think they were right. But they missed out on judging me. I need the money that Tom's job would pay, but I am an artist and not a cheap adventurer. I like Tom as a man and as an artist too well to make any profit as his expense.

"Tom Benton knows how to teach. He knows how to make students enthusiastic over difficult problems. He got the students of the institute to painting well enough to make a professional show in New York and sell $1,500 worth of their work. You cannot match that in any other school. In addition, he and his wife have the talented

Laurence Sickman. A product of the Fogg Art Museum at Harvard, he built up the museum's Oriental collection.

305

students always in mind. They have a gallery in their home where these students show their work. They sell that work and get real money for the students. They take no commission and do not ask anybody to wait on tables in return.

"Tom was just as generous with his fellow instructors at the institute. He got Reeves Lewenthal of the Associated American Artists to make a place for Wallace Rosenbauer's sculptures. He got a place for Fred James and he got a place for me. He would have gotten a place for Keith Martin's paintings I suppose if Keith had stuck by him. He is just friendly enough to have done that.

"This town is congealing. I think it's going to die of dry rot. Tom talks a lot. But he makes a lot of fun with his talk."

Unaware of de Martelly's blast, Keith Martin issued a statement the same day: "With reference to inquiries concerning the status of Thomas Hart Benton at the Kansas City Art Institute: I am very much surprised that Mr. Benton seems to assume that his immediate resignation has been called for. At a regular meeting of the board of governors last Wednesday preliminary consideration was given to questions of staff contracts for the year 1941–42. It is an administrator's duty, consequently, to look to the future. Therefore, confidential and unofficial conversations have been carried on with respect to the composition of the staff for next year."

Later that day, when he became aware that his words contradicted de Martelly's assertions, Martin rephrased his remarks. He told a reporter for the Kansas City *Times*: "The telephone conversation to which de Martelly refers was not a direct offer, but something for him to consider in view of the fact doubt had arisen in my mind as to whether Benton would be here next year. It is my duty to look ahead. I thought I would sound out John because I have a high regard for his technical competence."

De Martelly now qualified his earlier outburst: "It's true I had planned to be away from Kansas City next year anyway. But I was planning to come back, to take up teaching again, and perhaps to come back part of next year, at Mr. Benton's invitation. But the main fact remains the same, I'm not coming back at all. I'm through—because I don't like the underhanded way they offered me Tom's job before Tom had given it up."

The *Star* did not speak up on Benton's behalf, as it had in his struggle with Howard Huselton. The *Journal* and the *Journal-Post*, however, did what they could for his cause. On April 29, the *Journal* editorialized: "The witchburners are again out to get Thomas Hart Benton's position as instructor of painting at the Kansas City Art Institute. Mr. Benton overcame his critics the last time by the simple process of letting them make laughing stocks of themselves. Will they be accommodating enough to do so again?"

Benton published a long statement in the *Journal*, promising a fight: "After all the stuff in the papers yesterday, all the phone calls I've got and all the students who came over to my house, raising the devil, it looks like the art institute is going to oust me. All I can get out of the institute itself is that nothing official has been done. That means, so far as I can see, that they are waiting for summer, when I'll be out of the way, and they can fire me in peace and without risking any comeback on my part.

"Well, I'm fighting for that job up there. I don't really need it, but I want it anyhow for the sake of the students and for the help the 3,000 bucks that goes with it gives me in feeding and quenching the thirst of all the folks who come over to my house to listen to music and have a good time.

"I like Kansas City. It's a good place to live in. Rocks stick out of the ground and you have to look up and down hills to see things. Flowers grow easily and there's a lot of redbud in the spring. There are also plenty of regular men and women who live here—men and women you like because you can be yourself with them.

306

"But a lot of the people in this town who go in for Art with a capital A are different. They seem friendly enough when you meet them, but you get the feeling after a while that they are not quite regular in the plain American sense and that they want to live by pretending things are different from what they really are. Oftentimes, when I meet these people, I feel they are afraid of me.

"The people I thought were my friends have turned out not to be so. They sided with those whose lately offended vanities, pretensions and habits made them want to separate me from the school I had built up.

"OK. It looks like I'm going out.

"Do you really want to know why I'm going out? It's because I say in public what every other American artist says in private—and not only artists, but lawyers, critics, newspaper writers, businessmen and psychologists. They also know that what I said with a belly laugh has a serious side.

"If the youth of America is to grow up strong and build a virile art in this country he must first break with the colonial notions of these effete and precious dwellers in the Ivory Towers of theory, who have a stranglehold on the American art world. Lately, with the aid of a highball or two, I punctuated my convictions in this matter. I stand by them—the most of them—even though I'm flooded with letters from museums telling me how big are the chest measures of their directors.

"All this is a little storm in the teapot of aesthetics. But it has been said with authority that a civilization is reflected accurately by its art life. Are the strong men of Europe right when they speak of 'the rotten corpse of democracy'? Speak up—you people who still have a belly laugh and remember your granddad!"

On the day this statement appeared, the Kansas City *Times* polled the board of the Art Institute. Louis P. Rothschild stated that he was in favor of renewing Benton's contract. The other fourteen board governors gave a remarkable demonstration of bureaucratic buck-passing:

Robert B. Fizzell, first vice-president of the Institute, said he thought it would be unfortunate if the impression was created that de Martelly was leaving over the Benton

"They Back Their Teacher,"
Kansas City Star, *1941.*

affair. He explained that de Martelly had made known his decision about six weeks before that he would not be returning the next year.

Gordon T. Beaham, Jr., stated that he was "not in a position to act as a spokesman for the board."

John T. Harding said that he was not able "to crystallize an opinion."

Charles T. Thompson asserted that the situation appeared "to be well established," and added: "Benton is a difficult man to lay yourself open to."

Mrs. Wallace B. Richards said: "Whether Mr. Benton is important enough as a teacher to be retained is up to the director and to the school committee."

Paul Gardner, director of the Nelson-Atkins Museum of Art, said that he had not been present at the last meeting of the board of governors and did not feel that he was able to comment on the situation.

Parker B. Francis said that "because of the trend the situation has taken," he did not want to comment. He added that any statement about the situation should come from W. T. Kemper, president of the Institute.

Six other board members either were out of town or simply withheld comment.

As for the views of the faculty, Wallace Rosenbaur, instructor of sculpture, announced: "It has been suggested it is better for us not to think." Similarly, Bob Mays, fashion design teacher, suggested: "Put me down as a blank."

On April 30, fifty current and former students of the Art Institute demonstrated in front of the school, carrying placards with such messages as: "We Don't Care What Benton Says: We Like What He Does." "Is This School Run for Stuffed Shirts or the Students?" "Let's Have a Belly Laff," And one placard featured a drawing of a large pansy and the words: "We Don't Want These."

When Keith Martin appeared, several protestors greeted him politely. He commented to a reporter: "Well, I hope you get your story. I suppose you paid those kids a quarter each to stage that." The reporter denied the allegations.

Mingling with the protestors was Chris J. Gove, an oldtime fiddler, who often posed for Benton's classes. He pulled out his instrument and played. "I don't know what it is all about," he said, "but I guess they know what they're doing. They're a hard-working bunch of painters, ordinarily." There was a brief flurry when a lone first-year student tacked anti-Benton slogans to a tree: "Good-by Benton," and "We want Martin." The signs were hurriedly torn down by three or four vehement female Benton-boosters.

On May 1, the Kansas City *Journal* contacted Thomas Craven, whom it described as "America's most famous art critic," at his home in Great Neck, New York. Craven responded: "Mr. Benton may be too sweeping and undiplomatic in his statements, sometimes, but regardless of the opinions on the subject, they are losing the best art teacher in the country. I should think that instead of investigating Benton, those interested would inquire into what underlay his remarks, since he made almost specific allegations. They wanted somebody to adorn the social set and they got an art teacher who didn't play that side of the game."

On May 2, Benton announced that he would not speak as scheduled at a Sunday "fireside chat" at the Art Institute. "In just a few days I will be doing all the talking you will want to hear out of me." On the same day, he outlined his notion of an ideal art museum, where plain folks could lounge in comfortable chairs, smoke, and enjoy a living American art.

On May 3, at his home on Belleview Avenue, he spoke to Mike Amrine of the Kansas City *Week-End Feature Journal.* "It's a funny thing," he said. "In the East I said good-by to the pantywaists in Art. The phoneys. The screwballs. The hot-air circuit. I came home to Missouri to paint American pictures. I painted them and sold them and made money—and a little fame. I was asked to take over this painting school, and I taught my students to say good-by to the goofy 'modern art' schools that have no connection with people and living. They went out to their homes, down in the Ozarks, back at the forks of the creeks. And they painted pictures and sold them, and at the same time learned something about Art and a little about life.

"And now after six years the Art gang here in Kansas City is after my scalp. And I'm going to get the gate here from the same kind of Art gang that I thought I had shut the gate on when I said good-by to Paris and New York. It's a small thing. My losing my job doesn't mean much. But when you think that the fathers and grandfathers of these same people were horny-handed two-fisted men who built the Empire of the West—you wonder where we're going."

He gripped his stubby brier pipe more firmly, leaned back in his chair, and gazed off into the distance. "I wonder what's happening in America," he said. "What do you think?"

On May 5, the governors voted unanimously to fire Benton and issued a statement noting that it "was influenced by Mr. Benton's recent public pronouncements which, in the opinion of the board, reflect generally on American art and art education. . . . In fairness to Mr. Benton, as well as to the Institute, the board decided that he should be released from those minimum restraints which are imposed on anyone affiliated with an organization, where a certain degree of cooperation is essential." According to W. T. Kemper, the pressure to fire Benton came not from Keith Martin, but from the board itself. (Martin, who was ill with measles, did not even attend the meeting.) Many of the governors felt that Benton's attacks on the Nelson-Atkins, if left unchecked, would sabotage the Art Institute's efforts to gain financial support from the community.

Newsweek quoted the artist's reaction: "Stuffed shirts and sissies have won over the will of my students . . . I predict their victory will be a sour one."

Benton also prepared a typewritten statement, which he probably intended to

Billy Rose and a chorus girl pose with Persephone *at the Diamond Horseshoe, 1941. After Benton declared he wanted his paintings to hang in bars and brothels, Billy Rose borrowed* Persephone *for his "saloon."*

Benton painting in his studio.

Cal Alley, "A 'Twist of His Wrist' Could Regain Him His Job," Kansas City Journal *cartoon, May 5, 1941.*

release to the press. If he ever did so, the papers did not print it. "This business doesn't come as a surprise to me," he wrote. "There's always been a bunch of respectable brothers and sisters in the Kansas City Art Institute who got sick every time I laughed. When I first came out here, there were too many cowtown aesthetes using art to temper the smell of the stockyards on papa's boots, and too many would-be Ziegfeld boys, male ballet dancers, interior decorators, and played-out imitations of the Klondike. And there were too many goony women who thought Art was something that occurred at tea parties. And there were too many fat men pussyfooting around whose brains were fatter than their bellies. . . .

"But I wanted to live in Missouri. I thought Art needed to remember a little the smell of the stockyards. Maybe I can get all these phoneys out of the way and take the stigma off the art business in this town. I painted a mural that got everybody talking about Art, a living American art that said things American people understood. Then I built up a strong painting school in spite of a succession of dimwit presidents who looked on me as a wild radical. . . .

"Without me the Kansas City Art Institute will drop back to the kind of third rate joint it was before I came. It'll be just a place where girls hang around between high school and marriage. Of course, the tea parties will start again. Their idea of a living Art [is] a Glee Club boy in a frock coat [i.e., Keith Martin] sweetening up display portraits of vanitous women while he sips a cup of tea.

"But in spite of this degradation, Art will not go back on the bum in Kansas City. I'm staying here."

Although he may well have never released this remarkable statement, on the evening of May 5 Benton lashed out in an address to the Kansas City Young Democratic Club at the Hotel Phillips. In choosing this forum, he probably intended to contrast his own Democratic affiliations with the predominantly Republican loyalties of the governors of the Art Institute.

After a few of his customary cracks at reactionaries, dilettantes, and homosexuals, he went on: "The walls of the museums say in no uncertain terms, 'Look what I got that you ain't got.' That kind of stuff doesn't sit well in a democracy—but we've got it." In the question-and-answer session that followed, he added to his attack on museums, claiming that "Most of the stuff in them is not genuine, but a restoration nothing like the picture as the artist first painted it." He also noted that a check had shown that the average length of time a person spends looking at an old master in a museum is seventeen and a half seconds. "That is why I recently said I would like my pictures hung in saloons. I know plenty of men, myself included, who have spent and are willing to spend two or three hours regarding a painting behind a bar. Another good place to hang paintings is in your children's rooms." (No doubt this last thought was a consequence of Barbara Barton's comment that children were not allowed in bars.)

He concluded: "Change of form is just as much the essence of a true democracy as it is of a living art. It is the will and ability to change forms under the pressure of new needs and new experience in a living, going environment, that proclaims the very reality of democracy and makes it technically serviceable in real government. That is one great truth that Franklin D. Roosevelt has seen. It is for seeking that truth that conservatives most hate him—and the living, going people love him. We must say that although we do not believe ultimate democracy is presently attainable we are still going to see how far toward it we can get."

Thomas Hart Benton, Threshing Wheat, *egg tempera and oil on canvas mounted on panel, 1938–39. Benton showed an old steam thresher, which he sketched at a farm on the outskirts of Kansas City. The clouds echo the rolling curve of the landscape.* •

*Frank Lloyd Wright and
Thomas Hart Benton, 1941.*

The day after this speech, the Kansas City *Times* editorialized that "the Tom Benton affair is hardly to be taken tragically. There is no deep question of liberty of teaching or artistic expression involved." Still, the paper followed with a cartoon showing "Tom Benton remodeled to suit the Institute." His wrist was bent limply, he wore a floppy artist's tie, and the words "O, tush!" came from his lips. In a painting of *Susanna* on his easel, the girl was coyly peeking from behind a tree. The caption read: "A 'Twist of the Wrist' Could Regain Him His Job."

By no means silenced, Benton announced that he planned to "set up shop" in a school of his own. He and his students would make plans for it during their annual sketching trip on the Arkansas River, which would begin on the morrow. "Plans are nebulous but one thing is certain—it won't cost a cent to go to my school and I won't get a cent of pay out of it."

On May 10, the board announced that Fletcher Martin had been engaged to replace Benton. He had been awarded a two-year contract. The appointment was obviously intended to defuse Tom's claim that the Art Institute supported only effete, limp-wristed Harvard types, for Fletcher Martin was a muscular tough guy, over six feet tall, with a drooping, sad-dog mustache and a boxer's broken nose. He had grown up in frontier Colorado and Idaho and had never graduated from high school. But this Regionalist "hit man," who previously had replaced Grant Wood at Iowa, had attended the school of hard knocks, supporting himself as a farmhand, lumberjack, sailor, and boxer before he turned to painting. His most famous creation, *Trouble in 'Frisco* (1938), directly reflects his "tough-guy" persona; it shows a bruising fistfight between two sailors. Shortly after his appointment, a piece in *Parnassus* editorialized: "It was a wise and fortunate choice and should clear up all criticism."

Meanwhile, the controversy simmered on. On May 3, the *Star* published a letter from a physician who confessed that a visit to an art gallery generally left him cold. Benton's paintings, on the other hand, gave him something he could understand and relate to. Somewhat pathetically, to illustrate his point, the doctor cited a painting of three chickens, *Adolescence*—which was by Grant Wood. Benton's strongest supporter was his old friend Frank Lloyd Wright. On May 7, the architect was in town to inspect the progress of work on the Community Church on Main Street, a commission he would later angrily repudiate because of conflicts over the building code with city authorities. "If a creative artist can't have the privilege of free speech," Wright said, "and still be a teacher, we already are Hitlerized in some kind of Fascist society, whatever its name. . . . The average museum is a morgue, a cold storage place."

"Just put 'me too!' whenever he says things like that," Benton chimed in.

"I think it's just plain silly," Wright continued, "for an American man to take American money and model an art gallery after a Greek temple."

Tom nodded.

"Most museums are sarcophagi," Wright continued. "In such stilted, unnatural places you can expect to find stilted, unnatural people." Wright observed that his three hundred–odd buildings had been better understood by American businessmen than by their wives, who had been more exposed to old-world culture.

"There are plenty of male wives running around too," Benton added.

On June 1941, Benton wrote an essay, "Art vs. the Mellon Gallery," for *Common Sense*, in which he continued his battle against museums, this time singling out Andrew Mellon's new National Gallery for attack. "Judgements of the creative mind are very unstable," he wrote, "but they are alive and, even when time may show them to be erroneous, tend to stimulate creativeness."

In October, a piece in the *Star* noted that Benton was back home in Kansas City after a "reflective" summer on Martha's Vineyard, during which he had completed eighty-seven illustrations for a limited edition of *Huckleberry Finn*. He had taken a pledge to quit teaching art in institutions, and had turned down six offers, including one from the Brooklyn Museum. He confessed that his previous teaching plans had been destroyed by the Selective Service Act. His most promising young students had all been drafted.

But he wouldn't have any trouble staying busy, he added. He had a lecture series lined up, he planned to roam around the White River country, and he also wanted to take a look at a new military training center being set up in his hometown. "Incidentally," he noted, "I'm staying here in Kansas City. For the next five years at least."

In the final evaluation, both Benton and the Kansas City Art Institute were losers in this conflict. At the Institute, things moved on smoothly, despite his absence. Never again, however, did the school attract the national attention that it had when he taught there. Neither Martin remained at the Art Institute very long. Hardly more than a year after Benton's departure, Keith Martin left to join an army camouflage unit in Nebraska. Apparently army work proved more enjoyable than running an art school, for Martin did not return to Kansas City after the war and seems to have abandoned painting for some other pursuit. Fletcher Martin proved popular with his students, but in 1943 he accepted a commission from *Life* to document American war activity. He never returned to Kansas City.

The greatest loser was Benton. The informal art school he talked of creating never materialized. He never again did any regular teaching, and his vitalizing contact with young artists came to an end. Through the 1940s, he continued to win national attention with his work; but he did so as an individual. His claims to represent an artistic or a cultural movement grew increasingly tenuous; his place in the American art world grew increasingly isolated.

Benton lost one of his great dreams when he was fired from the Art Institute—the hope that Kansas City could become a creative art center of national importance. He had believed that the community would support the growth of a tough-minded Midwestern form of art. As Dan James once humorously expressed it, Tom hoped to create a "middle American Athens." But Kansas City rejected this ideal. "It must have been damn disappointing," James has commented, "not to have had that happen."

Benton's artistic program had been squelched by the forces of civic virtue. Howard Huselton must have been pleased.

Fletcher Martin. Regionalist "Hit Man" Martin replaced Grant Wood at Iowa and Thomas Hart Benton in Kansas City. A muscular "tough guy," Martin had supported himself as a farmhand, lumberjack, sailor, and boxer before he turned to painting.

Benton relaxing on a float trip.

Fletcher Martin, Trouble in 'Frisco, *oil on canvas, 1938.*

313

Chapter Eighteen
Afterward

Thomas Hart Benton, album cover for Saturday Night at Tom Benton's, *1941. In the fall of 1941, Benton performed on the harmonica for a three-record set released by Decca. He was backed by his son, T.P., who played the flute, and by an orchestra of professional musicians. Benton's drawing for the cover of the album shows his family: at the far left, little Jessie; in the center, T.P. on the flute and himself on the harmonica; and at the far right the dog Jake and the cat Buia.*

"He was fifty years old when I was born, and I always thought he was in his twenties."

The War Years

Two projects filled up Benton's time in the summer after he was fired: a professional recording for Decca of his harmonica music and an illustrated edition of *Huckleberry Finn*. Neither project was an unqualified success. Rather than let Benton toot away on his own, Decca set him off against a small orchestra of professional musicians. This caused great difficulties, for Benton had no formal musical training. The orchestra used conventional musical notation; he employed his own system; and the two found it difficult to harmonize or keep in time. More than that, the orchestral accompaniment adds a schmaltzy sentimentality to the effect. A few informal recordings exist of Benton playing for his own amusement, and they reveal a fire and vigor lacking from the Decca production.

Benton's *Huckleberry Finn* illustrations seem less successful than those earlier for *Tom Sawyer*. For one thing, he shifted from pen and ink to watercolor, and as a consequence the drawings harmonize less well with the printed page.

By the time summer ended, Benton realized that he was losing direction, and by late autumn, the international situation had grown so grim that he found it difficult to concentrate on painting. As an outlet for his restlessness, he set out on a lecture tour. He was on the stand in Cincinnati when the Japanese struck Pearl Harbor on December 7. Promptly stepping off the stage, he telegraphed to his agency to cancel all further engagements and returned to Kansas City. Within a few weeks, he had completed a series of gigantic cartoonlike posters of the horrors that threatened the United States —paintings unlike anything he had created before. He titled the series *Year of Peril*. *Again* showed German and Japanese soldiers spearing the crucified Christ; *The Sower*, a Nazi sowing the earth with human skulls; *Starry Night*, a freighter being sunk by an enemy submarine; and *Invasion* showed a Midwestern farm being attacked by invaders, who rape a woman and bayonet a farmer in the mouth, as if in an act of oral sodomy. The largest of the paintings, *Exterminate,* showed two GI's in hand-to-hand combat with Hitler and Tojo, amidst a landscape of carnage and dead bodies and a sky filled with burning planes. They violently disembowel the Japanese leader, whose intestines are formed of the chains with which he enslaves mankind. Roger Medearis recalls that at this time Benton advocated melting down the Statue of Liberty to make bullets.

No doubt these hate-filled paintings served as an emotional catharsis. It was not just Hitler but Howard Huselton and his kind that Benton wished to annihilate. Even admirers do not claim that these canvases constitute great art. "That was Tom at his worst," Bill McKim has commented. Oddly enough, though, the paintings were more widely reproduced than any in Benton's career. Reeves Lewenthal showed them at

Thomas Hart Benton in the doorway of his studio on Martha's Vineyard.

Associated American Artists in New York, where they attracted some seventy-five
thousand people; and he sold them to Abbott Laboratories in Chicago, which reproduced them in a propaganda booklet with a foreword by Archibald MacLeish. Because
of their topical nature, the paintings were featured in newsreels and newspapers across
the country. In all, they were reproduced some fifty-five million times.

Through the remainder of the war, Benton struggled to paint subjects related to
it. He painted GI's embarking for North Africa and a black soldier in the front line of
battle. He accompanied a submarine crew on maneuvers. He sketched the construction
of a troop ship in Pittsburgh, watched it being launched, and followed it down the
Mississippi to New Orleans, where it joined the fleet. His drawings of oil refineries at
Baton Rouge were the basis of the painting *Catalytic Crackers,* which he always
considered "one of my best pictures."

Unlike *Year of Peril,* these paintings did not simplify their messages into propaganda or in any way glorify the ugliness of war. They were not popular. The embarkation scene, for example, presents the soldiers as sheep being led to slaughter. The
last man in the line looks backward sorrowfully, knowing that he will never return.
The government declined to reproduce the painting, even when Benton changed the
title from *Prelude to Death* to *The Departure. Negro Soldier* is filled with ambiguity.
Did Benton intend the brutish features of the black man as a comment on the brutality
of war? Or did he intend a social criticism, showing how the black man, although
mistreated in America, was the first to be drafted in the fight for "freedom"?

Much as he struggled to keep up with the young soldiers, Benton felt most at
home with the subjects of an earlier period. Throughout the early forties, concurrently
with these war-related pictures, he continued to paint peaceful rural subjects. In 1942
he created *July Hay,* a Midwestern farm scene reminiscent of the work of Breughel.

The Music Lesson, in 1943, showed his Vineyard neighbor Gale Huntington teaching his daughter to play the guitar; and in the same year he completed one of his most ambitious treatments of a country music song, *The Wreck of the Ole '97*. In 1944 he produced *Spring Tryout*, a memory of his visits to Pappy Wise's Texas farm when he was a child, as well as *Tobacco Sorting*, one of a series of paintings for the American tobacco industry. In 1945 he painted the large canvas *Rice Threshing*.

After the war ended, Benton clearly hoped that the Regionalist movement would be revived. To further this objective, Reeves Lewenthal held a major show of Benton's work in Chicago in February of 1946. The painter drank heavily, stayed up late, and issued his usual pronouncements to the press. Both publicity-wise and commercially, the venture was a booming success, although Lewenthal was disappointed by his failure to sell *Persephone* to the Art Institute.

Benton's elation did not last long. Without pausing, he rushed off to Hollywood to work for Walt Disney in planning a cartoon operetta based on the life of Davy Crockett. Although he had some memorable conversations with Salvador Dali, who was also on the Disney payroll, he found it impossible to create anything satisfying within the constraints the studio imposed. After a few weeks, he returned to Kansas City, exhausted and unhappy. In August his dog Jake died of a heart attack in his sleep, and he published a long and moving obituary, almost worthy of Senator Vest, in the Martha's Vineyard *Gazette*. A few weeks later, Nat Benton also died unexpect-

Thomas Hart Benton, Fluid Catalytic Crackers, *egg tempera and oil on canvas mounted on masonite, 1945. This view of an oil refinery near Baton Rouge resembles the precisionist factory paintings of Charles Sheeler. Unlike Sheeler, Benton made drawings of the subject on the site rather than painting from photographs.*

edly of a heart attack. This time Benton did not compose an obituary; his brother's death sent him into a full-scale depression.

By a trick of fate, these personal tragedies coincided with a moment of artistic crisis. The work of Benton, Curry, and Wood began to be subjected to savage criticism in the press. Rather abruptly, Benton came to realize that he stood alone in the art world and that the Regionalist movement, which he had so vigorously promoted and fostered, had come to an end.

What Killed Regionalism?

As early as 1940, Benton confessed that the rural America he knew best had begun to change. "Things are different back in the hills," he commented. "Ten years ago I'd start out with a pencil and a notebook and a harmonica. I'd head for the country

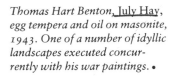

Thomas Hart Benton, July Hay, egg tempera and oil on masonite, 1943. One of a number of idyllic landscapes executed concurrently with his war paintings. •

roads, cut across pastures and fallow fields, working along the way. Along about dark I'd stop at a farmhouse, ask for a meal and a night's lodging, and even pay for it sometimes with my harmonica playing. We'd all sit around the parlor and play and talk. When I left, the whole family would stand on the front porch waving and calling to me to come back sometime. You can't travel like that now. After the hazards of the Depression too many persons are bitter and suspicious. So many families are on relief you're like to be taken for a WPA snooper sent out by the government to see if the families deserve their $23 a month."

The Second World War accelerated the transformation of American life. By the time the war ended, the United States had emerged as a world power, eager to focus its attention on international rather than local issues; Benton's rural America had largely vanished.

During and just after the war years, Benton lost his two major allies in the artistic world. Early in 1942, Grant Wood died of liver cancer, probably caused by his heavy drinking; in 1946, John Steuart Curry died of a stroke brought on by high blood

Thomas Hart Benton, After Many Springs, egg tempera and oil on masonite, 1945. Benton often used a foreground element to comment on what occurs in the far distance. Here a rusting revolver and a human skull, left over from a battle or a suicide, hint at the hardships of the farmer's life and comment on the futility of human existence. The bitter mood of the painting doubtless reflects the artist's revulsion over the carnage of World War II. •

Thomas Hart Benton, Water-boy, tempera with oil glazes on canvas mounted on plywood, 1946. •

pressure. Curry had been deeply depressed for some time because of the public's hostile response to his murals for the Kansas State Capitol in Topeka.

In May 1946, the noted art historian Horst Janson published a violent attack on Regionalism in *The Magazine of Art*. He began by stating: "The movement is essentially anti-artistic in its aims and character." Going further, he maintained that it was essentially Fascist in outlook: "Since the regionalists profess to be so suspicious of any alien influence, it is unfortunate that their own views should bear an embarrassing resemblance to certain European ideologies. These, to be sure, are not the product of the much hated French: their home is on the other side of the Rhine." In his view, Regionalism had been "nourished by some of the fundamental ills of our society—that same ills that, in more virulent form, produced National Socialism in Germany."

Not content with casting sweeping general aspersions of Babbittry and fascism, Janson slipped in a number of sarcastic personal digs. Speaking of Benton, he wrote unkindly: "He seems to go through life in constant fear of being called 'Shorty,' a condition not unfamiliar to psychologists." The violence of this attack is matched by no other essay in the canon of Janson's writings and undoubtedly reflects a personal animosity toward Grant Wood, who had schemed to have him fired from the University of Iowa after he took his class on a field trip to see a Picasso show in Chicago.

As if to further rub Benton's nose in the dirt, *Look* magazine published in 1948 a list of the "ten best painters in America today," based on a poll of museum directors and critics across the country. John Marin, the painter whom Stieglitz most vigorously promoted, was awarded first place; Stuart Davis was listed fourth. Thomas Hart Benton was not mentioned.

In April 1951, in conjunction with an exhibition of work by contemporary artists, Benton took the stage at the University of Illinois to debate with "my old friend, Mr. Davis" the question "Does Modern Art Make Sense?" Davis, looking plump and relaxed, answered the questions deftly in his tough, gravelly voice. The Hitler-Stalin pact had tarnished his love affair with Marxism, and he had largely abandoned political activity, but he was still a vigorous advocate of modernist art. Public opinion had begun to swing in his favor, and he was producing the best paintings of his career. Benton, on the other hand, found himself on the defensive and was going through an artistic dry spell. Alan Weller, who curated the exhibition, recalls that he looked worn and tired, and that many of the questions from the audience were loaded against him, in a fashion similar to the old trick question "How often do you beat your wife?" For example, one man asked Benton: "Why should the contemporary artist appeal to the lowest common denominator of his audience, as you do, rather than attempt to raise the general aesthetic response?"

In the spring of 1952, Benton's mother died, after a series of strokes. Mildred, her youngest child, did most the work of caring for her at the end. "I think that in a way it was a great relief to him," she comments. "If she had died as a younger woman the relief would have come earlier." Benton himself suffered a severe heart attack a few months before his mother's death, in January 1952. For a while it looked as if he would depart from the struggle, like his friends John Curry and Grant Wood.

A month before his heart attack, Benton publicly confessed that the Regionalist movement was over. In December 1951, in the *Saturday Review of Literature*, he published a sad account of the last days of his two fellow Regionalists: "By the time we moved over into the Forties, both Wood and Curry were in a pretty bad way physically and even psychologically. They had their good moments, but these seemed to be rare and shortlived. In the end, what with worry over weighty debts and artistic self-doubts, Wood came to the strange idea of changing his identity. He was a man of many curious and illusory fancies; when I went to see him in 1942, as he lay dying of a liver cancer in an Iowa hospital, he told me that when he got well he was going to

321

change his name, go where nobody knew him, and start all over again with a new style of painting. This was very uncanny because I'm quite sure he knew quite well he would never come out of the hospital alive. It was as if he wanted to destroy what was in him and become an empty soul before he went out into the emptiness of death. So far as I know, Grant had no God to whom he could offer a soul with memories.

"John Curry died slowly in 1946, after operations for high blood pressure and a general physical failure had taken his big body to pieces little by little. He made a visit to Martha's Vineyard the autumn before he died. Sitting before the fire on a cold grey day when a nor'-easter was building up seas outside, I tried to bolster his failing spirits.

" 'John,' I ventured, 'you must feel pretty good now, after all your struggles, to know that you have come to a permanent place in American art. It's a long way from a Kansas farm to fame like yours.'

" 'I don't know about that,' he replied, 'Maybe I'd have done better to stay on the farm. No one seems interested in my pictures. Nobody thinks I can paint. If I *am* any good, I lived at the wrong time.' "

The Break with Reeves Lewenthal

Although his paintings were falling increasingly out of step with the art world, Benton prospered through the 1940s, thanks to the entrepreneurial genius of his dealer. In 1947, however, just at the time when Regionalism began to fall out of favor, Benton broke off his association with Reeves Lewenthal and his gallery.

The event that triggered this break was curiously trivial. The Scruggs-Vandervoort-Barney department store in St. Louis commissioned a series of paintings of Missouri, and Lewenthal put together a list of artists for the project that included no one resident in the state except for Benton. Benton resigned from the gallery in protest, even though Lewenthal revised his list to include Fred Shane and several other Missouri artists. In fact, the Scruggs commission seems to have been simply an excuse for Benton to clear out. The real motive for his departure was his dissatisfaction with the increasingly commercial nature of Lewenthal's sales strategy.

Lewenthal had been an innovator in devising lucrative schemes that blurred the boundaries between high and popular art and expanded the support of art to new markets. His gallery began as a publisher of original prints by American artists. He called the venture Associated American Artists, but it was not a true association, since the artists played no role in the management. Lewenthal sold the prints he published for extremely low sums (in the first catalogue, in 1935, they were priced at five dollars each) and marketed them in department stores and by mail order, advertising in popular magazines. In short, he aimed his sales pitch at the middle class.

Lewenthal paid his artists two hundred dollars per edition of one hundred to two hundred fifty prints, with a bonus if the edition sold out. Modest as this sum sounds today, it represented a significant increase over what artists had been earning when they attempted to publish prints on their own. Throughout the 1930s and early '40s, Benton received a steady income from the sale of his prints. He was undoubtedly pleased that this income came from a democratic venture, which made art affordable for almost everybody.

In 1939, as has been noted, Lewenthal expanded his gallery to include paintings. As with prints, he was not content to limit himself to the selling strategies of the past. He sought a broader market, this time by trying to forge connections with corporate America. He arranged for commissions from Hollywood moguls, such as the one for Benton and other artists to paint a scene from *The Long Voyage Home*. He sold Benton's *Year of Peril* series to Abbott Laboratories, to be used in connection with their patriotic war campaign. Most insidiously, he tried to interest his painters in advertising, turning them into servants of American industry. In the early 1940s, he

arranged for Benton to execute a series of paintings for the tobacco industry, and Benton, eager to reach out to the broadest possible audience, threw himself enthusiastically into the scheme.

One would have expected a Regionalist such as Benton to prove adept at advertising; after all, his art dealt with the imagery of popular culture. But in fact, he found the whole tobacco enterprise exasperating. He submitted some sketches of black people working in the cotton fields of Georgia, only to be told that American blacks would raise protests if he depicted blacks as field hands, whereas American whites would object if he showed them as well dressed. Frustrated, he shifted the locale to North Carolina and sketched a hillbilly farmer sorting tobacco with his daughter. This was better, he was informed, but the girl was not pretty enough. To satisfy this complaint, he replaced the hillbilly girl with the pretty young daughter of a neighbor. But this was not quite right either, although everyone agreed that the finished painting, *Tobacco Sorters*, was one of his most technically polished works. The girl was too skinny. "Everything about tobacco must look healthy," he was advised.

Unwilling to compromise further, Benton decided to bypass the admen and appeal directly to the president of the American Tobacco Company, George Washington Hill. Perhaps, with Hill's intervention, the painting could be used without change. Hill received him cordially, chatted about river floating and fishing, and seemed most sympathetic to his tale of woe. "Why, Mr. Hill," Benton insisted, convinced that he was about to win his case and get his painting accepted for the ad campaign, "this picture is marketable for itself. Anybody would buy it as a straight work of art."

"How do you know that?" Hill inquired.

"Why, I'd buy it myself!" Benton burst out with conviction.

"Well, then, Mr. Benton," Hill responded, looking him directly in the eye, "I'll just sell it to you. It's yours."

To save the remainder of his contract and to show that his word was good, Benton had to pay up—to the tune of three thousand dollars.

Thomas Hart Benton, Tobacco Sorters, *egg tempera and oil on canvas mounted on panel, 1944.* •

Thomas Hart Benton, The Oboe Player, *oil on canvas mounted on cradled panel, 1951. One of Benton's most sympathetic late portraits showed his son's music teacher, a member of the Boston Symphony.* •

Thomas Hart Benton, Achelous and Hercules, *egg tempera and oil on canvas mounted on panel, 1947.* •

In 1951, when Benton wrote his *Saturday Review* essay on the demise of Regionalism, he placed the chief blame for its collapse not on the art critics but on American advertising, which had trained the public to distrust "realistic art." "One of the best reasons," he wrote, "for the persistence of Parisian modernism in artistic and intellectualist circles in the United States today lies, I believe, in the retreat it provides from the picture horrors of the advertising trade. . . . It is perhaps questionable whether any serious publicly directed art of a realistic nature can permanently sustain itself in America as long as the advertising trade in its present form exists."

Whatever the abstract merits of his case, Benton's break with Lewenthal made his financial situation extremely precarious. He had no New York dealer, no effective way

Thomas Hart Benton, Trading at Westport Landing (Old Kansas City), *egg tempera and oil on canvas mounted on panel, 1956. The first of a series of historical murals.* •

of promoting his work. The market for his paintings pretty much dried up, except for a few supporters in Kansas City. He had no one to distribute his new lithographs. His income suddenly dropped off to almost nothing. A year or so after the break, he and Fred Shane were having a drink together in the Benton home in Kansas City. "Fred, I'm scared shitless," Tom commented. Shane was astonished, for it was the first time he had ever heard his friend voice any fear.

The 1950s

Benton didn't die of his heart attack; but in the years around 1950, he began an artistic retreat: a retreat into the wilderness and into the past.

Because of the controversy over the Jefferson City project, it took more than a decade for him to get another mural commission. He finally received one in 1947, from his friend Lester Siegel, the proprietor of Harzfeld's, a women's clothing store in Kansas City. Even Siegel apparently had some qualms, for when he awarded the project to Benton, he warned: "Tom, I'm not going to start interfering with what you paint for my store, but for God's sake, try to let me stay in business." Obligingly, Benton avoided controversial political or social imagery and turned to classical mythology, presenting it, as he later explained, "without introducing any naked female backsides or frontsides."

The subject he chose, *Achelous and Hercules,* showed Hercules wrestling with a bull and breaking off a horn, which became a cornucopia. According to Bulfinch's *Mythology,* the unruly bull in the Greek myth symbolized a river, which provided irrigation but often overflowed in dangerous floods. Benton intended a parallel with Kansas City, whose prosperity depended on the flood-prone Missouri.

Such classical themes, of course, were common in turn-of-the-century mural painting, such as those Benton encountered as a boy at the Library of Congress. In the 1940s, they were undergoing a revival, thanks to a new interest in the relationship between myths and the unconscious. The surrealists often dealt with mythical subjects, and Picasso made innumerable renditions of the Minotaur. In the Harzfeld mural, Benton seems to have responded directly to the modernist challenge and sought to grow beyond the limits of Midwestern subject matter. This experiment with mythology, while intriguing, was only a qualified success. The subject matter is too esoteric to understand without a crib sheet. The effect is decorative but bland; Benton's heart was not in it.

In his subsequent murals, Benton gave up the attempt to respond to what was happening in the art world and returned to historical themes. In 1955 he painted *Old Kansas City* (or *Trading at Westport Landing*) for the exclusive River Club, located on the exact site of Lewis and Clark's encampment. A year later, the New York Power Authority commissioned a large mural of Jacques Cartier and the Indians of the Great Lakes for a huge hydroelectric dam in Massena, New York. No sooner was that completed than he undertook two murals simultaneously: one for the New York Power Authority at Niagara Falls and the other for the Truman Library in Independence, Missouri. Despite a crippling attack of bursitis, he completed both of these in the spring of 1961. In 1972 he painted a mural of *Turn of the Century Joplin*, showing himself in the center as a seventeen-year-old newspaper draftsman. "After I took the lines out of my face," he ruefully noted, "there wasn't much left." These successive murals provided the bulk of his income and largely freed him from depending on the sale of easel paintings.

Unlike his mural programs of the 1930s, Benton's later works did not form a three-dimensional surrounding. Placed on a single wall, they functioned essentially like large easel paintings. Indeed, with the exception of the Truman mural, which was painted directly on the wall, they *were* large easel paintings, executed in Benton's studio and transported to the final site. Also unlike the cycles of the 1930s, these later works presented undiluted patriotism, without undercurrents of cynicism or social commentary.

With the exception of the Joplin mural, the late works all presented historical reconstructions rather than events Benton himself had experienced. He undertook impressive historical research. For the Cartier mural, he limped through Cartier's *Relation* in the original old French (with the help of a modern English translation), located old costumes and tools, and even traced the Seneca Indian tribe Cartier en-

Thomas Hart Benton on the Buffalo River. At the age of eighty-one, Benton and his friend Harold Hedges ran through a section of unusually rough water on the Buffalo River, which was swollen from spring rains. Benton's canoe was the only one in the party that did not capsize.

Thomas Hart Benton, Independence and the Opening of the West, *Truman Library, Independence, Missouri, acrylic polymer on linen mounted on panel, 1959–62. Benton's most ambitious late mural was this design for the Truman Library. It was featured on a United States postage stamp in 1971.*

countered to the Oklahoma reservation in which it had been resettled, so that he could represent the right physical type of Indian. As he commented to his sister Mildred: "With Indians, if you place one bead on a moccasin wrong, somebody will let you know." The Truman mural represents his greatest technical tour de force in the field of history painting: literally thousands of objects, each carefully researched, are assembled into a flowing, organized composition.

Harry Truman once termed Benton "the best damned painter in America." Art critics, however, for the most part have not been kind toward his later work. Professor Marilyn Stokstad, for example, condemned the "bland idealization" of the Truman Library mural, which she described as "an exquisitely painted decoration, a thousand-piece interlocking jigsaw puzzle." Hilton Kramer castigated the "sickly sweetness" of these later paintings and declared that their textures resemble marzipan.

Benton himself came to realize that he was on his way to becoming "just another sober and respectable elder, not substantially different from the kind I had so often laughed at." Thanks to this new respectability, however, his local popularity reached new heights. In 1962, in an unprecedented gesture, Neosho staged a lavish homecoming in Benton's honor. Former President Truman accompanied him on the train down to his hometown and insisted that Benton disembark first. "This is your day. Go and take it!" he said, and poked Benton off the train.

During these late years, Benton concentrated increasingly on the natural landscape. Nearly every spring, right up to the year of his death, he took a float trip in southwest Missouri or northwest Arkansas. These excursions inspired a number of idyllic landscapes, such as *Cave Spring,* which shows his friend Lyman Field relaxing on the bank of the Current River. In 1948 he took a trip west to New Mexico, Utah, and Wyoming, and from then on, the wilderness of the Far West began to replace the Middle West and the South as the chief location of his paintings. His investigation of the Western landscape culminated in the early 1960s in two large and ambitious mountain paintings, *The Sheepherder,* a view of the Tetons in Wyoming, and *Trail Riders,* which shows Mount Assiniboine in the Canadian Rockies, where he went on a horseback trip with Lyman Field. In these mountain scenes, human activity is dwarfed and almost swallowed up by the grandeur of the landscape.

Thomas Hart Benton, Cave
Spring, *polymer tempera on canvas mounted on panel,* 1963. •

Thomas Hart Benton, Jessie
with Guitar, *egg tempera and oil
on canvas mounted on panel,*
1956. •

Thomas Hart Benton, Butterfly Chaser, *egg tempera and oil on canvas mounted on panel, 1951. In a composition of unusuallly complex visual rhythms, Benton showed his daughter, Jessie, chasing butterflies. He gave the painting to her on her twelfth birthday.* •

In keeping with the increasingly private character of his art, Benton also produced a number of paintings of his intimate surroundings. *Picnic* of 1952, for example, shows a family gathering on Martha's Vineyard, with his friends Fred and Diana James and Henry and Peggy Scott. Whenever his daughter, Jessie, had a birthday, he gave her a canvas painted for the occasion. For her fourth birthday, the subject was four flowers; for her eleventh, an easel and eleven brushes; for her twelfth, twelve seashells; and for her thirteenth, thirteen pearls. Two of his finest paintings were executed for this "birthday" series: *Butterfly Chaser* of 1951, which shows Jessie chasing a butterfly in the distance, and *Jessie with Guitar* of 1956. Benton once commented that Jessie would soon have the largest and most valuable collection of his work. "But there's this disadvantage," he added. "She'll never be able to lie about her age."

Long after the point at which most men retire, Benton continued to work long hours. Every day, seven days a week, without fail, he went out early in the morning to his studio, and except for a brief break for lunch, stayed there until the light began to

Thomas Hart Benton, Trail Riders, *polymer tempera on canvas, 1964–65. A view of Mount Assiniboine, painted after a riding trip with Lyman Field in the Canadian Rockies.* •

fade. The folksinger Burl Ives notes that Benton carefully controlled his life so that his mind would not be distracted from his work. Every evening, so he told Ives, he would read *The Arabian Nights*—the book his father had forbidden him when he was a child. "We were talking about sleep, for some reason," Ives recalls. " 'Well,' he said, 'I'll tell you the way I go to sleep.' He said, 'I have a beautiful edition of the thousand and one tales of *The Arabian Nights*. I read a chapter every night. Then I go to sleep. It leaves my mind full of color and excitement and a beautiful world so that my mind stays within that condition. When I get up in the morning, I'm ready to go.' He added, 'I read it through and through. When I get through a thousand and one nights, I start back to number one.' "

Mildred recalls that Benton could be "drunk as a coot" in the evening but was always up at five o'clock the next morning, looking fresh and cheerful as a baby. "He never had any hangover. I don't know why this was. I have never seen anybody else who was always without a hangover. I've known quite a few heavy drinkers."

His former colleague at the Art Institute, Vincent Campanella, has suggested that Benton's work decayed after his return to Missouri, as he retreated from the art world into his own private world. "But the dedication to his craft is something honorable," Campanella adds. "To me, it's inspiring. He worked at his business. By craft I mean the business of putting on paint, designing the picture, completing the picture. It was a day-to-day job, which people don't understand. They think it's some emotional thing that comes out of the sky."

"I have no young apprentice artist," Benton told Edward R. Murrow on "Person-to-Person" in 1959, just before his seventieth birthday. "The young artists these days have been taught in the schools that their own individual souls are so important that they might damage them if they come and help an old fellow like me, an old-fashioned painter. That's the great trouble with modern teaching. Everybody has too much of a soul."

"Jack the Dripper"

"Even the most emotional color splashing calls into play very special forms of knowledge."—Thomas Hart Benton, "Form and the Subject," 1924

By a curious irony, the leading figure in the new Abstract Expressionist movement, which overshadowed Regionalism, was Benton's former student Jackson Pollock. Although Pollock's long relationship with Benton is well documented, the supporters of both men have preferred not to explore the artistic connections between them. Such a comparison raises troubling questions of artistic value. Benton communicated through representational form, in a manner derived from the old masters. The narrative quality of his paintings makes them accessible to a broad spectrum of the general public; but many New York critics have condemned them as mere illustration—or worse. Pollock, on the other hand, abandoned representation and pushed painting to the extreme outer limits of formal order and intelligibility. He became the darling of the New York art world; but to much of the general public, his work seemed meaningless—a case of the emperor with no clothes. Thomas Craven, not one to mince words, once declared of Pollock's work: "All Pollock does is drink a gallon of paint, stand on a ladder and urinate."

Yet the strong tie between the two men is inescapably evident. Pollock received his only formal art training from Benton and lived in close proximity to the Bentons for six years, modeling himself in every way on Tom and becoming infatuated with Rita. It is not too much to say that every element of Pollock's mature work that was significant and original, that was more than a second-rate imitation of European modernism, can in some way be traced back to Benton's influence.

In the early thirties, Jackson Pollock was virtually a member of the Benton family, and in 1934 he lived with them year-round, spending the summer months at their place in Chilmark. With Benton's help, he converted the chicken coop behind the house to a sleeping area, which became known as "Jack's Shack." He helped the family with simple chores, painting the trim on the house and weeding the garden, went swimming and sailing with T.P., and also painted a number of small landscapes of Menemsha Pond, in swirling rhythms reminiscent of Ryder. "I am inclined to believe," Benton later wrote, "that he was happier during his Martha's Vineyard visits than in any other time in his life. Contented maybe is a better word."

Because Pollock was extremely poor, Rita taught him to decorate ceramics, which he was able to sell for modest sums. In the fall of 1934, she opened a small display area in the basement of the Ferargil Galleries, where she sold Pollock's paintings and ceramics, along with the work of other impoverished Benton students. On one occasion, Pollock exchanged a painting for a suit of clothes.

In retrospect, the enormous attention that Benton gave to Pollock seems odd, for outwardly he was among his least promising pupils. As Benton once commented: "Jack Pollock never learned to draw. He never could grasp anything that depended on logical connections, like anatomy or perspective. He was the most unintellectual man who ever lived. That doesn't mean he wasn't intelligent." Pollock could never locate a single outline but created webs of lines. His gift was for overall compositional rhythm. The cartoonist Whitney Darrow, Jr., recalls that, like Benton, Pollock made clay models of his designs, which he would paint in black and white, "swirling things with interesting curves and forces."

Pollock remained close to the Bentons until 1935, when they moved to Kansas City. After they left, he fell into a deep depression. "He was truly a lost soul," Pollock's high school friend Manuel Tolegian wrote to Benton many years later. "When you and Rita left New York, he took to heavy drinking, even spoke to me of suicide a number of times."

Dan James remembers that in 1935, when he moved from Kansas City to New York, Benton told him to look up the Pollock brothers, who had moved into his old apartment on Eighth Avenue. It was a time of transition for Pollock: "Jackson Pollock . . . was very ambiguous in his feelings about Tom and was deeply attached to Rita. Tom Benton had started Jackson painting. But there came a time—it was just about the time I was in New York, in '36 and '37—when Jackson was breaking out of this chrysalis. He was torturing the Benton shapes beyond, much beyond, anything that Benton did to them. It was a time when Jackson was terribly unsure of himself. He was destroying one lithographic stone after another. He was working on the Arts Projects. He was involved in all the Artists Union strikes at the time. Between strikes he would get drunk and go out and fight cops. He was a very strong, powerful guy, and he could usually beat one cop, but there would always be two. So poor old Jackson would be in and out of jail a good deal, beaten up. He hated his own work.

"His younger brother—who called himself Sandy McCoy so there wouldn't be too many Pollocks in the art world—really mothered him, and Sandy's wife did. They looked after him. On very slight evidence, it seemed to me at that time, they felt he was going to be the great artist of the family, and they were really pushing him along. I have somewhere an old lithograph of Jackson's which is much worse than one of Sandy's. It was caught between two things. He was busy destroying his stuff until Lee Krasner came into his life."

During this period of separation from the Bentons, Pollock's drinking problem became increasingly noticeable. On July 21, 1937, for example, he made his last visit to Martha's Vineyard. He took the ferry to Oak Bluffs and purchased a bottle of gin to give to Tom as a present. Since the Bentons had no phone, he called the Chilmark general store to leave a message that he had arrived. After waiting around for an hour or so, he got bored, opened up the bottle of gin, and drank it. He then used his last bit of cash to rent a bicycle, and wobbled down the main street. Every time he saw a group of girls crossing the street he headed after them, yelling like a banshee. As the gin did its work, he grew more and more unsteady, and finally he lost his balance and fell off, cutting his face. By the time the Bentons arrived, the police had arrested him. The next morning, Tom paid the ten-dollar fine and released Jack from jail.

Pollock's drinking had become even worse by the next winter, when he took a leave from the Federal Arts Project to spend Christmas with the Bentons in Kansas City. One morning, he returned home in such bad shape that Rita took him to a doctor. At a New Year's Eve party, he drank a great deal, broke up some furniture, and locked Fred Shane in an upstairs bathroom. "He began escaping with alcohol quite early," Benton later wrote, "though my wife and I did not recognize this as a disease until he visited us in Kansas City."

This was the last time that Pollock stayed with the Bentons. He was unable to obtain leave from the Federal Arts Project to accompany Benton on a six-week sketching trip that summer; and he was becoming increasingly incapacitated. By June 1938, he had been institutionalized for alcoholism in the Bloomingdale Hospital.

Pollock and Benton saw each other for the last time in the spring of 1944, when Benton came to New York on business and visited Pollock's studio. They had not met for several years, although they had followed each other's careers in the art magazines.

It proved an awkward encounter, for Pollock knew that Benton did not approve of his recent work, despite his efforts to speak politely of it. Nonetheless, in October 1947, when Pollock applied for a Guggenheim grant, he asked Benton to write a letter of recommendation. Benton did so, describing him as "Very much an artist. In my opinion one of the few original painters to come up in the last 10 years."

By that time, Pollock's work was much discussed in the art world. Two years later, on August 8, 1949, *Life* ran a feature story on him, and he gained national attention. There was only one precedent in American art for such a rapid rise to national fame; that of his teacher, Thomas Hart Benton, after he was featured on the cover of *Time*.

Despite his public repudiation of Benton (which he was probably pushed into by his wife, Lee Krasner), Pollock continued to call the Bentons right up to a few days before his death, asking for support and reassurance. Mildred Small comments: "I don't know that there was any break. . . . Jack used to call Tom—in the middle of the night it always was; he didn't think what time it might be—asking, really begging, for Tom's approval. Tom never gave it. He said, 'Jack, it's all right, whatever you want to do. . . . It's successful, you're successful, don't bother yourself about it. It's all right.' Then he'd hand the telephone to Rita and let her cut him off." Bill McKim remembers several occasions when Pollock called very late. Tom and Rita would be ready to turn in, so they'd hand the phone to Bill. "It was just like listening to any drunk," he recalls.

On a warm summer afternoon in August 1956, as Benton sat on the steps of his Martha's Vineyard cottage, two men came walking up the driveway to deliver some bad news. One was his former student Herman Cherry; the other, whom he had never

Thomas Hart Benton, Poker Night *(scene from* A Streetcar Named Desire*), egg tempera and oil on canvas mounted on panel, 1948. Benton painted the original theatrical cast of* A Streetcar Named Desire *on commission from Louis B. Mayer as a surprise Christmas gift for his daughter, Irene Selznick.* Look *magazine wanted to photograph the cast of* Streetcar *posed like the painting, but Jessica Tandy refused. She objected that Benton had painted from the standpoint of Stanley, the male protagonist, rather than of Blanche, the female victim. "I share your admiration for Benton as a painter," she wrote to Tennessee Williams, who had urged her to pose. "But in this painting he has chosen to paint, it seems to me, the Stanley side of the picture. . . . There has always been a part of the audience who obviously expects a sexy, salacious play. I don't want to do anything which will lead future audiences to think they are going to see sex in the raw, as it were."* •

met, was the Abstract Expressionist Willem de Kooning. Cherry reported that Jackson Pollock had been killed the previous evening in an automobile accident. He tried to persuade Benton to fly down with them to the funeral, but Benton was too upset to do so. "He said he just couldn't take it," Cherry recalls. "Rita, I remember, opened a drawer, and it was filled with Pollock clippings and reproductions. They saved *everything*."

Benton always refused to speak out against the work of his former pupil. Once, when pressed to do so, he commented loyally: "Jack never made a painting that wasn't beautiful." Privately, he was undoubtedly hurt by his student's great success. The painter Nene Schardt, who knew them both, has observed: "Tom never reconciled himself to their break. That father/son relationship . . . made it traumatic for Benton. He never quite understood or accepted it."

Pollock was less circumspect than his teacher. Once he had developed his distinctive drip technique, he noisily repudiated Benton's influence. "Benton was important to me as something to react against," he declared; and he once commented that Benton "had come face to face with Michelangelo . . . and lost." Privately, Pollock seems to have conceived himself as the figure who supplanted Benton and deposed him as the leader of American art. Dr. Raphael Gribitz recalls that when he urged Pollock to go to Paris, Pollock replied: "It's here. It's not in Paris. It used to be with Benton, but now it's with me."

For all his struggles to break free, the key elements of Pollock's artistic persona can be traced back to Benton: his hard drinking, his sometimes comical overassertions of his masculine identity, his chauvinistic attitude toward women, his anti-European stance, and his identification with the American West and the cowboy. As with Benton, much of this identity did not represent actual realities but was a form of theater. Pollock, for example, made much of the fact that he was born in Cody, Wyoming, but never volunteered that he left the place at the age of three and grew up in suburban California. Pollock the "cowboy" never learned to ride a horse.

Unlike Benton, Pollock repudiated representation and sought to give expression to the unconscious rather than the rational mind. After his "rejection" of the representational style of Benton, he was influenced by a series of other artists: the Mexican muralists (particularly Orozco and Siqueiros rather than Rivera) and, later on, Picasso and the Surrealists. These influences were undoubtedly significant, but none of them greatly affected his notions of pictorial structure; their effect was to loosen his technique and to make his pictorial style more gestural. Significantly, Pollock never developed a grasp of Picasso's early Cubist work but was influenced by the free shapes of his paintings of the late thirties and early forties, such as *Night Fishing at Antibes*. The underlying structural principles of Pollock's work remained those that had been drilled into him by Benton, through years of repetition and study.

Benton's principles of formal organization have already been discussed, and as has been noted, Pollock's fundamental principles of order, of rhythmic movement, of gestural rhythm, of swirling shapes arranged around invisible poles, can all be traced back to Benton's articles and teachings concerning the organization of form. From Benton, Pollock learned the expressive power of size. His interest in creating wall-size compositions, rather than easel paintings, obviously reflects Benton's interest in the mural.

A distinctive feature of Pollock's paintings is their absence of strong visual direction. This is related to his practice of painting them on the ground and working on them from all sides. Benton made many compositions of this type in the decorative sphere—for example, for rugs and tiles—during the 1920s. Pollock, however, pushed these principles toward disorder. As Benton once observed: "The fully developed Pollock rhythms are open and suggest continuous expansion. There is no logical end to Pollock paintings. . . . The Pollock structures may defy the 'rules of art,' but they do correspond to the actual mechanics of human vision, which is also without closed peripheries. Jack Pollock's work represents, not the objects we experience in the act of seeing, but the *way* we see them, in continuing, unending shifts of focus."

Many of Pollock's specific artistic devices and interests can be traced back to Benton. His first use of the drip technique occurred in glazing ceramics, which he learned to do from the Bentons. Reuben Kadish has noted: "On the Vineyard, Benton showed Jackson how to make drawings on ceramic plates and bowls. The way he did it was to take the glaze and pour it; though this was long before the drip work, maybe that's where Jackson got the idea."

Benton introduced Pollock to the work of Albert Pinkham Ryder, the mystic painter of seascapes, who Pollock once declared was the only American artist who interested him. Benton often praised Ryder and in the twenties made several nocturnal seascapes that recall Ryder's work. Thomas Craven devoted a chapter to Ryder in *Men of Art*—the only American artist to be included.

Pollock also learned from Benton about Navajo sand painting, which provided an inspiration for him at many levels. Like the Navajos, Pollock employed sand as a material, executed his paintings flat on the ground rather than tipped up on an easel, and aspired in his paintings to establish a mystical union with the forces of nature. He learned about this art form from a volume of Smithsonian Institution reports on the Navajos. Benton gave the book to the City and Country School, from which Pollock stole it.

Rather surprisingly, Pollock's interest in Jungian symbolism and "archetypes" again reflected the influence of Benton. He was introduced to Jungian ideas through Helen Marot, a close friend of Benton's. An editor of *The Dial,* Marot turned to psychology after she became disillusioned with Marxist efforts at social reform, and she worked on the Bollingen translation of Jung's collected works. She provided emotional support to Pollock until her death in June 1940 and was one of the first to believe that he possessed artistic genius. In 1939, when Pollock sought professional help for his alcoholism, he went to a Jungian psychotherapist, Joseph Henderson, a friend of Helen Marot's. Under Dr. Henderson's guidance, he produced a series of "psychoanalytic drawings" and learned the rudiments of Jungian terminology. When Dr. Henderson left for California, he referred Pollock to another Jungian analyst, Violet Staub de Laszlo, who had studied directly with Jung.

Interestingly, Pollock's involvement with Jungian ideas ended soon after he became involved with Lee Krasner, who felt threatened by Dr. de Laszlo's hold on her paramour. Krasner took Pollock to her own "healer," Elizabeth Hubbard, who treated him with various herbal remedies, including one put together with bird droppings. Undoubtedly, however, Pollock's exposure to psychotherapy had a lasting influence on his struggle to express the forces of the unconscious.

Benton outlived Jackson Pollock by nearly twenty years and witnessed his apotheosis as a major American master. Robert Wernick, who rafted down the Missouri River with Benton in 1965, noted that Pollock was repeatedly evoked. If Benton saw a particularly pleasing formation of lichen on a rock out in the Montana wilderness, he would say mischievously, "Just like Jack Pollock." While he always spoke warmly of Pollock, Benton clearly felt irked that his student had become famous by repudiating many of his own most cherished artistic principles.

At one point, he commented: "Lots of these abstract expressionists' works were made so carelessly that they're cracking and falling to pieces already. That's the trouble when you're just interested in pure expressing yourself, you don't give a damn what you're doing.

"And if you notice: The careers of abstract artists so often end in a kind of bitter emptiness. It's the emptiness of a person looking into himself all the time. But the objective world is always rich: there is always something round the next bend of the river."

Memories

"He had a wonderful gruffly voice," Jessie Benton recalls of her father. "He was very handsome. He had a very rich face and wonderful hair, black as could be. He was fifty years old when I was born, and I always thought he was in his twenties. Other people's fathers were always so old and kind of dried up, and he was so young and vibrant. When we went swimming I would ride on his shoulders. I was afraid of the cows, so someone always had to carry me. He taught me how to play baseball and ride bicycles. He was a very athletic, energetic man, so he was fun to be with.

"I think people have a view of him that he was very aggressive and spunky. But at home he wasn't like that. He was very quiet, very personal, very gentle, very fair. I don't know if the world knows that part of him. He liked to talk big, and he had millions of friends, but every day at home he was like silence. We had to be quiet, my brother and I, most of the time. The house was very still because he was very intense and he thought about things; and he thought about his paintings. Then in the evening he would kind of let that part of his life go and be very social.

"I used to love to go in that studio because of the smells of the paint. My father used to always whistle when he painted. Always. Constantly. It was rich being in there. I had my crayons and I used to sit on the floor and paint my pictures, which he would put up on the walls—if they were good.

"He didn't want people to think that he was complicated, that he was involved psychologically with things, which he was. He was a great reader. He read constantly. He also read in French. In the sixties, his favorite poem was 'Howl.' You know, he loved Allen Ginsberg. He loved all that kind of fresh . . . You know, like Henry Miller, for instance. He didn't like Henry very much, but he liked what Henry was doing with literature in the twenties and thirties and forties. He loved that. He loved new ideas.

"He was the most fair person. He felt that any effort with conviction was worth something, and he never criticized Picasso, for instance. He always had something good to say about him. But he wasn't into that kind of art. When he left Paris, he gave that all up. He believed in America. He believed in a spirit that was in the country, and he felt that the art should come from the country—not necessarily regionalistic but to be clear, like the American soul is, and articulate in a simple way; not abstract, but down-to-earth and real.

"He had plenty of demons. Who doesn't? Getting a word in edgewise might be one of the problems. He dominated a room, a group of people, a conversation. I think his own worst demon—this is deeply personal—was his inability to share his feelings with another person. I think he was frightened of human emotion. He came from a generation that felt that any kind of outside emotional showing was embarrassing.

"He had a thick skin. Criticism irritated him sometimes, but it didn't hurt him. He had an enormous sense of justice, my father; I can't say that enough. He felt that people had a right to criticize him. After all, he'd stuck himself out there in the middle of all this, and he expected it. I think what hurt my father the most, and he used to talk to me about it much, much later—not when we were kids—was loneliness. He said it was his great motivator. He said in his youth, most of his youth, until he was in his late fifties—up until then he was lonely.

"He would have something in mind for a painting, and sometimes it didn't work. He couldn't get it down on the canvas and he would be deeply depressed. Grumpy. Sometimes it would last for weeks, and sometimes, in terms of murals and things, if it

wasn't coming out right, it would be in terms of months. He would be deeply depressed. In despair.

"Controversy is stimulating, and he did like stimulants, you know. He loved to fight. He was a warrior. Sometimes he regretted things he said. Very deeply. A slow fuse and a spectacular temper. Yes, he lost his temper—oh, maybe I can remember four or five times. Never with the children, never with us. I said he had a thick skin, and he did, but there were certain people who would keep at it and keep at it and finally he would flip; and when he did, it was forever.

"I think he got better and better. I love his mountain pictures. He took aside many years to paint the mountains. He said it was the damnedest hardest thing he ever did—that mountains are impossible to paint. It took him years to finally paint a picture that he was satisfied with. He paid no attention to all those critics because he would get these things that he had to do. While they were still quibbling over *Persephone,* he was off in Wyoming trying to paint the Tetons for three, four, five years. He was always going off on sketching trips and going off here and there. He'd always come home. That's all you'd have to know was that he was coming home.

"My mother was something else; she was the Rock of Gibraltar. I don't think he or any of us would have survived without her. She was warm and friendly; she was an artist, too, and a dancer. She kept the family at one solid level so that we always had something to eat when we were poor. My father had absolutely no regard for money whatsoever. If he had it he spent it. And if he didn't have it, he didn't care.

"My grandmother did not speak to my mother because she was a foreigner and my grandmother was a snob. I thought my grandmother was fascinating. She lived right up the hill here, and I used to go visit her every morning. She would be covered with her diamonds and her black lace gowns, and every morning she would brush this long white hair that came down past her waist. It was very ritualistic, and of course I loved it. I would go up there and watch her brush out her hair.

"I have run into my father's critics all my life. I used to get angry, as a matter of fact, because people used to tell me that [his work is] no good. But also I've run into people who adore the paintings in a mystical way, even more than I do. I've lived with them all my life. I don't think I could live without them. They're my protection. They keep bad things away from me; I don't ever part with them; I carry them with me wherever I go.

"To the world, he was a little scrapper. To me, he was like a warrior and an innovator. He taught me all kinds of things. How to be fair, how to accept, how to accept other people's feelings. He was always for the underdog. He wasn't afraid of anything, and subsequently the house was full of all kinds of things and ideas and people.

"I think people should remember him as a man who put life into art. And art into life. I think he revitalized—he churned up something at the right time. I think he'll be remembered. I think the controversy will probably go on and on and on. But his paintings are alive, and they have no time. If a painting he did twenty years ago is still as vital thirty years from now—that is what he wanted to do."

The Sources of Country Music
In April 1973, just before Benton's eighty-fourth birthday, Mike Wallace interviewed him for *60 Minutes.*

Wallace: "Well, you still work?"

"Still work."

"You still walk around?"

"Yeah."

"Still do a little drinking?"

Thomas Hart Benton, The Sources of Country Music, *acrylic on canvas mounted on panel, 1975. Benton completed his last mural when he was eighty-five years old.*

"Yeah, still drinking. Not too much anymore, though."

"And you still can paint."

"Yeah, still paint. I think I paint better than ever."

"Do you hate getting old?"

"No, I feel good. I feel fine. I don't hate getting old. I don't even hate to die. I don't give a damn. I don't care."

"You mean, when your toes turn up?"

"That's it. That don't ever bother me. People say when you get old, you get to thinking about death. As the lawyers put it: 'in contemplation of death' that you make a move. I make no moves in contemplation of death."

Three months earlier, Benton had been approached by the cowboy singer Tex Ritter, who asked him to create a mural for the Country Music Hall of Fame in Nashville. While the two sipped Jack Daniel's together, they mused over an appropriate subject. "The sources of country music—that's it," Tom commented. "It should show the roots of the music—the sources—before there were records and stars." Over the next few months a contract was worked out, and in the fall of 1973, Benton began planning the painting; by December he had plotted the general composition.

At the same time, as background for his next big project, a mural for a suburban bank, he read up on the Dalton gang and their Coffeyville, Kansas, bank heist of 1892.

In late January 1974, when the board of the Country Music Foundation met to discuss Benton's sketches, they unanimously voted to dedicate the mural to Tex Ritter, who had died just a short while before. Soon afterward, Benton wrote to Bill Ivey, executive director of the Country Music Foundation: "I go for the idea that the mural should in some way be a tribute to Tex Ritter. Why don't we symbolize Tex in the cowboy singer?"

As usual, the artist constructed a clay model of the design and carried out painstaking research for every element and figure. Richie Guerin, a member of the commune in which Jessie Benton lives, recalls that Benton took care to have the musicians all striking the same chord, so that a musically trained viewer would recognize that they are playing in key. Not satisfied to use only friends and professional models, he took a trip out to Branson, Missouri, to locate some surviving country musicians. After searching a few days, he found several men who pleased him: Raymond Bruffet, who lived in a dilapidated cabin surrounded by junked cars; old Nick Clark, a left-handed

Thomas Hart Benton and Rita Benton.

fiddler; and Chick Allen, who performed percussion on the jawbone of a mule. "I guess I could use the face of an actor," Benton commented. "But sometimes what people do for a long time in their life—their occupations—shows in their faces. Or is suggested. That might be true in a musician. The emotions he has experienced might show. I don't know. I just have to see the face."

One of the elements that caused Benton most concern was the Wabash Cannonball, the train on which Casey Jones took his last ride, which he incorporated into the background to symbolize railroad music. The train serves as a harbinger of death in two famous railroad ballads, "Casey Jones" and "The Wabash Cannonball." As the latter song laments:

> Just listen to the jingle,
> The rumble and the roar
> Of the mighty rushing engine
> As she streams along the shore.
>
> The mighty rushing engine,
> Hear the bell and whistle call,
> As you rumble off to heaven
> On the Wabash Cannonball.

As late as December 1974, Benton was still trying to establish the exact appearance of the train. He asked his St. Louis friend Lyle S. Woodcock to help him out, and on December 19, Woodcock wrote back: "According to the Transport Museum records, and the Norfolk and Western Railroad (successor to the Illinois Central), Engine No. 382, the one driven by Casey Jones, was scrapped many years ago. The Museum of Transport in St. Louis has an engine which they say is identical to Engine No. 382. It is a 'Ten Wheeler' with a wooden cab, and is No. 635. It was a Missouri Pacific Engine, built by Baldwin Locomotive Co. in 1889."

Benton asked Woodcock to photograph the St. Louis train, and he based the engine in his painting on these snapshots. On January 18, 1975, he completed the mural, a considerable feat for a man of eighty-five, as it measured six by ten feet and contained seventeen nearly life-size figures. It seems to have displeased him, however, that he had painted the locomotive in the background from a secondhand source. On the afternoon after he completed the mural, he had drinks with his young friend John Callison and suggested that they drive to St. Louis together soon to look at the train.

But they never made the trip. After dinner that same evening, Benton walked out to his studio after dinner, to chew tobacco and look over his painting. He announced to Rita that if he was satisfied with how it looked, he was going to sign it.

At eight-thirty, the hour at which he usually returned to the house, he did not come back. Rita went out to the studio to fetch him and scold him for staying out so late. She found him lying dead on the floor with his spectacles on, directly in front of the Nashville mural. Stricken by a massive heart attack, he had fallen on his watch, which had stopped at the exact moment of his death: five minutes past seven o'clock. The mural, incidentally, remained unsigned.

Benton's closest friend, the lawyer Lyman Field, delivered the eulogy at the funeral. Benton's son, T.P., did not attend, but Creekmore Fath reports that the most poignant moment of the service came when Jessie sang her father's favorite hymn, "Amazing Grace," accompanied by a lone harmonica. In the weeks that followed, Rita found herself unable to face what she described in a letter to a friend as "the great emptiness without Tom." Joe Wershba of CBS recalls that when he phoned Rita with his condolences, she responded furiously: "He wasn't supposed to have died." "Oh, my mother—it was terrible," Jessie remembers. "She died three months later. She couldn't live without him."

Not long after Benton's death, a group of his friends formed the Benton Associates to keep his memory alive. Each year, they hold a party for his birthday at Kelly's Bar, the oldest structure in Kansas City, the place from which Francis Parkman set off on his journey over the Oregon Trail.

Summing up the achievement of Thomas Hart Benton is not easy, for he was an artist of different faces, whose work embodied some of the deepest conflicts of American culture. He was a politician's son who scorned politics yet struggled all his life to become a public figure. He was a sophisticate who pretended to be simple. He was a foe of abstract painting who made major contributions toward the mastery of abstract form. He was a rebel who fled from his Midwestern roots and then came back to celebrate them in his art. Above all, he was a painter of America and American life.

Although fifty years have now gone by since the battles of the 1930s, hostility toward his work remains as intense in some quarters as it was then. Hilton Kramer, for example, has declared: "I think Benton was an artist who got away with murder."

Karal Ann Marling has observed: "He constantly approaches the condition of the politician, the windbag, the professional windbag; and the lawyer, the professional nitpicker, the professional arguer, the professional persuader. That's inherent in everything he does."

"I think he was looking for the Chaplin audience," Dan James has commented. "He felt that he could set certain strings vibrating in America, among American people, that would give art the immediacy that perhaps it had in the Renaissance. Where it became a fighting thing; and when somebody finished something, the whole damned population would turn out to see it."

"Well, of course beauty is in the eye of the beholder," says Earl Bennett, "but he painted beauty. It could be an old farmer. It could be hogs. It could be an old beat-up steamboat. But he saw the beauty of, the need of these things. There isn't any beauty unless there are fulfilled needs; and there was a need for people that picked cotton, a need for people that went around doing minstrel shows. People needed that; and he was there; and he saw the beauty of it, and recorded it for us."

Benton lived three decades longer than the two other key members of the Regionalist movement, John Steuart Curry and Grant Wood. He lived to see his work pass entirely out of fashion as young critics and artists became entranced with abstract movements. Then, gradually, the tide began to turn. At the time of his death, although

Thomas Hart Benton, Wheat, oil on panel, 1967. This late painting showing full stalks of wheat standing beside two harvested rows resurrects Benton's subject matter of the 1940s but transforms it into a mythic reflection on life and death.

his work was still controversial, he was beginning to be enshrined as a classic. "Old age is a wonderful thing," Benton declared in 1972, at the dedication of the Joplin mural. "You outlive your enemies."

Despite the hostility of the critics, he managed to continue painting. As he wrote in *An Artist in America:* "I know there is no such thing as failure in the pursuit of art. Merely to survive in that pursuit is a success. Pictures may fail to please, movements may fail to survive, but the artist has his rewards anyway. He may lose his public and his market and still get full compensation for his efforts. Quite apart from the public values of art—those which give it significance in the social history of a people—the act of artistic creation has its own psychological payoff and a very considerable one. The rewards of art, for the artist himself, are concomitants of its practice. They lie in the life-heightening acuteness of his everyday occupational experience. The only way an artist can *personally* fail is to quit work."

With regard to the public significance of his painting, Benton saw his achievement as rooted in his understanding of American culture. "I have a sort of inner conviction," he wrote, "that for all the possible limitations of my mind and the disturbing effects of my processes, for all the contradicting struggles and failures I have gone through, I have come to something that is in the image of America and the American people of my time. This conviction is in me pretty deeply. My American image is made up of what I have come across, of what was 'there' in the time of my experience—no more, no less."

Thomas Hart Benton was a small man with a big name to live up to. Indeed, in the final summing up, the painter and his senatorial ancestor had much in common. Both were frequently involved in controversy. Both lost their jobs because they outspokenly expressed their views. Both enjoyed ridiculing East Coast ways and both, believing in the future of the Midwest, brought it to national attention. In many respects, Thomas Hart Benton the painter simply redirected the bombastic Midwestern Populist tradition of his family from politics to cultural affairs. Perhaps the most persuasive evidence of his success is that today, when one hears the name Thomas Hart Benton, one thinks not of the senator but of the artist.

Bibliography

For the benefit of scholars, a completely footnoted typescript of this manuscript has been placed in the Spencer Research Library of the Nelson-Atkins Museum of Art. In addition, the museum's Department of American Art has kept on file the working draft of this book (also footnoted), which is about twice as long as the final version. The draft contains many additional citations from Benton's letters and writings; fairly extensive quotations from the reviews of his exhibitions; additional information on some of the supplementary figures in the story; and occasional sidesweipes at the work of other scholars. Much of this extra material is tediously detailed; but some of it may well prove helpful to scholars who wish to explore some specialized aspect of Benton's work.

While working on this project we have compiled an extensive collection of materials relating to Benton. This includes a wide-ranging collection of articles concerning him, filed chronologically; a collection of his published and unpublished writings, including a fair number of items not previously listed; a chronological listing of exhibitions with their catalogues; files on individuals associated with Benton, such as Thomas Craven; and files on subjects of related interest, such as "Populism" or "Missouri Mules." At some point in the future we hope to publish a comprehensive annotated bibliography on Benton, perhaps accompanied by a chronology of his life. In the meantime, the collected materials are freely accessible to interested scholars, unless they are restricted by their original owner, as is the case with the materials from the Thomas Hart and Rita P. Benton Testamentary Trusts, United Missouri Bank of Kansas City, MO.

We are eager to expand our collection of materials and hope that anyone with information about Benton or his work will send it to the Thomas Hart Benton Project, Nelson-Atkins Museum of Art, 4525 Oak Street, Kansas City, MO 64111.

An extremely useful, although by no means complete, bibliographical guide to the literature on Benton and Regionalism is Mary Scholz Guedon's *Regionalist Art: Thomas Hart Benton, John Steuart Curry, and Grant Wood: A Guide to the Literature* (with a foreword by Karal Ann Marling), Metuchen, NJ, & London, Scarecrow Press, 1982. Matthew Baigell's monograph, discussed below, also contains a useful bibliography.

Benton's Principal Writings

I have drawn so extensively on Benton's memoirs and interviews that he might almost be considered a coauthor of this book. In fact, in many instances, particularly in the first three chapters, I have used Benton's own words and phrases without quotation marks or any other attribution. All full-sentence quotations, however, are indicated by quotation marks.

During his lifetime Benton published two autobiographies. *An Artist in America*, first issued in 1937 and updated in 1951, 1968, and 1983, provides an anecdotal account of his life, with particular attention to his travels around the United States. *An Artist in America* was originally published by Robert M. McBride; the fourth revised edition is now available from the University of Missouri Press, and page numbers in these notes refer to this latest edition. The book grew out of Benton's article "America's Yesterday: In the Ozark Mountains of Arkansas—Life and Customs on a Forgotten Frontier," which appeared in *Travel*, (62), July 1934, 7–11, 45–46.

An American in Art, Benton's second autobiography, published in 1969 by the University of Kansas Press, Lawrence, KS, describes his artistic development and techniques. In 1951 Benton published "American Regionalism: A Personal History of the Movement," *University of Kansas City Review*, (18) 1, Autumn 1951, 41–75. This was reprinted in 1969 as an addendum to *An American in Art*.

At the time of his death, Benton was at work on a third autobiography, *The Intimate Story*, which contains a great deal of highly personal material that he understandably left out of the earlier accounts. The project began with "Ali," a short note on his arrival as a young art student in Paris, which was published in *New Letters: A Continuation of the University Review*, University of Missouri, Kansas City, (38) 1, Fall 1971, 75–91. Encouraged by the favorable response to this, Benton then set out to write a complete autobiography. The most polished chapter is the one on his childhood, which survives in typescript. The other chapters, "Chicago," "Paris," and "The Thirties," survive in longhand. Although Benton never wrote up a chapter on his years in New York, he did compose several pages that outline, in somewhat fractured sentences, the major events of the teens. Apparently he also wrote a

chapter titled "The Twenties," for he alludes to it at various places in the surviving manuscript, but this chapter cannot be found among the papers in the Benton Trusts and may have been destroyed.

The Benton Trusts contains many of Benton's early letters sent home to his parents and siblings, written when he lived in Joplin, Missouri; Alton, Illinois; Chicago; Paris; and New York. While this correspondence does not mention many events recorded elsewhere, it helps establish a firm chronology and provides many delightful insights into Benton's personality as a young man. This correspondence ends when his mother moved to New York, although it picks up again during the months he spent in the Navy.

An important biographical source is a long interview between Benton and Paul Cummings, held on July 23 and 24, 1973, a 68-page transcript of which is in the Archives of American Art in Washington, DC. Cummings published an extensively edited version of this interview in *Artists in Their Own Words: Interviews by Paul Cummings*, New York, 1979, 25–46. Many of the most interesting sections of the interview, however, do not appear in the published version. Robert S. Gallagher also published an interview with Benton which contains much interesting material. See "An Artist in America," *American Heritage*, vol. 24, June 1973, 40–48, 90.

Creekmore Fath's *The Lithographs of Thomas Hart Benton*, Austin and London, 1st ed. 1969, 2nd ed. 1979, contains Benton's own comments on his lithographs and provides much useful information on the dates of his cross-country excursions. Benton's own *Benton Drawings: A Collection of Drawings by Thomas Hart Benton*, Columbia, MO, 1968, is less useful, for it contains few annotations, although it does reproduce drawings from all phases of Benton's career.

Matthew Baigell has edited *A Thomas Hart Benton Miscellany: Selections from His Published Opinions, 1916–1960*, Lawrence, KS, 1971. This contains twenty-five of Benton's most significant articles and statements.

Interviews

In this account I have drawn heavily on interviews conducted by Ken Burns during the creation of our PBS documentary on Benton. Complete transcripts of these interviews were made by Camilla Rockwell of Flor-

entine Films, and I have often used those that were not included in the final cut of the film. Copies of all these transcripts are on file in the Nelson-Atkins Museum of Art. The people interviewed were Matthew Baigell, art historian and biographer of Benton; Earl Bennett, student of Benton at the Kansas City Art Institute; Jessie Benton, daughter of the artist; John Callison, young friend and helper; Vincent Campanella, painter and colleague at the Kansas City Art Institute; Ann and Lee Constable, next-door neighbors; Richard Craven, son of Thomas Craven; Lyman Field, lawyer and personal friend; Edward Fry, art historian; Lloyd Goodrich, museum director and art historian; Pam Hoelzel, model; Burl Ives, drinking companion and friend; Dan James, writer, friend, and model for Benton; Hilton Kramer, hostile New York art critic; Sid Larson, painter and assistant on mural projects; Karal Ann Marling, art historian and expert on American mural painting; Bill McKim, student of Benton at the Kansas City Art Institute; Roger Medearis, student of Benton at the Kansas City Art Institute; Dorothy Miller, art historian associated with the Museum of Modern Art; George O'Maley, acquaintance of Benton; Eleanor Piacenza, second wife of Rita Benton's brother, Louis Piacenza; Santo Piacenza, Rita Benton's brother; Raphael Soyer, painter; Mildred Small, Benton's sister; Henry and Peggy Scott, friends of Benton both in Kansas City and on Martha's Vineyard; and Andrew Warren, the model for the figure of Johnnie in the Jefferson City mural.

I have held many informal interviews with Lyman Field, the Constables, Bill McKim, Duard Marshall (a pupil of Benton's), George O'Maley, Jessie Benton, and Santo and Eleanor Piacenza. I have also corresponded with Roger Medearis and with Jesse Charles O'Neill, who was the monitor in Benton's advanced painting class at the Kansas City Art Institute when Benton executed *Persephone*. Because this book focuses heavily on Benton's early years, I held a series of interviews with Mildred Small, during which I took notes that I have placed on file.

Previous Scholars

It is a pleasure to pay tribute to the efforts of previous writers on Benton, whose work has proved invaluable to me. The pioneer scholar of Benton's work is Professor Matthew

Baigell of Rutgers University, whose monograph *Thomas Hart Benton*, New York, 1974, remains the indispensable introduction to Benton's work. Because Benton was still alive when the book was written, his career is handled with careful tact. In partnership with Allen Kaufman, Baigell has also composed a provocative study of the leftist undercurrent in Benton's work: "The Missouri Murals: Another Look at Benton," *Art Journal*, (36) 4, Summer 1977, 314–321.

Karal Ann Marling has written a lively, fact-filled account of Benton's drawings: *Tom Benton and His Drawings: A Biographical Essay and a Collection of His Sketches, Studies, and Mural Cartoons*, Columbia, MO, 1985. I wrote a brief review of this in *The Winterthur Portfolio*, (23) 1, Spring 1988, 102–106. Marling has also written a somewhat florid but masterful study of Benton's first "Regionalist" canvas: "Thomas Hart Benton's *Boomtown*: Regionalism Redefined," in Jack Salzman, ed., *Prospects: The Annual of American Cultural Studies*, (6), New York, 1981, 73–137.

The oddest but one of the most informative books on Benton is Polly Burroughs, *Thomas Hart Benton: A Portrait*, Garden City, NY, 1981, a chatty account focusing largely on his association with Martha's Vineyard. On the positive side, this book presents an enormous amount of new material, much of it based on interviews with Benton and other old-timers on Martha's Vineyard. It also draws extensively from a cache of letters and sketches owned by Benton's sister, Mary Briggs, which Burroughs purchased from Mary's two children. On the negative side, the book contains many obvious and embarrassing errors, such as mistaking reviews of Benton's Whitney murals for reviews of his work at the New School. In a number of instances, such as the discussion of Rita Piacenza's arrival in the United States, the information is factually incorrect.

Wilma Yeo and Helen K. Cook, *Maverick with a Paintbrush: Thomas Hart Benton*, Garden City, NY, 1977, a children's book on Benton, draws on numerous interviews with the artist and presents a number of facts not recorded elsewhere.

Just as this manuscript was nearing completion, Richard Gruber submitted his doctoral dissertation at the University of Kansas, "Thomas Hart Benton: Teaching and Art Theory," April 1987. Despite the title, this account contains surprisingly little information on either Benton's teaching or art theory. It does, however, present a good account of his artistic development, based largely on materials in the Benton Trusts.

The Use of Dialogue

In the interests of readability I have standardized spelling and punctuation in all the quotations, except for a few rare instances where a misspelled name or word adds a significant nuance of meaning.

I have not made up any of the dialogue in this book. In the first three chapters (and occasionally later on), I have made use of Benton's reconstructions of conversations, mostly from *The Intimate Story*. Benton himself confessed in a marginal note that his memory of these conversations was by no means perfectly exact. Nonetheless, Benton had a remarkable ear for dialogue and was able in many cases to capture the speech patterns of his friends. Thus, for example, I have listened to several recordings of Stanton Macdonald-Wright; these demonstrate that Benton accurately captured the general flavor of his speech and remembered his characteristic tricks of phrasing. Some of the conversations Benton records were so memorable that it seems to me quite possible that he could remember them almost word for word, even many years later.

Even if they are not strictly accurate, I feel, as Benton did, that these conversations convey the flavor of artistic life in the period. It would be a false sort of pedantry to attempt to make them more "accurate" simply by transferring them to indirect discourse.

The remaining portions of dialogue come either from contemporary newspaper accounts or from the interviews for our documentary film. In presenting this material I have aimed for clarity and readability rather than a pedantic standard of scholarly accuracy. In transcribing the interviews from the film, for example, I have deleted "um" and other unnecessary words; in one or two cases I have added a noun, where the referent was unclear. In transcribing newspaper interviews, I have often omitted the reporter's question and presented Benton's answers as a continuous dialogue. I have sometimes changed the sequence of paragraphs to present a smoother flow of ideas.

Accuracy

Since a good portion of this text is based on information provided by Benton himself, it is natural to ask whether he was accurate as an informant. My own belief is that he usually was. Because of Benton's tendency to turn experience into art, he sometimes grew confused between the original event and his later transformation of it into a painting or a literary account. But on the whole, except for a few matters of dating or detail, I have accepted Benton's memories as accurate.

A careful reading of *The Intimate Story* suggests that in some portions Benton recorded events that were burned into his memory. In others he struggled to remember what occurred and in what sequence. In making use of Benton's testimony, I have relied in part on my own "hunches" about his accuracy, on the basis of the overall texture of the narrative. As often happens with events remembered many years later, Benton sometimes grew confused about the exact sequence of events. Thus, for example, he misdated the swimming accident that nearly killed him to the period before he studied in Chicago. Errors of this type, however, do not seem to me to invalidate the general accuracy of his record.

The chief motive for *The Intimate Story* seems to have been a desire to confront the embarrassments of his early life, such as the conflicts between his parents, the incident with Hud, and his affair with Jeanette. An impressive aspect of Benton's memoir is his consistent effort to deal sympathetically with figures who had hurt him or whom he disliked, such as Hud or Stuart Davis.

I think Benton did his best to be honest in his presentation of these key episodes; if evasiveness crept in, it was in his handling of subsidiary incidents. It seems amusing, for example, that Benton could work up the courage to describe the incident with Hud, but not to confess that it was through his mother, and not through his own initiative, that he finagled his way into the Navy. Benton's account of his family life, while mostly accurate, seems to have consistently softened his conflicts with his father and downplayed his mother's role. Mildred Small, who sided with her mother, has helped me supply a more balanced account.

Attempts at personal confession, of course, are always somewhat self-defeating. Benton's remarkable revelations naturally make us ask further questions, and make us wonder what additional information he may have withheld. Similarly, Benton's ability to evoke the personalities and motives of his friends and associates leaves us unsatisfied. We want to know more about them, and more about *his* motives for describing them as he did.

In *An Artist in America*, Benton sometimes seems to have added details to lend vividness to the story, although he did not actually remember them. Thus, for example, the text describes an adventure that took place at "Pete's Lunch," although he labeled the place "Jim's Lunch" in the accompanying illustration.

In describing his artistic battles of the thirties, Benton attempted to be fair-minded but often omitted significant points or indulged in unconscious exaggeration. His account of his dispute with Juliana Force is a singularly shocking instance of his untruthfulness, but he also undoubtedly exaggerated the hostile reception to his New School murals, blurring their reception with that of his later work. Fortunately, Benton's conflicts of the thirties are amply documented in the public record.

On artistic matters Benton seems to have been remarkably reliable. Unlike many artists, he does not seem to have attempted to redate his works; he never made any effort, for example, to date his Synchromist paintings back to his stay in Paris. Similarly, he never attempted to revamp the motives for his work to suit current art historical fashion. He always made it clear, for example, that his cubified figure drawings were based chiefly on the example of Luca Cambiaso rather than the Parisian Cubists. Benton's retrospective account of his artistic disputes with Stieglitz is fully supported by surviving letters. On occasion, particularly late in his life, Benton made errors of identification or dating—for instance, dating drawings made during his travels of 1926 to his trip in 1928. Such errors, however, are rare.

Chapter Notes

As far as possible, the references follow the form used by *Art Bulletin*. Many of the citations that follow come from newspaper clippings. These were gathered from various sources: the Missouri Valley Room of the Kansas City Public Library; the Kansas City Art Institute Library; the Benton home; the Benton Trusts; the clipping files of the Kansas City *Star/Times*; the Newton County Historical Society, Neosho; the scrapbooks of John Callison, Fred McCraw and others; and the curatorial files of museums that have lent works to the Benton Centennial Exhibition. The identification of these clippings is often incomplete, for example, page numbers are often unavailable. In the citations that follow I have not attempted to follow a consistent form but have given the identification found on these clippings. I have used the following abbreviations: "KCAI" for Kansas City Art Institute; "KC" for Kansas City; and "AAA" for Archives of American Art. Volume numbers of periodicals are enclosed in parentheses.

Chapter One: Neosho

The general framework of this chapter follows *The Intimate Story*, from which all the historical dialogue is taken except for the interview at the Joplin *American*, which combines this source with Richard Beer's interview, "As They Are: The Man From Missouri," *Art News*, (32) 14, January 6, 1934, 11. A briefer account of Benton's childhood is given in *An Artist in America*, 12–13, 19–20. The float-trip accident is described in Benton's "The Ozarks," *Travel and Leisure*, (3) 3, June-July 1973, 30–33; the barn-burning quotation, from Fath, 1979, 148. The quotations from Mildred Small come from Ken Burns's and the author's interviews with her; those from John Robison, Phil Ratcliff and Jack Rushmore are found in Robert Sanford, "Neosho Makes Big Plans for Tom Benton's Homecoming," KC *Star*, Sunday, April 15, 1962. See also: Yeo and Cook, 4; Winifred Shields, "Benton's Art at Age 9 Won an Early Admirer," KC *Star*, May 12, 1956; Sylvan R. Wood, *Locomotives of the Katy*, Boston, 1944, 8–9, 50; Theodore Roosevelt, *Thomas Hart Benton*, Cambridge, 1888; John D. Hicks, *The Populist Revolt*, Minneapolis, 1931; Richard Hofstadter, *The Paranoid Style in American Politics and Other Essays*, New York,

1965, 238–315; quotation on Vest from Dumas Malone, ed., *Dictionary of American Biography*, vol. 10, New York, 1936, 296; Edwin M.C. French, *Senator Vest: Champion of the Dog*, Boston, 1930, 40, 33–34; unidentified clippings on early Neosho and Benton's fight with Hargrove in the Newton County Historical Society, Neosho, MO; Dolph Shaner, *The Story of Joplin*, New York, 1948; A. H. Rogers, "Two Famous Men Start Different Careers While Working for Newspaper in Joplin," Joplin *Globe*, Sunday, April 29, 1962. Benton misremembered the number of his house on Q Street; it is given correctly in *The Elite List*, Washington, DC, 1900. All Benton's quotations not otherwise identified come from *The Intimate Story*.

Chapter Two: Chicago

All the Benton letters quoted are from the Benton Trust, with the exception of those to Fay Clark, which belong to Crowder College, Neosho, MO. The general framework of the chapter comes from *The Intimate Story*. The quotations about Hud come entirely from this source, as does the historical dialogue, except for the Timmons incident, which is found in one of Benton's letters to his parents of March 24, 1907. Benton's account in *The Intimate Story* is supplemented by *An Artist in America*, 30–33. John Vanderpoel wrote a book on figure drawing, *The Human Figure*, New York, 1st ed. 1935, 2nd ed. 1958, which outlines Benton's method of teaching. Oswald's teaching is described in the Paul Cummings interview, AAA, 7, 26. Vytlacil quote is from Burroughs, 40. The Phil Ratcliff and Jack Rushmore quotes are from Sanford, "Neosho Makes Big Plans"; the swimming accident (misdated by Benton in *The Intimate Story*) is described in an unidentified clipping dated August 15, 1907, in the Newton County Historical Society. See also Jan Dickerson, "A Different Tom Benton 50 Years Ago," KC *Times*, May 10, 1958; and *Thomas Hart Benton: A Personal Commemorative*, Spiva Art Center, Joplin, MO, 1973, 23–24. For Frank Lloyd Wright and Japanese prints see Gruber, 25; and Julia Meech-Pekarik, "Frank Lloyd Wright and Japanese prints" in *Frank Lloyd Wright at the Metropolitan Museum of Art*, New York, 1982.

Chapter Three: Paris

The chief source for the Paris years, including all historical dialogue, is *The Intimate Story* (including "Ali," *New Letters: A Continuation of the University Review*, University of Missouri, Kansas City, (38) 1, Fall 1971). Benton gave an extensive account of his artistic exposure in France in *An American in Art*, 12–28. The Gruber dissertation contains a helpful synthesis of this material. See also Cummings interview, AAA, 8–14; Thomas Craven, *Thomas Hart Benton*, Associated American Artists, New York, 1939, 11; Abel G. Warshawsky, *The Memories of an American Impressionist*, Kent, OH, 1980, 47; transcript, Betty Hoag's interview with Macdonald-Wright, April 13, 1964, AAA, 4; the author's interviews with Mildred Small, as well as her typescript entitled "Thomas Hart Benton in Paris," in her possession, 1–2, 4, 9–10. For memories of John Thompson the author is indebted to Professor John Haskins at the University of Pittsburgh and Colonel Frederick F. Sager, both of whom studied with Thompson in Denver, and to Linda Lebsack of Rosenstock Fine Arts, Denver. The best account of Thompson's work is Charles F. Ramus, "John E. Thompson, Dean of Colorado Painters," *Art Education*, Colorado State Art Association, April 1943, 4–10. See also James Mills, "Two Colorado Artists," Denver *Post*, November 13, 1977. The best general source on Macdonald-Wright is Gail Levin, *Synchromism and American Color Abstraction: 1910–1925*, Whitney Museum of American Art, New York, 1978. Also helpful is David Scott, *Stanton Macdonald-Wright*, National Collection of Fine Arts, Washington, D.C., 1967; four articles on Wright in *The American Art Review*, (1) 2, January-February, 1974, 49–68; and William C. Agee, *Synchromism and Color Principles in American Painting, 1910–1930*, New York, 1965. The author has also benefited from conversations with William Agee. Wright's memory seems to have been unreliable and there are inconsistent accounts of when he arrived in Paris; Benton's statements are followed. The identification of Gabriel Bernadou was based on a letter from Guy Quincy, Directeur des Services d'Archives de la Corrèze, Tulle, France, to Jennifer Hardin, November 14, 1987, and letters and a telephone conversation between René Brun, a specialist on artists of the Limousin, from Paris, and Jennifer

Hardin, November 1987. The Duc de Trevise wrote a memorial note on Bernadou in *Les Arts*, June 1914; Bernadou's work can be seen at the Musée du Cloître in Tulle.

Chapter Four: The Misfit Years

Benton did not write a chapter in *The Intimate Story* on his early years in New York, but left several pages of notations, which provide a general chronology of events. My interviews with Mildred Small established some of his changing residences, as did the New York street directory. Benton did not specify the name of Frank Zimmerer, but we have made the identification on the basis of these sources: the Kansas City Art Institute catalogue, Summer 1911–12; "It Happened in Kansas City," KC *Star*, June 23, 1946; and records of enrollment provided by Mary McIsaac, registrar, the School of the Art Institute of Chicago. Benton's comments on the drag party come from Robert S. Gallagher, "An Artist in America," *American Heritage*, (24) 4, June 1973, 40–48, 90. For Benton's early years in New York see: Thomas Craven, *Paint*, New York, 1923, 7, 18; Thomas Craven, *Modern Art: The Men, the Movements, the Meaning*, New York, 1934, 3–5, 245–250, 332; Carl Bode, *Mencken*, Carbondale, IL, 1969, 63, 66, 116, 132–133, 151–52; Liam O'Leary, *Rex Ingram: Master of the Silent Cinema*, New York, 1980; Richard Merkin et al., *The Jazz Age as Seen Through the Eyes of Ralph Barton, Miguel Covarrubias, and John Held, Jr.*, Rhode Island School of Design, Providence, 1968; Dorothy Giles, "Death was Sweeter," *College Humor*, (11) 100, Chicago, IL, April 1932, 76–77, 92; Betty Hoag's interview with Macdonald-Wright, AAA, 3–4; Royal Cortissoz, New York *Tribune*, March 12, 1916; Levin quote from Gail Levin, "Thomas Hart Benton, Synchromism and Abstract Art," *Arts*, (56) 4, December 1981, 144; catalogue, *The Forum Exhibition of Modern American Painters, March 13–25, 1916*, reprinted by Arno Press, New York, 1960; Jacqueline Hall, "Benton Briefly Used Style of Synchromists," Columbus, OH, *Dispatch*, August 25, 1971; Willard Huntington Wright, "The Forum Exhibition," *The Forum*, (55), April 1916, 457–471; "Modern Art: An American Painter of Promise," *The International Studio*, (61) 243, May

1917, 95–96; Laurie Lisle, *Portrait of an Artist: A Biography of Georgia O'Keeffe*, Albuquerque, 1986, 116, 120; John Weichsel (grandson of Benton's friend), "The People's Art Guild," unpublished master's thesis, Hunter College, New York, January 1965; John Weichsel, "Cosmism or Amorphism," *Camera Work*, (42–43), April-July 1913; John Weichsel, "Rampant Zeitgeist," *Camera Work*, (44), October 1913, 20–24; letters from Benton and Wright to John Weichsel, Weichsel Papers, AAA; Gruber, 71–75; letter of February 12, 1916, Weichsel Papers, AAA. Benton's account of the Parisian gangster episode is confirmed by Levin, *Synchromism*, 1978, 124, note 4. My thanks to John Weichsel for his help in locating a photograph of his grandfather. The film Benton acted in at Fort Lee has been lost and was not *The Upper Hand* as has been stated by Karal Ann Marling and Erika Doss.

**Chapter Five:
My Husband Is a Genius!**

Craven, *Modern Art*, 252–253, 333–334; "Whistler and Others on Exhibition," *New York Times*, December 22, 1918, Sec. 4, 6; "T. H. Benton's Naval Pictures Unique in Expressing Force," New York *Herald*, December 22, 1918; Thomas Hart Benton, "The New American Art," St. Louis *Post-Dispatch*, December 11, 1938, 14. The articles by Craven in *The Dial* that I have cited are "An Illustrator," (68), January 1920, 121–125; "Mr. Roger Fry and the Artistic Vision," (71), July 1921, 101–106; "The Progress of Painting," (74), June 1923, 581–593; "Imitation Again," (75), August 1923, 192–195; "Living Art," (76), February 1924, 180–183; "Making Modernism Difficult," (76), April 1924, 357–360; "Henri Matisse," (76), May 1924, 404–406; "A Neglected Master," (77), September 1924, 260–263. Benton's works were reproduced in *The Dial*, (79), July 1925, 30, and (79), September 1925, 194. The account of Benton's life on Martha's Vineyard is largely derived from the Burroughs biography. See also: Michael Bezdek, "Book Relates History of Deafness on Island," Boston *Globe*, November 29, 1985; Gilberta Goodwin, "The Art of Thomas Hart Benton," unpublished college paper, May 3, 1939 (typescript in Nelson-Atkins Museum); Albert Christ-Janer, *Boardman Robinson*, Chicago, 1946, 42–45; Janet L. Holladay, "An Artist and His Gift,"

The Dukes County Intelligencer, Dukes County Historical Society, Edgartown, MA, (17), 4, May 1976, 131–138; "Thomas Hart Benton, Famed Muralist, Speaks at College," *The Christian College Microphone*, February 4, 1936. Information on Alfred Raabe in a letter to Jennifer Hardin from Raabe's son-in-law, March 29, 1988. For the Barnes episode see George Biddle, *An American Artist's Story*, Boston, 1939, 260; William Schack, *Art and Argyrol*, New York, 1963; and Benton's correspondence with Schack, AAA. For Ethel Whiteside, *An Artist in America*, 50–60. Thomas Craven quote on Benton's father from Craven, *Thomas Hart Benton*, catalogue, Associated American Artists, New York, April 18–May 15, 1939, 14; Lloyd Goodrich, "In Missoura," *Arts*, (6) 6, December 1924, 338.

**Chapter Six: The Mechanics of
Form Organization**

Willard Huntington Wright, *Modern Painting: Its Tendency and Meaning*, New York, 1915, 18, 21–22, 93, 160, 342. Thomas Craven, "The Progress of Painting: The Modern Background," *The Dial*, (74), April 1923, 357–367; and "The Progress of Painting: Individual Tendencies," *The Dial*, (74), June 1923, 581–593. Thomas Hart Benton, "Mechanics of Form Organization in Painting," *Arts*, (10) 5, November 1926, 285–289; *Arts*, (10) 6, December 1926, 340–342; *Arts*, (11) 1, January 1927, 43–44; *Arts*, (11) 2, February 1927, 95–96; *Arts*, (11) 3, March 1927, 145–148. Edward Fry, letter to Fred McCraw, April 22, 1987. Jeffrey Potter, *To a Violent Grave: An Oral Biography of Jackson Pollock*, New York, 1985 (Ossorio quote, 106; Harry Jackson quote, 150–151). Cummings interview, AAA, 22; Gruber, 221; Milton F. Perry's interview with Thomas Hart Benton, April 21, 1964, Benton Trust; on use of clay models, Benton's letter to Betty Chamberlain of *Time* in reply to telegram of August 15, 1940, the Benton Trust. John Canaday, "Young Artist En Route to the USA," *New York Times*, December 10, 1972, D27; Benton, "Form and the Subject," *Arts*, (5) 6, June 1924, 303–308; Benton, "New York Exhibition," *Arts*, (10) 6, December 1926, 343–345; Thomas Craven, "Daumier and the New Spirit," *The Dial*, (78), March 1925, 240–245. Matthew Baigell, introduction, catalogue, *Thomas Hart*

Benton: Synchromist Paintings 1915–1920 from a Private Collection, Salander-O'Reilly Galleries, New York, 1981, unpaginated; Gail Levin, "Thomas Hart Benton, Synchromism, and Abstract Art," *Arts*, (56) 4, December 1981, 144–148; Helen K. Cook, "Friends Treasure Benton Tapestry," K.C. *Star*, May 30, 1976; Clement Greenberg quote from the panel discussion during the Benton Symposium, the Nelson-Atkins Museum, Kansas City, MO, April 11, 1987; Hilton Kramer, "Benton: The Radical Modernist," *New York Times*, January 10, 1982; Kay Larson, "The Secret Suitcase of Thomas Hart Benton," *New York*, December 21, 1981, 60–61; Helen Lieban, "Thomas Benton: American Mural Painter," *Design*, (26) 6, December 1934, 26–35; Frederick Kiesler, *Contemporary Art Applied to the Store and Its Display*, New York, 1930, 23; Michael Komanecky, "The Screens and Screen Designs of Donald Deskey," *Antiques*, (131) 5, May 1987, 1064–1077; Michael Komanecky et al., *The Folding Image*, Yale University Art Gallery, New Haven, 1984, 229–232.

Chapter Seven: On the Road

Most of the account of Benton's travels comes from *An Artist in America*. See also Sally MacDougall, "Benton the Artist a Wild Man to His Critics But a Lamb to His Wife Who Doesn't Nag," New York *World-Telegram*, undated clipping, c. April 1942; Thomas Craven, "Our Art Becomes American," *Harper's Monthly Magazine*, (171), September 1935, 430–441; John I.H. Baur, *The Inlander: The Life and Work of Charles Burchfield, 1893–1967*, Newark, DE, 1982, 133, 147, 149; Dick Fowler, *Leaders in Our Town*, Kansas City, MO, 1952, 29; "Carol Dilley Watched Benton Sketch Painting," *Borger News-Herald*, October 5, 1976, 3; "Borger: Changing Faces," *Shield*, Phillips Petroleum, 1st quarter 1984, 33–36; *Borger's Fiftieth Birthday: 1926–1976*, Borger, Texas, 1976; Lieban, "Tom Benton: American Mural Painter," 32–33. On many occasions Benton dated his Borger visit to 1926; Benton's date has been followed (Mrs. Dilley gave the date as 1927). Quotes from Frank Pollock, Tolegian, Hayter, Pavia, McNeil, Wilson, Busa, Jules, and Elizabeth Pollock from Potter, *To a Violent Grave*, 31–32, 34–38; Axel Horn, "Jackson Pollock: The Hollow and the Bump," *Carleton Miscellany*, (7)

3, Summer 1966, 80–87. Calder quote from Jean Lipman, et. al., *Calder's Universe*, New York, 1976, 111. Lewis Mumford, "An American Epic in Paint," *New Republic*, (50) 644, April 6, 1927, 197; Thomas Craven, "American Month in the Galleries," *Arts*, (11) 3, March 1927, 151–152; "Thomas H. Benton—American Modern," *Survey*, (57) 1, October 1, 1926, 31–34; "An Author and Art Critic Acquire Bentons," *Art Digest*, (4) 4, November 1929, 8; Lloyd Goodrich, *New York Times*, October 27, 1929, Sec. 9, 13; Lloyd Goodrich, "Exhibitions: The Delphic Studios," *Arts*, (16) 3, November 1929, 183–186; Marling, "Thomas Hart Benton's Boomtown,"; Bode, *Mencken*, 264–269; *An Artist in America*, 100–101; catalogue, *The South*, Delphic Galleries, New York, October 14–November 15, 1929; Lewis Mumford, "The Theory and Practice of Regionalism," *The Sociological Review*, (20) 1, January 1928, 18–33, and (20) 2, 131–141. Much of the analysis of the Southern identity and the quotes from Toynbee, Faulkner, Thornton Wilder, and Eudora Welty come from C. Vann Woodward, *The Burden of Southern History*, Baton Rouge, LA, 1986, 6, 8, 17, 22–24, 30, 32–33, 36.

**Chapter Eight:
The New School Mural**

I have made extensive use of Emily Braun's superb study, *Thomas Hart Benton: "The America Today Murals,"* The Equitable Life Assurance Society of the United States, New York, 1985 (with a supplementary note on the conservation of the murals by Thomas Branchick). Benton described the commission in *An American in Art*, 61–63. Information on Alma Reed is from Cummings interview, AAA, 32. Benton mistakenly stated she was involved with Zapata rather than Felipe Carillo Puerto, governor of the Yucatan. See also: José Clemente Orozco, *An Autobiography*, Austin, TX, 1962, 127; Alma Reed, *Orozco*, New York, 1957, 163–165. Background of New School murals and conversations with Benton and Ralph Pearson from Alvin Johnson, *Pioneer's Progress*, Lincoln, NE, 1960, 310–312, 328–329. Edward Alden Jewell, "Orozco & Benton Paint Murals for New York," *New York Times*, November 23, 1930, Sec. 9, 12; Suzanne La Follette, "Art: America in Murals," *The New*

Freeman, (2), February 18, 1931, 540–543; Lloyd Goodrich, "The Murals of the New School," *Arts*, (17), March 1931, 399–403; Forbes Watson incident from Ken Burns's interview with Lloyd Goodrich; "Artist Likens Trial Scenes to Burlesque," New York *World-Telegram*, January 3, 1935; Leo Huberman, *We, the People*, New York, 1st ed. 1932, 2nd ed. 1947; Florence Loeb Kellogg, "The American Scenes—Plural," *Survey*, (65) 5, December 1, 1930, 271–273. For Stuart Davis the best sources are John R. Lane, *Stuart Davis: Art and Art Theory*, New York, 1978; and Karen Wilkin, *Stuart Davis*, New York, 1987. My comparison of Benton and Davis is exactly opposite in its conclusions to those of Thomas Somma, "Thomas Hart Benton and Stuart Davis: Abstraction versus Realism in American Scene Painting," *Rutgers Art Review*, (5), Spring 1984, 46–55.

Chapter Nine: The Whitney Mural

George Eagle, " 'Water Story Mural': Benton's Grassroots Chronicle Uncovered," Washington *Post*, July 8, 1975, B1, B5; Henry Clay Gold, "Soda Fountain Mural by Benton Turns Up," KC *Star*, July 8, 1975; catalogue, Christie's, New York, December 5, 1986, lot no. 264. The correspondence between Benton and Juliana Force is preserved in the files of the Whitney Museum of American Art. A more detailed analysis of this exchange is provided in my longer typescript, which preceded this text; portions of the letters are quoted in Burroughs. Milton Brown provided the words for "Oh the eagles, they fly high" at a symposium on Benton at Williams College, April 12–13, 1985. See also: Barbara Goldsmith, *Little Gloria, Happy at Last*, New York, 1980; Gloria Vanderbilt, *Once Upon a Time*, New York, 1985, 226; Avis Berman, "Juliana Force: Visionary Champion of American Art," *Architectural Digest*, (45) 2, February 1988, 86; Beer, 11; Anita Brenner, "Art and American Life," *The Nation*, (136) 3524, January 18, 1933, 72–73; John Dewey, *Art and Experience*, New York, 2nd ed. 1958, 5–6; Edward Alden Jewell, "The Arts of Life in America Are Portrayed in Murals of New Library at the Whitney Museum," *New York Times*, October 6, 1932, Sec. 1, 24; Ralph Flint, "New Benton Murals at Whitney Museum Now

on Exhibition," *Art News*, (31) 3, December 24, 1932, 9; Louis Kalonyme, "The Arts in New York: The French and American Arts of Life as Celebrated by Matisse, Picasso & Co., and also Thomas Benton," *Arts and Decoration*, 38, February 1933, 50–51, 58; Henry McBride, "Foremost American Decorator Does Some Forceful Murals," New York *Sun*, December 16, 1932, 22; Paul Rosenfeld, "Ex-Reading Room," *New Republic*, April 12, 1933, 245–246; Brenner, "Art and American Life," 72–73. Mervin Jules quote from Potter, *To a Violent Grave*, 37; information on Architectural League medal from "About Ben Benton," *Art Digest*, (7) 8, January 15, 1933, 6; Arthur Le Duc, "Painters Deny Whitney Art Perils Child," New York *Journal*, November 9, 1934.

Chapter Ten: The Indiana Murals

Benton described the Indiana project in *The Intimate Story* and in *An American in Art*, 251–256. In addition, the Indiana University Archives, Bloomington, hold a typescript by Ross Teckemeyer describing the project. The subject matter of the mural is described in David Lawrence Chambers, *Indiana: A Hoosier History, Based on the Mural Paintings of Thomas Hart Benton*, Indianapolis, 1933 (includes "A Dream Fulfilled" by Benton at the end of the book). See also "Indiana's Mural," *Art Digest*, (7) 16, May 15, 1933, 20; Jay Diskey, "Populist Camp or Great Art? Benton's Indiana," *Indiana Alumni Magazine*, Indiana University, Bloomington, October 1983, 9–13; Arch Steinel, "Let's Have an Artist's Truce: Indiana's World Fair Muralist Prefers Work to War," Indianapolis *Times*, January 25, 1933, 1; "Benton in Indiana," *Art Digest*, (7) 11, March 1, 1933, 20; Beer, 11; Craven, *Modern Art*, 339; Askew and Morehouse quotes, Diskey, 12; Virginia Gardner, "Indian's Art Stirs Conflict at World Fair," Chicago *Tribune*, June 8, 1933.

Chapter Eleven: Hitting the Big Time

The visit with Ruggles is described in *The Intimate Story*. See also: Charles Seeger, "Carl Ruggles," *The Musical Quarterly*, (18) 4, October 1932. Karl Freund, "Thomas Hart Benton—Realist," *Ringmaster—The World in Caricature*, (1) 4, November 1936, 45–46; John Kirkpatrick, "The Evolution of Carl Ruggles,"

Perspectives on New Music, (81) 1, Spring-Summer 1968 (cites Browning poem). *Minstrel Show* and *Lord, Heal the Child* are described in *An Artist in America*, 92–95, 102–110; Edward Alden Jewell, "Art Works Shown by Thomas Benton," *New York Times* (late city edition), April 12, 1934, Sec 1, 21; Royal Cortissoz, "Things Static and 'Mobile,' " New York *Herald Tribune*, April 15, 1934; Henry McBride, New York *Sun*, April 14, 1934; "Benton Holds First Show in Four Years," *Art Digest*, (8) 14, April 15, 1934, 15; Bill C. Malone, *Country Music U.S.A.*, Austin, TX, 1968, 61–64. Thomas Craven, "The Curse of French Culture," *Forum*, (82) 1, July 1929, 57–63; Thomas Craven, *Men of Art*, New York, 1931, 512–513; Craven, *Modern Art*, 160–176 (chapter on Matisse), 237 ("The modern movement has come and gone," quote), and 311–312 (discussion of Stieglitz). "Thomas Craven Embalms Modern Art and Buries it on the Left Bank," unidentified clipping from 1934; Virgil Barker, "Modern Art & Its Personalities," *Saturday Review*, May 12, 1934; "Midwest Is Producing Indigenous Art," *Art Digest*, (7) 20, September 1, 1933, 10. Maynard Walker's papers are in AAA; he left a collection of paintings and some papers to the public library, Garnett, KS. For information about him I am indebted to Jane Feuerbarn of Garnett, KS, and George L. Dein, Jr., of Hawley, PA. See also "Walker Galleries," *The Waldorf Astoria Daily Bulletin*, June 10, 1936, Walker Papers, AAA; statement by Walker, *Art Digest*, (7) 20, September 1, 1933, 10; "U.S. Scene," *Time*, (24) 26, December 24, 1934, 24–27; M. Sue Kendall, "Maynard Walker and the First Kansas Campaign," in *Rethinking Regionalism; John Steuart Curry and the Kansas Mural Controversy*, Washington, D.C., 1986, 17–34 (letter to White from Mrs. Henry J. Allen, 31); Edward Alden Jewell, *New York Times*, November 4, 1928; Thomas Craven, "Our Art Becomes American," 430–441; Edward Alden Jewell, "Beware the Pendulum! Chastening Thoughts Anent a National Habit—Variety on the Calendar," *New York Times*, November 17, 1935; Baur, *The Inlander*, 166, 168, 169; Benton, *An American in Art*, 173.

Chapter Twelve: Stieglitz, Davis and the Communist Front

Waldo Frank et al., eds., *America and Alfred Stieglitz: A Collective Portrait*, Garden City, NY, 1934; Thomas Hart Benton, "America and/or Alfred Stieglitz," *Common Sense*, (4) 1, January 1935, 22–25; exchange between Benton and Stieglitz in the Beinecke Rare Book and Manuscript Library, Yale University; Craven, *Modern Art*, 1934, 312. See also Edward Abrahams, "Alfred Stieglitz and/or Thomas Hart Benton," *Arts*, (55), June 1981, 108–113. Benton gave a generalized account of the dispute with Davis in *The Intimate Story*. This includes a description of the tumultuous lecture after his Midwestern trip. I have filled in the details of what occurred from contemporary sources: Frances Kramer, "Thomas H. Benton on Vacation Flays Propaganda in Fine Art," *The News* (Dallas?), July 31, 1935; Thomas Hart Benton's speech to the John Reed Club at the Irving Plaza Auditorium, "Should Art Be National?" February, 1934; typescript prepared from the shorthand notes of Henry A. Clausen, files of the Nelson-Atkins Museum of Art, later published as "Art and Nationalism," *Modern Monthly*, May 8, 1934, 232–236. Information on Davis from Wilkin, *Stuart Davis*, 127, 142, 144–46, 160. Stuart Davis, "The N.Y. American Scene in Art," *Art Front*, (1) 3, February 1935, 6; "Radical Art Trend Seen in Midwest," *New York Times* (late city edition), February 8, 1935, 23; Thomas Hart Benton, "On the American Scene," *Art Front*, (1) 3, March 1935, 3, 8; Thomas Hart Benton, "Benton Answers," *Art Digest*, (9) 12, March 15, 1935, 20–21, 25; Jacob Burck, "Benton Sees Red," *Art Front*, (1) 4, April 1935, 4, 8; Thomas Hart Benton, Letter, *Art Front*, (1) 5, May 1935, 7; Stuart Davis, "Davis' Rejoinder," *Art Digest*, (9) 13, April 1, 1935, 12–13, 26–27; Thomas Hart Benton, "Benton Cries Quits," *Art Digest*, (9) 14, April 15, 1935, 10; Thomas Hart Benton, "Reply to Rivera," *The University of Kansas City Review*, (2), Winter 1935, 71–78; Thomas Hart Benton, "Confessions of an American I: Why I Don't Like Marxism," *Common Sense*, (6) 7, July 1937, 7–9; "Confessions of an American II: Marx and the Jeffersonian Ideal," *Common Sense*, (6) 8, August 1937, 10–12, 14; "Confessions of an American III: Class Rule vs. Democracy," *Common Sense*, (6)

9, September 1937, 19–22. Virginia Dabney, "Civil War Murals Assailed, South's Pride Is Sorely Hurt," *New York Times* (late city edition), January 20, 1935, Sec. 4, 7.

Chapter Thirteen:
Farewell to New York

Benton described his Midwestern lecture tour in *The Intimate Story;* the Canaday anecdote comes from Cummings interview, AAA, 51. See also: KC *Star,* January 12, 1935. For Curry and Wood see Thomas Hart Benton, "John Curry," *The University of Kansas City Review,* (13), Winter 1946, 87–90; M. Sue Kendall, *Rethinking Regionalism: John Steuart Curry and the Kansas Mural Controversy,* Washington, D.C., 1984; Thomas Hart Benton, "Death of Grant Wood," *University of Kansas City Review,* (8), Spring 1942, 147–48; Darrell Garwood, *Artist in Iowa,* New York, 1944; Wanda Corn, *Grant Wood, The Regionalist Vision,* New Haven, 1983; James M. Dennis, *Grant Wood: A Study in American Art and Culture,* Columbia, MO, 1986; Karal Ann Marling, "Don't Knock Wood," *Art News,* (82) 7, September 1983, 94–99. Bob Priddy, *Only the Rivers Are Peaceful: Thomas Hart Benton's Missouri Mural,* unpaginated manuscript (see note, page 349). Includes John Christy statement and description of the various bills associated with Benton's mural. Benton's statement on unconventional subjects from *The Intimate Story;* the payoff to Barbour is described in *The Intimate Story* and Burroughs, 123. Information on *Preparing the Bill* from *An Artist in America,* 78, correspondence in the curatorial file on the painting at Randolph-Macon Women's College, Lynchburg, VA, and correspondence with Benton's nephew, Thomas Hart Benton v. The Post Office mural is discussed in *The Intimate Story* and in Karal Ann Marling, *Wall-to-Wall America: A Cultural History of Post-Office Murals in the Great Depression,* Minneapolis, 1982, 140, 141 (illustration of Benton's design), and 184. "Benton to Institute," KC *Times,* March 30, 1935; "Mr. Benton Will Leave Us Flat," New York *Sun,* April 12, 1935; "U.S. Scene," *Time,* December 24, 1934, 25. Grant Wood's "Revolt Against the City" was originally printed as a pamphlet, Iowa City, IA, 1935, reprinted in Dennis, *Grant Wood,* 229–235. The authorship of the piece is discussed

by Corn, *Grant Wood,* 46, 153, note 85. Edward Alden Jewell, "Growth of Benton Seen in Art Show," *New York Times,* April 13, 1935; Edward Alden Jewell, "In the Realm of Art: Controversy and Exhibitions," *New York Times,* April 7, 1935, Sec. 9, 8; Royal Cortissoz, "Realism," New York *Herald Tribune,* Sunday, April 7, 1935; "Benton and Wood from the Middle-West Hold New York Show," *Art Digest,* (9) 14, April 15, 1935, 12; Lewis Mumford, "The Three Bentons," *New Yorker,* (11) 10, April 20, 1935, 48, 50, 53; correspondence with Ruggles from Yale University Music Library; "Benton to Quit Hectic City for Missouri Calm," New York *American,* April 2, 1935. Thomas Hart Benton, "American Artists Have Won Fight for Realism, Asserts Tom Benton," unidentified clipping, c. November 1940; Thomas Craven, "Love in Smokey Hill, *The Dial,* (72), January 1922, 1–16. "Craven never minced words" from Benton, *The Intimate Story;* H. L. Mencken, "The Sahara of the Bozart," in James T. Farrell, ed., *Prejudices: A Selection made by James T. Farrell and With an Introduction by Him,* New York, 1955, 69–81; Thomas Craven, "Men of Art: American Style," *The American Mercury,* (6), December 1925, 425–432; quote on Pascin from Thomas Craven, "Living Art," *The Dial,* (76), February 1924, 183; Royal Cortissoz, *American Art,* New York, 1923, 18; "French Artist Spur on American Art," New York *Tribune,* October 24, 1915, Sec. 4, 2; Matthew Baigell, "American Art and National Identity: The 1920s," *Arts,* (61) 6, February 1987, 48–55; Malcolm Cowley, "Benton of Missouri," *New Republic,* (92) 1196, November 3, 1937, 375; "Thomas Hart Benton, Muralist, Visits City," St. Louis *Post-Dispatch,* November 11, 1937; Cummings interview, AAA, 30, 53–54; Charles A. Beard and Mary R. Beard, *America in Midpassage,* Vol. II, New York, 1939, 803; Potter, 37; "Critics Disapprove of Benton," *Art Digest,* (8) 15, May 1, 1934, 14; Edward Alden Jewell, "In the Realm of Art: Controversy and Exhibitions," *New York Times,* April 7, 1935, Sec. 9, 8; Benton correspondence with Seth Low in the files of the New Britain Museum of American Art, New Britain, CT.

Chapter Fourteen:
The Jefferson City Mural

I am particularly grateful to Bob Priddy, who generously allowed me to consult the typescript of his forthcoming book on the Jefferson City mural, *Only the Rivers Are Peaceful: Thomas Hart Benton's Missouri Mural.* He is currently negotiating with the Independence Press, Independence, MO, to publish this account. Priddy, a journalist in Jefferson City, not only has assembled many contemporary sources but also has conducted interviews with Jackson Lee Nesbitt, Mary Humphrey, Sam Blair, Forrest Scrivener, Harold Brown, Jr., Mary Tunnell Wherritt, and others. A great deal of this chapter is based on his research. A much shorter but well-organized account of the mural is Nancy Edelman, *The Thomas Hart Benton Murals in the Missouri State Capitol,* Missouri State Council on Arts, Jefferson City, MO, 1986. A stimulating interpretation is Matthew Baigell, with Allen Kaufman, "The Missouri Murals: Another Look at Benton," *Art Journal,* (36), Summer 1977, 314–321. Gruber, 299–302; Ruth Pickering, "Thomas Hart Benton on His Way Back to Missouri," *Arts and Decoration,* (42) 4, February 1935, 20; "Benton Answers," *Art Digest,* (9) 12, March 15, 1935, 25; "An Art Call to Benton," KC *Star,* March 20, 1935; "Art News," unidentified clipping dated March 24, 1935, KCAI Library; "Benton Undecided, Painter Considering K.C. Art Institute Offer," unidentified clipping dated March 27, 1935, KCAI Library; "Muralist Quits New York for Midwest," Los Angeles *Times,* April 1, 1935; Joseph Hanlon, "Thomas Hart Benton to Live in Missouri," St. Louis *Post-Dispatch,* March 19, 1935; "Benton Goes Home," *Art Digest,* (9) 14, April 15, 1935, 13. "Painted autobiography" quote from *The Intimate Story.* See also: Gallagher, 87; Burns interview with O'Maley; lemonade anecdote from Fred Shane tapes, AAA; background on Kansas City largely from Darrell Garwood, *Crossroads of America: The Story of Kansas City,* New York, 1948; Howard E. Huselton, "Kansas City's Art Museum Plan," *American Magazine of Art,* (20) 9, September 1929, 502; *A Brief History of the Nelson-Atkins Museum of Art,* Nelson-Atkins Museum, Kansas City, MO, 1983; "Paul Gardner Issues Warning Against Too Much Sordidness in Art Today," *Lincoln State Journal* (Nebraska), March 9, 1936; Thomas

Hoving, *King of the Confessors,* New York, 1981, 92, 165 ff.; KC *Star,* September 24, 1935; "Cross Section of Life in Missouri: Found in Courts," unidentified clipping, July 12, 1935, KCAI Library; "Thomas Hart Benton Tours State for People and Scenes for Drawings," KC *Star,* June 18, 1936; the author's interview with Duard Marshall; *An American in Art,* 75; "In the Gallery and Studio," KC *Star,* January 7, 1937, 16; St. Louis *Star-Times,* July 15, 1936; Lisa Massoth, "Remember KC's Hottest Summer? Residents Sweltered in Disbelief in 1936," KC *Times,* August 14, 1986, 1, 16; Benton's letter to the visitors is reproduced in Nancy Edelman; "A Barrage of Questions," KC *Star,* February 3, 1937, 20; Malcolm Vaughn, "Up From Missouri," *North American Review,* (245), Spring 1938, 83; Otto Fuerbringer, "Living Missourians' Faces Used in State Capitol by Artist Benton," St. Louis *Post-Dispatch,* July 19, 1936; Paul Watkins, "Thomas Hart Benton Remembered," *Missouri Life,* March-June 1975, 75; "The Boss in Paint," St. Louis *Post-Dispatch,* December 9, 1936; editorial, *Daily Capital News,* December 19, 1936; Craven, *Modern Art,* 353; *An American in Art,* 152; Marling, *Tom Benton and His Drawings,* 135. Interpretive lecture by I. G. Morrison, September 1940, annotated by Benton, September 14, 1940, cited by Priddy. *An Artist in America,* 243–245; Bode, *Mencken,* 287; Bob Priddy's interview with Forrest Scrivener (see note, page 349); "Random Thoughts," KC *Star,* January 17,1937; *Missouri Times,* Jefferson City, January 10, 1983; C.H.T., "The Furor," KC *Star,* March 21, 1937; Priddy's interview with John Christy; "Thomas Benton Paints a History of His Own Missouri," *Life* (2) 9, March 1, 1937, 32–37; Burroughs, 125; "Recalls Bulger on Art," KC *Times,* January 29, 1937; "Murals Allow No Rest," KC *Star,* May 6 (?), 1937; Walter G. Heren, "You Either Like 'Em or Don't, There's No Half Way on New Capitol Art," KC *Journal-Post,* January 8, 1937; "Mural Debate is Nipped," KC *Star,* undated but with dateline of Jefferson City, March 11, 1937; Benton description of Stark meeting in *The Intimate Story;* "Murals Win Stark's OK," KC *Times,* March 19, 1937; KC *Star,* December 21, 1936; Holland from "Artistic Storm Brewing Over Benton Murals," KC *Star,* Saturday, January 2, 1937; letter to *Star* from T. C. Field, January 3, 1937; KC *Journal-Post,* January 7, 1937; Huselton from "Murals Split Art Ranks," KC *Times,* January 5, 1937; "No, the Eggs Didn't Cost $2,571," KC *Times,* January 12, 1937; "Eggs' Use in Murals Arouses Missourians," *New York Times,* January 13, 1937, Sec. 1, 19; "More Moot Murals— And Missouri's Fowl," New Orleans *Tribune,* January 23, 1937; Independence (MO) *Examiner* quoted in St. Louis *Post-Dispatch,* February 7, 1937; *Tulsa Tribune* cited in *An Artist in America,* 243–245; "Thomas H. Benton Paints the History of Missouri—Starts Civil War," *Art Digest,* (11) 9, Feb. 1, 1937, 10–11; "Thomas Hart Benton Takes the Stand," KC *Star,* January 15, 1937; "Ol' Elmer's Art Lesson," KC *Star,* January 24, 1937; "Benton Defends Murals, Wins Plaudits," KC *Journal-Post,* February 3, 1937; "A Barrage of Questions," KC *Star,* February 3, 1937; "Benton's Candor Holds," KC *Times,* March 1, 1937; copy of program from the Community Church, February 28, 1937, KCAI Library; Huselton's questions for Benton, typescript, KCAI Library; "Benton, Native Artist, Defends State Capitol Mural," St. Louis *Globe-Democrat,* March 8, 1937; "Talk on Mural for Fee," KC *Times,* March 11, 1937; "Frankie Had Her Ideals," KC *Times,* April 15, 1937; St. Louis *Post-Dispatch,* April 15, 1937; letter to KC *Star,* April 14, 1937; "You Win, Benton," KC *Journal-Post,* March 3, 1937; "Adams Defends the Benton Murals," *Columbia Missourian Feature Section,* April 15, 1937; Beaux-Arts ball interview from KC *Journal-Post,* March 7, 1937; Joseph Hanlon, "Thomas Hart Benton to Live in Missouri," St. Louis *Post-Dispatch,* March 19, 1935; "Study Faces to Know the Real American," KC *Journal-Post,* November 8, 1936, 8B; Malcolm Cowley, "Benton of Missouri," 375.

Chapter Fifteen: Howard Huselton and His Campaign of Hate

"The Great Flood in Missouri as Seen and Recorded by Thomas Hart Benton," KC *Star,* February 14, 1937; "Artist Thomas Hart Benton Hunts Communists and Fascists in Michigan," *Life,* (3) 4, July 26, 1937, 22. Original title of *An Artist in America* in Frances Kramer, "Thomas H. Benton, on Vacation, Flays Propaganda in Art," *The News*

(Dallas?), July 31, 1935. See also John Selby, "Thomas Hart Benton Writes Autobiography of Candor," Dallas *News,* October 25, 1937; Bruce Catton, "A Book a Day," *Call* (Piqua, OH), November 2, 1937; Clifton Fadiman, "Books," *New Yorker,* (13) 36, October 23, 1937, 89; Sinclair Lewis, "Slim, Jim, and Lem," *Newsweek,* (10) 18, November 1, 1937, 25; Margaret Miller, "Artist Describes Life, Observations," San Diego *Union,* October 24, 1937; J.D.W., "The Story of Thomas Hart Benton as 'An Artist in America,' " KC *Star,* October 23, 1937; Anna Jane Phillips, "Art Exhibit Prize Called Salute to Past," Pittsburgh *Post-Gazette,* October 19, 1937; "The Fortnight in New York," *Art Digest,* (12) 4, November 15, 1937, 22; "Greater America in the Drawings of Thomas Hart Benton, *Art News,* (36) 5, October 30, 1937, 16; Eleanor Jewett, "Benton Exhibit Worthy of Public Notice," Chicago *Tribune,* October 31, 1937; Grant Wood's visit described in "As Painters View Art," KC *Star,* January 3, 1938; "Life Goes to a Party," *Life,* (4) 12, March 21, 1938, 62–65; KC *Star,* March 4, 1938; KC *Star,* March 6, 1938; introduction, *Catalogue of a Loan Exhibition of Drawings by Thomas Hart Benton,* Lakeside Press Galleries, Chicago, 1937, 6–7. Reviews of *An Artist in America* include Meyer Schapiro, "Populist Realism," *Partisan Review,* (4) 2, January 1938, 53–57; Forbes Watson, "A Portrait of the Artist by Thomas Hart Benton," *New York Times Book Review,* November 28, 1937; Grant Wood, "Hard-Hitting Artist," *Saturday Review of Literature,* (18) 2, November 6, 1937. Benton briefly mentioned Huselton in *An Artist in America,* 271. The references to Fred Shane's memories of the affair come from Fred Shane tapes, AAA. Benton's sketch and letter to Shane is in the Archives of the University of Missouri, Columbia. Throughout this chapter Huselton's correspondence and memoranda have been used, as well as the letters of support to him cited at the end of this chapter, from the KCAI Library. Marianne Berardi established Huselton's birthdate from the National Census Archives, Kansas City, MO. See also "H. E. Huselton to Real Estate," KC *Star,* October 2, 1910; "Meet After 30 Years," KC *Times,* May 29, 1930; "Tribute to His Friend," KC *Times,*

February 28, 1948; "An Art Idea Budding," KC *Star,* June 23, 1938; KC *Star,* May 9, 1926. See also "Benton Roams in Bliss," KC *Times,* June 23, 1938; "A Naughty Mr. Benton," KC *Star* or *Times,* June 16, 1938; "Much Smoke, No Fire," *Art Digest,* (12) 18, July 1, 1938, 27; "Benton Loses Job," KC *Star* or *Times,* June 22, 1938; "An Art Idea Bubbling," KC *Star,* June 23, 1938; "Shabby Treatment," KC *Times,* June 23, 1938; "Benton Says, 'As I Am,' " KC *Star,* June 24, 1938; "In a Plea for Benton," KC *Star,* June 26, 1938; "Art School Alumni Back Thomas Benton," St. Louis *Post-Dispatch,* June 26, 1938; "He Holds Himself In," unidentified, undated article in KCAI Library; "Outside View of Benton," St. Louis *Post-Dispatch,* June 27, 1938; "Benton to Be Retained," KC *Star* or *Times,* June 27, 1938; "Benton Back by Oct. 1," KC *Star* or *Times,* June 28, 1938, KCAI Library.

Chapter Sixteen: Two Too-Nude Nudes

"Nude by Benton Arouses Ire of Woman Pastor," New York *Post,* February 6, 1939; Erika L. Doss, *Regionalists in Hollywood,* unpublished doctoral dissertation, University of Minnesota, 1983, Chapter 4, "Thomas Hart Benton Goes to the Movies," 122–169; Marling, *Tom Benton and His Drawings,* 59, 125, 168–169, 195; *Hollywood,* reproduced in *Life,* (5) 24, December 12, 1938, 74–75; Benton quote on Hollywood from "Thomas Hart Benton, Muralist, Visits City," St. Louis *Post-Dispatch,* November 11, 1937; letter to Bert Granet from Thomas Hart Benton, November 1, 1954, AAA; Benton, "I left nothing out" quote from *An Artist in America,* 280–281; " 'Very Nude' Girl Irks Art Critics," Indianapolis Sunday *Star,* February 19, 1939; Archie Musick, "West of the Mississippi," *Magazine of Art,* (31) 9, September 1938, 538–539; Archie Musick, *Musick Medley, Intimate Memories of a Rocky Mountain Art Colony,* Colorado Springs, 1971, 86–88; Mark Gabor, *The Illustrated History of Girlie Magazines from National Police Gazette to the Present,* New York, 1983; Roger Medearis, "Student of Thomas Hart Benton," typescript, 1986, files of the Nelson-Atkins Museum of Art; the author's interviews with Duard Marshall and Jesse Charles O'Neill; "The Metamorphosis of Thomas Hart Benton," *Art Digest,* (13) 14, April 15, 1939;

Nancy Heller and Julia Williams, *The Regionalists,* New York, 1976, Fig. 9; Lea Rosson DeLong, *Nature's Forms/Nature's Forces: The Art of Alexandre Hogue,* Philbrook Museum of Art, Tulsa, OK, 1984; Paul Bird, "The Fortnight in New York," *Art Digest,* (13) 15, May 1, 1939, 18; Milton Brown, "From Salon to Saloon," *Parnassus,* (13) 5, May 1941, 193–194; "Benton's Nude a Little Late in Being Hung at Art Exhibit," St. Louis *Post-Dispatch,* February 1, 1939, 3A; " 'Very Nude' Nude Hung in Art Exhibit," New York *News,* February 2, 1939; "Benton Art, Out & In," KC *Star* or *Times,* February 2 (?), 1938, KCAI Library; "Nude by Benton Arouses Ire of Woman Pastor," St. Louis *Post-Dispatch,* February 6, 1939; "Benton's Nudes People the Ozarks," *Life,* (6) 8, February 20, 1939, 39; Thomas Craven, *A Treasury of Art Masterpieces,* New York, 1939, *Persephone* illustrated, 296; Harry Hansen, "The First Reader," New York *World-Telegram,* October 10, 1939; "Benton Rejoices as Art is Hung in 'Saloon'; 'Persephone' Adorns Diamond Horseshoe," *New York Times,* April 9, 1941, Sec. 1, 27; Burns's interview with Sid Larson; Thomas Craven, catalogue *Thomas Hart Benton,* Associated American Artists, New York, April 18–May 15, 1939; Henry C. Haskell, "A Changing Benton appears in Gallery's New Show," KC *Star* or *Times,* March 1939, KCAI Library; "Benton in His Home Town," KC *Star* or *Times,* March 29, 1939, KCAI Library; "Artist Ends Exile—Finds City Still Boring," New York *Post,* April 17, 1939; "Benton Turns Mind to Mules and Vegetables," New York *Herald Tribune,* April 18, 1939; Paul Bird, "A Fortnight in New York," *Art Digest,* (13) 5, May 1, 1938, 18; "Benton's West in East," KC *Star,* July 9, 1939; "Wood, Benton Work Exhibited Here," Des Moines *Register,* September 17, 1939; J.D.W., "Benton Continues His Discovery of Missouri With Mark Twain," KC *Times,* November 15, 1939; "New York Critics Accept Benton's Challenge," *Art Digest,* (15) 5, December 1, 1940, 13; "Tom Craven Lauds the Work of Art Institute Students," KC *Star* or *Times,* November 29, 1940; information on Ben Nichols from the author's interview with Bill McKim; "Art Into Newsreel,"

November 20, 1940; Fath, 102, 106; Harry Salpeter, "Art Comes to Hollywood," *Esquire,* (14) 3, September 1940, 64, 173–174; "Allan Keller, "Movietown is Fascinating to Thomas Hart Benton," New York *World-Telegram,* July 13, 1940; "Thomas Hart Benton Paints Scene from Motion Picture," KC *Star,* July 28, 1940; "New Laurel to Benton," KC *Star,* February 11, 1940; "Pistol Packin' Gal Gets Adopted by Highbrow Art," New York *Journal-American,* November 3 (?), 1940; Berton Rouche, "Rare Adventure for Art Students on Journey to Ozarks with Benton," KC *Times,* May 13, 1940; letter to Reeves Lewenthal; and "the model was a beautiful girl" from "Benton Says Art Belongs in Cafe, Not in Museum," New York *Herald Tribune,* April 6, 1941, 40.

Chapter Seventeen: Getting Fired

Mike Amrine, "Tom Benton Lives as Sincerely as He Paints: No Pretense About World-Famed Artist," KC *Journal-Post,* May 3, 1941, 1D. On Keith Martin see KC *Star,* October 26, 1939; KC *Times,* November 30, 1939; KC *Star,* November 28, 1939; and Fred Shane tapes, AAA; friction over Benton's sketching trips, the author's interview with William T. Kemper, Jr.; the grading conflict was recalled by Benton in Cummings interview, AAA, 50–51. Fletcher Martin and the Midwestern exhibition described by Medearis and KC *Star,* January 24, 1941, and January 30, 1941. Floyd Taylor, "Thomas Hart Benton Says Art Belongs in Clubs & Barrooms, Not Museums," New York *World-Telegram,* April 5, 1941, 1, 4; Richard Gruber's interview with Herman Cherry, February 2, 1983, cited by Gruber, 349; conversation with Mrs. Milton McGreevy; "A Museum Chief Resents Benton's Deprecations," New York *Herald Tribune,* April 7, 1941; Peyton Boswell, "Benton Sounds Off," *Art Digest,* (15) 14, April 15, 1941, 3; "Take That! Mr. Benton," KC *Times,* April 8, 1941; Henry C. Haskell, "Two Bentons Discuss Museums with Extraordinary Results," KC *Star,* April 11, 1941; letter by Thomas Hart Benton, "Inconsistency a Useful Item for Tom Benton and Science," KC *Star,* April 25, 1941; Thomas Hart Benton, "The Dead and the Living," *University of Kansas City Review,* March 1941, 171–176; "Artist Benton is Out," KC *Star* or *Times,* undated clipping, KCAI Library; " 'I'll Lick 'em,' Says Artist Tom

Benton with Job at Stake Because of his Frankness," undated clipping, Arkansas *Democrat;* "Benton, Critic of Museums, Says Ouster Is Sought by Kansas City Art Institute," *New York Times,* April 29, 1941, Sec. 1, 21; "Cross About Tom Benton's 'Double Cross'—De Martelly Quits; Blasts Institute," KC *Journal-Post,* April 28, 1941; "One Nod to Mr. Benton," KC *Times,* April 29, 1941; "Art Must Be Kept Off the Bum in Kansas City—Thomas Hart Benton Defies Institute; Will Aid Young Even If Ousted," KC *Journal-Post,* April 29, 1941, 1–2; "Benton and His Critics," KC *Journal-Post,* April 29, 1941; student demonstration in KC *Journal-Post,* April 30, 1941, and "In an 'All Out' for Tom," KC *Star,* April 30, 1941; Thomas Craven, "Famous Critic Declares Benton 'Best Teacher,' " KC *Journal-Post,* May 1, 1941; "Tom Benton Will Not Give 'Fireside Chat,' " KC *Journal-Post,* May 2, 1941; "Artist Benton Is Out," KC *Star* or *Times,* undated clipping, KCAI Library; *Newsweek* quote from "Benton Ousted," *Art Digest,* (15) 16, May 15, 1941, 14; the typescript statement by Benton, found among his letters to Thomas Craven, is described by Kenneth Rendell, *Newsletter* (Newton, MA), 182, 1987; "Benton Has Art Plan," KC *Star* or *Times,* May 6, 1941; "Benton Art School to Be 'Workshop,' " KC *Journal-Post,* May 6, 1941; editorial, KC *Times,* May 6, 1941, KCAI Library; cartoon of Benton, KC *Journal-Post,* May 6, 1941; hiring of Martin in KC *Star,* May 11, 1941; "Fletcher Martin Replaces Benton," *Parnassus,* (13) 5, May 1941, 191; "Local Doctor Praises Benton," KC *Journal-Post,* May 5, 1941. On Frank Lloyd Wright, "It Happened in Kansas City," KC *Star,* May 20, 1941; see also: "A Mutual Echo in Art," KC *Star,* May 7, 1941; KC *Journal-Post,* May 7, 1941. Thomas Hart Benton, "Art vs. the Mellon Gallery," *Common Sense,* (10) 6, June 1941, 172–173; "Painting His Job Now," KC *Star,* October 1, 1941; Hereward Lester Cooke, Jr., *Fletcher Martin,* New York, 1975, 31–33, 223–224; Keith Martin's departure, KC *Star,* December 13, 1942.

Chapter Eighteen: Afterward

"Painting His Job Now," KC *Star,* October 1, 1941; Mark Twain, *Adventures of Huckleberry Finn,*

edited and with an introduction by Bernard De Voto, illustrated by Thomas Hart Benton, New York, 1942; *An Artist in America,* 288–290, 297–300, 294–296, 298–307, 311–313, 321, 324, 362–363; Medearis, "Student of Thomas Hart Benton"; The author's interview with Bill McKim; "Benton's War Paintings," *American Artist,* (6) 5, May 1942, 20; "The War and Thomas Benton," *Art Digest,* (14) 15, April 15, 1942, 13; drawings in the Navy Combat Art Center, Washington, DC; Quentin Reyonlds, "Take 'Er Down," *Collier's,* (114) 19, 1944, 16–19; " 'Spring on the Missouri' in Benton's Chicago Show," KC *Star,* February 24, 1946; "Chicago Views Benton, Midwest Dickens," *Art Digest,* (20) 11, March 1, 1946, 14; "Jake, the Dog With a Smile, Takes His Last Trip with the Tom Bentons," KC *Times,* August 28, 1946; Thomas Hart Benton, "Death of Grant Wood," *University of Kansas City Review,* (8), Spring 1942, 147–148; *Demcourier,* (12) 3, May 1942; H. W. Janson, "Benton and Wood, Champions of Regionalism," *Magazine of Art,* (39) 5, May 1946, 184–186, 198–200; Wilkin, *Stuart Davis,* 7; "Are These Men the Best Painters in America Today?" *Look,* (12) 3, February 3, 1948, 44–48; transcript of radio broadcast, "Does Modern Art Make Sense?" *Town Meeting,* (16) 50, April 1951, 2–13; "Benton Makes Point," KC *Times,* April 11, 1951; the author's interview with Alan Weller; the author's interview with Mildred Small; Thomas Hart Benton, "What's Holding Back American Art?" *Saturday Review of Literature,* (34), December 15, 1957, 9–11, 38. Scruggs project is discussed Fred Shane tapes, AAA; see also: "Benton Quits Art Project," *New York Times,* August 20, 1946, Sec. 1, 26; Fath, 17–19; Thomas Hart Benton, "Business and Art," and Reeves Lewenthal, "The Artist Has Never Been So Busy," In Elizabeth McCausland, ed., *Work for Artists,* New York, 1947, 21–26, 123–128. Benton's comments on advertising from "American Regionalism: A Personal History of the Movement," *University of Kansas City Review,* (18), Autumn 1951, 41–75; Burns's interviews with Hilton Kramer, Henry Scott, and Burl Ives; Leonard Lyons, "Age," New York *Post,* February 28, 1953; transcript of Edward R. Murrow interview, April 10, 1959. Craven quote from Deborah Solomon, *Jackson*

Pollock, New York, 1987, 61; Benton quote from Solomon, 70. Benton quotes on Pollock's drawing and abstract expressionism from Robert Wernick, "Down the Wide Missouri with 'an Old S.O.B.,' " *Saturday Evening Post,* (238), 21, October 1965, 92–97; Tolegian letter to Benton, August 21, 1964, Benton Trust, also Solomon, 77; Burns's interview with Dan James; Burroughs, 114–118; Benton quote on escaping with alcohol from Solomon, 90, 147; Burns's interview with Bill McKim. Cherry remarks from Potter, 251; Schardt, 61; Gribitz, 115; Kadish, 99. See also: Friedman quote in Potter, 213; Ruth Kligman, *Love Affair: A Memoir of Jackson Pollock,* New York, 1974, 154. Benton letter for Guggenheim fellowship, Solomon, 171; Benton quote on Pollock rhythms from *An Artist in America,* 667. For Marot, Henderson, Lazlo, and Hubbard see Solomon, 71–72, 94, 98, 93–99, 104–105, 145, 226. Ken Burns's interview with Jessie Benton; "60 Minutes" transcript, (5) 18, Sunday, April 8, 1973; Marling, *Tom Benton and His Drawings,* 3; William Ivey, *The Making of "The Sources of Country Music,"* brochure, Country Music Foundation, Nashville, TN, 1975, unpaginated; Robert Sanford, "Sketch of Benton in the Ozarks," St. Louis *Post-Dispatch,* January 24, 1975, 1D, 3D; the author's interview with Richie Guerin; Benton's correspondence with Woodcock supplied by Lyle S. Woodcock, St. Louis, MO; Fath, xxii; Rita's letter from Fath, xxii, also cited in Jules Loh, "Thomas Hart Benton," typescript, reprinted with changes as "Unforgettable Thomas Hart Benton," *Reader's Digest,* March 1976, 74–78; Ken Burns's interviews with Kramer, Marling, James, and Bennett; *An Artist in America,* 369; Thomas Hart Benton statement on his rendition of America in Thomas Craven, *Thomas Hart Benton,* Associated American Artists, New York, 1939. See also: Robert Bly, "Visiting Thomas Hart Benton and His Wife in Kansas City," *The Morning Glory,* New York, 1975, 61–63.

Credits

i Dedication page. *Thomas Hart Benton sketching on the beach, Martha's Vineyard,* photograph, The Kansas City Art Institute.

1 Frontispiece. Alfred Eisenstadt, *Thomas Hart Benton painting Persephone,* photograph, Alfred Eisenstadt, Life Magazine, c. Time Inc.

2 *Maecenas Eason Benton,* photograph, The Kansas City Art Institute.

3 *Neosho Courthouse,* photograph, Collection of Mr. Larry James. M. E. Benton giving a speech, detail from Missouri Mural, Missouri State Museum, Department of Natural Resources.

4 *Senator Thomas Hart Benton,* engraving. *Thomas Hart Benton (age 3),* photograph, The Kansas City Art Institute.

5 *Elizabeth Wise Benton,* photograph, Collection of Mildred Benton Small. *Aunt Maria Watkins,* photograph, Newton County Historical Society, Neosho, MO.

7 *Spring Tryout,* lithograph, 9½ x 13⅝", Lyman Field and United Missouri Bank of Kansas City, NA., Trustees of Thomas Hart and Rita P. Benton Testamentary Trusts. *Fire in the Barnyard,* lithograph, 8¾ x 13⅜", Lyman Field and United Missouri Bank of Kansas City, NA, Trustees of Thomas Hart and Rita P. Benton Testamentary Trusts.

9 *Oak Hill,* photograph, Collection of Mildred Benton Small. *The Benton children,* photograph, Private collection.

10 *Steam locomotive, Vinita, Oklahoma,* pencil on paper, 4⅜ x 7½" (sight), Private collection. *Custer's Last Stand,* 1896–1898, pencil on paper, 4¾ x 7¼" (sight), Private collection.

11 *"The Minerva of Peace,"* Mosaic Mural, photograph, Library of Congress.

15 *Christmas Card,* watercolor on paper, Private collection. *Valentine,* watercolor on paper, Private collection.

17 *Turn of the Century Joplin,* acrylic on canvas mounted on panel, 5½ x 14', c. 1973, Joplin Council for the Arts, Joplin, Missouri.

18 *Ben Reese and Thomas Hart Benton,* photograph, Courtesy The Joplin Globe, Joplin, MO.

19 *Joplin's Main Street looking South from Third - Elk's Parade,* photograph, Reprinted from *The Story of Joplin,* by Dolph Shaner, NY, Stratford House, Inc., 1948.

20 Clifford Berryman, *Teddy Bear,* pencil on paper, Library of Congress.

21 *Western Military Academy Football Team,* clipping, Lyman Field and United Missouri Bank of Kansas City, NA, Trustees of Thomas Hart and Rita P. Benton Testamentary Trusts.

25 *Caricature of the Quartermaster of the Western Military Academy,* pen and ink on paper, Private collection.

28 *Self-portrait in Caricature,* pen and ink on paper, 4¾"·x 3¾", Gift of Mr. Gil Stadeker. Courtesy of the Art Institute of Chicago. All Rights Reserved. *Self-portrait,* pen and ink on paper, 6¼ x 3", gift of Mr. Gil Stadeker. Courtesy of the Art Institute of Chicago.

30 *Classroom drawing under the instruction of Peixotto,* pen and ink on paper, 11¾ x 8¾", Location unknown. Reprinted from *Thomas Hart Benton: A Personal Commemorative* (1973: Joplin Council for the Arts.)

30–31 *Upper and Underclassmen,* illustration, Special Collections, Ellis Library, University of Missouri-Columbia, Columbia, MO.

31 *The Art Institute of Chicago: Illustration Department,* photograph, The Art Institute of Chicago.

32 *Baseball,* illustration, Special Collections, Ellis Library, University of Missouri-Columbia, Columbia, MO.

33 *Central Park,* watercolor on paper, 14⅞ x 17¾", Collection of Peter R. Blum.

36 *Self-portrait,* pen and ink on paper, 7 x 4½", Private collection.

37 *Chataignier—Contre Soleil,* oil on canvas, 20⅛ x 16⅛", Lyman Field and United Missouri Bank of Kansas City, NA, Trustees of Thomas Hart and Rita P. Benton Testamentary Trusts.

38 *Abe Warshawsky,* photograph, Reprinted from *The Memories of an American Impressionist* by Abel G. Warshawsky, Kent State University Press, Kent, Ohio, 1980. *John Thompson,* carte de visite, Private collection. *At the Terrace of the Cafe du Dome,* photograph, Reprinted from *Arts Magazine,* April 1980, Vol 54, #8.

39 *Self-portrait in the artist's studio,* pen and ink on paper, 4½ x 7", Private collection. *The Park Bench,* pen and ink on paper, Private collection.

44 *Landscape, Southern France,* pencil on paper, 12 x 8", C. *Thomas Hart Benton: A Portrait* by Polly Burroughs, Doubleday & Co., Garden City, NY 1981.

45 *Self-portrait,* oil on canvas, 20¼ x 16¼", Lyman Field and United Missouri Bank of Kansas City, NA, Trustees of Thomas Hart and Rita P. Benton Testamentary Trusts.

48 *Stanton Macdonald-Wright,* oil on canvas, 20 x 16", Lyman Field and United Missouri Bank of Kansas City, NA, Trustees of Thomas Hart and Rita P. Benton Testamentary Trusts. *Thomas Hart Benton painting Stanton Macdonald-Wright,* photograph, Courtesy the Nelson-Atkins Museum of Art, Kansas City, MO.

49 Robert Delaunay, *La Tour Eiffel,* oil on canvas, 79½ x 54½", Collection, Solomon R. Guggenheim Museum, New York. Photo by Carmelo Guadagno.

51 *Stanton Macdonald-Wright, Cassis, France,* photograph, Reprinted from *American Art Review,* Jan.-Feb. 1974.

54 *Morgan Russell,* photograph, Illustration in Gail Levin's *Synchromism and American Color Abstraction: 1910–1925* (New York: George Braziller in association with Whitney Museum of American Art, 1978), figure 1, page 10. *Sculpture in Morgan Russell's Studio,* photograph, Illustration in Gail Levin's *Synchromism and American Color Abstraction: 1910–1925* (New York: George Braziller in association with Whitney Museum of American Art, 1978), figure 10, p. 13.

55 *Gertrude, Leo and Michael Stein,* photograph, The Baltimore Museum of Art, Cone Archives, Baltimore, MD.

58 *Portrait of Maecenas E. Benton,* oil on canvas, Private collection.

59 *Self-portrait,* oil and tempera on canvas, 31½ x 22¾", Lyman Field and United Missouri Bank of Kansas City, NA, Trustees of Thomas Hart and Rita P. Benton Testamentary Trusts.

60 Balcom, *"Tommy Benton, Late of Paris,"* illustration, Reprinted from the Kansas City Star, February 4, 1912.

61 *Benton's friends and family walking about Neosho,* photograph, Newton County Historical Society, Neosho, MO. *Oak Hill on fire,* photograph, Collection of Mildred Benton Small.

62 *Fish Hatchery, Neosho (Girl in Park),* oil on canvas, 18⅝ x 23⅝", Collection of Mr. William N. Bush.

63 *Upper Manhattan,* oil on canvas, 28¼ x 28¼", the Cleveland Museum of Art, Anonymous Gift.

64 *Jack Armstrong and model,* photograph, Art from the Archives of Brown & Bigelow.

65 Ralph Barton, *Caricatures of Benton and Ingram,* pen and ink on paper, Collection of Diana Barton Franz. *Ralph Barton,* photograph, Courtesy of Museum of Art, Rhode Island School of Design.

66 *Portrait of Thomas Craven,* oil on canvas, 23¾ x 17¾", Collection of Richard Craven. *Still Life with Fruit and Vegetables,* oil on board, 25½ x 23¼", Collection of Mr. William N. Bush.

68 *Portrait of the Artist's Sister,* oil on canvas, 48½ x 27½", Collection of Mildred Benton Small.

69 *Sketch of Willard Huntington Wright,* drawing, (Now lost.) Princeton University Library, Department of Rare Books, Special Collections. Willard Huntington Wright scrapbooks.

71 *Constructivist Still Life,* oil on cardboard, 12½ x 8", Lyman Field and United Missouri Bank of Kansas City, NA, Trustees of Thomas Hart and Rita P. Benton Testamentary Trusts. *Constructivist Still Life,* oil on paper, 17½ x 13⅝", Columbus (Ohio) Museum of Art. Gift of Carl A. Magnuson.

72 *Figure Organization No. 3,* oil on canvas, (location unknown) Reprinted from *The Forum Exhibition of Modern American Painters,* New York, Arno Press, 1968.

73 *Figure Organization,* oil on canvas, location unknown, photograph private collection. Pierre Puvis de Chavannes, *Doux Pays,* oil on canvas, 10⅛ x 18⅝", The Yale University Art Gallery. The Mary Gertrude Abbey Fund.

74–75 Illustrations from *Europe after 8:15.* H. L. Mencken et al., New York, John Lane Co., 1914.

76 *Three Figures,* oil on canvas, 25 x 24⅛", From the private collection of Mrs. Deen Day Smith.

77 H. L. Mencken, photograph, reproduced by permission of the Enoch Pratt Free Library, Baltimore, MD, in accordance with the terms of the will of H. L. Mencken.

78 Stanton Macdonald-Wright, *Abstraction on Spectrum,* oil on canvas, 30⅛ x 24³⁄₁₆", Des Moines Art Center, Coffin Fine Arts Trust Fund, 1962. *John Weichsel,* photograph, Courtesy of John Weichsel.

79 *Bubbles,* oil on canvas, 21¼ x 16½", the Baltimore Museum of Art. Gift of H. L. Mencken.

80 *Rex Ingram with Clara Kimball Young,* photograph, Permission granted by Barnes & Noble Books, Totowa, NJ.

81 *George Hart, Walt Kuhn and Gus Mager at Fort Lee, New Jersey,* photograph, Walt Kuhn papers, Archives of American Art, Smithsonian Institution. *Rita Piacenza Benton,* photograph, The Kansas City Art Institute.

82 *Bust of Rita,* bronze, 14½ x 11¼ x 19½", Collection of Mr. and Mrs. John W. Callison.

85 *Self-portrait, South Beach,* oil on canvas, 49½ x 40", National Portrait Gallery, Smithsonian Institution, gift of Mr. and Mrs. Jack H. Mooney.

86 *Benton in his navy uniform,* photograph, Collection of Mildred Benton Small.

87 *Norfolk Harbor,* watercolor on paper, 7¼ x 11⅞", Collection of James and Margaret Smith. *Impressions, Camouflage, WWI,* watercolor on paper, 23⅜ x 28", Private collection.

89 *New York Construction,* charcoal on paper, 18 x 11", Collection of Mr. and Mrs. John W. Callison. *New York Stock Exchange,* ink and wash on paper, 15 x 18", Collection of Mr. and Mrs. John W. Callison.

91 *Thomas Craven,* oil on canvas, 38⅛ x 30⅛", Collection of United Missouri Bancshares, Inc.

92 *Construction,* oil on masonite, 19¼ x 21", Lyman Field and United Missouri Bank of Kansas City, NA, Trustees of Thomas Hart and Rita P. Benton Testamentary Trusts.

93 *Tom Benton, Ella Brug and Tom Craven,* photograph, c. *Thomas Hart Benton: A Portrait* by Polly Burroughs, Doubleday & Co., Garden City, NY,1981.

94 *Martha's Vineyard,* oil on canvas, 16 x 20", Collection of Whitney Museum of American Art, New York.

95 *Chilmark,* oil on canvas, 30 x 24", The Golovin Collection.

96 *Portrait of Dan,* oil on canvas, 23½ x 17¾", Lyman Field and United Missouri Bank of Kansas City, NA, Trustees of Thomas Hart and Rita P. Benton Testamentary Trusts. *Portrait of Frankie,* oil on canvas, 29¼ x 24½", Lyman Field and United Missouri Bank of Kansas City, NA, Trustees of Thomas Hart and Rita P. Benton Testamentary Trusts.

97 *The Lord is My Shepherd,* tempera on canvas, 33¼ x 27¼", Collection of Whitney Museum of American Art, New York. Gift of Gertrude Whitney.

98 *Frank Flanders,* oil on canvas, 24 x 19", Courtesy, Canajoharie Library and Art Gallery, Canajoharie, NY. *Tom, Rita and T.P.,* Martha's Vineyard, photograph, courtesy of Jessie Benton Lyman.

99 *Embroidery designed by Benton,* textile, 48½ x 36", Collection of Mr. and Mrs. Lelon Constable. *Study for Embroidery,* mixed media on board, 16⅛ x 12¾", Collection of Mr. and Mrs. Lelon Constable.

100 *The Cliffs,* oil on canvas, 29 x 34⅝", Hirshhorn Museum and Sculpture Garden, Smithsonian Institution. Photo by Peter Harholdt.

101 *Waves,* charcoal on paper, 20¼ x 23", Photograph copyright 1989 by The Barnes Foundation.

102 *Picnic,* oil on canvas, 38 x 36", Private collection.

103 *The Piacenza Family,* photograph, The Kansas City Art Institute. *Study of Rita,* pencil on paper, 11 x 8½", Private collection, Kansas City, MO.

104 *Dr. Alfred Raabe,* photograph, Private Collection.

105 *New York. Early Twenties,* oil on canvas, 34 x 25", Private collection.

106 *Dr. Alfred Barnes,* photograph, UPI/Bettmann Newsphotos.

107 *Ethel Whiteside and Those Pickannies,* photograph, New York Public Library at Lincoln Center. Billy Rose Theatre Collection.

111 *Color Study, Martha's Vineyard,* oil on paper mounted on board, 6¾ x 7¾" (sight), Collection of Harvey and Françoise Rambach.

113 *Landscape with Cow,* charcoal drawing, reprinted from *The Dial,* July, 1925. *The Tunnel,* charcoal drawing, Reprinted from *The Dial,* July, 1925.

115 *Organization* (Cubist Still Life), oil on metal panel, 6¾ x 4¼", Lyman Field and United Missouri Bank of Kansas City, NA, Trustees of Thomas Hart and Rita P. Benton Testamentary Trusts. *Twelve Planes and a Silver Egg,* egg tempera on board, 5½ x 4¾", Lyman Field and United Missouri Bank of Kansas City, NA, Trustees of Thomas Hart and Rita P. Benton Testamentary Trusts.

116 *Illustrations from the Mechanics of Form Organization,* Reprinted from *Arts Magazine,* November 1926-March 1927.

118 *Illustration to* WE THE PEOPLE, by Leo Huberman, Harper Brothers, 1947 edition. Jackson Pollock, *Going West,* oil on gessoed composition board, 15⅛ x 20¾", National Museum of American Art, Smithsonian Institution. Gift of Thomas Hart Benton. Jackson Pollock, *Troubled Queen,* oil and enamel on canvas, 1984.749, Charles H. Bayley Pictures and Painting Fund and gift of Mrs. Alfred J. Beveridge and Juliana Cheney Edwards. Collection by exchange. Courtesy Museum of Fine Arts, Boston, MA.

119 Jackson Pollock, *Summertime,* oil and enamel on canvas, 50 x 34", The Tate Gallery, London, England.

120 *Flight of the Thielans,* oil on panel, 8½ x 11½", Collection of Mr. & Mrs. Henry C. Schwab.

121 *Rhythmic Construction,* oil on canvas, 28 x 22", Lyman Field and United Missouri Bank of Kansas City, NA, Trustees of Thomas Hart and Rita P. Benton Testamentary Trusts.

122 *Garden Scene* (Figure Composition), oil on canvas, 42 x 60", The Crispo Collection, New York.

123 *People of Chilmark,* oil on canvas, 65⅝ x 77⅝", Hirshhorn Museum and Sculpture Garden, Smithsonian Institution. Gift of Joseph H. Hirshhorn Foundation, 1966. Photo by Lee Stalsworth.

124–131 *The American Historical Epic,* oil on canvas, *Discovery;* 60 x 48", *Palisades;* 72 x 84", *Aggression;* 72 x 36", *Prayer;* 5½ x 6', *Retribution;* 60 x 48", *The Pathfinder;* 69 x 48", *Over the Mountains;* 72 x 84", *Jesuit Missionaries;* 72 x 36", *Struggle for the Wilderness;* 72 x 84", *Lost Hunting Ground* 60 x 48", Collection of the Nelson-Atkins Museum of Art, Kansas City, MO, (Bequest of the artist). *The American Historical Epic,* oil on canvas, *Planters;* 66⅜ x 72⅜", *The Axes;* 59¼ x 41¼", *Religion;* 59¼ x 41¼", *Slavery;* 66¼ x 72⅜", Lyman Field and United Missouri Bank of Kansas City, NA, Trustees of Thomas Hart and Rita P. Benton Testamentary Trusts.

131 *Bootleggers,* egg tempera and oil on canvas, 65 x 72", Reynolds House Museum of American Art, Winston-Salem, NC. *Brideship,* egg tempera and oil on canvas, 62¼ x 43⅞", Collection of Mr. and Mrs. R. Crosby Kemper.

132 *Abstract Screen,* mixed media (location unknown), Reprinted from *Contemporary Art Applied to the Store and Its Display* by Frederick Kiesler, Brentano's Publishers, NY, 1930. *Autumn Leaves,* oil on panel, 15½ x 8¾", Collection of Gerald Peters Gallery, Santa Fe. *Cookie tin,* Oil on tin, 10" diameter, C. *Thomas Hart Benton, A Portrait* by Polly Burroughs, Doubleday & Co., Garden City, NY, 1981. *Two Trains,* design for a rug, Exhibition and catalogue "Hand-Hooked Rugs by Contemporary American Artists" from Ralph M. Pearson Gallery, NY, 1930.

133 *Tile with Abstracted Floral Design,* ceramic, 6 x 6", Private Collection, Kansas City, MO.

135 *Cotton Pickers,* egg tempera with oil glaze on canvas, 30 x 35¾", Metropolitan Museum of Art, NY. George A. Hearn Fund, 1933.

136 *Charles Burchfield,* photograph, Courtesy of the Burchfield Art Center, Buffalo, NY. Photograph by Herbert Appleton. *Cotton Hoeing, Arkansas,* pencil, ink and wash, on paper, 9 x 11½", Collection of Mr. and Mrs. John W. Callison.

137 *Lonesome Road,* egg tempera and oil on canvas, 25 x 34", Courtesy of Sheldon Memorial Art Gallery, University of Nebraska, Lincoln, NE.

138 *Borger, Texas,* photograph, Hutchinson County Historical Society, Borger, TX. *Oil Town,* pencil, ink and wash, 8½ x 11¾", Collection of James and Margaret Smith.

139 *Cattle Loading, West Texas,* oil and tempera on canvas mounted on panel, 18⅛ x 38⅛", Addison Gallery of American Art, Phillips Academy.

140 *Pulp, Paper and Sawmill Town,* pencil, ink and wash on paper, 8⅝ x 11¹¹⁄₁₆", Lyman Field and United Missouri Bank of Kansas City, NA, Trustees of Thomas Hart and Rita P. Benton Testamentary Trusts.

141 *Baptism,* pencil, ink and wash on paper, 9¼ x 12¼", the Art Museum, Princeton University, Princeton, NJ. Gift of Frank Jewett Mather, Jr. *Sharecropper's Shack,* Reprinted from the Kansas City *Star,* October 31, 1937.

142 *Louisiana Rice Fields,* egg tempera with oil glaze, 30 x 48", The Brooklyn Museum, Brooklyn, NY.

143 *Deck Hands' Crap Game,* pencil, ink and wash on paper, 12 x 9", Collection of Mr. and Mrs. John W. Callison. *Loading Cotton onto the Tennessee Belle,* pencil, ink and wash on paper, 10¼ x 14½", Collection of Mr. and Mrs. John W. Callison.

144 *Cotton Loading,* egg tempera and oil on canvas, 22 x 33", Private Collection.

145 *Lem,* pencil, ink and wash on paper. *Slim,* pencil, ink and wash on paper, Reprinted from *An Artist in America* by Thomas Hart Benton, University of Missouri Press, Columbia, MO.

147 *Rita and T.P.*, egg tempera and oil on canvas, 27 x 39¼″, from the collection of Nannette and Stephen Sloan.

148 *Folding screen with abstract sea motif*, oil on canvas with aluminum and painted wood frame, 6¼ x 8′2″, Private collection.

149 *Rita Benton, Jackson Pollock and others relaxing on Martha's Vineyard*, photograph, the Kansas City Art Institute.

150 *Benton on front page of "New York American"* (March 24, 1927), photograph.

151 *Lewis Mumford*, photograph, Courtesy Mrs. Sophia Mumford.

152 *Boomtown*, oil on canvas, 45 x 54″, Memorial Art Gallery of the University of Rochester, NY. Marion Stratton Gould Fund.

156 *José Clemente Orozco*, photograph, Photographs of Artists, Collection I, Archives of American Art, Smithsonian Institution.

158 *Third floor boardroom at the New School*, photograph, Reprinted from *Thomas Hart Benton, The America Today Murals* by The Equitable.

159 *Studies for America Today*, drawings, Courtesy of the Equitable Life Assurance Society of the US.

162–169 *America Today*, distemper and egg tempera on gessoed linen with oil glaze, *Instruments of Power*; 92 x 160″, *Coal*; 92 x 117″, *Steel*; 92 x 117″, *City Building*; 92 x 117″, *City Activities* with subway, 92 x 134½″, *City Activities with Dance Hall*; 92 x 134½″, *Outreaching Hands*, 17⅛ x 97″, Courtesy of the Equitable Life Assurance Society of the US.

169 *Leo Huberman*, photograph, Reprinted from book jacket, WE THE PEOPLE.

170–173 *Illustrations for* WE THE PEOPLE, from WE THE PEOPLE by Leo Huberman.

174 Stuart Davis, *New York— Paris, No. 2*, oil on canvas, 30 x 40″, Collection of the Portland Museum of Art, Portland, ME.

177 *Lassoing Horses*, watercolor on paper, 16 x 27″, The Brooklyn Museum, NY, 35.948 John B. Woodward Memorial Fund. *Wyoming Rodeo*, crayon on paper, 11¾ x 13″, Lyman Field and United Missouri Bank of Kansas City, NA, Trustees of Thomas Hart and Rita P. Benton Testamentary Trusts.

178 *Benton Transcribing Music for Harmonica*, photograph, Photo by Jack Wally. *Tom, Rita and T.P. playing music*, photograph, courtesy of Jessie Benton Lyman.

179 *The Engineer's Dream*, oil and tempera on canvas, 29⅞ x 41¾″, Memphis Brooks Museum of Art, Eugenia Buxton Whitnel Fund.

179 *Wreck of the Ole '97*, egg tempera and oil on canvas, 28½ x 44½″, Hunter Museum of Art, Chattanooga, TN.

180 *Gertrude Vanderbilt Whitney*, photograph, N.Y. Daily News Photo. *Juliana Force*, photograph, Photograph by Cecil Beaton, 1931, Collection of Whitney Museum of American Art, NY.

183 *Wilbur Leverett, Galena, Missouri*, pencil, pen and ink on paper, 11⅝ x 9″, Lyman Field and United Missouri Bank of Kansas City, NA, Trustees of Thomas Hart and Rita P. Benton Testamentary Trusts. *Dudley Vance, Fiddler, Bluff City, Tennessee*, pencil, pen and ink on paper, 11¾ x 9″, Lyman Field and United Missouri Bank of Kansas City, NA, Trustees of Thomas Hart and Rita P. Benton Testamentary Trusts.

185–191 *The Arts of Life in America, Arts of the West*; 96 x 156″, *Arts of the South*; 96 x 156″, *Indian Arts*; 96 x 84″, *Arts of the City*; 96 x 264″, New Britain Museum of American Art, Harriet Russell Stanley Fund. Photography by Arthur Evans, Williamstown Regional Conservation Laboratory.

188–189 *America Today, Unemployment, Radical Protest, Speed*, tempera on panel, 32 x 176½″. The Chrysler Museum, Norfolk, VA. Gift of Walter P. Chrysler, Jr.

189 *Political Business and Intellectual Ballyhoo*, egg tempera and oil on canvas, 56½ x 113″, New Britain Museum of American Art, Alix W. Stanley Foundation Fund. Photography by Arthur Evans, Williamstown Regional Conservation Laboratory.

192 *Richard Lieber*, photograph, Lilly Library, Indiana University, Bloomington, IN.

193 *A Hoosier History* (World's Fair Booklet Cover), Courtesy of The Nelson-Atkins Museum of Art.

194 *Tom Hibben*, photograph, Indiana Historical Society.

195–199 *Studies for the Indiana Mural*, Indiana University Art Museum.

200–204 *A Social History of Indiana*, egg tempera and oil on canvas, complete mural, 12 x 200′, Courtesy of Indiana University Auditorium.

209 *Self Portrait*, oil on canvas, 30 x 24″, Collection of Jessie Benton Lyman.

210 *The Sun Treader (Portrait of Carl Ruggles)*, 45 x 38″, oil on canvas, Collection of the Nelson-Atkins Museum of Art, Kansas City, MO. (Gift of the Friends of Art.)

212 *Minstrel Show*, egg tempera on canvas, 28⅜ x 35⅞″, Collection of the Nelson-Atkins Museum of Art, Kansas City, MO. (Bequest of the artist.)

213 *Lord, Heal the Child*, egg tempera and oil on canvas, 42¼ x 56¼″, Collection of Mr. and Mrs. John W. Callison.

214 *The Ballad of the Jealous Lover*, egg tempera and oil on canvas, 42¼ x 53¼″, Collection of the Spencer Museum of Art, University of Kansas, Lawrence, KS. Photograph by Jon Blumb.

216 *Maynard Walker*, photograph, c. 1933, Courtesy Mr. and Mrs. George Dein, Hawley, PA.

217 John Steuart Curry, *Baptism in Kansas*, oil on canvas, 40 x 50″, Collection of Whitney Museum of American Art, NY. Photography by Geoffrey Clements.

218 John Steuart Curry, 1929, *Tornado Over Kansas*, Oil on canvas, 46¼ x 60⅜″, Courtesy of the Muskegon Museum of Art, Muskegon, MI.

219 *Dr. McKeeby and Nan Wood beside "American Gothic"* photograph, Cedar Rapids Museum of Art Archives. Gift of John B. Turner in memory of Happy Young Turner. *John Steuart Curry and Grant Wood*, photograph, Cedar Rapids Museum of Art, Cedar Rapids, IA. John W. Barry Archives.

220 *Benton on cover of Time*, photograph, Copyright 1934 Time Inc. All rights reserved. Reprinted by permission from *Time*.

221 Grant Wood, *Daughters of Revolution*, oil on canvas, 20 x 40″, C. Estate of Grant Wood/ VAGA, NY 1988. Cincinnati Art Museum. The Edwin and Virginia Irwin Memorial.

222 *Alfred Stieglitz*, photograph, Philadelphia Museum of Art, Philadelphia, PA. From the collection of Dorothy Norman. Photographed by Eric Mitchell, 1985.

223 John Marin, *Movement No. 2, Related to Downtown New York (The Black Sun)*, watercolor on paper, 17½ x 22½″, Metropolitan Museum of Art, NY. Alfred Stieglitz Collection.

224 *Georgia O'Keeffe*, photograph, UPI/Bettmann Newsphotos.

225 *Diego Rivera*, photograph, Sophia Smith Collection, Smith College, Northampton, MA, and Mrs. Aubrey Niel Morgan.

229 *Stuart Davis*, photograph, The Peter A. Juley & Son Collection, National Museum of American Art, Smithsonian Institution.

233 Stuart Davis, *House and Street*, oil on canvas, 26 x 42¼″, Collection of the Whitney Museum of American Art, NY.

235 *Book cover design for "Thomas A. Edison,"* photograph.

237 *Preparing the Bill*, oil on canvas, 46 x 38″, Maier Museum of Art, Randolph-Macon Women's College, Lynchburg, VA.

238 *Grant Wood and Thomas Hart Benton*, photograph, State Historical Society of Iowa.

239 *Nat Benton and Thomas Hart Benton*, 1939, photograph, Law Office of the artist's brother, Nathaniel Wise, Springfield, MO.

242 *Mr. Benton Will Leave us Flat*, reprinted from New York *Sun*, April 12, 1935.

244 *"Revolt from the City"* pamphlet, photograph, University of Iowa Library, Iowa City, IA.

249 *Romance*, tempera with oil glaze on panel, 45¼ x 33⅛″, Archer M. Huntington Art Gallery, The University of Texas at Austin. Lent by James A. and Mari Michener. Photo by George Holmes.

250 *Plowing it Under*, oil on canvas, 20⅛ x 24¼″, Lyman Field and United Missouri Bank of Kansas City, NA, Trustees of Thomas Hart and Rita P. Benton Testamentary Trusts.

251 *A Lynching*, Reprinted from *Art Digest*, February 15, 1935. (Now lost.)

253 *Pioneer Days and Early Settlers*, 25 x 14′ 2″, Missouri State Museum. Department of Natural Resources.

254 *Kansas City Skyline*, photograph, Missouri Valley Room, Kansas City Public Library, Kansas City, MO.

255 William Merritt Chase, *William Rockhill Nelson*, oil on canvas, 59½ x 49¼″, by William Merritt Chase, the Nelson-Atkins Museum of Art, Kansas City, MO.

257 *Clay Models for a "Social History of Missouri,"* photograph, 2½ x 12′, Missouri State Museum. Department of Natural Resources.

259–261, 269 *Detail from Politics, Farming and the Law*, Missouri State Museum. Department of Natural Resources.

260 *Benton painting the murals in the Missouri State Capitol*, photograph, The State Historical Society of Missouri, Columbia, MO.

354

262–263 *The House Lounge, Missouri State Capitol* (overall view of room), Missouri State Museum. Department of Natural Resources.

266–267 *Politics, Farming and the Law*, 55 x 14′ 2″, Missouri State Museum. Department of Natural Resources.

272 *St. Louis and Kansas City*, 25′ x 14′ 2 ″, Missouri State Museum. Department of Natural Resources.

277 *Flood drawing*, pencil, ink and wash on paper, 9 x 12″, Lyman Field and United Missouri Bank of Kansas City, NA, Trustees of Thomas Hart and Rita P. Benton Testamentary Trusts.

278 *Discussion*, pencil, ink and wash on paper, 9 x 12″, Collection of Richard M. Levin. *Wood, Curry and Benton at the Beaux Arts Ball* (March 1938), photograph, Wide World Photos.

279 *Howard Huselton*, photograph, Copyright 1988. The Kansas City *Star*.

281 *Projection Room*, pencil, ink and wash on paper, 14⅜ x 18¼″, Lyman Field and United Missouri Bank of Kansas City, NA, Trustees of Thomas Hart and Rita P. Benton Testamentary Trusts.

282 *Missouri Painter and His Book*, photograph, St. Louis *Post-Dispatch*, June 23, 1938.

284 *Benton repainting Susanna*, cartoon.

285 *Persephone*, egg tempera and oil resin over casein on linen over panel, 72 x 56″, Collection of the Nelson-Atkins Museum of Art, Kansas City, MO. Acquired through the generosity of the Yellow Freight Foundation Art Acquisition Fund, Mrs. H. O. Peet, Richard J. Stern, the Doris Jones Stein Foundation, the Jacob L. and Ella C. Loose Foundation, Mr. and Mrs. Marvin Rich, and Mr. and Mrs. Richard M. Levin.

286 *Hollywood*, oil on canvas, 56 x 84″, Collection of the Nelson-Atkins Museum of Art, Kansas City, MO. (Bequest of the artist.)

288 *Susanna and the Elders*, oil and tempera on canvas mounted on panel, 60 x 42″, By permission of The Fine Arts Museum of San Francisco. Anonymous gift.

289 Alexandre Hogue, *Mother Earth Laid Bare*, oil on canvas, 44 x 56″, Philbrook Museum of Art, Tulsa, OK.

291 *Studies for Persephone*, pencil on paper, Collection of Dr. and Mrs. Gordon C. Sauer.

292 *Clay Model for Persephone*, Reprinted from *American Artist*, March 1940. *Study version of Persephone*, Collection of Mr. and Mrs. John W. Callison.

293 *Pussy Cat and Roses*, tempera and oil on canvas, 24 x 20″, The Art Museum, Princeton University. Gift of Mr. and Mrs. Morton L. Janklow, in honor of their daughter Angela LeRoy Janklow.

294 *Benton sitting on the Swing in front of his house*, photograph, The Kansas City Art Institute. *Benton looking at Weeds*, photograph by Jack Wally.

295 *Roasting Ears*, egg tempera and oil on canvas, 32 x 39¼″, Metropolitan Museum of Art, N.Y.

297 *Aaron*, egg tempera and oil on canvas, 30¼ x 2 ¼″, Courtesy of the Pennsylvania Academy of the Fine Arts, Philadelphia, PA, Joseph E. Temple Fund.

298 Jackson Lee Nesbitt, *Benton sketching at a farm sale*, Independence, MO, April, 1939, photograph, Courtesy of Bill McKim. Photograph, *Benton in front of his painting "Instruction". Reprinted from* KC *Star*, April 6, 1941.

299 *Rita Cutting Grass*, photograph, The Kansas City Art Institute.

300 *T.P. and Jake*, egg tempera on canvas mounted on panel, 50½ x 35½″, From the collection of Nannette and Stephen Sloan.

301 *Benton's sketching trip with students to the Ozarks*, cartoon, Kansas City *Star*. Courtesy of the Kansas City Art Institute. Jackson Lee Nesbitt, *Bill McKim, Thomas Hart Benton and Lewis Bogart looking at damage to their car*, April, 1940, photograph, Courtesy of Bill McKim.

302 *The Nelson-Atkins Museum of Art*, photograph, courtesy of The Nelson-Atkins Museum of Art, Kansas City, MO. *Keith Martin*, photograph, Reprinted from the Kansas City *Star*, September 20, 1940.

303 *The Hailstorm*, tempera on panel, 33 x 40″, Joslyn Art Museum, Omaha, NE, Gift of the James A. Douglas Foundation.

304 Arnold Newman, *Paul Gardner*, photograph, C. Arnold Newman.

305 *Laurence Sickman*, photograph, courtesy of The Nelson-Atkins Museum of Art, Kansas City, MO.

307 *Benton smoking*, photograph, The Kansas City Art Institute.

308 *"They Back their Teacher,"* Reprinted from the Kansas City *Star*, April 30, 1941.

309 *Billy Rose and a Chorus Girl pose with Persephone*, photograph, Wide World photos.

310 *"A twist of the wrist could regain him his job,"* Reprinted from the Kansas City *Journal-Post*, May 7, 1941. *Benton painting in his studio*, photograph, The Kansas City Art Institute.

311 *Threshing Wheat*, egg tempera and oil on canvas mounted on panel, 26⅛ x 42⅛″, collection of the Sheldon Swope Art Museum, Terre Haute, IN.

312 *Frank Lloyd Wright and Thomas Hart Benton*, photograph, Reprinted from the Kansas City *Journal-Post*, May 7, 1941.

313 *Benton relaxing on a float trip*, photograph, Collection of Jessie Benton Lyman. *Fletcher Martin*, photograph, Reprinted from *Art Digest*, May 15, 1941, p. 15. Fletcher Martin, *Trouble in Frisco*, oil, 30 x 36″, Collection, The Museum of Modern Art, New York. Abby Aldrich Rockefeller Fund.

314 *Album Cover for "Saturday Night at Tom Benton's,"* photograph, Courtesy of the Thomas Hart Benton Home and Studio State Historic Site, Kansas City, MO.

315 Fritz Menle, *Thomas Hart Benton in the Doorway of his studio on Martha's Vineyard*, courtesy of Jessie Benton Lyman.

316 *Exterminate!*, oil and tempera on canvas mounted on panel, 154½ x 82½″, The State Historical Society of Missouri, Columbia, MO.

316 *Negro Soldier*, oil and tempera on canvas mounted on panel, 58¼ x 70¼″, The State Historical Society of Missouri, Columbia, MO.

317 *Fluid Catalytic Crackers*, oil on canvas mounted on masonite, 48 x 58″, Permanent Collection, Massachusetts Institute of Technology, Cambridge, MA. Gift of Standard Oil Co. of New Jersey.

318 *July Hay*, oil and egg tempera on canvas mounted on panel, 38 x 26¾″, The Metropolitan Museum of Art, NY.

319 *After Many Springs*, oil and tempera on masonite, 30 x 21½″, Lyman Field and United Missouri Bank of Kansas City, NA, Trustees of Thomas Hart and Rita P. Benton Testamentary Trusts. *Waterboy*, oil on board, 35½ x 29″, Lyman Field and United Missouri Bank of Kansas City, NA, Trustees of Thomas Hart and Rita P. Benton Testamentary Trusts.

321 *Spring Still Life with Peony*, oil and tempera on canvas mounted on panel, 25⅜ x 19⅛″, Collection of Mr. and Mrs. R. Crosby Kemper.

323 *The Oboe Player*, oil on canvas, 28 x 34″, Collection of Mrs. Fred Chase Koch. *Tobacco Sorters*, Tempera on canvas mounted on canvas, 30 x 35⅞″, Private collection.

324 *Trading at Westport Landing*, egg tempera on canvas mounted on panel, 51½ x 89¾″, Private collection.

324–325 *Achelous and Hercules*, egg tempera and oil on canvas mounted on panel, 62⅞ x 264⅛″, National Museum of American Art, Smithsonian Institution. Gift of Allied Stores Corporation, and Museum Purchase through the Major Acquisitions Fund, Smithsonian Institution.

326 *Thomas Hart Benton canoeing at age 80*, photograph, Courtesy of Harold C. Hedges.

327 *Independence and the Opening of the West*, acrylic polymer on linen mounted on panel, 19 x 32′, The Harry S. Truman Library.

328 *Cave Spring*, polymer tempera on canvas mounted on panel, 30 x 40″, Collection of Edward J. Lenkin. *Jessie with Guitar*, egg tempera on canvas mounted on panel, 42½ x 30½″, Collection of Jessie Benton Lyman.

329 *Butterfly Chaser*, oil and tempera on canvas mounted on panel, 39½ x 30″, Collection of Jessie Benton Lyman.

330 *Trail Riders*, polymer tempera on canvas, 56⅛ x 74″, National Gallery of Art, Washington. Gift of the artist, 1975.

333 *Poker Night* (from "A Streetcar Named Desire"), 36 x 48″, egg tempera and oil on canvas, Collection of The Whitney Museum of American Art, NY.

337 *Self-portrait*, polymer tempera on canvas, 39½ x 29½″, Lyman Field and United Missouri Bank of Kansas City, NA, Trustees of Thomas Hart and Rita P. Benton Testamentary Trusts.

339 *The Sources of Country Music*, acrylic on canvas mounted on panel, 72 x 120″, from the Collections of the Country Music Foundation, Nashville, TN.

340 *Tom and Rita Benton*, photograph, Courtesy of Jessie Benton Lyman. Photographer unknown.

343 *Wheat*, acrylic on panel, 20 x 21″, Collection of Mr. and Mrs. James Mitchell, in celebration of their steadfast friendship with the family of Robert H. McDonnell.

Index

A note on the type

The display type is Tower.

The text of this book was set in
Sabon, a type face designed by Jan
Tschichold (1902 – 1974), the well-
known German typographer. Because
it was designed in Frankfurt, Sabon
was named for the famous Frankfurt
type founder Jacques Sabon, who
died in 1580 while manager of the
Egenolff foundry.

Based loosely on the original designs
of Claude Garamond (c. 1480 –
1561) Sabon is unique in that it was
explicitly designed for hot-metal composition on both the Monotype and
Linotype machines as well as for film
composition.

Composition by
Dix Typesetting Co. Inc.

Manufactured in Italy by
Sagdos S.p.A., Brugherio (Milano)

Designed by WGBH Design